"Schools of Tomorrow," Schools of Today

History of Schools and Schooling

Alan R. Sadovnik and Susan F. Semel
General Editors

Vol. 8

PETER LANG
New York • Washington, D.C./Baltimore • Boston
Bern • Frankfurt am Main • Berlin • Vienna • Paris

"Schools of Tomorrow," Schools of Today

What Happened to Progressive Education

Edited by
Susan F. Semel
and Alan R. Sadovnik

PETER LANG
New York • Washington, D.C./Baltimore • Boston
Bern • Frankfurt am Main • Berlin • Vienna • Paris

Library of Congress Cataloging-in-Publication Data

"Schools of tomorrow," schools of today: what happened to progressive education /
edited by Susan F. Semel and Alan R. Sadovnik.
p. cm. — (History of schools and schooling; v. 8)
Includes bibliographical references and index.
1. Progressive education—United States—Case studies. 2. Education—United States—
Experimental methods—Case studies. 3. Alternative schools—
United States—Case studies. 4. Educational change—United States—
History. 5. Dewey, John, 1859–1952. Schools of tomorrow.
I. Semel, Susan F. II. Sadovnik, Alan R. III. Series.
LB1027.3.S33   371.04'0973—dc21   98-30470
ISBN 0-8204-2666-0
ISSN 1089-0678

Die Deutsche Bibliothek-CIP-Einheitsaufnahme

"Schools of tomorrow," schools of today: what happened to progressive education /
edited by Susan F. Semel and Alan R. Sadovnik.
–New York; Washington, D.C./Baltimore; Boston; Bern;
Frankfurt am Main; Berlin; Vienna; Paris: Lang.
(History of schools and schooling; Vol. 8)
ISBN 0-8204-2666-0

Cover design by Nona Reuter

To Basil Bernstein

Mentor and Friend

ACKNOWLEDGMENTS

We are indebted to a number of colleagues and friends who have helped us in the completion of this book. At Hofstra University, Linda Merklin provided secretarial assistance; Keston Lall, our research assistant for two years, provided essential research and computer assistance, as well as moral support. Dean Eugene Ingoglia and the staff of Hofstra Academic Computing were always available to solve technical problems. Dean James Johnson, Associate Dean Penny Haile, Michael O'Loughlin, Mary Anne Raywid, Diane Schwartz and Sharon Whitton helped to create an environment at Hofstra conducive to scholarship.

At Adelphi University, Dale Snauwaert, Shirley Steinberg, and Pierre Woog provided feedback on a number of issues. We are grateful to former President Dolph Norton and Provost Lou Starkey who gave the second editor a sabbatical in Spring of 1998, which accelerated the completion of the project.

The Spencer Foundation provided support for the research on the City and Country School through its Small Grants Program. From 1993 to 1998, the American Educational Studies Association, the American Educational Research Association, and the John Dewey Society, especially Philip Jackson and Eliot Eisner, provided an ongoing forum for feedback on many of the chapters in the book. In April of 1993 at AERA and November of 1994 at AESA we began to present symposia on various chapters; in April 1998, the John Dewey Society sponsored a symposium at AERA on the entire book. We thank all of the participants and the thoughtful feedback from the audiences throughout this period.

A number of chapters (or sections of chapters) were originally published elsewhere and have been revised and adapted here. We are grateful to the publishers for permission to include material from the following:

Alan R. Sadovnik, Peter W. Cookson, Jr. and Susan F. Semel, *Exploring Education: An Introduction to the Foundations of Education* (Needham Heights, MA: Allyn and Bacon, 1994);

Susan F. Semel, *The Dalton School: The Transformation of a Progressive School* (New York: Peter Lang, 1992);

Susan F. Semel and Alan R. Sadovnik "Lessons from the Past: Individualism and Community in Three Progressive Schools,"

Peabody Journal of Education, Volume 70, Number 4, Summer 1995, pp. 56–84.

Daniel Perlstein, "Community and Democracy in American Schools: Arthurdale and the Fate of Progressive Education," *Teachers College Record* 97 (Summer 1996), pp. 625–650.

Mary Anne Raywid, "A School That Really Works: Urban Academy," *Journal of Negro Education*, Vol. 63, No. 1 (1994), Copyright 1994, Howard University.

In addition, the photographs of the schools and their students are included by permission of the following archives: The Francis Parker School Archives; The Marietta Johnson Museum Archives; The City and Country School Archives; Millbank Library of Teachers College, Columbia University; The Dalton School Archives; The Elsie Ripley Clapp Papers, Special Collections/Morris Library, Southern Illinois University of Carbondale; and the Urban Academy Archives.

We are grateful to the contributors who have been patient during the long gestation period. We know they are now saying, *finally at last*, as they read this. Their hard work, timely responses to our queries, and dedication to this project are greatly appreciated.

We are especially grateful to John Swinton for his elegant and diligent copyediting of the manuscript. His love of the English language is evident on every page. We have learned a great deal from him. The book is a better one because of his efforts.

At Peter Lang, we thank Christopher Meyers for his encouragement and steadfast belief in this book and our *History of Schools and Schooling* series. At the 1994 AESA meeting in Chapel Hill the series was born during a pleasant dinner and we are pleased to see both this book and the other volumes in the series begin to be published. Lisa Dillon provided excellent support throughout the production process.

Finally, we are grateful to Basil Bernstein, Karl Mannheim Chair Emeritus at the Institute of Education, University of London, to whom this book is dedicated. Basil has been a mentor and friend to both of us. During our many visits to London, he has listened carefully to our discussion of progressive education, provided insightful commentary and critique, and given us the opportunity to listen to him think out loud about the relationship between his work and our own. His analysis of the relationship between social class and pedagogic practice has shaped our own.

CONTRIBUTORS

Mary Bushnell is Visiting Assistant Professor of Education at the College of William and Mary.

John M. Heffron is University Professor of History and Director of Educational Research Programs, Pacific Basin Research Center, at Soka University of America.

Cynthia McCallister is Assistant Professor in the Department of Teaching and Learning at New York University.

Joseph W. Newman is Professor of History and Education at the University of South Alabama.

Daniel Perlstein is Assistant Professor of History and Education at the University of California, Berkeley.

Eugene F. Provenzo, Jr. is Professor of History and Education at the University of Miami.

Mary Anne Raywid is Professor Emerita of Education at Hofstra University.

Alan R. Sadovnik is Professor in the Department of Education Studies and former Dean of the School of Education at Adelphi University.

Susan F. Semel is Associate Professor in the Department of Curriculum and Teaching at Hofstra University. She attended the Dalton School during the Durham administration and taught there during the Barr and Dunnan administrations.

Sam Stack is Associate Professor in the Program in Education Foundations at West Virginia University.

Marie Kirchner Stone is a teacher of English at the Francis W. Parker School and formerly Chairperson of the English Department, Dean of Students, and Head of Curriculum.

Arthur Zilversmit is Professor of History at Lake Forest College.

CONTENTS

FOREWORD

As I walked the grounds of the Organic School in Fairhope, Alabama with Joe Newman, I was fascinated by the juxtaposition of this historically progressive school with the conservative environs of greater Mobile. Joe understood the history of the school in great detail and showed me pictures of a mid-fortyish John Dewey posing with founder Marietta Johnson, teachers and students from the school. Dewey encounters the "Heart of Dixie" I kept thinking, as I imagined the Father of Progressive Education in early twentieth century Southern Alabama. I couldn't help thinking of Paulo Freire's trips three-quarters of a century later to my own rural Tennessee to visit Myles Horton and his Highlander Center. What did these two innovative educators think as they observed such non-traditional programs in such conservative contexts?

Such thoughts are central to Semel and Sadovnik's *Schools of Tomorrow, Schools of Today* as they and their authors explore a variety of progressive schools constructed and maintained in radically different contexts—from the shores of Mobile Bay—to the immigrant-filled turn of the century Chicago—to New York City's artsy Greenwich Village, affluent Upper East and West Sides, and Washington Heights with its new immigrants—to rural West Virginia. How did Dewey's vision of democracy play out in these different contexts? What did schools as embryonic democracies mean to the various leaders of the progressive schools? If progressive education was not already a complex topic with its multiple impulses and contradictory articulations, the editors and authors here contribute to our understanding of the specific textures of that complexity. After *Schools of Tomorrow, Schools of Today* any educational historian who attempts to lump all progressive schools into a single category will have missed the important points made here. We have long understood the diversity of progressive education around categories of efficiency, child-centeredness, and social reconstructionism; now we can understand progressive non-uniformity in relation to location, place, and local social and cultural forces.

The excellent work of the editors and authors published in this book can play a dramatic role in the contemporary conversation about school reform. The progressive precursors of contemporary efforts to rethink education are generally unknown by school reformers. Such historical amnesia is apparent in their efforts, as we observe the results of their failure in their inability to anticipate the problems progressive innovators tend to encounter. What passes as a new strategy often originated in the schools studied here. What problems did these progressive teachers run into in the 1920s? What successes did they enjoy and celebrate? The exclusion of educational historians from the present conversation about educational change is intolerable—the voices in this book need to be heard in diverse venues.

Joe L. Kincheloe
Belle Zeller Distinguished Chair of Public Policy and Administration
Brooklyn College

PREFACE

The idea for this book began in 1988 in the office of the late historian of education Lawrence A. Cremin while Semel was working on *The Dalton School: The Transformation of a Progressive School*. Professor Cremin urged her to begin work on a comparative history of the early progressive schools in order to remind contemporary reformers of the practices that began in these and to ensure that their histories would not be forgotten. We only wish he were here to see the culmination of the project.

During the six years we have worked on this book, its original organization has changed greatly. As it was conceived in Cremin's office, the book was only to examine some of the schools founded in the early twentieth century. Based on our discussions, as well as feedback from audiences at AERA and AESA we decided to expand it to include some contemporary schools. This decision was based on the critique of many of the private, progressive schools as elitist and therefore not worthy of scholarly investigation. Therefore, we decided since many of the contemporary public, progressive schools mirror many of the pedagogic practices of the early schools, we needed to show the historical connections between them.

We have been struck by the reactions of many colleagues in Schools of Education to our work on private, progressive schools. During a job interview one faculty member asked Semel, "What can you possibly teach prospective public school teachers based on your years of experience at the elite Dalton School?" To which another faculty member ironically responded, "You mean unlike the white privileged public schools where we send many of our student teachers." This view is by no means an isolated one. A colleague refused to read our article in the *Peabody Journal of Education*, "Lessons from the Past: Individualism and Community in Three Progressive Schools," because it was about private schools. Many of our colleagues do not believe there is anything to be learned from private, progressive schools. Further, they rarely distinguish between different types of public schools, some of which are more elite and segregated than the private schools they criticize; nor do they acknowledge the pernicious effects of many urban, suburban, and rural public schools in the reproduction of race, class, gender, and ethnic inequalities.

These attitudes were also responsible for this book. We wanted to provide lessons to be learned from many of the early private, progressive schools and to show the historical links to current public school reforms. Although many contemporary reformers eschew the word progressive, it is ironic that their practices often mirror what occurred almost a century ago. We fervently believe that these practices should be available to all children and that the history of progressive education has much to teach us about public school improvement.

As a volume in our *History of Schools and Schooling* series, this book seeks to look to the past for what it can teach us today. School reformers often reinvent the wheel with little or no knowledge that many of their practices have rich historical precedents. The history of education is too often overlooked by contemporary practitioners, policy makers, and reformers. The lessons from the past about what has happened to progressive education hopefully will inform contemporary debates.

COVER PHOTOGRAPHS

Clockwise from upper right
1. The Lincoln School at its west side location (reproduced from Earl R. Glenn, Charles W. Finley and Otis W. Caldwell, *A Description of the Science Laboratories of the Lincoln School of Teachers College* (New York: Lincoln School of Teachers College, 1925).
2. Arthurdale: Scotts Run. Reprinted by permission of the Elsie Ripley Clapp Papers, Special Collections/Morris Library, Southern Illinois University of Carbondale.
3. Urban Academy: Student exhibition on the Civil Rights Movement. Reprinted by permission of Urban Academy.
4. The Dalton School: Picture of School Entrance, c. 1980s. Reprinted by permission of the Dalton School.
5. The City and Country School: Front of Building. Reprinted by permission of the City and Country School.
6. The Francis W. Parker School, c. 1961; The Old School original building 1901. Reprinted by permission of the Francis Parker School.
7. The Organic School Bell Building, 1996; the main building on the original campus, now restored as the Marietta Johnson Museum. Reprinted by permission of the Marietta Johnson Museum.

Figure 1:

The original two-story Francis W. Parker School Tudor building, fondly referred to as the "The Old School," was financed in 1901 by Anita Blaine McCormick and not replaced until 1962. From the Francis Parker School Archives. Reprinted by permission of the Francis Parker School.

Figure 2:

An enlarged photograph made by John Dewey (1913) showing Marietta Johnson with her students at the Organic School. This photograph was featured as the frontispiece of *Schools of To-Morrow*. From the Marietta Johnson Museum Archives. Reprinted by permission of the Marietta Johnson Museum.

Figure 3: Organic School Folk Dancers, 1956. From the Marietta Johnson Museum Archives. Reprinted by permission of the Marietta Johnson Museum.

Figure 4: City and Country School students and block play, c. 1980s. From the City and Country School Archives. Reprinted by permission of the City and Country School.

Figure 5: City and Country students and block play, 1970. From the City and Country School Archives. Reprinted by permission of the City and Country School.

Figure 6:   Classroom in the original Dalton School, c. 1920s. From the Dalton School Archives. Reprinted by permission of the Dalton School.

Figure 7:   Dalton students at George Dillman's farm in Otis, Massachusetts, c. 1960s. From the Dalton School Archives. Reprinted by permission of the Dalton School.

Figure 8:

Second Grade Village, Arthurdale. From the Elsie Ripley Clapp Papers, Special Collections/Morris Library, Southern Illinois University of Carbondale. Reprinted with permission of the Elsie Ripley Clapp Papers, Special Collections/Morris Library, Southern Illinois University of Carbondale.

Figure 9:

The Doddridge family in the cabin. Fourth grade play. Elsie Ripley Clapp Collection. From the Elsie Ripley Clapp Papers, Special Collections/Morris Library, Southern Illinois University of Carbondale. Reprinted with permission of the Elsie Ripley Clapp Papers, Special Collections/Morris Library, Southern Illinois University of Carbondale.

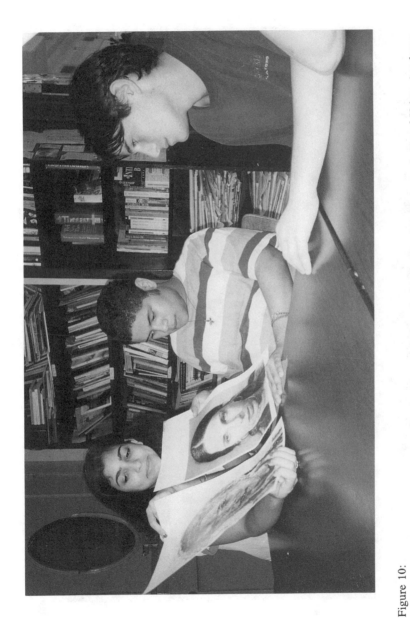

Figure 10:

Students at Urban Academy. From the Urban Academy Archives. Reprinted by permission of Urban Academy.

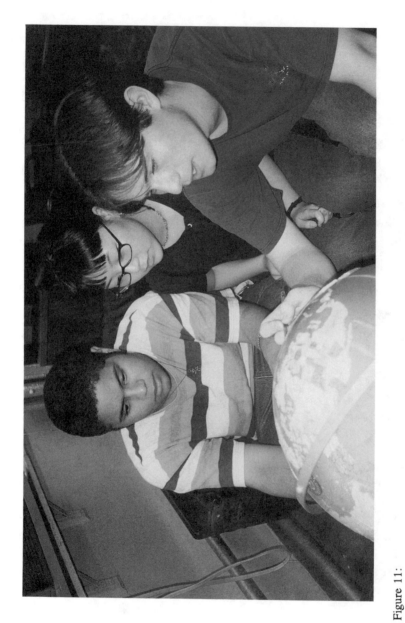

Figure 11:

Students at Urban Academy. From the Urban Academy Archives. Reprinted by permission of Urban Academy.

1

INTRODUCTION

Susan F. Semel

Few educational movements have been as maligned and misunderstood as progressive education.[1] As recently as 1996, critics of American education such as E.D. Hirsch have placed the blame on the putative failure of American schools on progressive education, although significantly, he often avoided the word, "progressive."[2] Recalling the conservative judgments of such critics as Arthur Bestor in the 1950s, Hirsch and his Core Movement followers see progressive education as the enemy of academic rigor because of its allegedly "soft pedagogy," which places the needs and interests of the child ahead of a rigid content-oriented set curriculum.[3] Nevertheless, we currently find a renewed interest in child-centered practices in public and private education, much of it reminiscent of the child-centered practices in some of the earliest progressive schools at the turn of the twentieth century. Those who now champion these progressive practices rarely acknowledge and may be altogether unaware of their historical antecedents. This book, therefore, addresses both the current critics of progressive education and its practitioners, and in so doing provides examples of progressive schools that worked and continue to work, as well as those that failed.

More specifically, this book documents some of the child-centered progressive schools founded in the first half of the twentieth century and provides histories of some more contemporary examples of progressive practices. Its title evokes John and Evelyn Dewey's 1915 book, *Schools of To-Morrow*, which examined early examples of schools explicitly designed to promote growth in children.[4] Not coincidently, three schools discussed in the Dewey's book appear in Part I of this book: The Francis W. Parker School, The Organic School, and The City and Country School. Part I discusses, in all, seven progressive schools founded in the first part of the twentieth century, tracing them from their beginnings to the present, or until their regrettable demises. Part II examines four more contemporary schools, showing how progressive practices gained momentum from the 1960s onward, sometimes, however, without a clear historical perspective.

Part I discusses the following seven schools: The Francis W. Parker School in Chicago, an example of an independent, progressive school with much to teach current educational reformers about teacher education and curriculum; The Organic School in Fairhope, Alabama, a school that has undergone dramatic transformation since its progressive origin; The Park School in Buffalo, a progressive school struggling to attract its share of students in a dwindling market; The City and Country School in New York City, one of the few current progressive schools following a curriculum and pedagogy that reflects the philosophy of its founder; The Lincoln School of Teachers College in New York City, a short-lived but troubling example paradoxical of the progressive effort to provide a democratic education for the elite; The Dalton School in New York City, an institution sensitive to the demands of the marketplace; and Arthurdale, an extinct experimental community in West Virginia, whose schools attempted to reflect New Deal progressivism.

Part II examines the following more recent examples of progressive schools: The Butterfield School in Illinois, a contemporary progressive school with good intentions that fell victim to poor planning and haphazard implementation; Free Union Country School in Virginia, a parent-founded effort in a rural area to provide child-centered education; Urban Academy in New York City, a student-centered alternative secondary school serving mostly minority students; and the W. Haywood Burns School in New York City, an elementary school in the Inwood section of Upper Manhattan, heavily influenced by the work of Deborah Meier and notably respectful of its community.

Four recurring questions and themes, emerging from the histories of all these schools, underscore the importance of studying school histories in the light of particular reform movements, in this case, progressive education:

(1)   What happened to progressive education in the schools dating to the first part of the twentieth century? What factors contributed to their stability and change, including leadership, the market (especially as regards private schools), philosophy, neighborhood, and the relationship

between the politics of educational reform and its impact on the schools? Most important, how do the histories of these schools relate to the zeitgeist of the times?

(2)   How do the schools founded from the 1960s onward reflect some of the pedagogic practices of the earlier schools? To what degree were or are these schools aware of the progressive school traditions that preceded them? To what extent do they consciously mirror their practices? As with the earlier schools, what factors affect educational stability and change?

(3)   What lessons can these past and present schools provide for school reform? What insights does the history of education provide for contemporary practice?

(4)   How progressive was (and is) progressive education, with respect to issues of equity? Given the fact that a large number of the early, child-centered schools were private and served a mostly affluent white population, the issue of progressive education and equity naturally arises. Since three of our four more recent examples are public schools serving more diverse populations, issues of race, class, gender, ethnicity, and religion also appear. To what degree, then, was (and is) progressive education reserved for the upper middle classes as Basil Bernstein has suggested?[5] To what degree did (and does) progressive education disadvantage African-American, Latino, and working class students, as Lisa Delpit suggests?[6]

A Short History of Progressive Education

In the early decades of the nineteenth century, the First Industrial Revolution produced immigration and urbanization of unprecedented proportions followed in due course by enough poverty and oppression to attract social reformers willing to reveal and challenge the evils of American industrial life.

But if the beginning of the nineteenth century brought social problems, its close brought even more. The Second Industrial Revolution centered this time on steam-driven and electrically powered machinery. Factories gave way to huge corporations, under the control of such captains of industry as Andrew Carnegie, John D. Rockefeller and Cornelius Vanderbilt. Immigrant labor, of course, sustained both revolutions.

At the start of the nineteenth century, most immigrants came from the northwestern part of Europe—namely Great Britain, Scandinavia, Germany and the Netherlands. After 1890, an increasingly large proportion came from southern and eastern Europe and they brought languages and customs dramatically different from those of the previous group. They settled in closely crowded substandard urban living quarters and found work in factories. Thus, by the turn of the century, American cities contained enormous concentrations of both wealth and poverty. Indeed, the gap between rich and poor had never been as great as it was at the close of the nineteenth century.

The purpose of education has been seen in a variety of ways: religious, utilitarian, civic and, with Horace Mann in the Common School era, social mobility. The common school had been born in an age of reform, but between 1900 and 1914 a new reform movement, the Progressive Movement, swept the country. Progressive reformers insisted upon government regulation of industry and commerce, as well as the conservation of the nation's natural resources; moreover, progressive reformers insisted that national, state and local governments become responsive to the welfare of its citizens rather than to the welfare of corporations. The progressive reformers had a sweeping agenda, including the secret ballot and universal schooling. Just as reformers, like Horace Mann in the nineteenth century, had looked to schools as a means of addressing social problems, so reformers once again looked to schools as a means of preserving and promoting democracy, within the new social order.

John Dewey and Progressive Education

An American philosopher whose influence on education remains strong today, John Dewey (1859–1952), moved to the forefront of these reformers. The list included "Fighting Bob" La Follette, governor of Wisconsin and architect of the "Wisconsin Idea," which linked university expertise to the mechanics of state government; settlement workers, like Jane Addams and Lillian Wald; municipal reformers and labor leaders, like Henry Bruere and John Golden. Thus, progressive education, the movement John Dewey has become associated with, can best be understood, as both historians Lawrence

Cremin and Richard Hofstadter remind us, as part of "a broader program of social and political reform called the Progressive Movement."[7]

Just as the schools today are undergoing a transformation due in part to rapidly changing technology, altered life styles and new, massive waves of immigrants, it could be argued that the schools at the turn of the century were undergoing a similar transformation in their time. In 1909, for example, 57.8 percent of the children in schools in 37 percent of our largest cities were foreign born.[8] Suddenly, teachers were faced with problems of putative uncleanliness (bathing became part of the school curriculum in certain districts), and they began to teach basic socialization skills. Just how these socialization skills are now interpreted, whether skeptically by radical historians or benevolently by liberal and conservative historians, is beyond our concern here. What we consider instead is how Dewey proposed to shape education to meet these challenges and how his progressive disciples interpreted his ideas so as to alter the course of schooling in this country.

Although born and raised in Vermont, by 1894 John Dewey had become thoroughly enmeshed in the problems of urbanization as a resident of Chicago and Chair of the Department of Philosophy, Psychology and Pedagogy at the University of Chicago. Distressed with the abrupt dislocation of families from rural to urban environments, concerned by the loss of traditional ways of understanding the maintenance of civilization and anxious about the effects that unleashed individualism and rampant materialism would have upon a democratic society, Dewey sought answers in pedagogic practice.[9]

Dewey argued in *My Pedagogic Creed, the School and Society* and *The Child and the Curriculum*[10] for a restructuring of schools along the lines of "embryonic communities" and for the creation of a curriculum that would allow for the child's interests and developmental level while introducing the child to "the point of departure from which the child can trace and follow the progress of mankind in history, getting an insight also into the materials used and the mechanical principles involved."[11]

Dewey believed that the goal of education was growth but within the context of a democratic society. Thus, for Dewey, school was "that form of community life in which all those agencies are concentrated that will be most effective in bringing the child to share in the inherited resources of the race, and to use his own powers for social ends."[12]

To test and implement his ideas, Dewey created the Laboratory School at the University of Chicago.[13] There, children studied basic subjects in an integrated curriculum since, according to Dewey, "the child's life is an integral, a total one" and, therefore, the school should reflect the "completeness" and "unity" of "the child's own world."[14] Dewey advocated active learning, starting with the needs and interests of the child; he emphasized the role of experience in education and he introduced the notion of teacher as facilitator of learning, rather than the font from whom all knowledge flows. According to Dewey, the school was—or should be—a "miniature community, an embryonic society"[15] and discipline was a tool which would develop "a spirit of social cooperation and community life."[16]

Dewey's form of pragmatism, instrumentalism and experimentalism was founded upon the new psychology—behaviorism—and the philosophy of pragmatism. His ideas were influenced by the theory of evolution and by an almost eighteenth century optimistic belief in progress, but for Dewey, in the attainment of a better society through education. Thus, the school became an "embryonic community" where children could learn skills experientially as well as from books in addition to traditional information, which would enable them to work cooperatively in a democratic society.

Dewey's ideas about education, often referred to as "progressive," proposed that educators start with the needs and interests of the child in the classroom, allow the child to participate in planning his or her course of study, advocated project method or group learning and depended heavily upon experiential learning.

Dewey's progressive methodology rested upon the premise that children were active, organic beings, growing and changing, and they required a course of study that would reflect their particular stage of development. He advocated both freedom and responsibility for students since he considered both to be vital components of democratic living. He believed that the school should reflect the community, in order to help graduates to assume societal roles and maintain the democratic way of life. In short, Dewey venerated democracy and he believed it could be more perfectly realized through an education that continually reconstructed and reorganized society.

Dewey's vision of schools was rooted in the social order; he did not see ideas as separate from social conditions. He fervently believed that philosophy had a responsibility to society and that ideas required laboratory testing—hence, the importance of the school as a place where ideas can be tested, implemented, challenged, restructured, and reconstructed with the goal of improving the social order. Moreover, he believed that school should provide "conjoint, communicated experience"; that it should function as preparation for democratic social life.

In accord with the progressive political atmosphere at the turn of the century, Dewey viewed the role of the school within the larger societal milieu to which they belonged. Thus, we can understand Dewey's vision of schooling as part of the larger project of social progress and improvement. While he was certainly concerned with the social dimensions of schooling, he was also acutely aware of the school's effects on the individual. Thus, his philosophy of education incorporated a need to balance the social role of the school with its effects on the social, intellectual, and personal development of individuals. In other words, Dewey believed that the schools should balance the needs of society and community, on the one hand, and the needs of the individual, on the other. This tension, or what the philosopher of education Maxine Greene called the "dialectic of freedom" is central to understanding Dewey's work.[17]

The key to Dewey's vision is his idea that schools should integrate children into a democratic society, not just any type of society. In other words, Dewey premised this view of integration on the school as an embryonic democratic society itself, with cooperation and community as its goals. Dewey did not believe, however, that the school's role was to integrate children into a non-democratic society; rather, he believed that if schools instilled democratic and cooperative values in children, they would be prepared as adults to help democratize the social order. While he managed to articulate this central function of schools, he failed to solve the problem of integrating diverse groups into a community without sacrificing their unique characteristics. But one can hardly fault him since this problem is still hotly debated.

As the historian of education Diane Ravitch noted, Dewey's philosophy of education was often misunderstood and misapplied.[18] It was often misapplied as in Charles Prosser's "life adjustment education" and whenever learning through experience became simply vocational education. It was often misapplied, as well, in regard to freedom, with individual freedom often becoming confused with a license that takes precedence over other, more structured processes. Finally, it often became distorted by tailoring education to social class (for example, vocational education for the poor).

Despite these distorted applications, Dewey's philosophy of progressive education remained central to all subsequent educational theory. For Dewey, the role of the school was to be "a lever of social reform"—that is, to be the central institution for societal and personal improvement—by balancing a complex set of processes.

In a progressive setting, the teacher is no longer the authoritarian figure from whom all knowledge flows. Rather, the teacher assumes the peripheral position of facilitator, encouraging, offering suggestions, questioning, and helping to plan and implement courses of study. The teacher also writes the curriculum and must have a command of several disciplines in order to create and implement that curriculum.

Dewey observed that children learn both individually and in groups and he believed that children should start their inquiries by posing questions about what they want to know. Today we refer to this method of instruction as "problem solving" or "inquiry method." Dewey's laboratory school relied on books often written by teachers and students together, and field trips and projects, which reconstructed some aspect of the course of study. These methods became, in turn, the basis for other progressive schools founded in the Deweyan tradition.

Some of these schools abandoned formal instruction and dispensed with traditional blocks of time for specific discipline instruction. Regiments of desks bolted to the floor became tables and chairs that could be moved about and grouped as needed. Children could converse quietly with one another, could stand up and stretch if warranted, and could pursue independent study or group work. What might at first appear as chaos to a visitor used to formal pedagogy might actually be a carefully orchestrated classroom with children learning in non-traditional yet natural ways. Individualized study, problem solving, and the project method replaced lock-step learning and rote memorization.

Progressive schools generally follow Dewey's idea of a core curriculum, or an integrated curriculum. A particular subject matter under investigation—like whales, yields problems to be solved using math, science, history, reading, writing, music, art, wood or metal working, cooking and sewing—all the academic and vocational disciplines in an integrated, interconnected way. Progressive educators generally start with contemporary problems and work from the known to the unknown, or what we have come to call in social studies education, "the curriculum of expanding environments." Progressive educators also tend to resist a fixed curriculum; rather, the curriculum will change as the social order changes or as the children's interests and needs change.

Some lingering controversy centers on Dewey's ideas about the traditional discipline-centered curriculum. Some contemporary scholars believe that Dewey's emphasis on the need for the curriculum to be related to the needs and interests of the child suggests that he rejected traditional subject matter and favored a child-centered curriculum based on imagination and intuition.[19] Others, including Howard Gardner, believe that Dewey proposed a balance between traditional disciplines and the needs and interests of the child.[20] I concur with Gardner's interpretation and believe that Dewey considered an integrated curriculum the most effective means to this balance.

Strands of Progressive Education

Indisputably, John Dewey made important contributions to both philosophy of education and pedagogic practice, especially if we examine what happened in the field of education subsequent to Dewey's early work. And as we do so, we should keep in mind just how rapidly education had expanded in this period. For example, in 1870, about 6.5 million children from ages five through eighteen attended school; in 1880, about 15.5 million children attended school. By 1900, 31 states had enacted compulsory education laws. Thus, whatever occurred in schools was sure to influence large numbers of Americans.

While few can dispute Dewey's influence among educational reformers, most of them would agree that Dewey was often misread, misunderstood, and misinterpreted. Thus, his emphasis upon the child's impulses, feelings, and interests led to a form of progressive education that often became synonymous with permissiveness, and his emphasis upon vocations ultimately provided a rationale for the "life adjustment" curriculum reformers.

Psychologists as well as philosophers soon became actively involved in educational reform. In fact, two distinctly different approaches to "progressive" educational reforms became apparent: the child-centered pedagogy of G. Stanley Hall, and the social efficiency pedagogy of Edward L. Thorndike.

G. Stanley Hall (1844-1924), once referred to as "the Darwin of the mind," believed that in their development, children reflected the stages of development of civilization.[21] Thus, according to Hall, schools should tailor their curriculums to the stages of child development. Hall argued that traditional schools stifled the child's natural impulses, and suggested that schools individualize instruction and attend to the needs and interests of the children they educate. This strand of progressive reform became known as "child-centered" reform.

In contrast to child-centered reform we find the "social engineering reform" proposed by Edward L. Thorndike (1874-1949). Thorndike emphasized the organism's response to its environment. Working with laboratory animals, he came to the conclusion that human nature could be altered for better or worse, depending upon the education it underwent. Ultimately, Thorndike came to believe that schools could change human beings in a positive way and that the methods and aims of pedagogy to achieve this could be scientifically determined.[22]

Thorndike's work, Frederick Winslow Taylor's work in scientific management, and research contributed by other progressive thinkers encouraged educators to be "socially efficient" in the ways they went about educating students. In particular, this thinking led to a belief that schools should provide meaningful experiences for students while preparing them to earn a living. It also suggested that schools might begin to educate students according to their respective abilities or talents. A leading proponent of this view was educational reformer Franklin Bobbitt. An issue of particular relevance here (and although never really resolved) involved Bobbitt's scientific approach to curriculum design. A curriculum designer, he thought, was like a "great engineer" and the purpose of curriculum design was to create a curriculum that would include the full range of human experience and prepare students for life.

Whereas the child-centered schools often emphasized the individualism inherent in Dewey's "dialectic of freedom," and the social engineering branch emphasized helping the child adjust to society, a third branch of progressivism, "social reconstructionism," emphasized the community and especially the development of a more just, humane and egalitarian society. Based upon the work of Kenneth Benne and George Counts, social reconstructionists viewed schools as the key to building a new social order.[23]

Although the child-centered and social-reconstructionist strands of progressive education often amounted to separate movements, the child-centered schools discussed in this book, nonetheless incorporated many of the community-centered aspects of social reconstructionism as they attempted to meet their students' individual needs and simultaneously integrate them into a democratic community. The social engineering strand, however, dominated public education from the 1930s onward, with scientific management and administrative concern with efficiency resulting in such practices as tracking, intelligence testing, and separate vocational education. The child-centered, and to a lesser extent, the social-reconstructionist strands, were more likely to be found in independent, private schools. Paradoxically, although these schools implemented many of the progressive practices Dewey advocated, they served a primarily affluent population.[24]

Progressive Education: 1900–1945

Progressive education had so dominated educational thinking that "by the mid-1940s it was no longer referred to as progressive education but as "modern education" or the "new educational practice."[25] Nevertheless, its many often contradictory strands[26] make it difficult to provide a "capsule definition of progressive education."[27] One can say, however, that progressive education began as a movement about the same time as Progressivism began as a political reform movement and it must be discussed within this larger context.

As we have seen, John Dewey made important contributions to both the philosophy of education and pedagogic practice. But of particular importance here, he strongly influenced a group of practitioners who founded independent progressive schools throughout the country that mirrored his Laboratory School. This prototype school "tried to provide education that balanced the children's interests with the knowledge of adults, that engaged the children in cooperative, active work, and that integrated social and intellectual learning. . . . The concepts of growth and active learning imbued the curriculum."[28]

While progressive education may be difficult to define, Diane Ravitch concluded that "it was an attitude, a belief in experimentation, a commitment to the education of all children and to democracy in the schools."[29] More specifically, Lawrence A. Cremin suggested four dominant themes present throughout the movement:

(1)   a broadening of the school to include a direct concern for health, vocation, and the quality of community life;

(2)   the application in the classroom of more humane, more active, and more rational pedagogical techniques derived from research in philosophy, psychology, and the social sciences;

(3)   the tailoring of instruction more directly to the different kinds and classes of children who were being brought within the purview of school; and

(4)   and finally, the use of more systematic and rational approaches to the administration and management of the schools.[30]

Before the 1920s, progressive reformers tended to concentrate their efforts in public education, applying scientific management techniques to the administration of schools, reforming curriculum and creating secondary, vocational schools.[31] But Cremin suggested, during the 1920s many progressive educators began to focus "on a select group of pedagogical innovative independent schools catering principally to middle class children."[32] One such school was the Dalton School founded by Helen Parkhurst,[33] as World War I drew to a close and "a great divide in the history of progressive education"[34] was occurring—one in which the thrust toward "social reformism was virtually eclipsed by the rhetoric of child-centered pedagogy."[35]

Dalton also came into being at a time when "progressive private day schools began to emerge in growing numbers."[36] Often the creation of parent cooperatives or talented practitioners, these schools held to the common practice that, "each individual has uniquely creative potentialities and that a school in which children are encouraged freely to develop their potential is the best guarantee of a larger society truly devoted to human worth and excellence."[37]

Educators commonly referred to these schools as "child-centered." They were often founded by female practitioners "spurred by the revolt against the harsh pedagogy of the existing schools and by the ferment of change and new thought of the first two decades of the twentieth century."[38] While historians tend to group these child-centered schools together, each has a distinct philosophy and practice according to the particular vision of its founder. For example, City and Country founded by Caroline Pratt emphasized the idea of self-expression and growth through play—in particular, through play with wooden blocks.[39] Another school, The Walden School, founded by Margaret Naumburg who was heavily influenced by Freudian psychology, emphasized the notion of "individual transformation." Under the leadership of Naumburg's sister, Florence Cane, the school encouraged "children to paint exactly what they felt impelled to paint."[40] Other examples include The Bank Street School, founded by Lucy Sprague Mitchell,[41] and The Lincoln School, founded by Abraham Flexner, which became a laboratory school for Teachers College, Columbia University.[42] Outside of New York City, where the aforementioned four schools were located, other examples of progressive education sprang up. Among these were The Organic School in Fairhope, Alabama, founded by Marietta Johnson; Francis W. Parker School in Chicago, founded by one of the early pioneers of progressive pedagogy, Colonel Francis W. Parker;[43] the Putney School, a boarding school in Putney, Vermont, founded by Carmelita Hinton;[44] and The Shady Hill School in Cambridge, Massachusetts.[45]

Whereas these child-centered progressive schools were almost all independent, private schools, public education was dominated by the social engineering strand of progressivism. From the transformation of the high school from an exclusively academic institution at the turn of the century to a host for life adjustment functions by the 1930s, to the social class- and race-based tracking systems that separated academic and vocational education, public progressive education from the 1930s to the 1960s stressed life adjustment rather than intellectual functions and often helped to reproduce rather than ameliorate social class, race, and gender inequalities. Progressive experiments in public schools did exist, for example, in Gary, Indiana, and Winnetka, Illinois.[46]

In the 1930s and early 1940s, social reconstructionism had a limited effect on the school practice. Based upon the work of Harold Rugg, George Counts, and Kenneth Benne and the journal the *Social Frontier*, a number of schools adopted a philosophy that espoused a radical reconstruction of the social order, especially with regard to inequalities.[47] Examples of these schools include Malumet, Hessian Hills, Arthurdale and Downtown Community School.[48] Although they represented an important attempt to use schools to change society, they neither had a wide following, nor a lasting influence.

From 1945 to the Present

The patterns that emerged during the Progressive Era continued during the post-World War II period. First, the debate about the goals of education, that is to say academic, social, or both, and whether all children should receive the same education continued. Second, the demand for the expansion of educational opportunity became perhaps the most prominent feature of educational reform. Whereas the Common School era opened access to elementary education and the Progressive Era to secondary education, the post-World War II years witnessed a growing concern with expanding opportunities to the post-secondary level. They also focused on finding ways to translate these expanded opportunities into more equal educational outcomes at all levels of education. As in the first half of the twentieth century, so too, in the second half, the compatibility of expanded educational opportunity with the maintenance of educational standards would create significant problems. Thus, the tensions between equity and excellence became crucial in the debates of this period.

During the post-World War II years the debate over the processes that defined the development of the comprehensive high school continued. We can probably describe the debates over academic issues, begun at the turn of the century, as shifting between pedagogical progressivism and pedagogical traditionalism. This movement continued the turn-of-the century pattern focused both on the process of education and on its goals. At the center of these debates are the questions regarding the type of education children should receive and whether all children should receive the same education. While many of these debates centered on curriculum and methods, they ultimately became associated with the question of equity versus excellence.

Perhaps we can best understand these debates by examining those reform cycles of the twentieth century which revolved around progressive and traditional visions of schooling. On the one hand, traditionalists believed in knowledge-centered education, a traditional subject-centered curricula, teacher-centered classrooms, discipline and authority, and the defense of academic standards in the name of excellence. On the other hand, progressives believed in experiential education, curricula responsive to both the needs of students and the times, child-centered education, freedom and individualism, and the relativism of academic standards in the name of equity. One or the other of these polar positions attracted most of the allegiance and were rarely as extreme in practice as they have been described here. In fact, the debate seemed to move back and forth between them rather evenly. Meanwhile, between 1945 and 1955, the progressive education of the previous decades came under strong criticism.

These critics—including Mortimer Smith, Robert Hutchins, and Arthur Bestor—assailed progressive education for appearing to sacrifice intellectual goals to social ones. They argued that the life adjustment education of the period combined with an increasingly anti-intellectual curriculum destroyed the traditional academic functions of schooling. Arthur Bestor, a respected historian and a graduate of the Lincoln School, one of the early progressive schools in New York City, argued that "regressive education" rather than truly progressive education had eliminated the school's primary role in teaching children to think.[49] Like the other critics, Bestor assailed the schools for undermining the democratic goal that all students receive an education once reserved for the elite. He suggested that the social and vocational emphasis of the schools indicated a belief that not all students can learn academic material. Ironically enough many of the conservative critics agreed with the radical critique, namely that the Progressive Era distorted the ideals of democratic education by tracking poor and working class children into non-academic vocational programs.

Throughout the 1950s, the debate between progressives who defended the social basis of the curriculum and critics who demanded a more academic curriculum raged on until what was often referred to as "the great debate" ended when the Soviets launched the first space satellite Sputnik.[50] The fact that the Soviet Union won the race into space produced a national commitment to improve educational standards, in general, and to increase mathematical and scientific literacy, in particular. From 1957 through the mid 1960s, the emphasis shifted to the pursuit of excellence and curriculum reformers attempted to redesign curricula so as to reemphasize and reassert academic standards (although many doubted that such a romantic age ever existed).

By the mid 1960s, however, educational priorities had shifted back again toward the progressive side. This shift occurred in two distinct but overlapping ways. First, the Civil Rights movement led to an emphasis on equity issues. Thus, such federal legislation as the Elementary and Secondary Education Act of 1965 emphasized the education of disadvantaged children. Second, in the context of the anti-war movement of the times, general criticism of American society, and the persistent failure of the schools to ameliorate problems of poverty and racial prejudice, a "new progressivism" developed that linked the failure of the schools to the problems in society. Heartened and guided by the publication of A.S. Neill's *Summerhill* in 1960, a book about an English boarding school with few if any rules and dedicated to the happiness of the child, the new progressivism launched an intellectual and pedagogical assault on the putative sins of traditional education: its authoritarianism, its racism, its misplaced values of intellectualism, and its failure to meet the emotional and psychological needs of children.[51]

Throughout the 1960s and early 1970s a variety of books scathingly criticized American education. These included Jonathan Kozol's *Death at an Early Age*,[52] which assailed the racist practices of the Boston public schools; Herbert Kohl's *36 Children*,[53] which demonstrated the pedagogical possibilities of "open education"; and Charles S. Silberman's *Crisis in the Classroom*, which attacked the bureaucratic, stultifying mindlessness of American education.[54] These books, along with a series of articles by Joseph Featherstone and Beatrice and Ronald Gross on British progressive or open education, resulted in significant experimentation in some American schools.[55] Emphasis on individualism and "relevant" education, along with the challenge to the unquestioned authority of the teacher, resulted in "alternative," "free" or "open" education: schooling that once again shifted attention from knowledge (product) to process. But little evidence now suggests that the open classroom was a truly national phenomenon, and the historian Larry Cuban noted in his history of teaching, *How Teachers Taught*, that we have seen surprisingly little actual variation in the twentieth century in teaching methods.[56] (Despite the cycles of debate and reform just discussed, most secondary teachers still lecture more than they involve their students.) Nonetheless, the period from the mid 1960s to the mid 1970s produced great turmoil in the educational arena, a time marked by two simultaneous processes: (1) the challenge to traditional schooling, and (2) the attempt to provide educational opportunity for the disadvantaged. By the late 1970s, conservative critics had begun to react to the educational reforms of the 1960s and 1970s. They argued that these liberal reforms in pedagogy and curriculum and emphasis on educational opportunity had eroded authority and standards. Furthermore, they suggested that the preoccupation with using the schools to ameliorate social problems, however well intended, both failed to achieve its goals and encouraged mass mediocrity. The conservatives began to urge nothing less than a complete overhaul of the American educational system. While radical critics also accused the schools of failing to reduce poverty and inequality, they located the problem not so much in the schools, but in the society at large. Liberals, meanwhile, defended the reforms of the period by suggesting that social improvement takes a long time, and a decade and a half was hardly enough.

In 1983, the National Commission on Excellence in Education, founded by President Reagan's Secretary of Education, Terrel Bell, issued its now famous report, *A Nation at Risk*. This report provided a serious indictment of American education and cited high rates of adult illiteracy, declining SAT scores, and the low scores of American students on international comparisons of knowledge as examples of the decline of literacy and standards. The Committee stated that "the educational foundations of our society are presently being eroded by a rising tide of mediocrity that threatens our very future as a Nation and a people."[57] The report called for higher standards and a return to academic excellence.

A Nation at Risk inspired scores of lesser known reports that supported the criticism and called for reform. During the 1980s and 1990s significant attention was given to the improvement of curriculum, the tightening of standards, and a move toward the setting of academic goals and their assessment. In the 1990s, through such educational reforms and policies as Goals 2000[58] and school choice, the primary focus shifted to issues of content, standards and educational excellence, the progressive concerns with equity now taking a back seat.[59] In fact, implicit and sometimes explicit in the standards movement one finds the allegation that progressive education had been the enemy of standards (an echo of the critiques of progressive education in the 1950s).[60]

Contemporary Progressive Educational Reforms

Despite the conservative climate in the 1990s, one is nevertheless encouraged by a lively interest in progressive education, especially as it applies to attempts to address issues of both equity and excellence. After more than a decade of conservative domination of educational discourse, and during a period when school choice, tuition vouchers and widespread loss of faith in public education gave rise to Goals 2000, attention has begun to turn again to progressive practices, though they are rarely labeled as such.[61]

An examination of contemporary progressive educational reform suggests that many of the early concerns of progressive education retain their resonance. For example, the statement of principles of the steering committee of the Network of Progressive Educators drafted on November 10, 1990, reflects contemporary attempts to reintroduce at least these nine progressive ideas into public school reform:

(1) Education is best accomplished where relationships are personal and teachers design programs which honor the linguistic and cultural diversity of the local community.

(2) Teachers, as respected professionals, are crucial sources of knowledge about teaching and learning.

(3) Curriculum balance is maintained by commitment to children's individual interests and developmental needs, as well as a commitment to community within and beyond the school's walls.

(4) Schools embrace the home cultures of children and their families. Classroom practices reflect these values and bring multiple cultural perspectives to bear.

(5) Students are active constructors of knowledge and learn through direct experience and primary sources.

(6) All disciplines—the arts, sciences, humanities and physical development—are valued equally in an interdisciplinary curriculum.

(7) Decision making within schools is inclusive of children, parents and staff.

(8) The school is a model of democracy and humane relationships, confronting issues of racism, classism and sexism.

(9) Schools actively support critical inquiry into the complexities of global issues. Children can thus assume the powerful responsibilities of world citizenship.[62]

One can see these principles at work in a number of public schools, as progressive educators in the United States reemphasize the need for progressive education for children from diverse class, race and ethnic backgrounds.[63] One such school, Central Park East Secondary School (CPESS), established in 1985 by Deborah Meier, is a progressive public school in New York City's District 4, in East Harlem.[64] The school is guided by the principles of the Coalition of Essential Schools founded by Theodore Sizer.[65] In many respects, it mirrors the pedagogic practices of such early independent, progressive schools as the Dalton School and the City and Country School. It uses an integrated curriculum, child-centered teaching methods, and an advisory system, and it attempts to integrate students into a cohesive community of learners. Although this chapter forgoes a detailed description and analysis of CPESS, it notes the important point that unlike most of the historically independent, private progressive schools, CPESS is a public school with a predominantly working class African-American and Latino student population. Its success suggests that the type of progressive education that has traditionally been the province of the middle and upper middle classes can work effectively with students from lower socio-economic backgrounds. Thus, one should examine how lessons from the past can inform present practice.

Central Park East Secondary School is part of the Center for Collaborative Education in New York City, which consists of elementary, middle and high schools and is affiliated with the Coalition for Essential Schools. CPESS subscribes to the Coalition's twelve principles of education:

(1)   Schools that are small and personalized in size.
(2)   A unified course of study for all students.
(3)   A focus on helping young people to use their minds well.
(4)   An in-depth, intra-disciplinary curriculum respectful of the diverse heritages that encompass our society.
(5)   Active learning with student-as-worker/student-as-citizen and teacher-as-coach.
(6)   Student evaluation by performance-based assessment methods.
(7)   A school tone of unanxious expectation, trust, and decency.
       (8)   Family involvement, trust, and respect.
(9)   Collaborative decision making and governance.

(10)   Choice.
(11)   Racial, ethnic, economic, and intellectual diversity.
(12)   Budget allocations targeting time for collective planning.

In the literature of Central Park East, the Center for Collaborative Education, or the Coalition of Essential Schools one finds few direct references to progressive education, probably because of a continuing contempt for progressive education among mainstream reformers, especially those who control grant funds. Given the pragmatic concerns, one can understand why these educational reform groups hesitate to label themselves as "progressive," but it is also clear that their principles and practices have their historical origins in the Deweyan progressivism of the early twentieth century.

These progressive reforms now center for the most part on public rather than private schools (which comprised a significant number of child-centered progressive schools in the first half of the twentieth century). I have raised elsewhere one of the abiding paradoxes of progressive education: the contradiction between its philosophical commitment to equity and the reality of the social class and racial composition of private, progressive schools.[66] In the 1990s, with the resurgence of such progressive, diverse, public schools as Central Park East, and those to be profiled in this book, Urban Academy, and the W. Haywood Burns School, we have an opportunity to assess whether progressive education can work for all children, or whether it will continue to be the province of the upper middle class,[67] or whether it, in fact, disadvantages African American, Latino, and working class students.[68]

Finally, we should observe how contemporary progressive schools reflect the practices of the earlier progressive schools. Much contemporary reform reinvents the wheel, proceeding with little awareness of its historical antecedents. We can learn important lessons from the past, and especially from the history of progressive schools.[69] The chapters that follow teach some of these lessons.

Part I

"SCHOOLS OF TOMORROW"

THE FRANCIS W. PARKER SCHOOL: CHICAGO'S PROGRESSIVE EDUCATION LEGACY

Marie Kirchner Stone

The revolution in American education reached its height at the turn of the century, when in 1901, the Francis W. Parker School opened as an experiment in progressive education. Earlier, in the Chicago suburb of Englewood, Francis Wayland Parker began training teachers at the Cook County Normal School, where in 1882, he became principal. Meanwhile, on Chicago's south side, John Dewey introduced his experiment in elementary education in 1896, at the Laboratory School of the University of Chicago, where he served as Chairman of the Department of Philosophy, Psychology, and Pedagogy. In 1899, Mrs. Emmons Blaine, the founder of the Francis W. Parker School and a daughter of the wealthy industrialist Cyrus McCormick, inventor of the mechanical reaper, persuaded Francis Parker to plan a school that would enable him to advance his new educational ideas. Accordingly, Francis Parker designed and Anita McCormick endowed the Chicago Institute Academic and Pedagogic, which they located on Chicago's north side in the Turverein Building on Wells Street. After two years, President William Rainey Harper of the University of Chicago encouraged Francis Parker and Mrs. Blaine to incorporate the Chicago Institute into the School of Education at the University of Chicago so the Institute might draw upon "the resources of a great university with its fuller advantages and equipment."[1]

In 1901, Parker and Blaine agreed to move the pedagogic work of the Institute to a new Emmons Blaine Hall at the University of Chicago, which was named after Mrs. Blaine's husband and son. Thus, Francis Parker and John Dewey, who had worked together before, became colleagues. Before opening the Laboratory School, Dewey had sent his children to Parker's Cook County Normal School for their elementary education. Dewey had also invited Parker to assist him in the development of the curriculum for Dewey's experimental school. That same year, Parker also transformed the practice of the Chicago Institute into the Francis W. Parker School on Chicago's north side, a few miles from the site of the Chicago Institute. Francis Parker simultaneously became the director of teacher training at the University of Chicago and the director of the Francis W. Parker School for one year until his death in March of 1902. John Dewey served as the educational advisor to the Francis W. Parker School until 1904, when he left the University of Chicago to become a professor of philosophy at Columbia University in New York.

Anita McCormick Blaine had guaranteed the University of Chicago one million dollars for the training of teachers at the time of the transfer of the Chicago Institute and a second million dollars to the Francis W. Parker School for an experiment in progressive education for elementary and high school students. Blaine supported the work of Francis Parker and John Dewey but preferred the educational practices of the former. Nevertheless, because of her help with the Laboratory School, John Dewey dedicated his first book, *The School and Society* (1899), to Mrs. Emmons Blaine "to whose interest in educational reform the appearance of this book is due."[2]

The Dual Influence of Parker and Dewey

The story of the Francis W. Parker School of Chicago illustrates what happened when one school combined John Dewey's educational principles, perhaps the soundest since Plato's, with Francis Parker's congruent educational principles and pedagogical practices. The Francis W. Parker School became the product of the two seminal leaders of progressive education, both living at the time on Chicago's south side: John Dewey, the philosopher of progressive education, and Francis Parker, called by Dewey the Father of Progressive Education.

These two educators differed widely in their fundamental views of life. "Parker believed in ultimate reality—his philosophy was idealism, and Dewey believed in the experimental method—his philosophy was pragmatism."[3] Yet, approaching the question of education from their opposite perspectives—Parker was the practitioner and Dewey the theoretician—the two agreed on education principles at a time when Parker was ending his career in education and Dewey was beginning his. Parker's and Dewey's school experiments in Chicago agreed in principle but differed in purpose.

John Dewey was a philosopher of education, whose goal for the Laboratory School was to test his own educational theories. An historian of the Dewey School explained that it served as a laboratory for applied psychology where "Dewey's theories of education could be put into practice, tested, and scientifically evaluated."[4] To develop a new science of education, Dewey began with a hypothesis and devised methods and curricula to test it. Dewey explained his theories of education in numerous publications of major importance to educators throughout the world. His texts of chief significance to the Parker teachers included: *The School and Society* (1899), *The Child and the Curriculum* (1902), *Democracy and Education* (1916), and *Experience and Education* (1938).[5]

Francis Parker reversed the scientific process. He was a pedagogical pioneer, whose starting point was the students in the classroom, where he introduced and kept adjusting new teaching methods and new content to see what could be learned about education through trial and error. For twenty-five years, Parker experimented with new educational practices as a teacher of elementary students and a trainer of teachers. He was first recognized for his innovative educational practices in 1875, at the grammar schools of Quincy, Massachusetts. He introduced his second major experiment in 1883, at the Cook County Normal School, where he combined teacher training with the education of children in the first eight grades. His final experiment of 1899, at the Chicago Institute, became after two years the present Francis W. Parker School. Parker built the practices of each school upon his former experiments and determined their successes by the experimental results defined as the successes of his students. "Parker had begun in the realm of practice from which he derived his theory of concentration and correlation" in an attempt to create a science of education.[6]

Francis Parker's pedagogical principles bore remarkable similarities to John Dewey's original educational theories. Their interpretations of education paralleled in their new explanations of the relationship of the school to the society. Parker explained that a school should be "a model home, a complete community, and an embryonic democracy."[7] Parker's mid-nineteenth century rural background had fostered the idea that the school was the community.[8] Similarly, Dewey believed that the life outside of the school gave the school "a chance to be a miniature community, an embryonic society," but his was an urban fin-de-siècle perspective.[9] Conceptualizing school as "a model home," meant to Parker that the school did in "a systematic, large, intelligent, and competent way what households did in a comparatively meager and haphazard way."[10] Writing five years later, Dewey saw a different kind of home, one that resulted from the Industrial Revolution: "Back of the factory system lies the household and neighborhood system" with factors of discipline and character building, but "at present, the concentration of industry and division of labor have practically eliminated household and neighborhood occupations—at least for educational purposes."[11] The home-school-society relationship was a new theme introduced by both educators and addressed by the early progressive schools. A special opportunity to experiment and to define the relationship among these three institutions presented itself to the Parker School between 1980 and 1985. The School began to grapple with the challenge, but the trial was incomplete and a definition of the interrelationship remains unresolved today.

Both educators not only broadened the base of a school as pivotal between the home and society but also affiliated it with life itself, necessitating a new school organization and different principles of school discipline. The new education called for school organization and discipline that were more democratic than that of traditional schools. Discipline in the traditional school of the 1890s meant external discipline based on reward and punishment by the figures in authority. Parker and Dewey saw that from "doing things in a cooperative way, there is born a discipline of its own kind that comes from having a part to do in constructive work."[12] Inner discipline in the new progressive schools superseded external discipline in how the student was taught to function in the community, where children learned to balance freedom with responsibility and to conduct themselves by the norm of "everything to help and nothing to hinder."[13]

Parker's and Dewey's ideas on curriculum content were less congruent than their definition of the school and its discipline. In *Talks on Pedagogics*, Parker moved the child to the center of the educative process and interrelated the curriculum subjects, which he called "central subjects." But Dewey's curriculum theory, as he explained it in *The Child and the Curriculum* and later in *Experience and Education,* was more radical. Dewey defined the educative process as the interaction between two forces: the child, "the immature underdeveloped being"; and the curriculum, "certain social aims, meanings, and values incarnate in the mature experience of the adult."[14] Parker's theory enhanced meaning for the child, but Dewey's theory made the child the starting point, the center and the end of the education process.

Although Parker and Dewey agreed upon and dealt with many of the same educational principles, Parker's unique contribution was the set of pedagogical principles he derived through practice. Parker explained these practices in his 1883 book, *Talks on Teaching*, following his work in the Quincy schools, and in his 1894 book, *Talks on Pedagogics*, written at the height of the Cook County Normal School experiment. These two books revealed that Parker's educational principles were eclectic and derivative with their main focus on curriculum and instruction.

Parker's Principal Influences

The intellectual genealogy of Parker's educational principles stemmed from the ideas of European philosophers of education, especially the German educators, who reconstructed education along utopian lines and according to the new scientific principles. Parker's philosophy was heavily indebted to Comenius's seventeenth century viewpoint of natural education, to Rousseau's eighteenth century romantic view of the child, but mainly to the nineteenth century views of Pestalozzi and Froebel on teaching method and Herbart on psychology. In both books, Parker synthesized their different viewpoints in an attempt to develop a philosophy of the unity of the whole of education—purpose, content and method.

In *Talks to Teachers*, Parker acknowledged his debt to John Amos Comenius (1592-1670), the Czech philosopher of education, for his definition of the natural learning method. Parker quoted Comenius: "Let things that have to be done be learned doing them."[15] Learning by doing, or learning actively in preference to learning verbally or passively, dominated the educational process of the schools Parker headed.

Parker's child-centered philosophy was Rousseauean and like the French philosopher Jean Jacques Rousseau (1712–1778), Parker emphasized "the spontaneous tendencies of the child."[16] Parker, however, deviated significantly from Rousseau's view that the child should do as he or she wished. Parker emphasized the learning of self-control or inner discipline, which he defined as the child's ability to postpone reward and to learn to contribute responsibly to the community rather than for personal self-aggrandizement. Parker's child-centered philosophy was molded by his strong belief in a democratic society and by his passionate commitment to the democratic process. He diluted Rousseau's romantic child-centered ideas with two democratic goals for education: the development of character or inner discipline, as just explained; and the development of ideal citizenship, a student's constructive participation in community life. Parker explained the function of the community: "A school is a community and community life is indispensable to the mental and moral growth of the child."[17] A Parker school was more community-centered than the child-centered institution in the Rousseauean tradition.

For method, Parker drew strongly upon the Swiss philosopher Johann Heinrich Pestalozzi (1724–1827) for what both called "the grand principle of education—the generation of power."[18] "Generation of power" meant that education was an active process and that to be educative, an act had to produce another educative act. Education was not a passive process in which the teacher transmitted knowledge to the student or the student learned solely by reading a textbook. Books complemented rather than replaced experience as in traditional schools. To generate power, education relied heavily on developing the motive that encouraged the learner to transform experience into ideas and convert ideas into action. Parker concentrated on the social motive for education or the motive that results from student and community interaction.[19] The motive in the education process was of central and prime importance to Pestalozzi and to a Parker-trained teacher.

Other of Parker's views on teaching included direct adoptions of Pestalozzi's naturalism, described as learning in a natural way in contrast to the formal approach used in the traditional schools of the turn of the century. Parker appropriated Pestalozzi's view that education should take place in a natural environment of love and security, and the model for that kind of school was the home. The experiences for the child were to be found in the natural environment through inductive teaching rather than dogmatic instruction. Parker was also attracted to Pestalozzi's object learning, which meant that learning began with observation. Parker's instructional method denounced the formalism and verbalism of the traditional method and emphasized the learner's motives, interests, needs and experiences. Natural method, also called "quality teaching," became a dominant instructional vehicle for teachers at a Parker school.

Parker's educational principles were also an exponent of the pedagogy of Prussian-born Freidrich Froebel (1782-1852), the father of the activity movement and the kindergarten. To Froebel, Parker attributed his aim of education, which he called "the all-sided growth of the child"—physical, mental and moral—resulting in the primary purpose of the school being "not the acquisition of knowledge but the formation of character constantly realizing itself in practical citizenship."[20] Seeking the education of the whole child, Parker added new classes in health education, manual training, music, the visual and performing arts, all types of sciences and several foreign languages. The education of the whole child also meant that the traditional courses of reading, writing and mathematics were taught differently. Reading focused on primary works, namely myths. Writing in different genres and for different reasons occurred daily and was integrated with most other subjects. Geography was the central organizing discipline, and mathematics was taught with it and other subjects. Parker also borrowed Froebel's concept of learning as activity-centered rather than as verbal- and memory-centered. To Parker, learning began with concrete experience, continued with observations and comparisons, and proceeded through a variety of different kinds of activities—"oral, written, manual and artistic expression."[21] Parker believed that, "Expression acts to develop motive, makes the highest use of thought powers, and requires the most healthful exercise of the body."[22] This activity-expression principle placed the arts as a dominant instructional device; consequently, the arts were an essential part of the curriculum in a Parker School.

The origin of the one major education theory that Parker introduced, the theory of concentration and correlation, was also derivative, its source found in the writings of the Prussian-born philosopher become psychologist Johann Herbart (1776–1841). Parker was a strong advocate of the advancing discipline of psychology to which Herbart was a major contributor before the influence of William James at Harvard University. In his 1894 book, Parker stated, "The psychology of Herbart and the doctrine of concentration enunciated and applied by Herbart's disciples, Ziller, Stoy and Rein, have been a source of inspiration and a guide in the general direction of my work."[23] During Parker's lifetime, educational psychology still labored under the now disfavored faculty theory of the human intellect. Faculty psychology was based on the theory that specific mental faculties constituted the mind and that each faculty could be developed independently through exercise and self-discipline. Herbart attempted to make psychology into an autonomous science divorced from philosophy, viewing the mind as an integrated unit rather than with separate faculties. In keeping with the new psychology, Parker's doctrine of concentration and correlation was his attempt to unify all subjects in the curriculum. His word "concentration," which meant placing emphasis on a subject, came directly from Herbart, and correlation of subjects was Parker's way to effect that concentration. "Correlation" meant integrating subjects, like geography, sciences, and mathematics, into what was called a "central subject." The purpose of concentration and correlation was to achieve "quality teaching," the teaching of fewer subjects in a natural way, rather than "quantity teaching," the teaching of many subjects in a fragmentary way. Because mental processes were unified and the subjects naturally related to each other, Parker saw no reason to divide disciplines artificially in the curriculum. At a Parker school, the subjects were unified and concentrated. The learning activities the students used to understand the content were, however, numerous. In short, a few subjects but multiple activities characterized the pedagogical approach.

Parker translated this European intellectual heritage into five general principles: (1) learning by doing, (2) the generation of power through concentration and correlation of subjects, (3) child and community-centered education to create citizens for the democratic society, (4) education of the whole child for character development and not just for the acquisition of knowledge, and (5) education through concrete experience in a natural environment. To apply these principles, Francis Parker traveled several times between his native New Hampshire and Illinois, and in his travels, he raised controversy centered either on himself or the education revolution he instigated.

From New Hampshire to Chicago

To Francis Parker, teaching seemed both his destiny and dilemma: "I cannot remember the time when I had not made up my mind to be a school teacher. I did not see fame in it or honor," but neither did he foresee the battle. Parker was proud that his ancestors were "five strands of ministers" and two strands of teachers. His grandfather Rand was "the first school teacher recorded in the old town of Derryfield," now Manchester, New Hampshire, and his mother was a teacher, who "never taught as anyone else did."[24]

By age sixteen, when Francis Wayland Parker became a country schoolmaster in Corser Hills, New Hampshire, he had attended three different schools but completed only four years of education. At first, young Frank Parker, the name he used then, attended an old-fashioned village school in Piscatauquog, New Hampshire, where he was born in 1837. He begged to attend an academy for boys three years older because he felt as capable as they seemed. But after the early death of his father, a sickly man and a cabinetmaker of modest means, his uncle bound him out to a farmer at age seven. While working on the farm, he attended "very poor classes for only two winter months each year, without knowing as I learned anything in them."[25] Parker left the farm at age thirteen to join his sister for three years and attend school in Mount Vernon, New Hampshire. In this rural heritage lay the roots of his definition of school as community. During the nineteenth century, the country school belonged to the community in more than just a legal sense; the schoolhouse was the educational, social, dramatic, political and religious center of the community.[26]

On the farm, he studied in a spontaneous way everything in nature. He knew the animals, the butterflies and insects, a little mineralogy, and some physics in the work of logging. "If any teacher told me that it was true education I was getting on the farm, how it would have lit up the whole farm in a blaze of glory."[27] Little did he realize that the farm would provide the educational content for his pedagogy: the barn on the school campus, the garden adjacent to the city school, geography as the central subject, and the necessity for trips in the fields. In 1897, he described how influential the farm had been on his life and in his education in the article, "The Farm as a Center of Interest."[28]

In his twenties, Parker found himself without credentials or the money to earn them and on an uncharted odyssey that took him from the East to the Midwest and back several times. Between 1859 and 1861, he was principal in Carrollton, Illinois, where he was educationally popular, but as a Union man, politically unpopular in a pro-South city. He returned to New Hampshire to join the fourth division and fought in Civil War battles from Cape Hatteras to Virginia "for the preservation of the democratic ideal."[29] Near the James River in Virginia, when the leader of his regiment fell, Parker became the ranking officer but took a bullet that impaired his vocal cords and ended his military career. A passionate and often dramatic man with a thirst for justice, Parker entered the War a stern disciplinarian and left understanding that people cooperated better when they understood the mission. The "war lessons" in self-discipline and leadership proved to be a second major influence in his life.[30]

After the War, Parker returned to New Hampshire, where he recuperated and married Josephine Hall from Bennington, New Hampshire. A daughter Annie was born to the couple in September of 1865. During Parker's convalescence, New Hampshire's Governor Smyth honored him with the rank of Lieutenant Colonel, a title he preferred thereafter.[31] The Governor also recommended Parker for a position in Dayton, Ohio, as "one of the best educators in New England," and in 1869, Parker accepted a principalship in the Dayton School system. Educationally successful in Dayton as principal and head of the Dayton Normal School, Parker was plagued by personal tragedies: his beloved wife, who had joined him in Dayton, died; his daughter Annie moved away to live with relatives; and his mother, who had remained living in New Hampshire, died in November of 1872. Now recognized as the Father of the Normal School, he was nevertheless criticized by his colleagues for "his poor educational background" and even for being an "illiterate man."[32]

After two years in Dayton, Parker, using a small inheritance from an aunt, went abroad to study education as Horace Mann, one of his heroes, had done. He attended lectures at the University of King William in Berlin and traveled through Germany, Holland, Switzerland, Italy and France, observing the pedagogical innovations of the day. The new

pedagogy strongly influenced him when he guided teachers in the study
of scientific education in Quincy.

In 1875, Charles Adams invited Colonel Parker to Massachusetts to
examine and improve the Quincy schools, where Parker introduced his
first major school reform. With his faculty he changed the set curriculum,
abandoning the speller, the reader, the grammar and the copybook, and
devised new curriculum materials. Arithmetic was approached induc-
tively, geography was learned through field trips, and manual and fine
arts supplemented the educative process. Parker emphasized observing,
describing and understanding. Some 30,000 visitors and observers came
to call the approach the "Quincy Method," which Parker disclaimed as
any method at all. Educationally successful, he resigned in 1880, because
of an altercation with Charles Adams and a fear that conservative political
forces sought to dominate the School Committee.[33]

Colonel Parker then became a supervisor of schools in Boston, where
he married a colleague, Frances Stuart, before they traveled to Chicago.
Warned of the battles he might expect with the Cook County Board of
Education, he nevertheless accepted the principalship of the Cook County
Normal School in October, 1882. With an artistic corp of teachers,
Parker used "illustrative teaching," a method of planning, observing and
critiquing lesson plans between master and novice teacher, to unify the
curriculum; he also developed the theory of concentration, which he
credited to his Normal School teachers.[34] That loyal corps of hard
working faculty members applied psychological principles to teaching,
picturing for the first time the school as the community and exploring the
unification of purpose, method and content, which became the hallmark
of Parker's pedagogy. In a letter to the city superintendent of schools in
1899, Parker described the challenges and accomplishments of the
Normal School, which he said rose from crudeness by a "zigzag of
experiments" to a new approach to discipline, a new way to teach, and a
new parent-teacher association.[35]

With political conservatives and educational traditionalists continually
attacking, Parker found himself in a full scale war in 1894, when the
commissioners drastically cut his budget. One outspoken commissioner,
Charles Thornton, another critic of Parker's lack of academic credentials,
called the Normal School "Parker's Fad Factory pudding."[36] When
hiring for the Chicago Schools, the Board of Education refused to

differentiate between a graduate of the Normal School and a candidate bereft of professional training. But distinguished Chicagoans and national educators—William James of Harvard; Nicholas Murray Butler of Columbia; William Rainey Harper and John Dewey of Chicago; and Jane Addams of Hull House—supported the Normal School. The Germans, Jews, Catholics, union members and many of the city's prominent parents also supported his reforms.[37] The Normal School became "so notable an institution, with its splendid record, that a group of citizens demanded its acceptance by the Chicago Board of Education, and it was transferred to the city in January 1, 1896, and renamed Chicago Normal School.[38]

Parker embraced the public schools until he could no longer make educational progress. Parker, like Horace Mann, wholeheartedly subscribed to universal public education.[39] "There is," he said, "but one place where children of all nationalities and sects can come together, sit on the same benches, lay upon the same ground, live and work together, know each other, and that is the common school."[40] But the political battles with the Chicago Board of Education and the harsh, unfriendly political attitude in the city toward the new education under old Mayor Carter Harrison finally brought Parker's progress to a halt. Persuaded by his second wife, also an accomplished teacher, he finally conceded to Blaine's proposal for a private school, which she had offered earlier. On May 30, 1899, the *Chicago Times Herald* reported his resignation and on June 28, 1899, most of his teachers joined him at the Chicago Institute Academic and Pedagogic, the foundation of the Francis W. Parker School.[41] Parker's hope was that the private school would become a model for the common school. He also envisioned a second private school near Jane Addams's Hull House, "where a composite foreign population would provide a diversity of types for broader experimentation."[42]

The School's founder, Anita McCormick Blaine, a woman of keen intelligence, saw the need for educational reform in Chicago, but she understood the private sector approach as the only alternative. Blaine, who lived on Chicago's north side, was the product of a Presbyterian value system and of great wealth. After her father invented the reaper on his farm in Virginia in 1831, he marketed it in 1842, moved his family to Chicago in 1848, and by the time of the Chicago fire in 1871, he had amassed a large fortune, which continued to grow. Anita's birth in 1866 was celebrated by "fireworks, booming cannons, and parades," the day coincidentally being July 4. Mrs. Blaine was the wife of a Vice President of the United States and the mother of a young son for whom she desired a school on the north side of Chicago. More significantly, however, she had served on the Chicago Board of Education, which caused her to conclude, "The usual educational institution is so hampered by the weight of ignorant demand and blind conservatism it is seldom free to take steps toward better education. The rock of the school's foundation," she continued, "is the freedom to carry out such educational policies as should further a truer education."[43] To this end, Blaine's financial contribution to the Parker School between 1901 and 1934 approximated two million dollars, double her original estimate and perhaps the largest endowment ever to a pre-college school, when calculated in today's dollars. Blaine served as a trustee, donated the land on which the original school was built and eventually the entire city block, financed the first school building, and made up the operating deficit until 1934. Though not a trained educator, Blaine possessed the educational vision, the moral force and the financial resources to be the power that enabled the progressive principles of the Parker School to flourish during her lifetime.

New Education in Chicago

Dewey's and Parker's progressive vision—their new definitions of the school, the curriculum, and instruction—revolutionized education. In the 1890s, the public school curriculum concentrated on reading, writing and arithmetic in the elementary grades with literature, history and foreign languages added in the secondary grades. Curriculum material derived from uniform textbooks, which were morphological and encyclopedic compendiums of facts. The traditional purposes of the school included mental discipline, knowledge for its own sake and student evaluations relying on the written exam. The public of the 1890s viewed the school in relationship to the achievement of the individual student rather than in relationship to the democratic society the schools were to help create. Educators thought that the classes should be subject-centered, defining learning as rote memory and training students in language and mathematics skills.

Parker's pedagogy and later Dewey's educational theories launched the first attack on the traditional view of education that dominated American thinking before the scientific revolution. By the turn of the century, the new formula for an experimental or a progressive school included eight precepts: (1) a twentieth century democratic view of the school as society shaping itself; (2) a perception of the subject of the school as the child rather than knowledge; (3) a definition of education that included the whole child and character development; (4) schooling purpose redefined as the test of the child's ability in new academic and social situations, not just in exams; (5) a curriculum designed with new subjects organized in new ways; (6) discipline measured by community conduct rather than reward and punishment; (7) activity-centered learning based on direct experience prior to classroom investigation; and (8) progress in education equated with the creation of a science of education. For this new science of education, Dewey created the model in the form of a question: "What are ways by means of which the function of education in all its branches and phases—selection of material for curriculum, methods of instruction and discipline, organization and administration of schools—can be conducted with systematic increase of intelligent control and understanding?"[44]

The story of Francis Parker's final experiment in progressive education reveals how one twentieth century progressive school, now almost a hundred years old, functioned in terms of the three educational variables Dewey's question posed: (1) the selection of curriculum materials, (2) the choice of methods of instruction and discipline, and (3) the organization and administration of the school. These new concepts and other compelling forces shaped the history of the Francis W. Parker School into three distinct periods: the Foundation Years 1901-1932, with the accent on the first eight grades; the Stabilizing Years 1932-1967, with the accent on the high school experiment; and the Challenge of Progressivism 1968 -1986, with the accent on the middle school experiment. A progressive school is influenced by the society that shapes it, by the discovery of new educational principles in psychology and sociology, and by internal school forces. In some periods, national events and educational trends detracted from and in other eras enhanced the Parker School. Teachers applied Colonel Parker's basic educational principles to one of the three divisions of the School in each historical period and achieved good results. In each different period, administrative leaders—principals and trustees—reorganized the School, often increased the enrollment, and at times arranged for the construction of a new wing or building. Some periods were stronger than others, but the three experiments, which were based on Parker's educational principles, validated Colonel Parker's dictum, "Progress comes through the science of education."

The Foundation Years 1901–1932: Accent on the First Eight Grades

In retrospect the opening of the Parker School represented a momentous occasion for education, but the opening went uncelebrated in the city in 1901. The School was unaffiliated with any Chicago institution; it had neither a religious alliance, unlike the growing number of Chicago's Catholic schools, nor a university affiliation like the Laboratory School. Neither did it cater to the elite as did the Latin School for Boys and the Latin School for Girls, established in 1888 and located just a mile south of the Parker School. The vision for this new twentieth century school was an education for a democracy in a city of a growing and increasingly diverse population.

The School was built on the outskirts of the city on Webster Avenue, where newly constructed brownstone buildings stretched from the downtown Loop northward for twenty blocks. In 1900, the northern boundary of the city extended another twenty blocks beyond the School to Irving Park Road.[45] Tree-shaded Lincoln Park and the shore of Lake Michigan made up the School's eastern border, and small commercial buildings bordered it to the west. The Tudor-style building was compatible with the Victorian houses located also to its west. The little barn built on the School campus reflected a countryside as yet innocent of a city poised to envelop it. The new School hardly stood out on the urban landscape, which was in the process of being shaped by Chicago's great architects.

The School would depend for students upon the city's growing population and, of course, the financial aid Mrs. Blaine provided. In 1840, the Chicago population had been 4,470 residents, but by 1901, when the School opened, the population had increased to 1,698,575. The new Chicago citizens were mostly first generation immigrants, mainly ethnic whites from the Slavic countries, Ireland and Italy; freed slaves from the South to Chicago's South Side, and Midwesterners, moving from nearby small towns to seek their fortunes in the city.[46] Chicago had become a composite of foreign neighborhoods, each nationality speaking its respective language and clustered in a ghetto. Only two German cities had more Germans; only two cities in Sweden had more Swedes, and only two cities in Norway had more Norwegians.[47] Rising phoenix-like from the ashes of the 1871 fire it became both "a spectacular and awful place."[48] No city in history paralleled its meteoric growth: "not St. Petersburg rising out of the marshes at an imperial edict, not Berlin, the magic creation of a consolidated empire and a Caesar's power."[49]

This rapid growth and the growing non-English-speaking multi-ethnic populations quickly affected the schools. In April of 1901, in its first document, "Instrument Creating Trusteeship," Mrs. Emmons Blaine established two goals for the School: "the best education of the child" and "the effective training of teachers."[50] On October 7, 1901, the Francis W. Parker School experiment began when 144 students from different economic levels, nationalities and religions; thirteen experienced teachers and a principal trained at the Normal School; a generous benefactor; and Francis Parker himself walked through the doors of a new two-story building. The children, ages six to eighteen, entered classes on Monday morning at 8:45, carrying with them, according to age level, paint clothes and paint boxes, paste cups, brushes and general supplies. The School furnished writing, drawing, painting and colored paper, glazes and wood. The Opening Notice informed their families that parents would be involved in School activities and every Friday in October, weather permitting, they were invited to a day excursion, joined by teacher trainees from the School of Education at the University of Chicago. The first excursion was a boat trip in the Chicago Harbor.

At 10:30 the excited students gathered in the Assembly Hall for the first Morning Exercise, where a stout sixty-four-year-old Francis Parker, jovial with the children but a tyrant among his teachers, welcomed them. Several parents, apprehensive about sending their children to this new school, stood perplexed in the rear of the hall; experienced faculty members, familiar with each other, smiled reassuringly at the prospect of new possibilities; a determined Mrs. Blaine stood regally aloof; and guests at the first assembly were surprised by its informality. Like a patriarch fathering a long-delayed child, Francis Parker opened the assembly by reading a verse from I Corinthians 12: 12-27, about the importance of the parts of the body to the whole: "For the body does not consist of one member but many. If the foot should say 'because I am not a hand, I do not belong to the body,' that would not make it any less a part of the body." A Christian and an Emersonian transcendentalist, he considered it natural to combine a personal and educational philosophy. His reading of Corinthians established an unbroken school tradition, a reminder of the relationship of the individual to the community.

The daily twenty-minute Morning Exercise meeting of the entire school was "a place where all good things of class and grade are poured into the larger life of the whole."[51] The Morning Exercises, which continued throughout the century, changed daily but might include a physics class demonstrating an experiment, fourth graders dramatizing their favorite Greek myth, fifth grade medieval knights jousting, a Chicago Symphony musician performing, or a controversial speaker presenting a new viewpoint. The Morning Exercise provided a forum for an exchange of ideas, a place for sharing common experiences, and a time when the child became secondary to the community and could exercise the self-discipline that helped form character. The three central aims of the school—the all-sided development of the individual, the formation of character realizing itself in practical citizenship, and education through community—provided the rationale directing the discipline and conduct for the Morning Exercise.[52] The passage from Corinthians defined the philosophy of community, and the Morning Exercise epitomized and materialized that philosophy. Combining Corinthians with the Morning Exercise was the living embodiment of the educational principle of integrating thought with deed.

During these founding years, the Parker faculty based its curricula for the first eight grades on the educational principles applied at the Normal School. Instruction was child-centered and also based on these principles: "The being to be developed determines the subjects and methods; the value of the subject is determined only as it contributes to the child's interests, needs, and powers; each subject begins with first hand experience; and the learning process begins with observations and comparison and proceeds to inductive reasoning."[53] Curriculum subjects were organized as interrelated branches of each other to create a unified curriculum. This curriculum organization principle, called "central subjects," lay at the heart of Parker's theory of concentration, and as later adapted by the high school was called "interdisciplinary education." Subject unification became the School's pervasive curricular organizing principle.

The geography sequence illustrates a typical instructional pattern for central subjects. Geography class began in the form of nature study, a field trip conducted by a teacher through the Lincoln Park area or along Lake Michigan, where children made observations and comparisons, which they illustrated in their writings and drawings. The children moved from first-hand experience to investigation in the classroom and from observation and comparison to inductive reasoning. Geography was correlated with the other physical sciences and taught with mathematics, history, and literature to unify the curriculum. To its central subjects the School added German, Latin, and French classes and hygiene and physical education classes for the first eight grades.

The lower school curriculum concentrated on the centrality of expression in learning, and the instruction relied on different modes of expression—writing, reading, visual and manual arts, and music and drama—throughout the eight years. Children learned to read the way they learned to talk and used "reading leaflets," observations they themselves wrote and printed in the School's print shop. They learned written language largely through daily writing. Modeling, painting and drawing accompanied most classes. The centrality of the arts as expression and as discrete disciplines became the School's second pervasive curriculum principle.

A third curriculum principle was activity-centered instruction, which emphasized mental training in a variety of ways: animal husbandry and gardening, housekeeping and cooking, sewing and weaving, printing and bookmaking, and restoring dolls for the children of Hull House. Physical activities, including pageants, marches, athletics, corrective exercises or rhythmic movements often combined with artistic activities to culminate in outdoor festivals called Field Day and May Day. The activities became ceremonial traditions sustained throughout the School's history. Education in and out of the classroom held equal status.

The teachers of the central subjects were generalists, called "grade-heads," who trained grade-level teaching assistants. The arts were taught by specialists, called "special teachers," to differentiate them from the "gradeheads." Both generalists and specialists were called upon to be organizers of community instruction. Developing the School as a cooperative community was a difficult instructional task. It was based on the principle, "The only true education comes through the stimulation of the child's powers by the demands of the social situation in which he finds himself."[54] The social motive, empowering the child by meeting the demands of the community, was assumed to be the most effective and wholesome motive for work. But the teachers, "the organizers of community life," found arranging the community to balance freedom with responsibility, inner with external discipline, cooperation with competition, and selfishness with altruism to be problematic. Colonel Parker's child-centered objectives, often at variance with community-centered strategies, exacerbated the complexity. Thus, the principle of "moral training through community life" remained an untested aspect of Colonel Parker's education principles.

The strength between 1901 and 1932 resulted from both a curriculum based on central subjects and a unified faculty. Each year until 1930, the faculty jointly prepared a *Course of Studies*, a 100-page bound volume that informed the parents, teachers and other educators of the scope, policy, principles and purpose of the School. These volumes detailed the new education in terms of the problems of instruction, the concept of individual attention and student interest, discipline through self-control and the relationship of work and play.[55] In addition to these annual publications, the faculty wrote *Studies in Education*, a series of expositions of particular phases of the School work, either a vertical articulation of curriculum like *Social Science: the Course of History* (1918), or a pedagogical dissertation like *Expression as a Means of Training Motive* (1919).[56] The earliest of the ten volumes, *The Social Motive in Education* (1912), was "as compact and complete a statement of the postulates of the new education as yet had been written."[57]

The Parker instructors collaborated in developing the curriculum and instruction, which resulted in their increased grasp of and a close adherence to Parker's educational principles. Throughout the School's first thirty years, this collaboration established a standard for curriculum development. The *Course of Studies* became a method to achieving its purpose. Curriculum and instruction, developed through "illustrative teaching," trained assistants, interns, and practice teachers to construct well designed lesson plans for field trips, classroom investigation, use of expression and activity, and engagement with the community. The grade-level master and the specialists in the respective departments engaged the novice in the drafting, implementation, and critique of the teaching plan. This procedure taught the faculty to be methodical and experimental in the curriculum design process. A variation of "illustrative teaching" lingered at the Parker School in this and other eras but gradually became a shadow of the original. American colleges and universities, however, adopted the technique for their teacher training programs.

Teaching at the Parker School evolved as "a passing of the hands from a master teacher to an heir and from one generation to the next."[58] It began with the "teacher of teachers," Colonel Parker, who elevated the profession and defined the teacher's role in society: "to make life, the society, the state, and the nation what they should be."[59] Parker insisted that teachers must be "cultured, educated, and trained," and he called the history of the school "the history of its teachers."[60] The experience of the first thirty years indicated that a Parker teacher must care about the child and put the child first. A Parker teacher also had to possess expertise in the art and science of teaching, exhibit a thorough knowledge of one discipline, be acquainted with psychology and sociology as they relate to education, and be familiar with the arts as instructional techniques. Socially, a teacher had to be a team member and contribute to collective scholarship through faculty discussions, public speaking and writing. Personally, a teacher had to be energetic and willing to work demanding hours, capable of taking and giving criticism as a member of a deliberative body and courageous in experimentation as well as creative in the design and scientific in the process. In its first thirty years, the School sought to employ teachers likely to create an effective group in the same way that college admissions officers admit students to create a group complement.

The history of School practices between 1901 and 1932 shows that at least twenty percent of the faculty at any given time were long-term employees able to provide curriculum and instructional leadership for the other teachers. At least sixty-five percent of the teachers had to be capably engaged in the organization of community life to make the community an effective teaching device.[61] In the first ten years, the average term was twelve and a half years, but eight teachers hired in this first decade remained until 1932. The School hired its first teaching assistant in 1913, and by 1932, the first eight grades were all assisted by teaching apprentices learning with masters.

The Parker faculty influenced the direction of progressive education in a variety of ways: its numerous publications, constant School visitors, frequent conference presentations and support from the Progressive Education Association. Parker teachers and alumni initiated instruction and reorganized schools modeled on the Parker School's educational principles. In 1919, Perry Dunlap Smith, a 1908 alumnus and a Parker teacher from 1912 to 1916, became headmaster and reorganized North Shore Country Day School in Winnetka, Illinois. In 1921, Katherine Taylor, a 1906 alumna and a Parker teacher from 1917 to 1921, became director and reorganized Shady Hill School in Cambridge, Massachusetts. Another teacher, Elizabeth Moos of the class of 1907, who taught at Parker for one year, founded and became principal of the Hessian Hills School in New York in 1925. Ethel Dummer Mintzer of the class of 1913, but not a Parker teacher, founded and became principal of the Francis W. Parker School of San Diego, California. After Edward Yeomans founded the Ojai Valley School north of Los Angeles in 1923, Mrs. Gudrun Thorne-Thomsen became its director, aided by her husband, Georg Thorne-Thomsen, both recognized as gifted teachers previously from the Normal School and the Parker School. Himself a Parker student, Edward Yeomans became a teacher at Shady Hill School under Katharine Taylor from 1935 to 1939, and was later appointed Taylor's successor.[62] Principal Flora J. Cooke founded the Graduate Teachers College of Winnetka in 1932, with Perry Dunlap, a Parker graduate, and Carleton Washburne, a student at the Chicago Institute, for the short period it remained open. The Graduate Teachers College combined teaching theory with practice and sent its teachers for training to Francis W. Parker, North Shore Country Day, and the Winnetka Public Schools, three progressive educational institutions, each headed by Parker principals.[63] In short, by 1932, the Parker educational network had become large and its practitioners enjoyed an honored legacy.

The first principal of the School, Flora J. Cooke, served there for fifty years as teacher, trustee, and Educational Council member. Born near Youngstown, Ohio, in 1864, Flora Juliette Hannun took the name Cooke from the family that adopted her. At nineteen, Miss Cooke began her career as a country school mistress. She then took a teaching position in Youngstown before training at the Cook County Normal School in 1887, at the suggestion of Youngstown's principal, Zonia Baber, a Parker trainee and disciple. In 1889, Parker assigned Flora Cooke to teach the first grade and to supervise the practice work of other teachers at the Normal School. In 1899, Cooke was appointed principal of the lower school at the Chicago Institute before being invited to become the principal of the Francis W. Parker School.

When Cooke accepted the principalship, Parker told her, "You won't be duplicating our experiments; you will be on your own," reflecting his belief that as education advanced it would present new principles. Cooke, however, became noted for "carrying the Parker legacy to the next generation."[64] Her speeches to the faculty made frequent reference to Francis Parker's educational principles, and several of her articles about Colonel Parker appeared in educational journals between 1913 and 1937.[65]

As both teacher and principal, Cooke established a tradition for the School that emphasized the education process over the administrative process. She possessed an almost religious belief in Parker's philosophy, yet the trustees often criticized her for lacking it. Although she served as principal until 1934, Cooke was twice replaced—in 1909, for "letting the school depart too far from old principles and methods" and in 1913, because "the school was leaderless." She was twice reappointed because one replacement "had the methods of a cheap political boss," and the second man had an "unacceptable relationship with the boys."[66] Between 1906 and 1908, Mrs. Blaine made herself Cooke's assistant principal. From completely different backgrounds, their common belief in education and democracy bound them to the same principles, resulting in a positive and productive relationship.

A woman of intelligence, bravery, and boundless energy, Cooke involved herself in more than twenty educational, social, and cultural organizations. She wrote two books on instruction for first graders and numerous articles, and she directed the faculty in the publication of *Studies in Education*. She also lectured in Switzerland and Denmark. An active member of the Progressive Education Association, Cooke advocated the Eight Year Study and served as a director of thirty-six teacher institutes. A respected member of the Chicago community, Flora Cooke received many honors. She was made the director of her alma mater, then called Chicago Teachers College, in 1930, and was one of the founders of Roosevelt College (now University) in downtown Chicago in 1946. Two Chicago colleges, Lake Forest and Columbia, conferred honorary degrees upon her. When she retired after fifty years in education, she had earned the sobriquet, "The Grand Old Lady of Education."[67]

During this era, one principal and four trustees, wholehearted subscribers to Colonel Parker's educational principles, undertook the administrative tasks of the School. The School was a trusteeship until 1932, and three original trustees together with Mrs. Blaine constituted its board. Each trustee—a personal friend, business associate, or a relative of Blaine—contributed at least $5,000 to the School at its opening. Mrs. Blaine assumed the average annual School deficit of about $121,000 until 1932 and an additional amount until 1934.[68] The main cause of the deficit was student scholarship aid, or more accurately "financial aid" since the criterion was not scholarship but diversity, which Colonel Parker, Blaine, and the faculty considered an educational necessity.

From 1901 to 1932, diversity was ethnic and economic, not racial; few African Americans lived on Chicago's North Side, and although the School offered a carriage service, time and cost were prohibitive for Southsiders, where most African American families located.[69] The parents included uneducated and educated neighborhood residents, and more second-generation than first-generation immigrants. Jews constituted the largest group.[70] In the main, the intellectual elite, including a significant number of artists, sent their children to the Parker School, while Chicago's North Side moneyed elite, for the most part, sent their children to the Latin Boys or Girls Schools or to eastern boarding schools. Chicago's large Catholic population preferred Catholic schools. The parents of this diverse student body were made an integral part of the School, and were organized into a Parent Association, an innovation Parker had introduced at the Normal School.[71]

In this era, Mrs. Blaine financed the addition of an auditorium and a gymnasium. A barn was built to house the animals and the chickens, and the experience of raising and selling farm products provided the background for classes in science and mathematics. After World War I, the trustees authorized temporary portable classrooms, but they eventually became flimsy and more dangerous than the shed the eighth grade boys built behind the main building. Blaine purchased a building for a library and a lunchroom, and she bought a plot of land for $250 so city children could grow a garden to complement the School's science class.[72]

In these thirty years, the Parker School achieved its dual purpose: the education of children and the training of teachers. It also produced, as Dewey noted, a "systematic increase in control and understanding of the materials for curriculum and the methods of instruction and discipline" for the first eight grades. "Organization and administration" would not become part of the Parker experiment until later. The initial strength reflected an emphasis on the child and on the educative process. The continuity provided by one principal, the same trustees, and a well-trained corps of teachers, passionately committed to the same progressive ideals laid a strong foundation for the decades to follow.

Stabilizing Years 1932–1967: Accent on the High School Experiment

In the second period of the Parker School's history, between 1932 and 1967, America underwent major demographic, economic, cultural and educational changes, but the Parker School enjoyed relative stability. Nationally, progressive education changed quite a bit. It had implied all that was good in education by 1919; it peaked between 1932 and 1945, with the Eight Year Study; but by 1950 it had become a scapegoat for nearly all the problems in American education.[73] The analysis of progressive education in Diane Ravitch's book *The Troubled Crusade*, confirmed that by the 1940s, the ideals and tenets of progressive education had become the "dominant American pedagogy."[74] From 1932 to 1967, in fact, the Parker School remained a bastion of progressive principles, collaborating with thirty experimental high schools to examine the relationship of progressive schools to college achievement.

In April of 1930, two hundred men and women assembled in the nation's capital to consider how the American secondary schools might better serve young people. The Progressive Education Association, with support from The Carnegie Foundation and the federal government, supported an Eight Year Study of the Relationship of School and College to find an answer. Ralph W. Tyler, the study's Research Director, compared 1,475 students from experimental schools with their counterparts in traditional schools, tracing and measuring their performance in 600 colleges for eight years. The experimental focus became the high school curricula and, one of three schools that contributed $800 each to launch the experiment, the Parker School led the initiative.[75]

Between 1933, when the Parker School entered the experiment, and 1942, and then again between 1963 and 1971, a period of reassessment, the faculty assimilated Colonel Parker's proven educational principles from the lower school with Ralph Tyler's newer principles to the experiment with its high school curriculum. The emphasis remained on "materials for curriculum" and "methods of instruction," with however, the added dimension of a scientific approach to education. How teachers undertook curriculum development became as important as the actual course of studies they designed. The starting point was the question, How can progressive education extend more effectively to secondary education?[76] Tyler guided the faculty through a five-step sequence in which teachers (1) examined the goals, aims, and purposes of the school; (2) identified objectives from their three sources—the child, subject matter specialists, and studies of contemporary life; (3) selected learning experiences to meet the objectives; (4) organized the learning experiences vertically and horizontally to facilitate the student's transfer of training; and (5) developed different evaluative tools to measure whether the students achieved the established objectives.[77]

Then, at the height of the Great Depression, the faculty envisioned the kind of American society it wanted the Parker School to develop and arrived at eight goals for its experiment: (1) an improved living standard, (2) employment in productive work, (3) conservation of material and human resources, (4) cooperative planning, (5) training for leisure, (6) participation in the arts, (7) reason and arbitration to replace force in disputes, and (8) the application of scientific thinking.

In Step Two of the Tyler model, teachers identified and defined three different sources of objectives: (1) subject-centered, (2) child-centered, and (3) society-centered objectives, that provided ways the experimental goals might be realized. Since the course of the study was predominantly subject-centered, it was easiest to transform former content into the new. The subject-centered objectives differed for each discipline, but the teachers specified three overarching subject-centered objectives: to create critical thinkers, to use interdisciplinary organization, and to use different forms of expression. Familiar with the child-centered objectives of the first eight grades, it was remarkable that the teachers selected the fewest number of child-centered objectives. The high school faculty gave less emphasis to the School's founding purpose—"the formation of character and not only the acquisition of knowledge"—than the lower school teachers. Perhaps because of the Great Depression, the faculty identified the greatest number of society-centered objectives to achieve their eight goals.

In Step Three of this Tyler model, "the selection of learning experiences," the faculty compared the current curriculum with their eight new goals with a view to accepting, modifying, or replacing the curriculum. Social studies became the central high school subject to be coordinated with the other disciplines. Abandoning the traditional history sequence, the history faculty required a six-year sequence in social studies for all students. "Seventh through ninth grades focused on world history, including the Orient; and tenth through twelfth grades used their world history background for a careful analysis of the development of democracy, political, economic, and international."[78] The English faculty designed a curriculum based on concepts presented in the Francis Parker Yearbook, *Experience in English* (1934), and focused the reading on what literature could contribute to a broader and deeper understanding of human behavior. In the most experimental English course, a motion picture project, juniors and seniors between 1937 and 1939 produced fifty-seven short films for use by church groups, labor unions, public schools, and colleges. Research techniques designed to correlate writing with social studies supplemented the English sequence in composition.

The science teachers designed a science curriculum based upon the Parker School Yearbook, *The Course in Science* (1918). Long before it became fashionable, the science teachers framed the physical and biological sciences in a moral and social context through the correlation of science with social sciences. The School's eighth experimental goal, "the application of scientific thinking," strengthened the sciences, and the science department made critical thinking the pervasive pedagogy in most high school disciplines. The science faculty wanted to require a four-year sequence in science but met resistance because of the homework load. Their solution was to complete the science homework during the class period, which by implication introduced first- and second-class subjects.

This pragmatic decision gave rise to an inequity problem caused by the imbalance of time in the course schedule for different disciplines. The faculty learned that when the school scheduled less time for one course, the discipline became less important to the students, who quickly reflected what the values appeared to be.

The subject matter in other disciplines underwent a less radical change. The mathematics faculty implemented only minor alterations until the reassessment period, and the physical education curriculum remained as it was into the 1970s. The performing and visual arts continued to hold a central position in the high school curriculum, but now, without the consideration of college requirements during the Eight Year Study, the arts faculty was free to experiment. Two of the eight experimental goals—"the training for leisure and participation in the arts"—encouraged additions to and improvements in the arts courses, the construction of an art gallery, a renewed emphasis on non-verbal media, and more correlation between social studies and the arts. The objective of the fine arts in the social studies and in foreign languages was to explain the American and foreign cultures respectively through drama, music, and the visual arts. The art classes were strengthened by their correlation. The experiment resulted in the unification of content and method in the high school curriculum.

The child-centered objectives focused on the "formation of character" and other psychological principles, which indicated a need to introduce new strategies. The high school teachers introduced the first psychology class, graderooms, where all students met to discuss group issues, and an advisory system, where students met with teachers to discuss individual issues. In a group approach, four gradehead teachers for ninth through twelfth grades conducted daily meetings with the entire grade focused on community issues, thereby placing a greater emphasis on student activities. For the individual student, the high school introduced an advisory system to reinforce an awareness of individual differences and to offer pupils guidance and direction. For the school, the teachers and principal wrote a polity in 1942 that effectively integrated "Negro" students. The School received public recognition for its effectiveness in the 1950s, when integration became a more popular cause.[79]

After "identifying the objectives" and "selecting the learning experience," the faculty followed the next step of Tyler's model, "organizing the courses" and then undertook the last step of its evaluation. Ralph Tyler, whose specialties were statistics and evaluation, introduced evaluation as an instructional technique into the school.[80] The School declared neither class rank for seniors nor letter grades until the freshman year. Class ranking, it was thought, interfered with the School's educational principle of cooperation in preference to competition as a social motive. Dissatisfied with any grading system, the faculty eagerly designed and tried out alternative student evaluation methods: anecdotal records, paper-pencil tests, neutral observation, and the planned conference. Whatever device they tried, some grading system emerged. The School's principal then, Herbert Smith, experimented with college entrance testing reform. Smith, in fact, began the testing reform in 1943, at the end of the Eight Year Study, and continued it until he retired in 1956.[81]

The results of the Eight Year Experiment were significant for the Parker School and for the nation in advancing "intelligent control and understanding" of basic curriculum and instruction principles. The national results of the Study on participating schools reported about the Parker School that "the unification of the school within itself and with the community is now marked. The students have a genuine interest in ideas, relating everything automatically to its effect on human beings. They let little intellectual capital lie idle, tending to examine critically, to scrutinize implications, and to weigh things by comparison." The national results illustrated that (1) students from the most experimental schools had the highest achievement in college, (2) a scientific approach to curriculum was the best guarantee of progress and a basis for continual growth, and (3) evaluation provided valuable information. In college, the students from the experimental schools were academically successful, their grade point averages were somewhat higher than those from the comparison group, and in the field of social studies, the targeted area of experiment, students took nearly fifty percent more courses than members from the comparison group. Ralph Tyler reported that the Parker School "developed students who were devoted to democratic principles and able to think critically and to participate constructively in community life."[82]

Just as Colonel Parker's experiments with teachers in Quincy and at the Normal School resulted in theoretical publications, so too Tyler's experiment with Parker teachers resulted in *Basic Principles of Curricu-*

lum and Instruction (1949). Tyler first outlined the "basic principles" on a napkin, when he and Hilda Taba, a consultant in social studies, met for lunch. The "basic principles" then became Tyler's syllabus for a course he taught at the University of Chicago between 1937 and 1948, when he was appointed to Dewey's former position and where he also became University Examiner, and between 1948 and 1953, Dean of the Division of Social Science. In 1949, Tyler published the syllabus as a book, which became for decades to follow the theoretical basis for curriculum development nationally and internationally, with nine editions in several different languages.[83]

The Parker School sustained the unification of the high school curriculum, introduced in the Eight Year Study and reassessed when Ralph Tyler returned for a critical reappraisal, which began in 1963. Available consultants from the Eight Year Study and other subject matter specialists reevaluated each department in a sequence that ended in 1971.[84] The reassessment called for a strengthening of content, sequence, and instruction but suggested no major changes. Departmental concentration during this period strengthened the courses and resulted in effective curricular development. The departmental approach, however, also detracted from curriculum unification because interdepartmental communication eroded as a consequence. The strengthened departments eventually became self-serving and a source of future unrest among teachers. In this period, the high school curriculum experiment positioned the high school as the strongest division of the School.

From 1901 until 1950, the unified lower school curriculum flourished, but then began to stagnate. During those fifty years, little experimentation took place with the lower school curriculum, and it grew only by accretion. The unified curriculum concept faded, and fewer lower school assistants received training in the precepts of experimentation. Additionally, the School's two principals of the era permitted lower school teachers to approach the curriculum unscientifically, changing and adding courses at will. A hybrid central subject transformed the theory of concentration into topic-centered interdisciplinary studies focused on, for example, Japan, the Middle Ages, or the Greeks. The result was minimal grade-level coordination and little vertical curriculum unity from grade to grade. As lower school teachers were permitted to "do their own thing," the unified center disappeared and "fragmentation increased until there was no quilt, only patches that children were expected to sew together on their own."

New discoveries in the education field necessarily added to lower school curricular fragmentation. For example, the Gillingham Reading Program, introduced in 1949, had to be changed later to a Learning Improvement Program for the learning disabled. Computer instruction also had to be added as a new teaching strategy. Unified sciences taught by grade teachers now became a sequence in science taught by specialists as a separate subject. These and other innovations were effective in themselves, but the trend in the lower school like the departmental trend in the high school moved toward isolated rather than unified courses, in contradiction to the central subject at the foundation of curriculum organization. It was true that the course of studies had been stabilized, the innovations were effective, and instruction was strong, but experimentation was increasingly undertaken without a scientific base. Not until 1985 did the lower school, then directed by a new lower school principal, Norma Nelson, begin to gain the momentum it possessed in the first thirty years.[85]

Between 1932 and 1967, the effectiveness of the instructors overshadowed the slow diversion away from scientific experimentation. Near midpoint in the School's history, Principal Smith's report to the trustees described the faculty in approving terms: "The standards are extremely high and they show an unusual willingness to spend time and effort in order to produce quality. The intellectual curiosity of the Parker student comes in large part from the faculty. The teachers do not fear to step outside the usual adult conformity in the exercise of their work."[86] The data showed that among the thirty-eight second-generation faculty members, twenty-six held advanced degrees, the longest faculty term was thirty-six years, and the average term was eight years, four and a half years shorter than in the previous era. The number of old guard faculty members, the quality of most teachers, and a variation on "illustrative teacher training" continued to provide stability. The lower school faculty trained twelve teaching assistants, and the faculty from the School instructed at Roosevelt University, the Pestalozzi School, and the Graduate Teachers College. In one year, six teachers were published and twenty-four participated in professional organizations. The curriculum reports, however, became less complete and competent than their earlier counterparts as described in a *Course of Studies* no longer prepared by the faculty.

The principals who led the School in this era, Herbert Smith from 1938 to 1956, and Cleveland Thomas from 1956 to 1967, took seriously its dual mission—the education of children and teacher training. Both embraced the Cooke tradition of principal as headmaster, which meant providing educational leadership for the School. Smith and Thomas were both English teachers, published authors, and nationally known educational leaders.

After thirty-six years of continuous administrative succession, running from Miss Cooke for thirty-four years to her assistant, Raymond Osborne, the trustees appointed Herbert Smith principal. A "transplanted New Englander and a lover of Cape Cod" as well as a Harvard graduate and the former principal of New York's Fieldston Ethical Culture School, Smith knew about the Parker School through his participation on the Committee on Transfer to College in the Eight Year Study. Along the range of the principal's responsibilities, from educational leader to school manager, Smith struck a balance but inclined toward the former. He was democratic with teachers and a stern disciplinarian with students, speaking in "staccato, precise, and clean language that covered multiple subjects with brevity. A respected teacher of the Senior Seminar, he inspired a twelfth grader's love for Thackery and Frost."[87]

Principal Smith absented himself from the school for extended periods to provide national education leadership. He helped establish the National Council of Independent Schools in 1942, and the National Registration Office, housed at Parker School until 1953, to report on a comparison of student performance in thirty experimental high schools and 600 colleges in 1944. In 1949, Smith established the Committee on General Composition with the task of adding essay exams to multiple-choice questions for the college Scholastic Aptitude Test. In 1957, he also initiated the Tyler Commission Report on the Value to American Society of the Independent School. One of the results of Smith's many contributions to education was an Institutional Award in Human Relations granted to the Parker School by the Chicago Commission on Human Relations.[88]

After Smith's effective principalship of eighteen years, Cleveland Thomas, Dean of Faculty at the North Shore Country Day School, who had earned his doctorate in English at Northwestern University, accepted the position. Thomas's experience at North Shore, a school built in the Parker image, acquainted him with the School's principles and practices. His style was to engage in all aspects of the position; he did not delegate responsibilities. "Gadge," as many called him, was teacher, college counselor, admissions officer, business manager, fund-raiser, and principal. Thomas encouraged modest experiments in interdisciplinary curriculum, but he undertook no major projects. The teachers respected his decision making because he encouraged impersonal open debate for a limited time, then made a decision everyone was expected to follow.[89] He searched for and secured highly desirable teachers by offering generous salaries when necessary.

Between 1932 and 1967, new buildings were erected, the School became a legal corporation, and the principals increased the enrollment, which signaled a new kind of permanency. In 1942, Smith arranged for the construction of the Little School to serve the senior kindergarten and, in 1946, the new junior kindergarten, at a cost of $90,000, financed through fund raising. Eleven years later, in 1957, Thomas began fund raising for a new building to house the additional 200 students that had been admitted since the 1930s. The modern structure opened in 1962, at a cost of $2,200,000, but elements of the design remained incomplete because of a lack of funds. While on a college counseling trip in the East in April of 1967, Dr. Thomas, still a young and vibrant man, died unexpectedly. The new building became a memorial to his great vitality, and his successor, Jack Ellison, was a man he had chosen to be the dean of faculty four years earlier.

The reorganization of the School in 1932 created a corporation for which Mrs. Blaine, fearful of conservative forces ruining the education experiment, insisted on an Educational Council as influential in safeguarding educational principles as the Board of Trustees was in the school's financial welfare. She saw to it that the Educational Council was legally constituted as an advisory body to keep vigilance on educational changes and to recommend the firing of any principal who neglected to support the basic educational principles. Continually worried about conservative forces redirecting the School's mission, Blaine recommended that alumni constitute the members of both the Board and the Council. She expected the Council to carry forth the progressive mission she had launched and financed over three decades. Upon her death in 1954, Anita

McCormick Blaine's New World Foundation granted the School the remaining city block, which it had been leasing from her for four dollars a year.[90]

Responding to Blaine's attempt to make the School self-reliant, a Scholarship Committee made up of parents and alumni set an annual fund-raising target of $30,000 in 1932, to provide financial aid to students. The achieved its goal infrequently, but on average two-fifths of the 300 students in the 1930s and 1940s received financial aid. In 1955, of the 505 students enrolled, 169 received full or partial aid.[91] The significant amount of financial aid to students competed with a fair wage for the teachers, who twice accepted salary reductions in order to support a diverse school enrollment. In the mid 1930s, the teachers considered but eventually declined to join the AF of L even though they had no salary schedule, no pension plan, and no hospitalization at the time. Seven hundred students constituted the economically, ethnically, religiously, and racially diverse student body by the end of this era.

The School had now stabilized financially and legally, and it had committed itself to remain a city rather than suburban school, a move Principal Smith suggested. The completion of two new buildings on the campus attested to its stability. The School continued in its dual purpose of educating children and training faculty, but the latter goal received less attention than it had in the former era, and "illustrative teaching" all but disappeared. The School continued its "systematic increase in the understanding of the materials of curriculum and methods of instruction and discipline," but the focus shifted to the four high school years. It continued to emphasize the educative over the administrative processes and two principals, along with several trustees, served long terms and provided continuity for twenty-nine years. The School's educational principles, a supportive student and parent body, the accomplishments of the faculty, and the success of students earned the School continued acclaim. More important, the School gained recognition as a leader in primary and secondary education.

Challenge of Progressivism, 1967–1986: Accent on the Middle School

Between 1967 and 1986, progressive education, once in the avant garde, gradually became synonymous with "modern or good education."

Meanwhile, the Parker School lost much of its cachet and experimental significance. In its early history, forces outside of the School—new theory in education and psychology, the Progressive Education Association, other experimental schools—promoted progressive education. In this later period, outside forces—the transformation of family structure and life, the changing values of college campus youth, the focus of education on science and math following Sputnik—threatened progressive schools. From among these societal changes, two strongly influenced the Parker School's direction: (1) the changing definition of the home-school-society interrelationship integral to the School, and (2) the ever-increasing dominance of the colleges over secondary education. Although more than ninety-five percent of its graduates had attended college, Parker had never been a college preparatory school, per se, but was rather dedicated to the education of the whole child for character formation and for the creation of a democracy. These external forces became sources of controversy, and the School began to suffer a problem of definition, so that, at the era's end, it struggled between the progressive and traditional forces within and without the community.[92]

During these two decades, the School undertook three major projects: (1) a new middle school curriculum, (2) a high school experiment in Intensive Scheduling, and (3) a community reorganization initiative that ultimately failed. To advance curriculum development throughout, the School added two curriculum coordinators and curriculum committees for departmental and vertical curriculum organization. The principal reorganized the School into three divisions with grades six, seven, and eight constituting a new middle school just as, in the earlier periods, it had concentrated on the lower and then its high school. The middle school teachers and the curriculum coordinator designed a new curriculum, modeled on Ralph Tyler's *Principles of Curriculum and Instruction*. Following the Eight Year Study pattern, the faculty began by setting goals and from them, identifying subject-centered, child-centered, and society-centered objectives and selecting, organizing, and evaluating learning experiences.

The central organizing principle for the subject-centered objectives was the desire to prepare students with both reading habits and reading skills. In an experimental model, the teachers planned two different approaches to see which would better achieve the subject-matter objective. The first trial was a cross-graded, interdisciplinary activity-centered Group Reading Project.[93] In the second trial, a Developmental Reading Program, the teachers used the written word for instruction in their disciplines and thereby taught reading in their respective content areas. Both approaches achieved the objectives, but the latter appeared more effective for the subject-centered history, science, and English courses that remained from the past era. The subject-centered experimental results demonstrated that (1) curriculum changes should be made incrementally and slowly, (2) the addition of some classes necessitated the elimination of others, and (3) well designed curriculum projects, like group reading, deserved additional study.

The child-centered objectives were met through a series of experimental, month-long, cross-graded, interdisciplinary mini-course electives offered in one intensive morning and one afternoon session of two and a half hours each. The activity-based classes used experiential instruction and expression as a learning tool.[94] Teachers established the mini-course experiment following established principles of curriculum and instruction; therefore, when the experimental results indicated that the trial was inappropriate for this age level, they dropped the mini-courses from the curriculum. Many teachers were disappointed by the evaluation results since the mini-courses appeared to have been effective: the students welcomed the new approach, and the courses offered a variety of instructional opportunities. The data, however, revealed little transfer of training, and hence the decision to eliminate the experiment.

To meet society-centered objectives, the curriculum coordinator introduced a Community Service Program networked nationally with an Experiential Education experiment directed by Ralph Tyler.[95] Both the national evaluation data and the Parker data indicated a successful trial. The experiment became an effective middle school community service program, later expanded to the high school, and by 1994, community service had become a graduation requirement. Thus, curriculum unity and faculty collaboration positioned the middle school as the School's strongest division during this third era. In general, the School personnel learned that curricular strength resulted from experimentation; in fact, the experimental division of the School in each of the three eras became the strongest curriculum area.

While the middle school faculty advanced the curriculum for the reorganized sixth, seventh, and eighth grades, the high school teachers simultaneously implemented changes, but this time they disregarded the principles they had learned to use during the Eight Year Study. The result was a major curriculum change for grades nine through twelve undertaken unscientifically. Such societal influence as the knowledge explosion, the debate between multicultural and traditional content, college campus activism, the innovations of the curriculum from 1975 through 1985, college requirements, and other influences stimulated many minor changes but ultimately caused a major change in the high school.

The earliest curricular development the high school teachers initiated was a series of trials with interdisciplinary, team-taught ninth grade entrance and twelfth-grade exit courses. The goal was to introduce and to conclude the high school experience and to focus students on learning critical thinking skills in several disciplines. One trial course, focused on Galileo, combined science, history, and literature. Another trial focused on *Richard III* to contrast how drama presented a story differently from the way the Tudor and other historians interpreted the same tale. The foreign language department developed a new bilingual approach to Spanish. The chairperson of the physical education department effectively transformed year-long required courses into elective semester courses based on lifelong activities.[96] But because the high school curriculum now reflected more innovation than ever, a drastic overhaul seemed to be a necessity.

Responding to this challenge, in the mid-1970s several young teachers initiated a large-scale innovation with an experiment called Intensive Scheduling. They designed the new intensive schedule around a three-hour class offered three times weekly for one semester. Students reduced the number of courses they took at one time and concentrated instead on fewer disciplines simultaneously. Year-long forty-minute classes daily or three sixty-minute sessions weekly remained the schedule for the mathematics, foreign language, and music departments. Physical education adopted its own schedule. The general course content in science, English, or history became specific electives like Environmental Science, Writing and Fiction and Poetry, or Economic Theory. The experiment transformed the curriculum by altering course content, selection, sequence, and diploma requirements. The new Intensive Scheduling gave students flexibility in course selection rather than unity.

The Intensive Plan invigorated the School and offered many excellent educational opportunities. Most of the courses were well taught and followed valid instructional principles like activity, expression, and interdiscipline. Their isolated effectiveness was, however, eclipsed by curricular fragmentation, departmental inequities, little transfer of training from one subject to another, lack of teacher awareness of their students' progress, and numerous other problems difficult to address without an evaluation tool in place for the trial. Because the design proceeded unsystematically without formal evaluation to measure it, the project failed to "increase intelligent control and knowledge" of curriculum and instruction. Instead of resolving the curriculum problems the design addressed, old problems recurred each year and new problems surfaced. But, variations of the high school Intensive Schedule lingered, and unenlightened adjustments continued to be adopted without evaluation data.

Sidestepping a solution to the problems Intensive Scheduling caused, beginning in 1980, the experimentation focused on the development of a "cooperative community." Throughout the era, societal forces had been rearranging the community, and the School leadership, with a deliberative body of teachers and the advice of the Educational Council, reorganized community life by democratizing its governance. The goal was to identify, analyze, and solve those social problems that had damaged the community. The plan was to position representative members—administrators, teachers, students, parents, and experts—on each school committee as a first step in "democratization."

This democratization prevented many problems and solved others. The process used parents as chaperons to revitalize student activities and, in general, improved student-adult relationships. An innovative ninth grade Parent Night conducted by support service professionals and a new health curriculum for parents, teachers, and students strengthened the School and became part of its current curriculum. The democratization process helped the School recognize the new needs of adolescents in a changing society, and it acted upon those needs. For many parents and teachers in the community, democratization encouraged thought and reflection and produced new insights and growth.

But the democratization process proved difficult and its failures were many. The democratic strategies slowed down decision making and at times brought it to a standstill. The representation of constituent bodies on most school committees complicated meetings. The process increased a general awareness of social problems thereby intimidating many parents and teachers previously unaware of drug issues, new sexual behaviors, or racial tension. Participatory democracy engaged more people in the schooling process in new ways than ever before, making it difficult to define the boundaries "between home and school" and "between school and community."[97]

Dewey's theory of "the new kind of school discipline" and Parker's principles of "school government and moral training" were being given a trial. The process was educative, but many teachers, the ordained "organizers of community life," and some trustees resisted testing democracy so thoroughly. The frustration overwhelmed those adults who discovered that authoritarian governance was easier. The experiment in democratization died from a frustrated leadership, discouraged by those in the School hostile to the experiment and blind to the progress. The School had been positioned to discover and propound new principles for a new kind of experiment with "democracy and education." The progressive forces lost the battle over democracy, and it was a defeat for the Parker School.[98]

The faculty profile remained strong between 1967 and 1986. Thirteen faculty members taught at the School for twenty-five or more years, providing allegiance to basic principles.[99] Seven high school faculty members held doctorates, and a quarter of all the faculty members in this period had become published authors. But only forty percent, the lowest number since the school opened, involved themselves in professional organizations. Teacher training continued with assistants in the lower school and practice teachers from universities throughout the School. The teaching legacy continued to be transferred by "artistic teachers" many of whom were in leadership positions while also being classroom teachers. The curriculum coordinators introduced teachers new to the School to its history, educational principles, practices, and policies. Collaborative curriculum development with coordinators, department chairmen, and the curriculum committee continued throughout the era. Teachers' curriculum reports, now products of the departmental structure, were organized in a curriculum library by the coordinators for professional utilization by colleagues and other educators. Throughout the era, the faculty remained an accomplished and deliberate group, thoughtful in its tasks and responsive to student needs.

As the era came to a close, however, faculty members became less cohesive, and the department chairmen, who constituted the membership of the high and middle school curriculum committee, became increasingly contentious, voted from department interest, and argued about the schedule for their department courses. The lower school curriculum committee argued primarily two issues: the nature of faculty representation on their curriculum committee and an approach to reading upon which they could all agree. The three divisions of the School, previously unified, began to argue with each other. A majority of the faculty became disgruntled over real and perceived issues related to many aspects of the School: (1) the changing nature of trustee leadership from democratic to hierarchial, (2) the trustee shift in emphasis from school management to educational policy, (3) the diminished role of the faculty in the decision-making process, (4) the greater dominance of the parents in curriculum matters, and (5) increasing ambiguity over the goals of the School. The general mistrust among teachers caused them to organize a Parker Teachers' Association, which all but six joined. The non-faculty staff, many of whom had served the School in usual and unusual ways, was not invited to participate. The membership disagreed once again over affiliating with a national union. In the past, the principal had negotiated the contract with teachers, but now the trustees served as the bargaining agent. This new arrangement radically altered the relationship between the principal and the teachers and between the trustees and the teachers. Untrained as educational professionals, the trustees misplaced their emphasis on accountability and evaluation rather than on recruitment and development. The trustees assigned the administrators, most of them less qualified as teachers than the classroom masters, to implement the task. The School's emphasis shifted from students and education to business and bureaucracy.

Two experts in the educational principles of progressive education served as principals, Jack Ellison, from 1967 to 1972, and William D. Geer, Jr., from 1973 to 1986. Both subscribed to democratic school practices; Ellison's hallmark was his insistence upon intellectual rigor, and Geer's was his call for a visible faculty presence working democratically with the community.

Ellison preferred to guide through scholarship and to use the impetus of an idea to motivate. Understanding learning as self-effort, he wanted his faculty members and students alike to pursue it actively. Canadian born and educated, Ellison had completed his graduate work at the Graduate Teachers College in Winnetka. In 1937, during the Eight Year Experiment, Principal Herbert Smith had hired Ellison to teach ninth grade English and social studies, and in 1963, Cleveland Thomas had appointed him Dean of Faculty. Ellison introduced and taught anthropology to seniors, and, an authority on the teaching of social studies, he was made chairman of the Wingspread Conference on Social Studies, sponsored by the National Association of Independent Schools. A scholarly man, he was as comfortable debating a Marxian viewpoint with a history teacher as quoting Alfred North Whitehead to make an educational point with a student. A prodigious reader, Ellison ended his presentations and meetings by recommending an appropriate book, the starting point for the next meeting. Perhaps a bit of an intellectual snob, Ellison was also an egalitarian humanist. A progressive politically—some might call him a radical—he placed a high value on freedom and democracy, a value captured in his opening remarks to the faculty in 1971, when he quoted Albert Camus: "We have nothing to lose except everything, so let us go forward."[100]

Jack Ellison preferred the educative to the managerial aspect of the principalship, leading the school in a kind of seminar style with intergeneration groups congregating in the hall, in his office, or wherever he happened to be. He was "the headmaster," who mentored teachers by sitting unobtrusively in a classroom corner observing teaching, writing copious notes, and meeting afterwards to discuss and illuminate the lesson. His idea of administration was "to put the ineffective teachers in administration and keep the good ones in the classroom."[101]

Ellison's contributions were numerous and diverse, but his main interest focused on the relationship between the school and the community. He created Independent Study and May Month, which took the students into the community. His community outreach resulted in a summer play program organized at the School for neighborhood children; Parker Evening Courses, which shared resources with the community;

and public-private school exchanges. For five years, with Ellison at the head, the total environment became educative.

After Ellison retired, the trustees appointed a one-year acting principal until William D. Geer, Jr., began his fourteen years of service. Geer was a New Yorker and a Harvard graduate with experience in both private and public schools. Similar to Thomas in administrative style, Geer assumed responsibility for the whole, but the Parker School was a larger undertaking than it had been in 1956. Geer's understanding of progressive principles and practices enabled him to address challenges scientifically, logically, and creatively. He worked a twelve-hour day so he held Saturday morning meetings at his office and evening meetings in his home, where he served his own hot homemade bread. He taught English in the high school and child care in the lower school. He reorganized the school for instructional purposes and curriculum coordination. He espoused Tyler's "principles of curriculum and instruction" and insisted on faculty participation and leadership in local and national education issues.

Geer encouraged active student and faculty participation in extending the Parker outreach. Under his leadership, the health education curriculum became nationally recognized.[102] A student drug program culminated with a rally in Lincoln Park for students against drinking and driving with Governor Edgar of Illinois, a representative from the mayor's office, rock bands, and various speakers. A Martin Luther King Day celebrated community awareness of diversity in the School. Geer recruited minority teachers and insisted on Black teachers actively engaging in the community. One response to woman's issues, a topic that attracted his special attention as the father of four daughters, was an increase in girls' sports and early childhood education. Geer's great energy and his willingness to explore new ideas, to confront new problems, and to find innovative solutions often exhausted the School personnel.

During Geer's administration the built a new wing to house the middle school division, and he directed an extremely effective seventy-fifth anniversary celebration for some 6,276 Parker Graduates.[103] In the constellation of the principal's responsibilities societal issues dominated the Geer administration. Attendance of parents at school meetings flagged, and in the increasing absence of a close home and school association, the teachers and students struggled with decisions about language at Morning Exercise suitable for the entire audience and about clothing and behavior standards—holes in jeans, bra burning, and streaking—that violated the progressive school principle of discipline through freedom with responsibility. To address the attack upon the high school curriculum by the colleges, Geer engaged himself and the faculty in local, state, and national organizations. He refused to succumb to college pressure, but he heightened college counseling and engaged the parents of college-bound students more rigorously. To confront these societal issues impinging on the educative process, Geer applied progressive principles in a democratization experiment with the community. The experiment stopped, however, when Geer retired in 1986. He had poised the School to address a major progressive theme—the interrelationship of the home-school-society triad—an unresolved theme introduced at the turn of the century by both John Dewey and Francis Parker. Instead the School dissipated its energy while the trustees pondered the School's goals and the Educational Council became the handmaiden of the Board of Trustees.

The Francis Parker School in the 1990s

At the close of the Geer administration, the School floundered in indecision. In the mid-1990s, the Educational Council, the keeper of the progressive flame, declined into irrelevance, and the Board of Trustees became the dominant voice. Following a fierce battle against the faculty, waged by the majority of trustees and four appointed teachers unsympathetic to the School's legal charter of 1932, the Educational Council was dismantled. The Charter for the Reorganization of the School that charged the trustees operating the School and the Education Council with the progressive educational principles of the School had been abandoned.

Until 1995, the trustees vacillated over whether the school should remain progressive or become traditional, and they projected their irresolution in the hiring of principals. In less than a decade, the trustees hired two acting principals. The first was Fred Dust, who had been the head of the high school, and the second was John Cotton, whose education came from a traditional eastern boarding school. Cotton served as principal for a short term and, when he resigned, the trustees, remaining uncertain of their direction, engaged Timothy Burns as an interim principal for one year. The Parker School had not been founded as a traditional, elite college preparatory school; its prestige lay elsewhere; the legacy of Colonel Parker, Anita McCormick Blaine, and Flora Cooke languished in the decade of dispute.

Then in 1995, a search for a principal culminated in the appointment of a democratically oriented educator with a neo-progressive vision. Before coming to the School, Donald Monroe had been the Superintendent of the Winnetka, Illinois, Public Schools; he had earned his doctorate in education and his expertise lay in lower school education. Modern innovations appeared immediately: a desktop or laptop computer for each member of the faculty, experimental computer rooms for testing instructional arrangements, a strengthened video production class, an investigation into a collaborative mathematics and science approach, and a new middle school foreign language program. His presence stimulated new thoughts on old ideas. Colonel Parker's vision of the School as "a model for the common school" once again appeared in new outreach programs: the Chairman of the English Department introduced a collaborative summer community program for Parker School and public schools; an alumna implemented a new teacher training program with Northwestern University; several middle school teachers, working with a foundation, undertook to guide minority students through the transition to high school; and an African-American teacher assisted admissions with minority recruitment.

During his first year, Monroe directed school innovations designed to achieve a "unity of purpose, method, and content," the concept that had informed and energized the Parker School since 1901. He consulted with teachers familiar with School practice, held parent and student meetings, and engaged the alumni in reunion gatherings. As validated educational principles found themselves recast into designs for the future, a twenty million-dollar construction project began transforming the Francis W. Parker School for the twenty-first century.

Conclusion

In the first eighty-five years of its history, the Francis W. Parker School implemented the progressive principles espoused by Colonel Parker and John Dewey. Its greatest success during its first three decades was the development of a curriculum for the first eight grades. Four accomplishments marked this era: (1) the education of the whole child—mental, moral, and physical; (2) the experience-activity-expression learning and teaching method; (3) the integration of the curriculum through central subjects and, most significantly, (4) the development of the school as the instructor in character and democracy.

In the second era, the teachers implemented a less explicit version of the first three accomplishments with significant success in the high school. Bolder educational processes for the development of community were implemented in the ninth through twelfth grades. Until this era, the School mirrored the progressive theories and practices developed by Parker and Dewey. The students had learned by doing and the teachers had learned by teaching and collaborating. The School had advanced from applying psychological and sociological principles and had progressed through experimentation. Educators outside the school learned from the Parker School's contributions: a network of schools in the Parker image developed, numerous publications contributed to educational practice, many school visitors learned first-hand about the School, and faculty participated in many numerous conferences spreading its philosophy.

In the third era, the science of education continued to develop in the middle school, but other experiments like Intensive Scheduling were not scientifically tested. Others, like the democratization of all committees, proved difficult to support. From 1985 to 1995, progressive principles languished among the faculty, students, alumni, and parents, as the curriculum became more traditional. As the School approaches its centennial, the Parker School may be at a crossroads. Like many progressive schools founded in the early twentieth century, it can lose touch with its progressive heritage. Or its legacy, based on the art of teaching and the science of education, can be reaffirmed; and the School can be a platform for a moral education in a democratic society, consistent with Blaine, Dewey, and Parker's vision of a new kind of education.

EXPERIMENTAL SCHOOL, EXPERIMENTAL COMMUNITY: THE MARIETTA JOHNSON SCHOOL OF ORGANIC EDUCATION IN FAIRHOPE, ALABAMA

Joseph W. Newman

Half a mile from the shops and restaurants that line the business district of Fairhope, Alabama, the Marietta Johnson School of Organic Education sits tucked away down a side street, perched atop a piney-woods bluff. Once the very heart of a community of reformers, intellectuals, and freethinkers, today the school is set some distance apart, struggling to survive while it tries to recapture the spirit of its past.

The campus is attractive in a modern sort of way. Connected by covered walkways, four small red-brick buildings and a manual arts shop make up the physical plant, while a playground, woods, and open areas invite students out of doors. The four main buildings mimic the architecture of the white-frame Bell Building, the centerpiece of the old downtown campus the school occupied for eighty years before selling in the late 1980s in a bid for financial security.

The school still hums with the activity of sixty students, ninety-eight percent of them white, most of them upper-middle class and from the immediate area. All seem happy to be there. Some have had difficulty getting along in more traditional settings, but most have parents who simply want a different kind of education for their children, something less regimented, less hurried, less competitive. The Organic School tries to fill this niche in the educational marketplace of the 1990s—a small niche, apparently, even in an artsy community like Fairhope—by offering pupil-teacher ratios of ten to one, generous individual attention, and, yes, glimpses of Marietta Johnson's original vision.[1]

Directors have come and gone through a revolving door since Johnson's death in 1938, and with members of the governing board throwing their weight around, the school has zigged and zagged. Given this school's history, the future could hold almost anything. Still, the institution Lawrence Cremin described as "easily the most child-centered of the early experimental schools" remains child-centered today.[2] The school is much as it was in Johnson's day—only less so.

The Experiment

It was an *experiment*, she wanted people to understand, repeating the word until early visitors came away using it. Marietta Johnson was conducting an educational experiment as part of a larger community experiment. John Dewey explained in *Schools of To-Morrow* (1915) that he was one of the many "students and experts" who "made pilgrimages" to Fairhope to see the School of Organic Education. Fittingly, Dewey titled his chapter on the Organic School "An Experiment in Education as Natural Development," and he pronounced it a "decided success."[3] But despite rave reviews from Dewey and other notable pilgrims, and notwithstanding the true-believer optimism that seemed to be everywhere in Fairhope, it was too early to call either the educational experiment or the community experiment a success.

Marietta Pierce Johnson and her husband, Frank, moved to Fairhope in 1902, looking for change, which was just what the small village (population 100) on Mobile Bay had to offer. Like most others drawn to Fairhope in its early years, the Johnsons were not southerners—they were from St. Paul, Minnesota—and like many others, they were socialists. Fairhope had been established in 1894 as a single-tax colony devoted to the theories of Henry George, author of *Progress and Poverty* (1879). Of the millions who read George's late-nineteenth-century bestseller, a few disciples took his words seriously enough to put them into practice. This Deep South colony, which its founders believed had a "Fair Hope" of succeeding, was the first and largest single-tax experiment in the nation.[4]

The original colonists, most of them from the Midwest, resolved to make their new home a model of "cooperative individualism." Under the terms of the community experiment, the colony owned the land, with individuals and families holding ninety-nine-year leases on their plots. The annual rent paid to the colony constituted the "single tax" on land, which generated funds for such public amenities as parks, a beach, and a library. The colony also owned the utilities. These arrangements, George's followers believed, would help control the gap between rich and poor by preventing the wealthy from monopolizing the land and its resources.[5] George himself, though, doubted an experimental "single tax city" could succeed.[6]

From the very start, Fairhopers won a well-deserved reputation as an intellectual group united in their belief that the economic system of the United States was flawed. Beyond that central conviction, the early residents agreed to disagree. Spirited debates broke out in the many organizations they formed, societies like the Progressive League, Socialist Club, and School of Philosophy. Fairhope's single-tax founders, ardent defenders of individualism and other values central to capitalism, often found themselves at odds with the socialists who soon came to dominate the community. Participation in town-meeting politics ran high, and the climate grew particularly charged after the village incorporated in 1908 and a socialist defeated a single taxer in the first race for mayor.[7]

But even if Fairhopers took different sides on a wide range of issues, virtually all residents drew inspiration from the utopian idealism of *Progress and Poverty*. Working together in an experimental community gave them a sense of self-importance, an identity they enjoyed projecting to outsiders.[8] Upton Sinclair, who enrolled his son in the Organic School while wintering in Fairhope in 1909, captured the spirit of the early community in his *Autobiography* (1962):

> Here were two or three hundred assorted reformers who had organized their affairs according to the gospel of Henry George. They were trying to eke out a living from poor soil and felt certain they were setting an example for the rest of the world.[9]

Marietta Johnson added an educational dimension to the Fairhope experiment. In the early 1900s, Alabama was still in the process of building a viable state school system; it was easy for Fairhopers to make unfavorable comparisons between the midwestern and northern schools they had left behind and the schools they found in rural Baldwin County, Alabama. But beyond raising additional local funds and trying to attract better teachers, the colonists had no special ideas on how to improve schooling. Nor did Henry George have much to say on the subject. Marietta Johnson did.[10]

Born Marietta Louise Pierce on October 8, 1864, near St. Paul, Minnesota, she grew up in a close farming family that included a twin sister and six other siblings. Her parents, Clarence and Rhoda Martin Pierce, were devout members of the Christian Church and raised their children accordingly. The family's economic circumstances seem to have been comfortable. But Marietta's father died while she was still young, and her mother helped support the family by running a school at home for neighborhood children. Marietta later attended public school in St. Paul and graduated in 1885 from the State Normal School at St. Cloud. She began her work as a teacher with five years of service in rural Minnesota schools.[11]

Enthusiastic, charismatic, and ambitious, she quickly climbed the occupational ladder. She taught every elementary school grade and several high school subjects on her way to becoming a "training" or "critic" teacher in the normal schools at St. Paul, Moorhead, and Mankato.[12] Later, looking back on this stage in her career, Johnson painted an ironic portrait of the achievement-driven teacher she had been:

> It was a great joy to me when six-year-old children in the first grade could read through four first readers in three months!!. . . Of course, it was high pressure, but they could do it! The student teachers were thrilled with these results. . . . The parents were pleased. I was a success! And we all truly believed that the children loved to do it, and that it was good for them![13]

Although Johnson could be self-critical, as these remarks indicate, her faith in herself was always a hallmark of her personal style.

That faith shook in 1901 when she "underwent a conversion experience."[14] The religious imagery is appropriate, and Johnson herself used it to explain the intensity of her ordeal. It began when she read *The Development of the Child* (1898) by Nathan Oppenheim, a pediatrician at Mt. Sinai Hospital in New York City. "The world has a wrong idea of its children," Oppenheim insisted. Parents and teachers who think of children as "adults in small" and of childhood as a time for mastering adult behavior are causing children harm—in some cases irreparable harm. According to Oppenheim, children are "absolutely different from adults, not only in size, but also in every element which goes to make up the final state of maturity." Constantly changing, children need a "special treatment and environment" to guide and encourage their development.[15]

As Johnson read on, she began to question virtually everything she had learned about teaching; indeed, she felt appalled at what she had been teaching teachers. She convinced herself she had been a "child destroyer" whose efforts violated the "order of development of the nervous system. I realized that my enthusiasm was destructive, and the more efficient I was, the more I injured the pupils!"[16]

Now growing critical of organized religion, Johnson proceeded to repent of her educational sins. She took Oppenheim's book as her "educational Bible," soon supplementing it with works by Dewey and other child-centered educators. When she first arrived in Fairhope, she would stay up late at night, poring over these texts. She would revisit them for "inspiration" and "support" for the rest of her life. As the ideas in these books "took possession of me," she recalled, "I could not rest until I had started a school. I began experimenting with my own child and with other children of the neighborhood."[17]

Johnson's chance to experiment in a school setting came in January 1903, less than a month after her move to Fairhope, when the thirty-eight-year-old woman took charge of the colony's public elementary school. In what became a pilot project for her later work at the Organic School, she added gardening and manual arts to the curriculum, invited adults to school to make music and tell stories, and organized a normal course. At the start of the 1903–1904 school year, Johnson announced ambitious plans to expand the normal course, develop a high school program, and recruit out-of-state students.[18]

These plans were cut short by her husband's decision to move the family to Mississippi in 1904. Frank Johnson was a farmer and rancher, and at this time in their lives together, his work came first. But their attempt at pecan farming failed, his eyesight steadily worsened, and a fire destroyed most of their possessions.[19]

The Johnsons returned to Fairhope in 1907. From then on, her work came first. Although Frank would be elected mayor of Fairhope in 1912 on the Socialist ticket, his primary work outside the home was as a manual arts teacher in the School of Organic Education, where he used his skills as a carpenter and cabinetmaker. Frank stayed busy within the Johnson household. Until his death in 1919, he played a supportive role as "Marietta Johnson's husband," taking on a large share of domestic duties to enable his wife to spend long hours with her educational experiment.[20]

Across the nation during the early 1900s, women were emerging as leaders in local school reform. Marietta Johnson, like many of her counterparts, was a "quiet feminist."[21] Joyce Antler argues in her study of Lucy Sprague Mitchell, founder of the Bank Street College of Education in New York City, that the lives and careers of such women exemplify feminism as an "individual's struggle for autonomy, rather than a conscious, political strategy for altering the social order."[22] Johnson certainly achieved a strong sense of self-actualization as she rose to national prominence as an educator, but her daily life in Fairhope, a community where women voted and played active roles in the community, was the wellspring of her autonomy. Johnson may not have campaigned for women's rights, but she operated her school as a coeducational institution with few distinctions between male and female students.[23]

"An Original Demonstration"

Elated to be back in Fairhope after the discouraging sojourn in Mississippi, Johnson opened the School of Organic Education in November 1907. The school started modestly enough as a kindergarten in a small cottage. Lydia and Samuel Comings, the Johnsons' close friends in Fairhope, provided the cottage as well as a monthly subsidy of $25. Six kindergartners, two of them the Johnsons' own sons, enrolled the first day and were quickly joined by a handful of older elementary students. Additional financial support would soon be forthcoming from the colony council, enabling her to run the school as a quasi-public institution with no tuition for local children. Two tragedies dampened Johnson's joy at resuming her educational experiment: the death of her younger son in a freak accident just after school began, and the death of Mr. Comings on Christmas eve. Johnson handled the stress characteristically by throwing herself into her work. By the end of January 1908 she had enrolled more than 30 students, 20 of whom were in the kindergarten. Her optimistic spirit returned as the school prospered.[24]

Johnson was eager to attract older students, but her deepest concern was for the very young. Most Fairhopers thought of her first as a kindergarten teacher, an image that was accurate symbolically if not literally. Although she had taught people whose ages ranged up to young adulthood, a Fairhope friend insightfully observed that Johnson's approach amounted to the "kindergarten method carried through the entire school course," just as "Froebel intended it to be."[25] Johnson took that as a great compliment, for she cited Froebel more often than any other classical writer on education—more often, even, than Rousseau, whose *Emile* often came to the mind of visitors to the Organic School.

Johnson appropriated the concept "organic" from C. Hanford Henderson, former headmaster of New York City's Pratt Institute, whose book *Education and the Larger Life* (1902) became another of her educational bibles. Johnson advocated treating each student as a complete organism—a "whole child," as the progressive slogan would later have it—balancing the mental, spiritual, and physical.[26] As Dewey noted in *Schools of To-Morrow* (without acknowledging Henderson, for the two were rivals), organic education "follow[s] the natural growth of the pupil" and provides the "occupations and activities necessary at each stage of development."[27]

Johnson did not design her experiment as an empirical test of the "point of view" she synthesized from Oppenheim, Henderson, Dewey, Froebel, and others. As far as she was concerned, the "idea" of child development she got from these sources was "universally accepted."[28] Johnson was exaggerating, of course. Although there was a broad consensus by the early 1900s that children went through developmental stages, the very authorities she most admired often disagreed. They differed not only on methodological matters—which activities are appropriate at which stages?—but on basic principles—how many stages are there and how long do they last? Other scholars held even more divergent views.[29] But Johnson was simply not interested in running studies of child development, pitting different theories against one another to prove one superior. That was not the nature of her experiment.

Instead, she *accepted* a set of developmental principles that struck her as valid and incorporated them into the framework she adapted from Oppenheim during her conversion experience. Then she set about finding ways of putting the principles into practice. Johnson's experiment was not a theoretical test but a practical application. It was, in her words, an "original demonstration."[30]

Dewey Visits, Plays Santa Claus

The experiment was well underway by the time Dewey visited the Organic School in 1913. Now boasting an enrollment of 150 students, the school had attracted two-thirds of Fairhope's elementary-aged white children, who attended tuition-free.[31] As Dewey put it, "Mrs. Johnson is trying an experiment under conditions which hold in public schools, and she believes her methods are feasible for any public school system. . . . Any child is welcome."[32]

Dewey was exaggerating. The Organic School's enrollment *did* reflect public school conditions—which meant African-American children were not welcome. Racial segregation was so widely accepted throughout the nation during the early twentieth century, not even John Dewey saw fit to comment. Johnson held enlightened views on race for her day, going so far as to denounce racial prejudice in her speeches and writings. Some of Fairhope's nonsouthern founders shared her views but feared they would jeopardize their community experiment if they accorded blacks equal treatment. African Americans lived separate and decidedly unequal lives in Fairhope, and with respect to race relations, the Organic School upheld the status quo.[33]

Within the limits the white community established, though, Johnson worked to create an egalitarian climate at the Organic School. In addition to providing equal opportunities for female and male students, she accepted students from all socioeconomic backgrounds represented in the white population—a fairly narrow range in the early days of the community. She also recruited "backward" (disabled) children for whom public schools made no provision.[34]

Johnson also recruited students of a very different kind: well-to-do northern and midwestern children whose parents were enamored of what would soon be called "progressive education." Some of these students enrolled for just the winter while their parents vacationed in the South. Resort communities flourished along the Eastern Shore of Mobile Bay, and the single-tax aura of Fairhope, now a village with a New England look and more than 500 residents, held a special appeal for artists, writers, and intellectuals. The sunny weather, heady politics, and child-centered education were attractive indeed to the Sinclairs and would-be Sinclairs. The two younger sisters of Margaret Mead, for instance, spent time at the Organic School during the early 1920s. Tuition- and board-paying students made up approximately one-third of the enrollment and subsidized the attendance of local children.[35]

Johnson proved an effective recruiter for the school because she spent so much time spreading the gospel of organic education on the lecture circuit. She addressed women's and civic clubs, single-tax groups, education associations, and university audiences. She conducted teacher institutes, demonstration schools, and summer schools. She founded organic school societies. Eventually speaking throughout the nation and in several foreign countries, Johnson became particularly popular in the New York City area. *The New York Times* regularly gave her positive publicity, including a full-page interview in March 1913.[36]

Soon after the interview ran, a group of socially prominent women in Greenwich, Connecticut, formed the Fairhope League (later the Fairhope Educational Foundation) to support Johnson's work. Under their sponsorship, she conducted an ongoing summer school in Greenwich for teachers, parents, and others interested in organic education. For several years she also served as director of the Edgewood School in Greenwich, which gave her a chance to experiment with organic education in an elite suburban context.[37]

This group of well-connected friends from metropolitan New York persuaded Dewey to visit Fairhope during the Christmas season in 1913. Johnson knew the stakes were high, calling the visit "the most critical experience of my life!"[38] After she explained to her students the significance of Dewey's planned pilgrimage, they voted to hold school during the holidays, and boarders made arrangements to stay over. Although Dewey's daughter Evelyn made all the other site visits for *Schools of To-*

Morrow, Dewey himself went on this one, taking along his fourteen-year-old son Sabino, who attended the Organic School for a week and liked it so much he wanted to stay.[39] "Dewey in Fairhope" stories, still part of the local mythology, include a tale that has the bespectacled, white-haired philosopher playing Santa Claus and bouncing students on his knee.

Dewey's blessing catapulted the Organic School into the front ranks of progressive schools, but even before his visit the school was not only surviving but thriving. An $11,000 gift from soap magnate Joseph Fels underwrote much of the school's early growth, while revenue from boarding students and Johnson's earnings on the road provided critical operating funds. As the school grew, Johnson hired teachers, some of them graduates of the two-year normal program she started in Fairhope and some recruited in Greenwich and elsewhere.[40]

The Fels gift helped the school move in 1909 to a new location one block off Fairhope's main street, to a ten-acre site the colony provided rent free and with its utilities paid. Johnson, Lydia Comings, and four other Fairhope women signed papers incorporating the school that same year. The Bell Building, named for the school bell that rang out at regular intervals across the village, served as the campus focal point. Several other structures were either in place or under construction by the time Dewey visited. A total of ten buildings, including a revenue-producing dormitory called the School Home, would dot the campus by the early 1920s.[41]

Inside (and Outside) the Organic School

The school's facilities were handsome and well ventilated, to be sure, but Dewey and other visitors were even more impressed by the time the students spent outdoors. Students and teachers often took the pleasant half-mile walk down to the colony beach on Mobile Bay. Nature study and field geography brought them into the woods, fields, and streams. Dewey's camera caught students working math problems on the walls of a deep gully and exercising in a field they called "the gym." A photograph he snapped of Johnson and a group of students outside the Bell Building became the frontispiece of *Schools of To-Morrow*.[42] It would soon become fashionable for progressive educators to claim "the whole community is our campus," but during the early 1900s those words probably rang truer at the Organic School than at any other school in the nation.

Beyond the time spent outside, several other features seemed especially striking to visitors. Over the years, it became easy for Johnson to anticipate their questions and comments, which she worked into her speeches and writings. Why didn't students take reading or even use books until they were eight or nine? visitors wanted to know. Why were there no tests (until high school), no grades, and no report cards? Given the lively atmosphere of folk songs, folk dances, and arts and crafts, weren't Johnson and her teachers just letting students do as they pleased? Surely Johnson grew tired of the repetition, yet she continued to answer with a candor and simplicity even her critics found disarming.

Her insistence on postponing reading instruction deserved all the attention it got, for it symbolized the way her "idea" of child development permeated the Organic School. To parents who complained they could not prevent their children from reading at home, Johnson retorted, "You keep [them] from doing other unwholesome things, why not direct [their] attention away from books until you are sure such work is desirable?"[43]

Beg your pardon, Mrs. Johnson? Parents could hardly believe a *teacher*, of all people, would brand reading "unwholesome"—for any age group.

Once the shock wore off, Johnson explained that children's nervous systems were not sufficiently developed to handle reading before age eight or nine—actually age ten or twelve, according to Oppenheim, but Johnson faced strong parental pressure not to wait quite so long. She could recite a litany of all the damage caused by "excessive or too early use of books." From eyestrain and cramped posture to unclear thinking, unsocial attitudes, and nervous breakdowns, Johnson could supply endless anecdotal evidence to document each problem. In her lectures and writings, she returned again and again to the issue of reading, almost as if she enjoyed waving the red flag.[44]

Johnson frustrated and annoyed academic traditionalists, so sharp were her attacks on bookishness and so strong her preference for experience as a way of learning. On the printed page, moreover, her views sometimes came across as simplistic; and yet people who heard her speak, or better still visited the Organic School and watched her work, sensed something that was hard to put into words. Johnson had a gift. Somehow, she managed to lift her school high above the pedagogical jargon that mired the child development literature. She invited everyone to look at the results, and, yes, the students in her school *did* seem to read easily, naturally, happily. "The actual learning to read is hardly a problem," Dewey observed, when "children teach themselves."[45] When Johnson's students were ready to read, they read. And within a few years, as she loved to remind critics, her students' reading skills equaled or surpassed those of students who learned at earlier ages under traditional methods.

When pressed for evidence of a more empirical nature, Johnson usually tried to oblige, but always she made it clear that the standards she upheld—in reading as well as every other area of organic education—did not lend themselves to quantification and measurement. Were students doing their best? Were they reaching their potential at each developmental stage? If so, Johnson was satisfied. If not, students could sense her disappointment.

Johnson dominated the Organic School so completely she had to reconcile her rejection of "external, competitive" standards with her own powerful influence. Her goal was for students to cultivate "inner, human" standards: the feeling of "inner necessity" that developed, she believed, in the "absence of external demands."[46] In her school, students worked to satisfy themselves, not to please adults—or so Johnson intended. But she had to walk a fine line indeed when students and teachers confessed that part of their motivation for working hard was pleasing her.[47]

Still, Johnson tried to practice what she preached by eliminating many of the traditional yardsticks used to measure one student against another. With bluntness that delighted some people as much as it rankled others, Johnson explained,

> I am very happy to say that we do not have any report cards whatsoever. I am also delighted to say that we have no grades or standards for promotions and I am also pleased to tell you that we make no reports to parents either of scholarship or behavior.[48]

Such practices would be "destructive to the sincerity and unself-consciousness of the child." "Parents are not usually to be trusted" with school reports, she continued, because parents often put harmful pressure on children. "We have fallen back on the beautiful scripture, 'Judge Not.'"[49]

If critics understandably accused Johnson of allowing students to do as they pleased, Johnson predictably lost little time setting them straight. Trying to sound tough minded, just as Dewey did on occasion, Johnson flatly stated "children have no basis for judgment, they do not know what is good for them, or their desires are often quite unwholesome." Children need discipline, she readily admitted, always adding discipline "must really be for their good, not for the convenience of the adult!" She urged teachers to say "yes" to as many wholesome requests as possible to win student confidence and respect. Even more important, she structured the curriculum to provide activities and occupations appropriate to each developmental stage, which helped minimize discipline problems by keeping students interested and involved.[50]

As part of her curriculum plan, Johnson modified the single-year grade groupings used in other schools. Four- and five-year-olds she placed together in the kindergarten class, six- and seven year olds in the "first-life" class, eight- and nine-year-olds in "second life," ten- and eleven-year-olds in "third life," and twelve- and thirteen-year-olds in the "fourth life" or junior high class. For the last four years, students attended high school.

Just beginning to extend her experiment to older students when Dewey visited, Johnson tried to ensure that the high school curriculum continued the organic emphasis on folk music, folk dancing, drama, and handwork. These subjects were no less important than the academic subjects, she insisted, going into detail to explain how the daily work students did in manual arts, for instance, helped promote balanced development of body, mind, and spirit. "Our shop," she noted, sometimes with fond references to her husband, "is the most important place on the campus."[51] Seeing the pride students took in their ceramic and woodwork left a lasting impression on visitors, as did watching every student take part in daily folk dancing. Johnson played up these aspects of the curriculum so much she inadvertently reinforced a caricature of her school as a place where even the older students sang, danced, and made pottery all day.

An easy target for critics, the "playschool" image of child-centered progressive education drew attention away from a surprisingly traditional high school curriculum. Students took four years of literature, history, math, and science and two years of Latin and French. High school students did homework and took examinations.[52] Looking back on their experiences, members of the senior class of 1931 wrote in their yearbook, the *Cinagro*, "Remember the funny feeling we had the first morning we were in High School? . . . The first thing we remember is work. We really snapped out of being silly and got some backbone."[53]

Still, high school classes tended to be animated and engaging. Often they were project-centered, and students had considerable freedom in selecting and designing the projects. The only students who failed were those who absolutely refused to do their best.[54]

On balance, such preparation seemed to stand students in good stead at colleges and universities. True to form, Johnson was critical of American higher education, but she proudly cited her students' record in college as one indicator of the Organic School's effectiveness.[55]

Years of Success

Johnson and her school hit their stride during the 1910s and peaked during the 1920s. Dewey's praise in *Schools of To-Morrow* brought the school national attention; Johnson reached the apex of her personal influence during the twenties as well. A founding member of the Progressive Education Association in 1919, she tried with limited success to use the organization to promote organic education nationwide. With the support of the Fairhope Educational Foundation, she booked an exhausting schedule of lectures and demonstrations, soliciting contributions wherever she spoke. It seemed Johnson was always boarding the train for another round of speeches. Bolstered by a steady flow of students from the Northeast, Midwest, and California, enrollment at the school varied from 100 to 220 students, about a third of whom were usually not local residents.[56]

One of the school's greatest assets was its faculty. As Johnson's reputation spread, she attracted teachers who were willing to work for low wages in order to work with her. Now in a position to be selective, she hired teachers whose academic credentials matched their admiration for her. Johnson, who lacked a college degree, took special pride in assembling a faculty whose members held degrees from major state universities, the Ivy League, even Oxford and Cambridge. Some of these teachers came south to work at the Organic School and spent the rest of their lives in Fairhope; others served an apprenticeship and moved to other progressive schools; a few went on to found their own schools based on the organic model.[57]

The example par excellence of the caliber of teacher Johnson attracted was Charles Rabold. A student of the noted English folklorist Cecil Sharp, Rabold left a position in the music department at Yale to teach at the Organic School. During the 1920s he turned the already well-established dance program (which Sharp himself had helped Johnson develop) into one of the school's defining features. With a confident, outgoing personality that complemented Johnson's, Rabold could help even the most awkward students and teachers learn to enjoy English folk dancing—country, Morris, and sword. Rabold became Johnson's close friend and eventually the school's assistant director.[58]

Despite financially and professionally attractive offers to relocate, Johnson remained in Fairhope, wedded to the educational experiment that was part of a community experiment. She wanted to succeed with the original demonstration, which still enrolled about half of Fairhope's school-aged children and provided a "simple environment . . . to work out an idea which could not be approached in [a] more sophisticated community."[59] If the experiment worked in Fairhope, she believed, organic education could spread across the nation, carrying with it the egalitarian spirit of the single-tax movement.

As Fairhope's population grew from 853 in 1920 to 1,549 in 1930, Johnson redoubled her efforts to keep in touch with her neighbors. Despite her heavy travel schedule, she remained a highly visible presence in Fairhope—not only at the Organic School but on village streets, in colony and town meetings, and in the pages of the Fairhope *Courier*. The adult course on organic education she first conducted in 1921 turned into an annual winter event. By the end of the decade, it was pulling in people from throughout the nation—pilgrims who, like Dewey, wanted to learn about the educational experiment, the community experiment, or as

Johnson always emphasized, the connection between the two. Not every resident of Fairhope was a true believer in either single taxation or organic education, of course, but most locals felt proud that Johnson was putting their small town on the intellectual map.[60]

Years of Depression

In what should have been the crowning touch to a successful decade, Johnson published her first book, *Youth in a World of Men*, in 1929. At the urging of her Greenwich supporters, she tried to capture on paper the essence of her speeches and demonstrations. But the results of her efforts as a writer were as mixed as the reviews the book received.[61] She had won a well-deserved reputation as a practitioner—a doer—yet *Youth in a World of Men* struck most readers as detached from experience, even naive. Instead of offering insight into the Fairhope experiment, Johnson touted organic education as a panacea, promising more than she or it could possibly deliver. The charm, self-confidence, and powers of persuasion she projected so well in person fell flat in print.

Then the Depression hit, and the Organic School felt its impact almost immediately. The number of boarding students dropped sharply, decimating the operating funds from this vital source. The financial crisis reminded the school's supporters of how precarious its situation had always been, even in better days. In 1924, for instance, Johnson and other members of the corporation had been forced to mortgage the school in order to keep it open. Much of this debt remained outstanding when the stock market crashed in October 1929. As the decade of the thirties began, the school's economic position slipped from marginal to dangerous.[62]

A personal tragedy foreshadowed the trying years ahead. In February 1930 Charles Rabold was killed in an airplane crash. Rabold was the faculty member whose charisma and other qualities best matched Johnson's, and she was planning to turn the school over to him when she retired. Rabold's death, coming late in her life and at a difficult time for the school, was a loss she never got over.[63]

As the Depression wore on, Johnson had to work at maintaining her characteristic optimism. She managed to keep up her busy schedule of lectures and demonstrations, for they continued to generate money for the school. But while invitations to speak regularly crossed her desk, she had to face the fact that her name was losing some of its magic within the progressive education movement. As social reconstructionists seized leadership of the movement, they pushed aside Johnson and other child-centered educators. By the time she turned 70 in 1934, she was being dismissed as past her prime, written off as a "play schooler" despite her unwavering commitment to single taxation and other social reforms. No publisher would touch her manuscript for a second book, which she called *Thirty Years with an Idea*. Some of her New York and Greenwich friends remained loyal, but the collapse of the Fairhope Educational Foundation during the 1930s dried up yet another source of revenue for the school.[64] Desperate to save her school, Johnson had long since cut teacher salaries and reduced other expenses. What else could she do? Every summer it appeared the school would not reopen in the fall, but Johnson refused to give up, turning to donations from friends, supporters, and her personal savings to keep the school alive. Students and parents noticed a decline in the quality of instruction as key faculty members, trying to remain loyal but unable to survive on their salaries, reluctantly said goodbye. Johnson also became more lenient in accepting tuition and board-paying students with learning or behavioral problems.[65]

At last Marietta Johnson's struggle ended. In poor health, mentally as well as physically, she died on December 23, 1938, 25 years after Dewey's visit. The Organic School's struggle for survival would continue for years to come.

A Venture in Cooperative Management

Children cried when they heard Mrs. Johnson had died, not only because they respected her but because so many adults said the school would close at the end of the 1938–39 year. No one could fill Johnson's shoes, Fairhopers predicted. Besides, Johnson herself had barely managed to keep the school open during the 1930s. Enrollment had dropped to below 100. Cash flow had slowed to a trickle. Faculty morale had fallen. Students, parents, and alumni had every reason to worry about the future of the Organic School.

Rather than trying to replace Johnson with a strong individual, several experienced teachers convinced their colleagues to operate the school as a "cooperative venture"—an experiment in shared governance and shared financial risk.[66] Acting as a committee of the whole, the twelve-person faculty would run the school and, forgoing salaries, divide whatever money remained after paying the bills.[67] Here was an experiment in democratic school administration that surely would have intrigued John Dewey.

The cooperative venture at the Organic School was, on the one hand, well within the spirit of Fairhope's reformist heritage. The very word "cooperative," which the faculty consistently used to describe their endeavor, called up a rich aspect of that heritage. As part of the Fairhope community experiment, several major cooperatives sprang up during the 1910s and 1920s, including an ice house, transportation company, creamery, and general mercantile. The socialists who dominated the early community were among the prime movers in these ventures.[68]

But on the other hand, Fairhope was changing, and the days of the cooperatives were already over. By the early 1930s, all the cooperatives had collapsed—along with socialist influence in Fairhope generally. Prominent and successful single taxers, those whose families had gotten in on the community's ground floor, cloaked themselves in individualism and free enterprise, rejecting socialism and carefully distancing themselves from fundamental criticism of the economic order. With the town's population approaching 3,000 as the decade of the thirties drew to a close, more and more residents saw Fairhope as just a nice place to live rather than a community with a mission of experimentation and reform. Thus the faculty's decision to launch a cooperative venture at the Organic School was true to Fairhope's heritage but out of step with its recent past and present.[69]

Difficulties with the cooperative arrangement surfaced almost immediately as governance problems aggravated the school's longstanding financial woes. Teachers grew tired of sitting through long meetings and handling administrative chores. Parents missed having one person in charge of the school, a designated leader who could answer questions and make decisions. As the faculty explained in a 1940 newsletter, "the need was felt for centralizing administration."[70]

At a special parent-teacher meeting held at the end of the 1939–40 year, S.W. Alexander, a math and Latin teacher who had been at the school since 1930, reluctantly agreed to assume more control. Since 1935

Alexander had served as principal, which meant principal *teacher* or instructional leader at the Organic School. Now he was also administrator—the school's de facto director. Highly respected as a "veteran aide of Mrs. Johnson's," Alexander nevertheless resisted being drafted as her successor. He was a quiet man, a self-described "plain Alabama farmer" who lacked Johnson's personal charisma and political finesse. His reluctant acceptance of the role of administrator ended the school's brief experiment in cooperative management.[71]

The Corporation Steps Forward

Sensing a power vacuum, the Organic School corporation became more assertive in the affairs of the institution during the 1940-41 school year. Now composed of six members, the corporation still included Lydia Comings, who helped Johnson found the school in 1907 and incorporate it in 1909. Trying to lighten the school's debt burden, the members conveyed title to Comings Hall to the town of Fairhope. They rented the School Home, the dormitory that had housed boarding students, to the National Youth Administration in an attempt to generate operating funds. And in a move they made with misgivings, members of the corporation began requiring local students to pay tuition, partly in cash and partly by helping with the upkeep of the campus.[72]

Here was a major break with the school's past. Although some Fairhope families had paid tuition voluntarily while Johnson was director, she had always insisted the school operate free of charge to local students.[73] Now one of the ground rules of her educational experiment had been altered. Now only parents who could afford to pay tuition could choose an organic education for their children. Now the Organic School was truly a private school.

The opposition Alexander and the rest of the faculty expressed to local tuition strained their relationship with the corporation. Members of the corporation, pointing to the financial bottom line, insisted that local tuition offered the only hope of keeping the school alive. The faculty replied charging tuition would be counterproductive because it would drive local students away. Even with their jobs and salaries on the line, faculty members resigned themselves to closing the school—if the only alternative was to violate one of Johnson's most basic principles. The corporation regarded the faculty's attitude as negative and self-defeating.[74]

Determined to keep the school open, corporation members looked outside Fairhope for new leadership. In December 1941, just as the nation entered World War II, the corporation hired William E. Zeuch as director. With a Ph.D. from the University of Wisconsin and a broad background in university and government work—he had founded Commonwealth College in 1923—Zeuch brought practiced administrative skills to the position. While promising "no departure" from Johnson's idea of organic education, Zeuch ushered in fundamental changes in the school's organizational structure. These changes carried profound educational implications for the school's future.[75]

Understandably, the new director made stabilizing the school financially his top priority. Within two months after his arrival, Zeuch had launched a drive to establish an endowment he called the Sustaining Fund. Drawing on a long list of contacts from the Johnson era, the drive netted numerous small contributions from around the nation. John Dewey sent a check for ten dollars. But Zeuch concentrated on local alumni and friends, believing their support held the key to the school's survival. By February 1943 the fund had reached $4,000 of its $5,000 goal.[76]

The price Zeuch paid for this support was an expanded corporation with increased control over the school. The January 1943 issue of the school bulletin *Integration* announced a reorganized corporation of from 20 to 25 members. In addition to the six old members, the new corporation included representatives from faculty, parents and patrons, and alumni. The members appointed from the latter two groups included some of Fairhope's most influential citizens, and the bulletin foresaw "further expansion . . . through the inclusion of alert and progressive business men or women of the community." Members of the corporation elected a three-person board of trustees, soon to be called the executive committee, to "carry out the policies of the corporation and to manage the purely business affairs of the school." "All academic matters will continue in the hands of the teaching staff as at present," Zeuch promised.[77]

The new corporation kept a low profile at first, for Zeuch and Alexander worked well together as director and principal. Zeuch's business acumen impressed prominent Fairhopers. Constantly eyeing the balance sheet, he reopened the boarding department and helped persuade the Fairhope Single Tax Corporation to purchase the mortgage on the school. Overriding faculty objections, he kept local tuition in place and was able to boast that few families had withdrawn their children. As for Alexander, his devotion to organic education reassured those who wanted to see the school stick to Johnson's principles. Even with World War II pulling older boys away and complicating faculty recruitment and retention, the Organic School appeared to be on the rebound.[78]

But a major transition—a shift of power—was about to occur. Ill health forced Zeuch to resign during the summer of 1944. Alexander carried on as principal, but during the 1944-45 year he too became ill. Alexander's death in November 1945 left no one in charge—no one, that is, except the twenty members of the corporation and its three-person executive committee.[79]

With a revamped organizational structure in place, corporation members were both willing and able to take charge. And with no director or principal to run the school in 1945-46, the corporation quickly breached the line between "business affairs" and "academic matters." As the *Cinagro* explained, the executive committee "took over full responsibility."[80]

One member of the executive committee seemed particularly eager to play a leading role. Sam Dyson, a 1926 graduate of the Organic School and a successful Fairhope banker, pushed forward and began several decades of service. Dyson soon emerged as both the dominant force on the corporation and the most influential person in the affairs of the school. His wife Helen, a graduate of Johnson's teacher training program, served initially as a first life teacher and then as both vice-president and president of the corporation. As of 1995, half a century later, the Dysons and their family remained closely involved with the school.[81]

A Scapegoat and Two Saviors

Searching for a new administration, corporation members once again looked outside Fairhope, only this time they put the position of director on the shelf and hired just a principal. In 1946 they employed Edgar E. Ritter, who came from San Francisco with a background in journalism and a master's degree from Stanford.[82] The student editors of the 1947 *Cinagro* reported that "with Mr. Ritter as principal, we have had a very successful and smooth running year."[83] The corporation apparently thought otherwise. As financial problems returned to haunt the school, Ritter came under fire. At a special meeting called in May 1947 to deal with the budgetary crisis, the corporation accepted his resignation. In protest, parents withdrew as many as a third of the school's 100 students. Ritter became a scapegoat, the first but unfortunately not the last administrator to leave the school bearing the blame for its persistent financial woes.[84]

Unable to meet payroll and pay its other bills, the corporation considered closing the school. But Sam Dyson donated money to keep it afloat in the short term[85] and, after lengthy negotiations, the Fairhope Single Tax Corporation agreed to assume the debts and "sponsor the operation of the Organic School"[86]—provided the school corporation offered sufficient security. That security turned out to be all the school's property, which the corporation signed over in May 1947.[87]

With the school's very survival at stake, the corporation prevailed on two veteran teachers, John and Clara Campbell, to "reorganize the faculty and reopen the school."[88] Having moved to Fairhope in 1928 to work with Marietta Johnson, the Campbells had built a base of friends and supporters in the community. Corporation members persuaded John, who held a doctorate from the University of Wisconsin, to serve as principal, and Clara, a graduate of the University of Minnesota who enjoyed a reputation as an exceptionally fine teacher, to continue as a science and English instructor. The Campbells' direct ties to Johnson gave the husband-wife team great credibility in Fairhope.[89]

With John in the principal's office from 1947 through 1951 and with Clara at work in the classroom and behind the scenes, the school returned to its organic roots, thriving educationally and surviving financially. Student newspapers and yearbooks from the Campbell years depict a school that was, if anything, even more responsive to contemporary social issues than it had been in Johnson's day. Surely it would have made Johnson proud that students and teachers now enjoyed the academic freedom to advocate racial tolerance, call for a more rational approach to understanding communism, even speak out against war—all this in a southern community turning increasingly conservative during the McCarthy era.[90]

Johnson would also have appreciated the Organic School Caravans that went on several summer tours, publicizing the school outside as well as inside the South with one-act plays and performances by the Morris dance teams. Students thought of the caravans as updated versions of Johnson's own lecture and recruitment tours. But despite the students' best efforts, few out-of-towners enrolled. The caravans marked the last serious attempt to attract boarding students. The days when the Organic School could draw a national student body were over.[91]

Still, the Campbells were able to reestablish the school as a viable institution in Fairhope. Enrollment rebounded to 120 as some of Fairhope's more prosperous families, particularly those descended from turn-of-the-century colonists, rallied 'round the school and continued to send their children there. A spirit of optimism returned to the campus.[92]

The Corporation Centralizes Control

When age and health forced John Campbell to step down at the end of the 1950–51 year, another shift in power occurred. Once again the immediate cause was a financial crisis, and once again the corporation consolidated control at the expense of the faculty and administration. Business influence increased in the school's affairs when several local businesspeople who had staged a fundraising drive for the school took seats on the corporation. A new organizational chart unveiled in May 1951 showed the line of power extending downward from Sam Dyson, who now held the titles of president and general manager. Beneath Dyson lay a network of committees on which faculty members were represented but as a decided minority. The committees governed every aspect of the school's operation, from buildings and grounds to educational policy.[93] As a history of the school published in the Fairhope *Courier* put it, businesspeople now "took the responsibility of supervising [the] administration."[94]

It seemed "Mr. Sam," as Dyson was known, was always on campus. He took an interest in every task, great and small, from painting buildings to cautioning teachers not to stray from Mrs. Johnson's principles. At his best, Dyson was a tireless worker, a constant booster of the Organic School. At his worst, he seemed to regard the school as his pet project, brooking no opposition to his plans and tolerating no challenge to his and his wife's interpretation of organic education.[95]

Thus by the early 1950s, not even fifteen years after the founder's death, governance at the Organic School had evolved into something quite different from the strong director model of Johnson's day. An organizational theorist might dub the new model "strong corporation/variable director/weak faculty." There could be no doubt ultimate authority resided in the corporation, and it was just as clear the faculty had little control. With few veteran teachers remaining from the Johnson years, Sam Dyson and other corporation members felt the faculty needed close supervision.[96]

As for the directors, the succession who came and went found their power hinged on their relationship with the corporation. In 1951 and 1952, immediately following the Campbells, no fewer than three people served brief terms as director, including Kenneth Cain, Marietta Johnson's adopted son. None of the three pleased the corporation. Frederick Archer, who held a doctorate from Emory University, maintained somewhat better relations as director and managed to stay from 1952 through 1954. Retired public school teacher and administrator C.F. Taylor, by contrast, got along so well with the corporation he was elected president of that body—a feat unmatched at the school before or since. During Taylor's four years (1954–58) as director and principal, he displayed diplomatic and managerial skills that impressed the businesspeople on the corporation. The next director, David Howell (1958 –1960), scored points with the corporation by improving the Organic School's standing with the Alabama State Department of Education.[97]

In many respects the school appeared healthy during the 1950s. Enrollment climbed to 200 toward the end of the decade. Yearbooks portrayed a school adhering to some of the more obvious aspects of organic education. Folk dancing, for instance, remained a highly visible feature, and students continued to work in the shop. Visitors to the campus could never mistake the Organic School for a "typical" school, public or private.[98]

Yet the school had changed and was continuing to change in ways that disturbed many alumni from the Johnson era. Johnson's policy of delaying reading instruction until age eight or nine had fallen by the wayside during the 1940s. Her policy on student evaluation fell in 1951, a year of revolving-door directors when the corporation yielded to parental pressure and instructed teachers to grade students and issue report cards to parents. By the early 1960s, the school seemed to be drifting with the tides on Mobile Bay as directors and faculty members entered and exited and as the moods of the corporation rose and fell. Several times, for instance, the school switched back and forth between the life classes Johnson insisted on, which grouped younger students by two-year age cohorts, and the traditional single-year groupings known as first grade, second grade, third grade, and so forth.[99]

To be sure, the 1950s and early 1960s were hard times for progressive education in Fairhope no less than throughout the nation. But the market pressures on the Organic School were extraordinary. Trying to position the school to appeal to an increasingly conservative local clientele, those in charge gradually steered it away from Johnson's principles, charting a course that reflected uncertainty over where to go but determination to get there.[100]

Child Misfits and Republican Politics

The detailed records kept by Dr. Goodwin Petersen, director from 1960 through 1962, provide a snapshot of the school as it approached twenty-five years of operation without Marietta Johnson. Petersen, who held a doctorate in education from Stanford, repeatedly voiced concern over the quality of students and faculty and over the heavy-handed role of the corporation, now usually called the board of trustees or managing board.

Many students, Petersen contended, lacked the "academic and creative promise" to succeed at the Organic School.[101] In fact, the school was accepting probationary students from other schools, which reinforced the "child misfit" image Johnson worked so hard to counteract. With boys outnumbering girls by three to one, the institution was becoming a school of last resort for young males with academic or behavioral difficulties in more traditional settings. Petersen considered using a variety of psychological instruments, including standardized personality and intelligence batteries, to screen applicants and track students.[102] "Adhering to a minimum entrance (IQ) level" would be one way to "stabilize" the school, he suggested, adding "the image of the School may not be satisfactorily improved until this is done."[103]

Plagued with high teacher turnover, Petersen fretted over teachers who either misunderstood or disagreed with Johnson's principles. "At present the School of Organic Education has a weak faculty," a report prepared under his direction bluntly stated.[104] One of Petersen's solutions to this problem was requiring teachers to study Johnson's principles and read such works as Lawrence Cremin's just-published history of educational progressivism, *The Transformation of the School* (1961). Another solution Petersen tried, one that flew in the face of the insights teachers may have gleaned from Johnson and Cremin, was drawing up class schedules that specified what to teach during each time slot of the day. In several classes, Petersen tried to circumvent poor teaching by imposing programmed instructional materials.[105]

Hardly faithful to Johnson's principles, Petersen was nevertheless a strong leader and assertive director. Predictably, he locked horns with the corporation and resigned after two years to accept a faculty position at Northern Illinois University. A report he issued during his last year pointed out that the same group of people who made financial policy for the school also made educational policy—and without any expertise, the report implied, in the latter area. Petersen also pointed out that teachers had no personal representation on the board. Before he left the school, Petersen angered Sam Dyson by charging the board with violating a provision of its 1951 charter that required members to seek reelection after each three-year term.[106]

After Petersen's departure, the school entered a period of relative stability under Frances Hughes, who served as director from 1962 through 1969. Offering leadership in a lower key, Hughes tried to modernize the school while maintaining familiar icons of the Johnson era. As the editors of the 1965 *Cinagro* commented "She brought many ideas to the school," including a developmental reading lab that "increases a student's rate of reading and betters his comprehension."[107] While Hughes expanded the school's role as a remedial institution for struggling students, she also reemphasized folk dancing, which students demonstrated for residents of Fairhope at the annual field day. On that occasion each spring, the school pulled out all the stops to prove it remained true to the spirit of Marietta Johnson.[108]

The stability of the Hughes era paid dividends. Enrollment ranged between 110 and 140 students, down from the late 1950s but about the same as under Petersen. Hughes endeared herself to the managing board by returning her salary checks, a gesture at once admirable for the genuine dedication it reflected and troubling in its commentary on the financial affairs of the school. The board's acceptance of Hughes's generosity seems almost opportunistic because, during her administration, a major bequest from the estate of longtime school supporter Georgianna T. Ives gave the board the resources it needed to embark on a capital improvement program.[109]

The Dysons once again took charge, for Sam was named joint executor of the Ives estate and Helen served as president of the managing board from 1966 through 1974. In an era before historic preservation was an issue, the managing board demolished several architecturally significant wooden buildings from the Johnson era and replaced them with plain but serviceable concrete-block structures. Other parts of the physical plant were repaired and remodeled. The board was also able to reclaim the school's assets from the Fairhope Single Tax Corporation, which reconveyed title along with a new land lease in 1967.[110]

Fairhope's ninety-nine-year leases on colony land lingered as one of the last remnants of the original community experiment. Now downplayed by real estate agents as a "quirk," a "minor inconvenience" to those wishing to move to Fairhope, the single-tax leases had become a relic of turn-of-the-century idealism. Fairhope remained one of the likeliest places in Alabama to hear nonsouthern accents, but those who spoke them now tended to be comfortable retirees rather than committed reformers. By the end of the 1960s, stability and security had become the selling points of the community of almost 6,000. The town that had elected a socialist as its first mayor had become a stronghold of Goldwater-Nixon Republicanism.[111]

A Segregation Academy?

The Organic School entered the decade of the seventies with stable enrollment and a child-misfit image. What could it offer the community that the Baldwin County public schools, now considered good-to-excellent by Alabama standards, could not? Racial segregation, for one thing.

During the early 1970s, large-scale, court-ordered desegregation of public schools finally came to south Alabama. The Baldwin County school system, where only 10 percent of the students were African-American, complied with court orders in a relatively orderly and peaceful way. But across the bay in Mobile County, where the African-American population stood at almost 40 percent, massive resistance and white flight broke out. [112]

Like other private schools on both sides of the bay, the Organic School profited from the discord and reaped higher enrollment. As a newspaper reporter concluded in 1974 after interviewing director Barbara Zwayer and principal Mary Nell Avery, "There are 16 seniors in the school but the junior class is much larger, partly because of racial unrest that has plagued Mobile area schools in the past few years."[113] Enrollment climbed again during the early 1970s, peaking at 168 in 1973–74 when racial tensions ran highest. Although the managing board adopted and published a statement of nondiscriminatory admission policy, the Organic School remained virtually all white. [114]

Higher enrollment notwithstanding, keeping the school in operation was no easy task during the 1970s. Helen Dyson complained to a reporter how difficult it was to find teachers who were "totally dedicated and willing to take less salary in order that they might participate in the rewarding atmosphere of a truly creative, teacher-pupil relationship."[115] Meanwhile, the board continued to compromise Marietta Johnson's organic curriculum. In order to offer a wide variety of academic courses to larger numbers of students, the board made ceramics and folk music optional. For a time, the board closed the shop Johnson thought of as the "most important place on the campus."[116]

One constant in the school was the Dysons' involvement. The 1977 *Cinagro* devoted a full page to Marietta Johnson and another page to Sam and Helen Dyson. Mr. Sam, now chair of the board of Fairhope's largest bank, won praise as a "daily worker" at the Organic School, wearing his plumber's hat one day and his financial advisor's hat the next.[117] In 1976 he established a permanent trust fund for the school from the Ives estate. That fund, with a principal that reached approximately half a million dollars by 1995, still underwrites about half of the school's budget.[118] Administrators came and went as the Dysons developed a reputation for hiring and then firing directors. Zack Lee, for instance, came to the Organic School in 1975 from the assistant principalship of Bel Air Christian School in Mobile, an institution that lasted only a few years during the desegregation era. Mr. Lee lasted only two years as principal of the Organic School.[119]

Dashed Hopes of Revitalization

The experiences of Mike Kingsmore, principal from 1979 to 1982, paint a revealing portrait of the school forty years after Marietta Johnson's death. Arriving from Ohio with a military background and twelve years of service in teaching and administration, Kingsmore soon became a convert to organic education. To a greater degree, perhaps, than any other administrator since John Campbell in the late 1940s and early 1950s, Kingsmore tried to realign the school with Johnson's principles, only to run into the brick walls of insufficient funds and a domineering managing board.[120]

A controversy between the board and Kingsmore brewed at the start of the 1980–81 year and quickly boiled over into the pages of Fairhope and Mobile newspapers. At first the scenario seemed all too familiar. Enrollment had fallen below 100, and the board, as usual, was blaming the principal. Defending himself, Kingsmore pointed to the inflationary economy of the early 1980s and the board's recent decision to raise tuition by 31 percent.[121] What made this situation different, though, was the "flood of protest and indignation" Kingsmore's resignation announcement triggered, an outpouring that "left the school virtually paralyzed."[122]

Newspaper reporters investigating the controversy played up the concentration of power in the hands of the managing board. Readers learned the principal and faculty were rarely, if ever, allowed to attend the board's meetings.[123] How, then, could the board blame Kingsmore for the school's financial difficulties? One board member opined that the principal had an "inability to carry out instructions."[124] In response, Kingsmore's advocates accused the board of deliberately mismanaging funds so the school would close and its property revert to the Fairhope Single Tax Corporation.[125] The ten-acre downtown campus was now a prime piece of real estate, and rumors were already flying about what would happen to the property when—not if, but *when*—the school failed.

With the vocal support of parents and faculty members, Kingsmore weathered this storm. He spent the remainder of the 1980–81 academic year as well as much of the next year trying to shore up the school's commitment to organic education while also struggling with the budget. He wrote a series of articles for the *Courier* in an effort to reacquaint the community with Johnson's principles. Working with Johnson's adopted son, Kenneth Cain, and his wife, Dorothy "Mama Dot" Cain, Kingsmore arranged a traveling exhibition of the founder's scrapbook and other personal papers to publicize a benefit auction for the school.[126]

To little avail. Although Kingsmore remained popular with parents and teachers, early in 1982 he announced his plans to leave the school as part of an economy plan. "He's energetic and exemplifies the principles of Marietta Johnson," the president of the board confessed, but dollars were dollars, after all.[127] Kingsmore had already taken a 40-percent salary cut, yet the school was still losing $3,500 a month.[128]

In retrospect, it appears Kingsmore's departure dashed the school's best hopes since the early 1950s of recapturing Marietta Johnson's "idea" of education. The situation seems doubly tragic, for while the managing board was passing on Kingsmore's leadership, it was also passing up a chance to make the school economically self-sufficient. That chance came in the form of an offer from millionaire industrialist Harold Dahlgren.

A Texan who made his fortune in the printing business, Dahlgren discovered the Organic School in the late 1970s through his wife Emily, an artist and native of Fairhope. After befriending Dot and Kenneth Cain, the Dahlgrens enrolled their children in the school and began to contribute liberally. In 1981 they donated $70,000 to retool the shop and restore the old high school building, which was rededicated as Dahlgren Hall at the start of the 1981–82 academic year. The Cains looked hopefully to the Dahlgrens, envisioning them as modern counterparts of soap magnate Joseph Fels, the Henry and Edsel Ford families, and other philanthropists whose support Marietta Johnson had won for the school.[129]

The Dahlgrens offered to make the school financially independent—provided Harold received a seat on the managing board. The board declined. Dahlgren had been critical of the board's micromanagement of the school, speaking out as Goodwin Petersen had about its tendency to make educational decisions without the necessary expertise. In addition, the Dahlgrens' connection to the Cains made them suspect to the Dyson faction on the board, for the Cains and the Dysons headed rival camps of Organic School supporters. To this day, those associated with the school feel pressure to declare themselves as allies of either Mama Dot or Mr. Sam. The ill will between the two factions has cost the school dearly, in this instance a once-in-a-lifetime chance at financial security.[130]

Decline, Near Death, and Rebirth

After Mike Kingsmore left, the school went downhill fast. Kingsmore built up enrollment to 119 before his departure in 1982, but the number of students dropped steadily as the managing board scaled back the school in a series of economy moves. The last high school class graduated in 1983, after which the board phased out secondary programs. By the fall of 1986, a downsized Organic School could claim grades K through 6 only—and a mere 25 students. Many Fairhopers sensed the end of the school was in sight.[131]

Board members, though, were at work behind the scenes to keep the school alive. In August 1986 the board announced plans to sell the school's physical plant to the city of Fairhope and vacate the campus in May 1989. The city had made the board an offer it could hardly refuse: $334,000, which would be enough to rebuild the school at a new site, with money left over for other expenses. Relocating the Organic School, Fairhope's mayor explained, had become an important part of the city's master plan. Faulkner State Community College would open a branch on the old 'ten-acre campus and, after extensive building and renovation, draw as many as a thousand college students into downtown Fairhope, where the economy was already booming with the addition of trendy restaurants and boutiques.[132]

Because the Organic School had not served as the symbolic heart of Fairhope for several decades, it struck some supporters as sad but fitting when the school finally acknowledged its changed circumstances and moved out of the geographical heart of the community. The new campus, dedicated in 1989, sits hidden and isolated, plain and modern in its concrete-and-brick architecture, while downtown Fairhope displays rows of historic buildings for a steady stream of shoppers and tourists. Visitors to the old campus can see the restored Bell Building, which now houses the Marietta Johnson Museum and its rich collection of archival materials. Mama Dot Cain, who founded and developed the museum with her late husband, joins curator Sherold "Doc" Pope in greeting researchers, alumni, and other visitors.

Now a city of 9,000, Fairhope retains a refreshing spirit and a touch of the avant-garde. It is, by and large, a tolerant place of literate people. But the former experimental community, once the number one single-tax colony in the nation, now rates in *Money* magazine as the nation's number two retirement community.[133] Rising property values, the very prospect that vexed Henry George, are almost a source of pride in the new upscale Fairhope. In the late twentieth century, people who have money to invest in real estate can hardly be expected to play by the rules of a late-nineteenth-century social reformer. Can they? By the same token, people who have the money to invest in private schooling can hardly be expected to follow the rules of an early-twentieth-century educational reformer. Can they?

The results of Marietta Johnson's educational experiment parallel the results of Fairhope's community experiment. The rules have changed, yet a certain atmosphere remains. Students at today's Organic School no longer wait until they are eight or nine to learn to read. That rule is rendered obsolete, teachers explain, by the early exposure children get to print in the electronic media. Yet reading instruction still seems easy and natural. Dewey's observation that "children teach themselves" still fits.

So it is with the other features that once drew visitors' questions and criticism. Even though report cards now go home on a regular basis, teachers try to minimize competition and working for grades. Folk dancing remains part of an organic education, even if students now dance only two hours a week rather than the daily hour Johnson looked forward to. Students still work in the shop, but now for only one hour a week instead of one hour a day. Students continue to spend time outside—bicycle rides and walks in the woods are especially popular—although they spend less time than Johnson's students did.

The director in the late 1990s, Mordecai "Mawk" Arnold, a retired military officer, graduated from the Organic School during the 1930s, while Johnson was alive. More than any other recent director, he seems committed to her principles. He is even willing to negotiate special financial arrangements with parents of modest means who want their children to attend the school. With a less autocratic managing board apparently supporting him, Arnold is trying to recapture more of the founder's vision. But other directors have held similar goals, only to lose political battles with the board or economic battles with the balance sheet. Arnold's predecessor lasted less than one year. Despite encouraging recent signs, the results of Marietta Johnson's educational experiment remain mixed and small scale.[134]

Conclusion

Two features that set the Organic School's history apart from most of the other accounts in this book are the unusual community in which the school developed and Marietta Johnson's insistence that any white child in Fairhope could attend. From the very start, her educational experiment had a strong egalitarian element: progressivism for ordinary folk, we might call it. Her commitment to keeping that element central to the experiment struck visitors as remarkable. Given the exclusivity of many progressive schools—including the Organic School at certain stages of its history—Johnson's egalitarian spirit seems all the more admirable today, notwithstanding the racial constraints she reluctantly accepted.

Yet the "ordinary folk" who moved south to Fairhope in the early 1900s were clearly extraordinary by the standards of their day—or ours. Upton Sinclair, remember, sized them up as a self-anointed band of "assorted reformers" who "felt certain they were setting an example for the rest of the world."[135] Their children, too, were extraordinary, not so much as an economically privileged group (although Fairhope had few poor whites) but as an academically and ideologically stimulated group. In the years when one-half to two-thirds of Fairhope's white families chose to send their children to the Organic School instead of public school, just imagine what kinds of kids showed up on the steps of the Bell Building! Today that building houses their videotaped recollections, which form a highly personal documentary of how special they felt to be "living in utopia" and going to a progressive school.[136]

Mrs. Johnson added to these extraordinary local children a sizeable number of upper and upper-middle class students from outside the South. She attracted an extraordinarily talented group of teachers willing to work for almost nothing in order to work with her. With these elements in place, her school soon became, as Dewey put it, an educational "experiment station" that produced impressive results.[137]

"Under her direction," Dewey wrote in 1915, "the school has proved a decided success."[138] Eighty years later, I can add that Johnson's experiment proved *most* successful while she was alive and involved with the school. No surprise here. This chapter, like several others in this volume, confirms the conventional wisdom that institutions change, often for the worse, when they lose charismatic leaders—especially founders.

What may be surprising about the history of the Organic School, though, is that Johnson herself, founder and leader par excellence, had such a hard time keeping her experiment going. If she was never short of vision, her school was always short of cash. Operating the school on a free basis for local white children required Johnson to maintain a delicate balance among colony funds, outside philanthropy, and most important, the tuition and board of wealthy northern and midwestern students. In the best of times, this balancing act was difficult. During the Great Depression, the feat became all but impossible. Johnson's experiment was on the verge of falling apart throughout the last years of her life and on several occasions during the glory days of the 1910s and 1920s.

In concluding this history, then, I will resist the temptation of simply repeating the Fairhope wisdom that the Organic School has never been the same since Johnson's death because no one has been able to fill her shoes. Of course the school hasn't, and of course no one has. But to stress this truism is to minimize the contributions of S.W. Alexander, John and Clara Campbell, Mike Kingsmore, and a host of other capable teachers and administrators who deserve more credit than they have ever received for keeping the school alive and sticking fairly close to Johnson's principles. I will also resist overemphasizing the conclusion, also commonly voiced in Fairhope, that a lack of money has always been the Organic School's greatest problem. To be sure, this point helps explain much of the school's history, including some of the educational changes the institution has undergone over the last sixty years. When financial support from outside Fairhope slowed to a trickle after Johnson's death, the corporation responded by charging local tuition, thereby altering one of the most basic elements of her experiment. Recurrent financial crises then pulled the managing board deeper and deeper into the school's educational affairs, resulting in autocratic lay governance and a drift in first one direction and then another. Money is a key factor in virtually all institutional history. But as economists remind us, the way people choose to spend their money reflects their attitudes and values.

Looking beyond both the money factor and the Marietta Johnson factor, I offer the conclusion that the Organic School flourished in Fairhope because—and probably *only* because—the educational experiment was initially an integral part of a community experiment. Ideologically, the school and the community sustained each other in their early years. A strong reciprocal relationship developed. So long as a sufficient number of Fairhopers regarded their community as experimental—as a community with a point to prove—local ideology provided a critical margin of support for the school.

Fairhope changed, though, and as it did, the school also changed. The Depression knocked the wind out of the sails of the once optimistic community. Johnson lived long enough to see the consequences, and they ran much deeper than a weakening of the community's finances. She witnessed a weakening of the very spirit of the community: its commitment to reform. After her death, as Fairhope revived but became less and less extraordinary, so did the Organic School.

Instead of a quasi-public school with a clear mission, it became a private school in search of a population to serve, marketing itself at different times to Fairhope's local aristocracy, to the parents of child misfits, to segregation-minded whites, to almost anyone who could afford the tuition, and now to those who just want something different for their children. Over the years, the Organic School has sometimes drifted so far from Johnson's educational idea, she almost certainly would have disowned it. And although the school now seems to be returning to its original moorings, it still sits apart from the community. Appropriately so, for at the end of the twentieth century, Fairhope basks comfortably in the Gulf Coast sun, an antiquarian version of its heritage on display for a mix of suburbanites, retirees, good old boys and girls, New Agers, and, yes, a few never-say-die reformers who remember when.

4

AN ADVENTURE WITH CHILDREN: REFLECTIONS ON THE PARK SCHOOL OF BUFFALO AND AMERICAN PROGRESSIVE EDUCATION

Eugene F. Provenzo, Jr.

One of the most intriguing early experiments in Progressive Education in the United States, the Park School of Buffalo has been in continuous operation since 1912. Originally located in downtown Buffalo, it moved to its current location in the early 1920s. Visiting the campus today, one can still detect links to the past. The campus occupies an inviting park-like setting, many of its original buildings still standing. At the same time, there is evidence of significant change. Newer brick buildings lack the charm of the original, white clapboard administration building and Primary Village. The campus is smaller today, portions of it having been sold to build new homes; it is better manicured and less inviting to exploration and discovery than the original farm on which the campus was built.

The Park School has evolved beyond its original founding philosophy, becoming more modern while losing many of its ties to the progressive education movement, in 1912 the most modern of all types of education available in the United States. The present school nonetheless provides an extremely interesting case study of the rise and fall of private progressive schools. Its history supplies a lens through which one can study different aspects of the growth and decline of John Dewey's progressive educational experiment.

Dewey's influence on the development of both public and private education in the United States has, of course, attracted considerable interest among educational historians and philosophers. Beginning with Merle Curti's *The Social Ideas of American Educators*,[1] and continuing with studies such as Lawrence Cremin's *The Transformation of the School: Progressivism in American Education, 1876–1957*[2] and Arthur G. Wirth's *John Dewey as Educator: His Design for Work in Education (1894–1904)*,[3] both Dewey's educational experiments and his influence have been widely chronicled and analyzed.[4]

Despite this continuing interest, however, relatively little research has addressed the early educational experiments based on Dewey's work and the Park School of Buffalo certainly ranks among the most interesting of these.

The following discussion includes a general history of the Park School and the problems it faced in maintaining its progressive heritage and traditions. My approach will be highly personal. I attended the Park School of Buffalo from 1962 to 1968, when I graduated. My mother, Therese King Provenzo, worked at the school for twenty-five years—primarily as a second and fourth grade teacher, then as headmistress of the lower school, and finally as headmistress of the middle school. My younger sister, Anne Provenzo Freedman, attended the school as well, graduating in 1972.

In developing my analysis, I draw on historical sources, as well as my own memories and those of my mother, the administrators, and my classmates. Accordingly, this discussion extends beyond the boundaries of traditional educational history to include elements of both autobiography and participant observation. I expect these methodologies to reveal aspects of the school's character and history a less interdisciplinary model might neglect.

The Influence of Mary Hammett Lewis

Essential to any study of the Park School of Buffalo is Mary Hammett Lewis's 1928 book *An Adventure with Children*.[5] Lewis wrote *An Adventure with Children* after she resigned from the school as its headmistress and founder in 1926. Despite its charm and insight, her work has received almost no attention from the historians of the progressive education movement. Lawrence Cremin, for example, relegates it to a brief footnote in his *Transformation of the School*.[6] Lewis's work at the Park School descended directly from John Dewey's work at the University of Chicago and Teachers College, Columbia University. In 1896,

Dewey and his wife, Alice, had begun an experimental or "laboratory school" in Chicago sponsored by the University's Department of Philosophy, Psychology and Pedagogy. Dewey used the University Elementary School as the testing ground for his ideas as an educational innovator and philosopher. For Dewey, the school was literally, rather than figuratively a pedagogical laboratory. As he explained,

> The conception underlying the school is that of a laboratory. It bears the same relation to work in pedagogy that a laboratory bears to biology, physics or chemistry. Like any such laboratory, it has two main purposes: (1) to exhibit, test, verify, and criticize theoretical statements and principles; (2) to add to the sum of facts and principles in its special line.[7]

Dewey developed a curriculum that emphasized the interrelatedness of subjects and the need for children to "learn by doing." He designed the school to be a social environment—a real world for children where they learned and lived their day-to-day lives.

In 1904 Dewey resigned from the University of Chicago and took a position in philosophy at Columbia University, where he worked closely with Teachers College—the University's education school. Enormously influential there, Dewey largely set the agenda for the school's experimental school—the Horace Mann School—which was closely patterned after his experiments at the Laboratory School in Chicago.

Lewis came to New York from Cleveland to work at the Horace Mann School. As she recounted in *An Adventure with Children*, despite Dewey's fame and the school's obvious excellence, she found it less than a totally satisfactory place:

> We had a curriculum most completely and carefully worked out and handed down to us from the highest sources of authority in the university. . . . But there had been growing upon me a firm conviction that something was radically wrong with schools everywhere. All my life I had played with children and found them inventive, imaginative, full of ideas, with never quite enough time to carry them out. Yet here in this school, a leader in schools in this country, we felt stifled and suffocated. . . .[8]

Lewis began to innovate on her own. Her first step was to get "a big friendly rug" for her students and her to sit on. Moving her classes to the floor, she wanted to melt the rigid formality the desks and chairs created in her classroom. The introduction of the rug transformed her classroom:

> To tell the truth, it became sort of a magic carpet in my adventure. The attitudes of the children changed completely the moment they set foot upon that rug. Language lessons became confidential chats about all sorts of experiences. One day the rug became early Manhattan Island; another day it was the boat of Hendrick Hudson. Unconsciously it began to dawn on me that the thing I really wanted was to break up as far as possible the formality and artificiality of my classroom.[9]

The year following her introduction of the rug, Lewis took her class to the roof of the Horace Mann building, eight stories above Manhattan. On one of the windiest sites in New York City, she and her students set up schoolkeeping in a large canvas tent. Isolated from distractions caused by grown-ups and special teachers, Lewis created a rich learning environment for her children, and in this setting, she began to clarify her personal approach to education:

> [I]t was there, after many months of living alone with the children, undisturbed by any grown-ups, untaught by any special teachers, in the most primitive kind of environment, living day after day in the sunshine and doing all our own work, that it came to me. The thing above all else that these city children needed was a place to live which would suggest ideas of what to do or what needed to be done, and freedom to carry them out.[10]

Working with her students outdoors this way, Lewis concluded that more important even than learning multiplication tables was learning to love what one did:

> They learned to love work because they could see its real significance. They had to be ingenious because the poverty of their equipment demanded it; the simplicity and naturalness of their

surroundings made them their best children-selves; and they throve in that atmosphere of freedom and opportunity.[11]

In the Spring of 1911, shortly after her rooftop experiment began, a group of visitors from Buffalo came to visit Lewis's classroom. Headed by Nina Bull and Maulsby Kimball, the group expressed interest in establishing an innovative school for their children based on Deweyan principles.

Lewis agreed to come to Buffalo and start a co-educational school there. It opened in the fall of 1912 in a small rented cottage on Bird Avenue in Buffalo. The following year the school moved to a large colonial house at Main Street and Jewett Parkway and five additional small buildings were added on the property in the next six years. In 1920, the school purchased a sixty-acre farm on the outskirts of the city, in what is now the suburb of Synder, from the Hamlin family.

The Park School of Buffalo, which now included kindergarten through twelfth grade, soon achieved renown among those interested in progressive education and visitors came to the school from all over the world. By 1917, the school was attracting an average of six visitors a day:

One morning we had an MP from England, two physicians from Austria, two Japanese students from Columbia University, the president of a great college, a superintendent of schools from the Middle West, and a Harvard professor. . . .[12]

Among the more famous people to visit the Park School during this period was the writer Dorothy Canfield Fisher. Fisher came in 1915 when the school was still located on Jewett Parkway and she was particularly impressed by how the children helped to run the school:

In an ultramodern city, I stood in the midst of an old, old-fashioned home, where every process was open to the child's eye, where he took part in all that goes to make a home, where, above all, there was not a button to be pressed. And this old, old-fashioned home called itself the very latest thing in schools! With twentieth-century precision and accuracy it had analyzed the ideal of the old home and reconstructed everything thing in it of value to children.[13]

What Fisher observed at work in the Park School was Dewey's philosophy of the school as a social center: a place where the child lived and worked and learned. Yet the school represented more than just the implementation of John Dewey's philosophy; it was also the creation of Mary Hammett Lewis. Central to her philosophy of education was the belief that children needed a learning environment in which they could grow and flourish—a place where "a child's soul and mind might be at peace."

Lewis ratified her philosophy of education largely through the reality of the school she founded. She had placed herself firmly within the tradition of such charismatic progressive school founders as Helen Parkhurst at the Dalton School, Caroline Pratt at the City and Country School and Lucy Sprague Mitchell at the Bank Street School. And like many other progressive school founders, Lewis eventually developed major conflicts with her board of trustees.[14] In 1925 she became ill and spent the summer in France recovering. In her absence, conservative members of her board of trustees, evidently dissatisfied with the school's finances, took control of its overall operations. In the consequent conflict over board actions, all but two of the school's teachers resigned. When Lewis learned about the mass resignation, she resigned as well.[15] She subsequently went on to found the Park School of Cleveland.

The Park School after Lewis

Various distinguished headmasters succeeded Lewis at the Park School of Buffalo, including Morris Mitchell, Adolphus Cheek and Barton Chapin. When I attended the school during the 1960s, it still maintained its progressive traditions to a remarkable degree. Its setting and architecture contributed to its progressive environment. Much of the original sixty-acre campus had been sold off over the years. But the property still contained a barn with farm animals (including goats, sheep, chickens and ducks) and a pony. In a nearby pond, a child might discover tadpoles, catch sunfish, and observe an occasional muskrat.

The buildings erected at the Snyder campus during the 1920s were, in many respects, brilliantly designed. The buildings in the Primary Village, where my mother taught second grade for many years, contained two large, airy classrooms for the first and second grades, usually had between twenty-five and thirty students each. An assistant teacher helped the first and second grade teachers. A mud room with lockers provided a place for the students to leave their boots and hang their jackets. Bathrooms were adjacent to the mud room. A music room, which was also used for rest time and storytelling, was adjacent to the first grade classroom. Off the mud room, opposite the second grade classroom, was a simple kitchen with a stove, a sink, and a space to conduct science experiments. Storage space was available in a large attic. A small office allowed teachers to meet with parents in private and provided a quiet place for students who were sick or had to work by themselves.

Behind the Primary Village first and second grade building was a playground set in an apple orchard. It had a beautifully crafted playhouse with miniature furniture, sandboxes, swings, and other playground equipment.

As one of the first country day schools in the United States, the Park School's setting and environment reflect, at least in part, its philosophy. As Lewis recalled,

Our Primary Village stood in the orchard, its little houses quite literally the homes of the children who lived there. Children's houses they were indeed, each with its own out-of-door class-rooms, its shop with a loft overhead holding every sort of conceivable material which a child could want, each with its own tiny living room built around a fireplace, where one was apt to find a group of children reading poetry or planning the dramatization of a play, each with its own gardens and trellises and woodpile.[16]

During Lewis's administration, third-grade children "were actually running the chicken business on a large scale and making money on it."[17] Performances of *H.M.S Pinafore* took place on the banks of the pond, while potatoes from the school garden supplied the school's kitchen.

These progressive traditions remained as a vital part of the school culture well into the era when I attended. In sixth grade, one of my clearest memories is of helping the lower-schoolers pick apples from the orchard. Using an ancient cider press, we made our own cider. I had recently transferred from a rather unimaginative public school and found Park's philosophy of learning by doing both a novelty and thoroughly engaging and satisfying.

Take the cider making, for example. I remember that our cider was brown and sugary—nothing like the thin cider at the grocery store. We had the pleasure of selling it and making a little money for school projects. We also made the extraordinary discovery that when left to age, our cider would ferment and become effervescent and mildly alcoholic. We wrote about making and selling the cider, and of course, we had to keep records of our business venture and calculate our profits. The learning came naturally.

This approach to learning was consistent with Dewey's philosophy and Lewis's practice. Lewis emphasized that amid the discovery and adventure at the school, academic learning—learning linked to the real lives of the children—was also taking place. My education at Park School was, in fact, clearly serious. We were being shaped and groomed to become leaders in the community—people with a responsibility to make a better society. It was assumed that everyone in my class would go on to college and we tried to gain admission to the best colleges possible. But we were also a democratic community, and everyone had obligations and connections to each other.

In retrospect, I can say that the teachers at Park were far more influential than any of the others I have met. As an overall group, they were both talented and well-educated, and the more successful among them had a clearly defined image of the school and its purpose.

The tradition of hiring talented and creative teachers goes back to the time when Mary Hammett Lewis founded the school. In *An Adventure with Children*, she wrote that the school's teachers played an absolutely crucial role in maintaining its dynamism and energy. As headmistress, she scoured the country for imaginative and creative teachers. In selecting her staff, she explained how her own guiding principle was to discover, if I could, by talking with them, whether they were inclined to do their own thinking, whether they would tend to be creative, provided conditions were right. In no case during the early years of the school did I consult a teachers' agency, nor did I select teachers because they had taken any prescribed courses in education. This was not because I had not the greatest respect for the fine work which was being done in this line, but because I wanted above everything else to find a group of teachers free from any preconceived notions, then to place them in a school environment different from anything they had ever known and let them decide what to do with it.[18]

In researching and writing this chapter, I talked to administrators and classmates about their experiences at Park. Fred Keller (a prominent film and television director) recalled how important various teachers were in defining his experience there. He talked about William Hoyt, a history teacher both of us had. Hoyt had attended Park as a student, and his own children attended there as well. Keller explained how Hoyt had provided him not only with interesting instruction as a history teacher, but with fine soccer and hockey coaching and with a strong sense of what it means to be a member of a larger community as well.

I too remember Hoyt. Unlike Keller, who was a superb soccer and hockey goalie, I was an indifferent athlete. Hoyt, who was interested in sports, tended to treat me a bit dismissively at times, although I found his history classes consistently exciting. He is, in part, responsible for my decision to become a social scientist and historian. What I remember most clearly about Hoyt and several other teachers—people like Miriam Goldeen, a mildly eccentric Latin teacher; Allen Thomas, a thoughtful high school English teacher; Ed Barnes, a gifted hands-on science teacher; and Michael Stafford, a talented math and science educator—was their obvious dedication to the Park school philosophy.

This philosophy became critical to my experience as a student. I remember how discussions often came up in our weekly school assemblies about whether someone's actions had been consistent with the "school's philosophy." I constantly heard references to what it meant to be a "Park Schooler." Whenever confusion in this matter arose, we would refer to a teacher or sometimes to a parent who had attended the school. It did not necessarily matter if a teacher had always been at Park. Allen Thomas's experience with progressive education, for example, had come mostly from his work at the Putney School in Vermont. Miriam Goldeen's approach to teaching had been influenced by her experience at Mills College—a private woman's liberal arts college in Oakland, California.

Others had, of course, attended Park: Art Meyer—an admired headmaster of the Upper School—had gone to Park and returned to teach after serving in the Second World War and then completing his undergraduate degree at Princeton University on the G.I. Bill. Meyer had originally intended to pursue a career in the State Department, but just before taking the foreign service exam, Adolphus Cheek offered him a job teaching in the Middle School at Park.

After five years, Meyer moved on to teach at the high school level and then became headmaster of the Upper School in the late 1950s. This progression of teachers who had attended the school as students and then taught in the Middle School and worked their way up to the high school level occurred often. Peter Dow, for example, started attending Park in the fifth grade in the early 1940s and graduated in 1950. After earning a degree at Harvard and teaching at the Weston School in Cambridge, he came back to Park in 1958.

Dow initially taught seventh and eighth graders and then moved into the high school where he taught history. He left Park to work on a graduate degree at Harvard in 1962, and later returned to Buffalo to work in a family business and served on Park's board of directors for ten years during the early 1970s and early 1980s.

My discussions with classmates made it clear that the teachers like the ones just described most clearly embodied the school's values and traditions. According to Art Meyer, teachers in the 1960s and 1970s were deliberately recruited from among former graduates who had recently finished liberal arts degrees. Almost none of the teachers brought traditional pedagogical training, and although the administration and staff conducted their interviews the headmaster made the final decision. Applicants were selected according to whether they seemed to reflect the school's philosophy and whether they had a firm academic background.

To a certain extent, young male teachers often taught at Park School as part of a transitional experience between completing a college degree and advancing to other professional pursuits. When I was a freshman, for example, I had an English teacher named Roger Hooker. An heir to the Hooker chemical fortune, he attended the school and had come back to teach for a few years before entering the business world.

Attendance at a progressive school, or some experience with other alternative forms of private education, seemed to be a unifying experience among the majority of the Park teachers. This pattern was particularly evident at the high school level, although often at the lower and middle school levels as well.

When I attended Park in the 1960s, the school's headmaster, Barton Chapin, became largely responsible for defining the school's purpose and direction. Chapin always had a clear idea of the school's philosophy. He made frequent reference to John Dewey's work as an educational philosopher, often to Mary Hammett Lewis's work, and more specifically to *An Adventure with Children*. Yale-trained and originally an English teacher, he was for many of us the physical embodiment of the school. He had attended private school throughout his education, and while not strictly a product of the progressive school tradition, he had a clear vision of the importance of private education and the essentials of the progressive school model.

The informal activities that were an essential part of the school's culture communicated the important components of that model. We ate lunch family-style in a large dining room. We rotated through table assignments with different teachers and different students from various grade levels. For example, the high school students, grades nine through twelve, ate together. A senior sat at the head of the table opposite a teacher. Seniors had the privilege of drinking coffee. They also served the meal that had been carried from the dining window by one of the younger students. We never sat in the same seat for more than one day, and I remember the excitement of moving down the row to an end seat where I would have the chance to sit next to and talk with a teacher or upper classmate I admired. The Park School abandoned this tradition during the 1970s when they began serving lunch cafeteria-style and students chose where they wanted to sit.

When I attended the school, we discussed its purpose chiefly during these family-style lunches. Teachers interacted with students and older students with younger students. A similar procedure obtained in our sports programs, where members of the academic faculty undertook most of our coaching.

Other routines also contributed to communicating the school's philosophy and purpose. Lewis had established a number of practices that continued at the school fifty years later when I attended it. For example, every Wednesday the faculty stayed through dinner to discuss the curriculum and other issues related to the school. These meetings took place in the school's dining hall. Although more specialized meetings addressed the school's different levels, at these Wednesday meetings the faculty met as a total unit, pre-school through twelfth grade.

Another factor that tended to unify the school were the work days, when we completed various projects: painting the outside of the classrooms, cleaning out the drainage ditches to the pond, digging a fish pond, renovating a student lounge, or planting a garden. Everyone in the school—teachers, students, janitors, and administrators—participated in these projects. I clearly remember that the entire student population of over 400 would walk in the early spring across the campus in a giant human chain picking up all the trash and litter that had accumulated during the winter. Simple as these activities were, they provided a sense of purpose and community. They helped us understand that Park Schoolers made contributions beyond our regular lessons and activities.

Other activities were more artistic. For a week each spring we conducted an arts festival. Our regular classes were canceled while we staged plays, concerts, and art exhibits. Everyone participated from throughout the school. My own memories include exhibiting my sculpture for the first time, building and designing stage sets, and acting in plays.

But certain teachers failed to fit into the program and most of them left after a year or two. The young Mormon woman from Utah who taught me Geometry in my sophomore year was a graduate student at the University of Buffalo. She was attractive and always exquisitely dressed, but she had no idea of what the school was about. Her high heels and silk blouses hindered her participation in its many spontaneous, rough and tumble activities. I remember her stranded on a sidewalk, unable to follow a group of us across a soggy field.

Progressive Education Gradually Relinquished

My recent discussions with Paul Farber, now a Professor of Educational Philosophy at Western Michigan University, who graduated a year after me in 1969, reminded me that the school had begun to evolve into something different at about the time we left. The classes certainly presented different personalities, but something began to shift in the school's character in the late 1960s. My sister Anne Provenzo Freedman, who graduated in 1972, also noticed that the school had begun to undergo significant changes when she attended.

Some of these changes undoubtedly had to do with the Vietnam War and the crises of the late 1960s. In the spring of 1968—the year I graduated—Martin Luther King was assassinated and the day of my graduation, Robert F. Kennedy was shot. These events dampened what should have been an exciting time. The draft loomed before the boys who did not go on to college. Urban riots following the King assassination and the protests of our Vietnam involvement made us realize that our lives were less secure than our school made them seem.

Change seemed constant throughout the 1960s, 70s, and 80s. Whenever I visited the Park School while I attended college and graduate school and in my early years as a professor at the University of Miami, I sensed significant changes taking place. My mother, who stayed on as a teacher and headmistress until 1987, also kept me informed of the more substantive changes.

Financial problems persisted at Park throughout the 1970s and 1980s. Parents began to demand a more traditional curriculum and a movement started to make Park more like the other elite private preparatory schools in Buffalo: Nichols and Buffalo Seminary. College admission gradually became the principal goal of the school, yet it seemed as though the colleges to which Park graduates were admitted belonged increasingly to the middle level.

As Peter Dow reminded me, college admissions became more competitive during the 1970s and 1980s. Until the 1960s, most of the students attending the elite colleges across the country had come from private schools, their admission depending heavily on the recommendations of their headmasters and senior teachers. This practice began to shift during the 1960s as the Scholastic Aptitude Test and Advanced

Placement Course scores became increasingly important criteria for college acceptance.

Parents exerted pressure on the school to make sure its students would be prepared to score well on the standardized college admissions exams. What seems to have been lost in this process was the school's fundamental Deweyan philosophy of learning by doing. Park School no longer served as a miniature society where children lived and learned.

I observed this philosophical shift when I visited the school in 1985 to speak on the school's history at the Adolphus Cheek lecture. As a labor of love, I had just published with my mother a new edition of Lewis's *An Adventure with Children*. I expected the book at least to mildly interest educational historians, but mainly I hoped it would give those attending and teaching at the school access to its early history.

I presented a slide lecture on the history of Park in its early years, and discussed at length Dewey's and Lewis's philosophies of education. It was a cold and rainy night, but about 40 or 50 conscientious souls came to the lecture, and it generated a lively discussion. Yet as I listened, I saw that those attending (both teachers and parents) had little sense of the school's progressive roots and origins. Instead, Park had become a college prep school, rather like the other traditional elite schools in town. Interest, at least on the part of the parents attending my speech, seemed to focus primarily on assuring that their children entered a selective college rather than on their education, per se.

On that visit, my mother and I discussed at length how the character of the school had changed from when I graduated seventeen years before. She explained how various headmasters had tried to make the school more appealing to parents unconnected to the progressive tradition. As general economic conditions worsened in the Buffalo area during the 1970s and 1980s, competition among private schools intensified. My mother described how various headmasters had tried to market the school, evidently emphasizing the themes parents wanted to hear, mainly academic competitiveness.

Lewis had firmly resisted the influence of parents on the school's curriculum and environment fifty years earlier. She had considered it essential to make "the school convincing and absolutely irresistible to parents."[19] Yet in doing so, she adhered to the idea of a clearly articulated philosophy and vision. She felt that she had to demonstrate to parents that

> [W]e were doing our own thinking as a school and that we had a definite educational policy, a policy that was the result of an endless amount of thought and planning of teachers who were giving the best part of their lives to bring it about. This policy we should adhere to if we lost every child in the school.[20]

Under Lewis, parents were asked less what they wanted and more to see the progress their children were making. They could come to observe but not to interfere with the school's fundamental model or plan. As Lewis explained,

> Questions we asked parents were of this order: Is your child fatigued after his day's work? Is he becoming an investigator? What interests does he bring home? Does he show more initiative than he used to? Does he eat and sleep well? Is he eager to go to school? Parents came to know that we depended upon them enormously for help, and they gave it freely. They came to understand that on the other hand we should no more expect them to criticize a teacher for a method she was using in teaching the multiplication tables than they would expect one of us to ask them why they gave their child white bread instead of graham.[21]

The parents Lewis met were, of course, concerned that their children acquire the moral and disciplinary value they associated with traditional schooling. In addition, they wanted their children to acquire the requisite background in the basic subject matter.[22]

This concern remained important many years later during my experience at the school. When I took my high school general science and biology courses, I recall considerable concern about whether Ed Barnes, our science teacher, was really covering the curriculum. A Harvard graduate, Barnes had come to Park with his wife, Nadia, from an experimental Waldorf school. His classroom became an exotic collection of animals and equipment. We spent huge amounts of time keeping detailed notebooks of field observations, writing our feelings about dissecting a rat or pig, and developing reports on different aspects of science.

We learned a lot of science and biology. In particular, I learned to become an independent learner and a critical researcher, to care passionately about how systems worked, and to describe in writing what I saw around me. We also did well on our standardized tests, well above national norms. Yet despite this fact, parents continually questioned Mr. Barnes's unorthodox teaching methods. Art Meyer recalled having frequently to defend Barnes to parents who expected a more traditional approach.

Conclusion

In short, as modernity approached, the school changed, drawn gradually away from its progressive roots. The dearth of a certain renewable source of teachers trained in the progressive tradition no doubt contributed to its drift away from its founding principles. In addition, the pressure from parents to conform to standardized college admission requirements combined with a general social pressure to pursue a more conservative curriculum also contributed to the school's gradual departure from the progressive traditions of its founders.

To some extent, the history of the Park School of Buffalo probably resembles those of many other progressive schools across the country.[23] But the disassociation from their progressive roots and traditions raises a certain irony. Developmental psychologists who follow the likes of Jean Piaget and Lev Vygotsky contend that the hands-on experiential model Dewey and his followers advocated ideally meets the needs of children, both cognitively and in terms of their role as emerging members of the social system. Simply stated, one sees a high likelihood that schools like Park intuitively incorporated into their curricula key aspects of how children develop socially and psychologically.

I would like to argue that progressive schools like the Park School of Buffalo need to return to the Deweyan tradition of the school as a social center and to hands-on learning. In doing so, they would offer a positive alternative to elite models of private schooling they can, at best, only imitate. All romanticism aside, the progressive school tradition represents one of the most interesting experiments in the history of American schooling. Its curriculum was to a remarkable degree successful and well worth reinventing. But to do so, we must reexamine the work of John Dewey, as well as the contributions of the other charismatic leaders in the Progressive School Movement, like Mary Hammett Lewis, and consider its possibilities for helping to define education in years to come.

5

THE CITY AND COUNTRY SCHOOL: A PROGRESSIVE PARADIGM

Susan F. Semel

The City and Country School, located at 146 West 13th Street in New York City, occupies three connected landmark brownstones that appear to be a single building on a tree-lined street in the heart of Greenwich Village.[1] Visitors to the school, especially non-New Yorkers looking for a more traditional school building, often walk right by it. Indeed, the school is marked only by a modest, brown weather-beaten wooden sign bearing its name. To either side, stand more brownstones—some of them having seen better days, others having been renovated by the recent influx of affluent "baby boomers"—comprise the neighborhood. Current real estate prices are steep for prospective newcomers; brownstones often start at one million dollars. Apartments, especially the large ones that would accommodate growing families, are difficult to find and are usually sold or rented at top market prices. This neighborhood had traditionally attracted artistically inclined single people or couples without children who were drawn to its affordable rents, bohemian ambiance, and tolerance of alternative lifestyles and radical politics.

Today, in addition to its aging, long-term tenants on rent control or rent stabilization and its artists and writers, the neighborhood is home to newly affluent couples with children—that is to say "yuppies" attracted to the aesthetic atmosphere of the Village. Thus, independent schools in this area can now draw from a small but steadily growing applicant pool. Although competition for students remains stiff, City and Country School appears to enjoy a reliable stream of applicants either from parents who consciously seek a different kind of educational experience for their children than the traditional one they received or from alumni who expect their children to receive the same kind of education they experienced at City and Country.

To enter the school building, visitors ring a bell and are buzzed in by a receptionist located in a room to one side of the lobby. A sliding glass window gives her an unobstructed view of the lobby, a cozy rectangular space where parents and care-givers congregate at arrival and dismissal times. The lobby is probably the only space at City and Country that is not continually populated with children and adults for, as in most city schools and particularly at City and Country, space is at a premium. The enrollment figure for the school year 1996–1997 was 239. The school accepts children at age two and the students may continue through age thirteen. It is organized into three divisions: The Lower School, which consists of pre-school through second grade (Groups II through VII); The Middle School, which consists of third, fourth and fifth grades (Groups VIII through X); and the Upper School, grades six, seven and eight (Groups XI through XIII). Although enrollment tends to be heavier in The Lower School and tapers off in The Upper School, recent trends indicate that more students are remaining at City and Country through the eighth grade. On the whole, class sizes average around 18 and tuition runs from $7,300 for the two year olds in the morning group to $10,500 for the eight through thirteen year olds. Because money is an issue at City and Country there are fewer scholarships granted in the early groups, which tend to be in popular demand. Thus, the ethnic and racial composition of The Lower School tends to mirror that of the immediate neighborhood. Financial aid does exist, however, and at present about 20 percent of the student body at City and Country School receives some form of scholarship assistance.

The interior of the City and Country School building is modest. The walls, with their numerous coats of paint, show signs of age, and classrooms have what real estate brokers euphemistically refer to as "Old World charm." Little renovation has been done over the years save what was deemed essential to maintain the building. Nevertheless, the constant energetic flow of traffic on the single staircase leading to the upper floors; the giant block-building activity in the yard, visible from the passage off the front lobby; and the ground floor classrooms, amply stocked with such diverse educational materials as paint, clay, water, sand, and well-worn unit blocks, clearly indicate that the students are actively engaged in learning in a school that proudly calls itself "one of the oldest progressive schools in the United States."[2] Founded by Caroline Pratt in 1914, not far from its current location, City and Country consciously continues to practice the progressive philosophy and pedagogy Pratt developed, built upon block play, jobs, and an integrated, lived curriculum. At the same time, the school remains mindful that it is educating children who will live in the twenty-first century.

The history of the City and Country School provides us with an instructive study of a progressive school that still seeks to maintain its progressive roots and has worked to both preserve its philosophy, curriculum and pedagogy, often at times when progressive education had fallen under severe criticism. In fact, at one point in its history its conscious efforts to preserve its particular vision of progressive education brought the school to the brink of disaster. That City and Country School survived, and now successfully grapples with the tensions of continuity and change, speaks both to the vicissitudes of educational reform movements and to the timelessness, resiliency, and flexibility of progressive education. Moreover, it validates Caroline Pratt's vision of progressive education that began as an experimental play group in an assembly room at Hartley House, a settlement house on New York City's West Side in 1913.[3]

City and Country: The Influence of Caroline Pratt

The City and Country School is indisputably the creation of its founder, Caroline Pratt, and as the histories of other child-centered progressive schools indicate, it is always useful to examine the history of a particular institution as inexorably bound to the experience of its founder. In this case, we should note that Pratt was born in rural Fayetteville, near Syracuse, in upstate New York, in 1867, two years after the Civil War. As a child, she was exposed firsthand to the worlds of both farming, through her uncle, and commerce, through her father. Pratt noted in her book, *I Learn from Children*, that she was a participant in the process of breadmaking from the harvesting of wheat on her uncle's farm through the baking of bread for her family's consumption.[4] It seems probable that the interest in jobs and woodworking for children that appeared in her subsequent educational practice were shaped in part by both active participation in and observations of life in a small village that was both a prosperous farming community and, by nineteenth century standards, a stable, commercial center originally fueled by the trade from the nearby Erie Canal.

Pratt began her teaching career in the Fayetteville school in 1887; in 1892, as the recipient of a scholarship, she set off for Teachers College in New York City.[5] There she demonstrated her interest in woodworking and manual training and went on to teach manual training at the Normal School for Girls in Philadelphia, where she met her life-long companion, Helen Marot. Marot was a Quaker and a librarian, interested in social causes and co-founder of a library in Philadelphia devoted to economics and political science.[6] According to Pratt, Helen Marot's library provided a congenial refuge for radicals of all sorts to read about and discuss contemporary social and political issues.[7] In 1901, Pratt and Marot moved to Greenwich Village, where they believed they could better implement their ideas about social change: Pratt through education and Marot through social activism. Pratt's socialist politics and impetus to reform appear to have come from Helen Marot, whose radical politics led her to become co-publisher of *The Dial*, a periodical that had both John Dewey and Thorstein Veblen on its editorial board.[8] Marot's lifework revolved around improving working conditions of working class women and children.[9]

Caroline Pratt decided to open up her own school after a two-month experiment at Hartley House proved to be successful. Funded by her friend, Edna Smith, who had supported her efforts at Hartley House, she began her new play school in a three-room apartment in Greenwich Village, at the corner of 4th and 12th Streets in 1914, not far from the site of the present school. She determined that her school would serve young children from the neighborhood, particularly from working-class families, who through play, might come to understand their environment. Pratt's materials included blocks—like the ones Patty Hill's students used in her kindergarten at Teachers College—hammers, nails, saws, and the daily activities of the neighborhood. The first group of children included only four year olds, but by the second year of the school's operation, it had added a mixed-age group of fours and fives and a group of sixes. Then the school moved, this first time to a rented building on 13th Street;

then shortly after, to a converted stable in MacDougal Alley, owned by Lucy Sprague Mitchell, and located behind her house.

Mitchell, introduced to Pratt by Harriet Johnson, became closely affiliated with City and Country School as a teacher, as a parent, and most important as its primary benefactress.[10] When five years later, in 1921, Mitchell moved her family to West 12th and West 13th Streets, the school moved as well. She remained connected to Pratt until 1930, when she officially severed her ties with the school and sold it her real estate holdings—three buildings on West 13th Street and two buildings on West 12th Street—considerably below market price.[11] Mitchell's departure at the onset of the Depression represented a serious loss for the school. Her reliable generosity obviated the need for broad-based, systematic fund-raising by either Pratt or her successor, Jean Wesson Murray, and in the 1980s, dwindling funds almost forced the school to close.

While Helen Marot shaped Pratt's progressivism, targeting her educational experiment to working-class children—first in a settlement house and then, in a Greenwich Village apartment—John Dewey influenced Pratt's thinking about curriculum and pedagogy, particularly in the areas of child growth and development. As she so aptly stated, it was hardly surprising that the school she founded tried "to fit the school to the child, rather than as we were doing with indifferent success—fitting the child to the school."[12] Moreover, Pratt contemplated her child-centered pedagogy with an embryonic community within the school in which the child could actively participate. Thus, the child would move from making sense of the world with play blocks to performing actual jobs necessary for the maintenance of the school community.

Pratt began her school as a "play school"—that is, a pre-kindergarten school based on the premise that children learn by play and that for children, play was really hard work.[13] Play provided a way for children to learn how to negotiate the world in which they live and to understand how life situations work and how people live together. As an integral part of her pedagogy, Pratt emphasized the use of her ubiquitous plain wooden blocks to help children "sort out and make sense of the world around them."[14] She explicitly stated that the program for the younger children and later, the program for the older children, was formulated through

. . . work with blocks and kindred materials. Play with these
materials is an organizing experience. At three or four, children
come to block-building, for example, after a good deal of experiencing with their bodies. They themselves have been everything.
. . . cows, animals of all kinds, engines . . . everything that
moves. . . . Now they become interested in the details. What part
of the engine makes the whistle? What makes the movement?
Who pulls the throttle? Children are interested in these not as
mere facts, but as facts to be used in play; or it would be more
correct to say that what the information does to the play is to
keep it going and help it to organize as a whole, to raise new
inquiries and above all to offer new opportunities relationships.
This is what block-building means to us.[15]

For Pratt, play was far from static; rather, she believed that the play
experience leads to new opportunities for further experiences and,
therefore, as Dewey might also have concluded, growth.

In accordance with her reformist thinking, Pratt began her school
with six children from working-class families with tuitions funded by
outside benefactors; however, she had difficulty attracting and retaining
working-class families from the neighborhood. As she expanded both her
preschool and elementary school programs, in the West 13th Street
building she observed that

We did not get as many children as we had hoped. It was one
thing for parents to send their children to *play* school before they
were six, but quite another to keep them out of public school and
send them to us. They were afraid the children would not be
ready for public school later, and they were not far wrong. We
had no intention of pushing three R's on the children until we felt
they were ready.[16]

But if working class families avoided Caroline Pratt's pedagogical
experiment, artists and writers in the neighborhood enthusiastically
endorsed it. This group was far more willing to embrace unconventional
methods; thus, the composition of the student body changed dramatically
during the school's initial years to include the children of the Greenwich

Village intelligentsia, seeking an experimental school for their children, and some members of the local gentry interested in "the new education." Although Caroline Pratt began City and Country with a focus upon the early years, she eventually began to add more classes concerned with academic content, until the school accommodated children through age thirteen. In 1921, she changed the name of the school to the City and Country School to reflect its seriousness of purpose. The "Country" of the title referred to the summer farm program Pratt and Mitchell established in Hopewell Junction, New York, and which lasted for thirteen years. In 1924, the school became incorporated as a non-profit institution.

Pedagogic Practice at the City and Country School

The pedagogic practices Pratt developed at City and Country openly Deweyan in nature, reflected his idea of an "embryonic community" based on the needs and interests of children at various ages and heavily slanted toward both inquiry and experimentation, both book learning and experience. Pratt believed that young children should initially learn experimentally and experientially from their immediate environments, then, as they mature and as their horizons expand, they should be introduced to more sophisticated tasks and materials:

> As the children grow older, they carry their inherent experimental method into other fields with the help of a teacher and a loosely but positively organized program. Jobs require trips to stores to purchase things. A school store requires extended buying at wholesale and selling again at retail. Wholesalers need warehouses for supplies and the children visit there. Finally they begin to require books as sources of information; and through these, with the teacher's help, they extend their inquiries beyond the confines of their own city. They make maps instead of floor schemes. They are pushing back their own horizons.[17]

As Pratt further refined her thinking, block play remained the linchpin of the curriculum of the Lower School with a particular focus at each age group. The Threes, according to Pratt, would use blocks as their "raw materials" to help them make sense of their immediate world:

the world of themselves and their families. The Fours would use blocks as a way of understanding their immediate environment, particularly "as they observe such interesting activities as street-paving, excavation or construction work."[18] Clay, paint and woodworking would augment block play. As the groups become older and their horizons expanded, block play became more sophisticated, lengthier, more likely to reflect serious research into how processes work and to integrate reading and writing skills. By the time they became Sixes, the children would actively engage in trips around the city with their block construction mirroring its actual geography, and its workings. Finally, in the Sevens, the children would construct the city, working together to create neighborhoods and communities with running water and electricity.[19] The effect of this curriculum was and continues to be powerful: It encourages children to investigate their world, to work both independently and cooperatively, to pose questions and find answers, to solve problems, to conduct research, and to become independent learners.

As the curriculum of the school began to evolve, it became clear that after age seven more challenging content was needed to hold the students' attention. Particular historical periods and civilizations became the vehicles for an integrated curriculum that reflected the interests of the students and encouraged their acquisition of content and skills, while simultaneously immersing them in their course of study. A graduate of the class of 1928 recalled the process of creating curriculum:

> I was always convinced that at the beginning of each school year our class would (after reporting on our summer activities) decide what area of the past we would study: Middle Ages, the Vikings, Greece, Renaissance Italy, and so on. If there was manipulation by the teachers, it was extremely clever and subtle, for we were convinced that we were in charge. This was heady stuff that motivated our research and reading as well as our painting and clay work.[20]

Other graduates from the period of Pratt's tenure as Principal recalled the experiential nature of the curriculum: "When we studied the Vikings, we became Vikings. We dressed like Vikings, we built a Viking ship in the classroom." Another added, "when we studied the Westward Expansion, it was like travelling across this country much like the pioneers did."[21]

As block building was the focus of the primary groups, beginning in the Eights, so jobs became an integral part of the curriculum for students. The practice of assigning specific jobs of "actual service" to the different age groups evolved so that the school eventually functioned as a self-sufficient community. But as even more than a self-sufficient community, Pratt saw her school functioning as a democratic, self-sufficient community—that is, as a model for the future.[22] Informants readily point out that Pratt set the tone for a discernable socialist orientation present in the school from its inception through the 1970s. The school organized its jobs around the concepts of interdependence and community and used them to teach both academic and social skills. For example, Pratt described how the Eights ran the school post office:

> Mail boxes, made by the children and placed conveniently throughout the buildings, are used by the office staff, teachers, and the children of all the groups for their school communications. The Eights choose a postman who makes five daily collections and deliveries. Packages, too, are called for and delivered. An electric bell, installed by the children with the help of the science teacher, is used by the office to call a Special Delivery postman to carry important messages. The mailing material is sold by the Eights. They make stamps in the clay room, shop, or science room; post-office tables and counters are made in shop. A postmaster and his assistant are selected each week to sell the materials and to do the bookkeeping.[23]

Pratt further noted that field trips to the post office provided the students with a model and sparked their interest in postal routes. This interest might, in turn, lead to a study of "early post routes, the lives of early settlers and Indians, as well as into a study of present day methods of communication."[24] Thus jobs could be linked to the curriculum as a natural outgrowth of student inquiry.

The Nines ran the school store, supplying the entire school with its needs: They were responsible for purchasing inventory and then selling it, and their curriculum was heavily influenced by economics, especially how the capitalist system works. The idea was less to make a profit than to serve the community and provide valuable learning experiences for the children. Informants, however, recall the controversy the school store generated in later years when a number of parents and faculty members called into question the teaching of capitalist practices and their values.

The Tens were responsible for all of the hand-printed materials for the Sevens, like flash cards and reading charts. The Elevens ran the print shop and attended to all of the school's printing needs: attendance lists, library cards, stationery, and stamps. The Twelves first made toys, then weavings, until they settled upon the publication of a monthly magazine called *The Bookworm's Digest*, which reviewed new children's books sent to the group by publishers and included a popular "Old Favorites" column discussing familiar books.[25] As the students performed their jobs they also learned basic academic skills although it seems that social studies was (and still is) the core subject of the curriculum. For example, the Elevens studied the Middle Ages, which worked well with their job, given the emphasis on illuminated manuscripts and the invention of the printing press. What emerged from this model was a community of independent young children actively engaged in their learning, while concurrently contributing to the life of their school community.[26] In sum, these students were, in Deweyan language, "saturated with the spirit of service," while they learned to be self-directed in the context of the school community—"the best guarantee of a larger society which is worthy, lovely and harmonious."[27]

In addition to blocks and jobs, such "specials" complemented the educational experience as Library, Rhythms, Shop, Music, Art and Dramatics. Rhythms, in particular, established by Ruth Doing in the 1920s, continues to be an integral and unique part of the program. To the accompaniment of a pianist in a specially designated room, children use such materials as scarfs, ropes and rings to explore their movements and recreate their experiences.

The Organizational Structure of the City and Country School

The organizational structure of City and Country also bears examination, since the way in which it ran helped support and maintain Pratt's vision of progressive education long after her principalship ended. It also illustrates indirectly her socialist politics. In essence, Pratt set up City and Country as a teacher cooperative, and all faculty members who had taught in the school for one year gained membership. A five-member executive committee, which operated much like a board of trustees, governed the corporation created by parent and school lawyer, Timothy Pfeiffer. The five charter members of the executive committee were teachers in the school (many of them parents, too as there was a great deal of overlap). Among them were Lucy Sprague Mitchell and Jessie Stanton. As Pratt describes the procedure, "Each year the corporation would elect the principal, secretary, and treasurer of the school as its own president, secretary, and treasurer, respectively, and would accept as its board of directors the annually elected executive committee of the school."[28] The executive committee was elected by the principal and staff.

This organizational model resulted in charging a small group of faculty members with both educational and fiscal responsibilities. This arrangement eventually jeopardized the school's survival, for when Mitchell departed in 1930, the Executive Committee began to confront financial matters and managerial problems it was incapable of resolving without a strong leader. At the same time, the structure empowered teachers and encouraged them to maintain the particular pedagogic practices established by Pratt and refined by her successor, Jean Wesson Murray. Although the record remains unclear on how day-to-day school governance proceeded, it seems safe to conclude that Caroline Pratt insisted on at least a semblance of democratic structure in the executive committee, whose charge it was to oversee business and curricular matters. Sources generally agree that discussions were open, that Pratt took what was said under advisement, and that she had a way of making all the participants feel as if they were making valuable contributions.

Most informants agree, however, that while Pratt encouraged democratic governance she nevertheless had very clear ideas about how to implement her particular version of progressive pedagogy. Informants recall that she would enter a classroom and if she saw something amiss, she would share her distress with the teacher in full view of the students. In short, there was really only one way to do things: Pratt's way. One informant likened the way the school was run to "National Socialism in Russia." She further observed that, "When it came down to brass tacks, she [Pratt] made the decisions. She ran it like Stalin." Furthermore, this source noted that the Executive Committee members, although composed of teachers and parents, were "heavy duty guys who were very affluent" and that Pratt "would and did dominate these people."

Particularly, this informant pointed to the fact that the kind of women who served on the executive committee (not unlike a board of trustees) were upper-class or upper-middle-class women "who liked to come in and drink martinis." Executive Committee meetings, in fact, took place in Pratt's office, where participants were greeted by a uniformed maid, who served them cocktails and hors d'oeuvres, the latter usually catered by Luchows, an elegant neighborhood restaurant at the time. Pratt's talent for management lay in how she "let the women drink martinis while convincing them that she had listened to and taken up their ideas."

Like many women founders, Pratt had little tolerance for those who deviated from her philosophy. Thus, some City and Country teachers, in the words of another informant, felt that "the quicker I get out of here the better." Political differences as well discouraged some faculty members from continuing at City and Country, especially those who were "to the Left of Caroline." Some former parents and former students recall Pratt's highhandedness in her daily dealings with her constituency. Pratt noted these shortcomings herself, although somewhat vaguely, in *I Learn from Children.* Perhaps with Pratt's as with many other talented leaders in the pedagogical avant-garde, the Rousseauean idea of exerting force to achieve freedom was the most viable and expedient way to nurture and develop her particular experiment.

While Pratt's leadership style may have often been less than democratic, her creation of an educational community in which students contribute cooperatively toward its maintenance while learning both experientially and through traditional means exemplifies Dewey's idea of a school as a "democratic workshop."[29] Pratt believed that "a school's greatest value must be to turn out human beings who could think effectively and work constructively, who could in time make a better world than this for living in."[30]

Caroline Pratt remained Principal of City and Country until she retired in 1945 and held the title of Principal Emerita until her death in 1954. Following her retirement, an "outsider" ran the school in 1945 –1946, then a teacher from City and Country, Charlotte Pinco, served as

Acting Principal through 1948, when Jean Wesson Murray, a teacher under Pratt, assumed the leadership of the City and Country School.

Life after Pratt: Jean Wesson Murray, 1948–1977

Jean Wesson Murray emerged from the faculty in 1948 to lead City and Country as its Principal for almost thirty years until her health forced her into retirement in 1977. Whereas Pratt tended to be brusque in manner and mannish in dress, informants characterize Murray as "a lady dressed in tweeds and pearls." Unlike Pratt, who came from a rural town in upstate New York, Murray grew up in England, the child of affluent American parents, descended on her mother's side from the gunmakers, Smith and Wesson. Interestingly, Murray retained her British citizenship throughout her life. In the tradition of many upper-class aristocrats, she had been tutored at home and first attended school at the age of eight. Educated at Radcliffe College, she found her way to City and Country in 1934, first as a student teacher and then as a teacher of the Nines, Sevens, and Eights. Evidence suggests from both Murray's writings and numerous informants that she was committed to carrying on Pratt's vision. She cared passionately about the experiences of the child in learning situations, especially in the early years; additionally she was constantly mindful of Pratt's legacy:

> Every normal child is born with courage, curiosity, a desire to explore, to discover and try things out for himself. He experiments with everything, both animate and inanimate, and he should, for this is his way of growing. A school should therefore provide an environment in which such discoveries can be made. Nearly fifty years ago Caroline Pratt, with an unerring understanding of children's deepest needs, founded the City and Country School. Here children are helped to value themselves, other people, ideas, skills, responsibilities and hard work. They know the wonderful satisfaction of creative thought and action in a wide variety of mediums. Each child has an opportunity to develop at his own special pace in his own unique way. Each child may discover for himself the excitement and discipline of

learning and forge within himself a deep feeling of personal integrity.[31]

Murray appears to have been a model progressive teacher. As one informant recalled, "I remember vividly my year in the Nines with Jean Murray. It was the beginning of the year, she was sitting on the desk. For years, she said, people went across the country in wagons. Would anyone mind if we sailed to San Francisco? Sailing to San Francisco became math, science, etc. It became our passion. We decided the curriculum, but probably it was what Murray wanted to do."

Murray continued to follow the practice of an experiential, integrated curriculum emanating at least in principle from the child. She believed in giving children space and encouraging them to realize their full potential. As she wrote in 1958, "All really good education has and always has had as its aim the fullest possible development of each individual. Therefore, situations have to be found in which this development can best flourish. We at City and Country are fortunate in that we believe we have an almost ideal environment in which young children can start their education."[32]

During her thirty-year tenure as Principal of City and Country Murray managed to retain the progressive pedagogy Pratt established—the pedagogy she had been steeped in as a teacher at the school for fourteen years. She was aided first by the Executive Committee, which was by then composed of a group of teachers who had been at the school for between two and three years and who were themselves supported by a core of faculty members informants have referred to as "old timers." Collectively, this group possessed an institutional memory and a commitment to Pratt's vision. She was supported second by parents, most of whom resided in the Village and who had consciously chosen City and Country for their children because the education it offered matched their world-view. As one informant remarked,

The Village was composed of different people then and City and Country was heavily a Village School. When I first came here, it was the old Civil Defense days. We had to go across 13th Street to the basement of the Salvation Army for air raid drills. We had to pledge allegiance and sing "The Star Spangled Banner." It was always a joke that City and Country kids didn't know The Pledge of Allegiance, didn't recognize the flag because City and Country didn't have one, and couldn't find their hearts because City and Country had a weak science program. The point is that parents here wouldn't have stood for The Pledge of Allegiance or for having a flag.

Unlike other progressive schools that might now be unrecognizable to their founders, City and Country under Murray clung to its traditions. Perhaps the emphasis Pratt had placed on woodworking yielded a bit to Murray's interest in geography and map-making. Perhaps more importantly, Murray's interest in progressive education had not emerged from a political position like Pratt's but rather from a concern for the children themselves. Murray's starting point may have differed from Pratt's, but Murray retained her commitment to children through Pratt's child-centered pedagogy. Present throughout her writings, in interviews with those who knew here, and in the eulogies from teachers, parents and alumni is the theme of her singular focus on the developing child and on helping him or her reach full potential, unhurried, and aided by uncluttered classroom spaces and non-specific materials. As Murray observed in an often quoted sentence, "Growth cannot be hurried except at the risk of losing depth."[33] In sum, as one alumna remarked, "When I came back to visit as a grown-up with an infant child I was looking for what I had loved. This was the school I had gone to and loved; the way the kids moved with free will and yet purposely was there." This remarkable continuity became a hallmark at City and Country.

At the same time, City and Country remained an exciting place in which to work. Numerous informants spoke of the freedom teachers had to work classroom situations out for themselves. As one former teacher remarked, "I could be my own judge and see from the children's responses whether I was doing a good job or not." But serious responsibility accompanied this freedom: "There was a great risk if you did something wrong. Not only would Jean come down on you but [so would] everyone else. They isolated you, they whispered about you." Another informant observed, "She [Murray] never had a qualm about telling you what she thought you should do but allowed you to do what you wanted as long as you could defend it." Yet another stated, "She would listen, elicit, and encourage you to make your own decision"; and again, "Murray created the situation where we took it upon ourselves to make it better. Somehow this was very empowering." Finally, "Jean saw teachers as artisans, practicing their varied arts in varied styles, unobtrusively, all to enrich the growing up of each individual. The arts we were all expected to share were listening, watching, waiting, so that we best could guide the strengths of individual children into forging active, progressive, attentive, embracing groups."[34]

Under Murray's leadership City and Country survived as a progressive school, often despite virulent and systematic hostility to progressive education. Her leadership provided the school with a second female principal as dominant as Pratt but with a style somewhat softened by her upper-class background. She commanded loyalty and respect from parents as well as her faculty, although she, like Pratt, tended to be more attentive to the children and faculty at City and Country than to those who paid its tuition and bills. They appreciated her single-minded focus on the child and her commitment to the school as "a home away from home," a school that "nurtured the whole child," a school that respected physical, emotional, and developmental differences in children, and "a school that provided children with the resources to lead rich, imaginative, intellectual lives."

But while Murray provided educational leadership for City and Country, she failed to establish a solid financial foundation for the school in order to ensure its perpetuation. One can trace this failing, in part, to Murray's sense of noblesse oblige: If someone—a child or a teacher—needed something and the school could not afford it, she paid for it out of her own pocket. The school needed money desperately, but women like Murray and Pratt were educators, not fund raisers or business managers. Pratt had relied on a single benefactress, and Murray was never able to find a replacement for Lucy Sprague Mitchell. Nor was she ever comfortable asking for money. Thus, City and Country became cash poor and real estate rich, with its history and survival linked to the interplay of leadership, location and money. As if to illustrate the particular importance of location, City and Country managed to survive and insulate itself from educational fads and reform currents by drawing a steady group of applicants from among people living near the school who were interested in its particular approach to progressive education. But as the neighborhood began to change in the late 1960s, attracting fewer couples with children, this demographic shift hurt a neighborhood school like City and Country offering a strong early-childhood program. As well, the alternative-school movement of the period gave rise to a number of small schools, which provided stiff competition for City and Country among parents who either misunderstood the school's philosophy or thought its practices "too rigid." Enrollments began to decline as operating costs soared. One informant noted the probable effects on enrollments the parental grapevine exerted: "We were perceived badly in the playgrounds as a school that didn't teach reading and that took kids with learning disabilities." Jean Wesson Murray retired as Principal in 1977 and for the next fourteen years, City and Country became a school in search of leadership and financial stability.

The School after Jean Wesson Murray: Restructuring and Persisting

In the aftermath of Murray's retirement, when no strong principal emerged from the faculty ranks to assume leadership, the school edged toward the brink of disaster. It has since had seven principals, each averaging two or three years of service prior to Kathleen Holz in 1991. In one year, 1980–1981, the Executive Committee ran the school with a consultant, Rae Tattenbaum. During this time the Executive Committee considered a number of fund-raising options involving the school's main asset: its real estate. Nevertheless, it became painfully clear to the Committee, faculty and parents that the faculty members themselves were woefully underprepared to run a school, particularly one that required a serious infusion of cash for survival.[35] Then, early in 1980, the school announced its closing.

By 1981 it had become clear that no matter how dedicated it was to City and Country, the Executive Committee could no longer maintain the school's financial solvency while attending to pedagogical concerns. Operating with 108 students with fewer projected, the school could neither meet its payroll nor pay its bills. But to keep City and Country alive, the alumni came to its rescue, raising close to $100,000. They also suggested restructuring the school's governance, creating an "outside" board of trustees, consisting at first of alumni and teacher representatives (parents were added later), that would attend to financial matters so the faculty could concentrate on educational matters.

The restructuring began in earnest with the creation of City and Country's first board of trustees. The Corporation, consisting of everyone who had taught at the school for at least one year and governed by the Executive Committee, met on December 1, 1981. It voted to accept an interim board consisting of alumni and to change the by-laws to accommodate an outside board of trustees. In the school's lunchroom on February 23, 1982, a touching ritual marked both the creation of this outside board and the dissolution of the Executive Committee, as each teacher representative of the Executive Committee, in turn, relinquished his or her place to a newly appointed outside board member. The Executive Committee was recast as the Education Committee. The original governance of a school established as a teacher cooperative thus dissolved.[36]

Because the school required heroic measures to survive, the new board decided to sell the 12th Street building. In January of 1984, the sale gave City and Country a much needed infusion of cash. The board also began discussing the need to restructure the educational and financial arms of the school and to draft a long-range plan. To these ends, the board formed specific committees and an on-going effort to professionalize fund raising ensued. As the school began to rebound, however, space became an issue. It remained unresolved until, ironically, in January 1997 the school leased its old building back with first right of refusal for its purchase. At this time, the Principal of City and Country was still Kathleen Holz. In keeping with tradition, she is a woman and a former faculty member, having come to City and Country in 1978 as a teacher of the Fours, then the Sixes and Sevens. She appears committed to maintaining the school Pratt established; as a member of the Education Committee, she seems mindful of the delicate balance that the school must strike: preserving Pratt's ideas, "keeping City and Country experimental in practice as well as theory while preparing our students for the world in which they will live."[37] Equally at home presiding over a "downtown" gathering of both youthful and aging progressives at the school for an alumni night or at an "uptown" meeting of independent school heads, Holz seems to understand what both worlds demand of her and what she represents.

Holz forthrightly identifies City and Country as a progressive school and has presented its philosophy and pedagogic practices before such groups as the American Educational Research Association. As of 1997, the school's books were balanced, the enrollment had risen to 239 students, and the school has been accredited by the New York State Association of Independent Schools (NYSAIS), and it has joined the Independent Schools Association of Greater New York (ISAGNY). This new emphasis on outreach and membership signals an end to City and Country's self-imposed isolation from traditional, mainstream independent schools. Holz believes that her effectiveness is possible because "as an insider I was able to do that [preserve the school's progressive philosophy and pedagogy] more readily while looking to the needs of the outside world and the market."[38]

To this end, a number of important curricular reforms have been introduced, perhaps some of them long overdue. In 1980–81, the school installed computers. Spanish and Latin are now available as well. Preparation for the standardized tests that determine admissions to both selective public schools (like Stuyvesant High School, Bronx Science, Brooklyn Tech, and Hunter) and independent secondary schools is now offered in the upper grades. The Twelves and Thirteens now play basketball, a competitive sport, coached by the business manager.[39] An educational coordinator has been added to the faculty, and published curriculum overviews for each group are available to both faculty and parents.

Yet while the school moves forward, it retains its connection to its roots, and its sense of community. It still uses blocks and jobs as primary learning tools; its faculty still feels an allegiance to an historic past; and the intimacy of a school with small classes prevails. Particularly, blocks and jobs create a common vocabulary and forge a common set of experiences for the students who have attended the school. A small but significant group of faculty members, dating back to Jean Murray, evidence a strong personal commitment to the school. But these "old-timers," with their institutional memory, invaluable resources over the years for mentoring new faculty into the ways of the school, are now retiring. Concurrently, City and Country School now attracts achievement-oriented, first-time parents, oblivious of its history. Another concern voiced by some informants centers on how the school can preserve its sense of community and its small size under pressure to expand to meet rising operation costs. It has already committed itself to a new building.

Clearly City and Country consciously continues to draw upon its past. Nevertheless, it is a school in transition. It is at present financially healthy and in demand. It will be interesting to see how an "outside board" consisting now of more parents than alumni grapples with change and continuity and how it balances the vision of the Education Committee with its financial concerns. But above all, one waits to see to what degree "success" necessitates compromises with the vision of progressive education Caroline Pratt established and Jean Wesson Murray refined.

Postscript

During the 1997–1998 school year, Kathleen Holz announced her resignation as Principal to devote herself fulltime to her family. Jim Achterberg, with a background in Quaker schools and elsewhere as an interim head for five years, was appointed Interim Principal for the 1998–1999 school year. This marked the first time in the school's history that a man had been chosen Principal, even on an acting basis.

THE LINCOLN SCHOOL OF TEACHERS COLLEGE: ELITISM AND EDUCATIONAL DEMOCRACY

John M. Heffron

Did William Shakespeare really poach a deer in Stratford-on-Avon, and spend a night in jail for it? And what might this episode in the life of the great playwright have to do some 300 years later with a small, private experimental school located 3,500 miles away on the upper west side of Manhattan? For the Class of 1921, at least, the story was propitious, a fractured fairy tale shedding light on their school experience and on the foibles of a modern education. "The man who could really prove with printed evidence that Shakespeare did steal a deer, well, nothing would be too great a reward for him. And if he could prove that William walked off with a whole zoo, they'd probably make him Dean of Teachers College or something! Reader of the future, look within! The proof is all here. Of course, there were one or two little things; but we had to leave something for the scholars to grub."[1] This oblique, mildly irreverent excerpt from the foreword to the Lincoln School's first yearbook, *The Lincolnian* (1921), by "The Lincoln Imp," reveals as much about the school and its influence in progressive educational circles as most of the more conventional documents on the subject. It hints at the connection between the school and Teachers College, Columbia, a leader in the field of teacher education, founded thirty-four years earlier in 1887. It singles out the Dean of the College, who in the eyes of Lincoln School seniors was a symbol of the power and authority of "printed evidence," especially where the evidence is potentially damaging, as in Shakespeare's case. It snipes at scholarly pretensions and their outlandish rewards—all the emoluments that flow from being "right." It does all of this in good fun, but deliberately. The Class of 1921, the first graduating class of a school dedicated to "pioneering" curriculum research and development, had something it wanted to say.[2]

The difficulty Lincoln students had appreciating narrow, specialized research questions of the Shakespeare-and-the-deer sort says something important about the nature of their school experience and about their attitude toward the thirty-seven faculty members—the majority of them research scientists—who directed their studies. The playful rebelliousness of the Class of 1921, while a characteristic pose of graduating seniors everywhere, is especially poignant in the case of the Lincoln School where, according to its promotional literature, everything was based upon "real situations to the end that the school work may not only seem real to the pupils, but be so." The foreword to *The Lincolnian* indicates a tension, one felt directly by the students, between the school's apotheosis of "real life" and its primary function as a scientific experiment. Indeed, facile comparisons to "an institute of medical research" or "a laboratory of agricultural experiment" were as commonplace at the school as the dogma of direct and immediate experience. The boys and girls of Lincoln had their experiences interpreted to them in science and mathematics courses that emphasized the practical application of these subjects to life in the contemporary world, in community study that used nonacademic community resources—the fire department, markets, churches, transportation and communication facilities—as models for the reorganization of school life, and in music, language, art, and social studies where students imbibed "principles that are foundational to effective and upright living." The fixation on contemporary social issues—"problems" in the parlance of the day—meant that students had little contact with the great movements of the past, except as they served to illustrate the relative superiority of the present. Exotic topics like the Shakespeare escapade appeared in the Lincoln School yearbook because no other place existed for them in a curriculum that left little or nothing to the imagination.[3]

Experiences were rarely spontaneous in classrooms where, according to school authorities, "carefully planned experiments" guided every phase of the work and where teachers pushed the laboratory methods of collection, organization, and interpretation of data "as vigorously as they [could] be pushed." In keeping with the dual purpose of the school— experimental curriculum development and "training of an exacting character in the fundamental lines of modern interest, activity, and responsibility"—children were led through a sequence of avowedly modern courses in character. "Modern" meant practical and useful, with "a direct bearing upon the everyday work of the world" in finance, industry, agriculture, government and the arts. It also meant a great deal more science and mathematics instruction than one found in the traditional curriculum. Contemporary industrial life, the experts believed, was a knotty tangle requiring sophisticated problem-solving skills, a thorough understanding of the quantitative relations of "everything," and an ability to subject the information in any situation to systematic, rational analysis. Modern educators looked increasingly to the social and natural sciences to fulfill these needs.[4]

The Lincoln Imp advises a reader to "look within" for further clues to the inner life of the school, but serious students of Lincoln will be disappointed. Not one or two but many useful facts seem to have been left for future scholars "to grub." That is not to say material for a full-reckoning of Lincoln's legacy is missing or incomplete. For a school of its size, the Lincoln School left a long paper trail documenting its 23-year history: scores of research publications and textbooks by its faculty; long and frequent memoranda, annual reports, and promotional materials setting forth in excruciating detail the school's goals and objectives; popular newspaper and magazine accounts of its successes and failures; the papers and correspondence and a number of biographies of some of its major supporters and personnel, including the Director of the School, Otis W. Caldwell; and not least its annual yearbook, *The Lincolnian*. At the end of this trail, one can draw a number of informed conclusions about the school, but the journey also raises new and vexing questions about the nature and extent of progressive school ideas and practices, about the efficacy of experimentation and the laboratory method generally in education, about the value of private investment in public interests and concerns, and about the rights of students vis-à-vis the organized research conducted in their name.

A Brief Description of the Lincoln School: Ambiguous Purposes and Internal Contradictions

Founded in 1917 by the General Education Board (GEB), a Rockefeller philanthropy created originally to address the educational needs of the American South, the Lincoln School combined so many conflicting social, and inter-regional political forces that its overall contributions and significance to education are almost impossible to characterize. Was it a progressive institution, taking the socialized curriculum of Gary and other experimental schools to a new and higher synthesis? Or was it conservative, reflecting the interests of industrial philanthropists and so-called "administrative progressives" eager to reconcile rapid economic development with cultural and political stability, and the psychological re-ordering of educational priorities recommended by John Dewey and others with what one historian has called "the corporate reconstruction of American life?"[5] Or was it something else again, a school neither in the libertarian, social reconstructionist, or administrative mold? In the words of one of its faculty members, the Lincoln School

> commits itself to no one way of doing things. It is not a Dalton plan school, nor a Winnetka plan school, nor a socialized recitation school, nor a project method school, nor a visualization school, nor a play school. At various times and in various spots it may partake of all of these, but if it does so, it is always with experimental, not devotional intent.[6]

For Paul Shorey, a classics professor and the school's most articulate contemporary critic, the Lincoln School was emphatically "not an experiment." The experimentation its founders had in mind was not experimentation in any normal, least of all scientific sense of the word. The omission of Latin and Greek from the curriculum, a deliberate and certainly one of the most controversial policies of the school, disqualified it as an experiment in secondary education. On the other hand, the school's all-science curriculum made a sham of claims that it was an "experiment" in the efficacy of general science education. Shorey also worried about the involvement and enthusiasm of John D. Rockefeller, Jr., the school's benefactor. "In proportion," Shorey wrote, "as the enthusiasm or the personal ambition of such a founder or the exceptional resources at his command enable him to make a better school for a selected group of children, is its significance as a scientific and crucial experiment on the curriculum diminished."[7]

Other, harder questions raise doubts about the very origins and purposes of the school. It seems fair to assume, for example, that as a university laboratory school Lincoln reflected, in part at least, the needs and interests of its parent institution, Teachers College, Columbia. But how safe an assumption is this? Rockefeller philanthropies generally operated by posing as mere grant-making agencies, which did not initiate projects of their own or interfere with the institutions that won the grants. But the opposite was typically the case. The two principal architects of the Lincoln School, Charles W. Eliot and Abraham Flexner, were themselves members of the General Education Board. They shared only the most tenuous connections to Teachers College. When and under what circumstances did the purposes of these two groups clash? And with what outcomes?

Then, too we find the niggling questions, the questions historians of education find themselves asking when confronted, for example, with someone like Charles W. Eliot, himself a bundle of contradictions. What was an old mental disciplinarian like Eliot doing supporting an institution like the Lincoln School, stumping the country on its behalf and lobbying for its acceptance within the country's oldest bastion of educational traditionalism, the New England Association of Colleges and Secondary Schools? Not only had Eliot's young protégé, Abraham Flexner, dealt the doctrine of mental discipline a fatal blow in "The Modern School," his Occasional Paper for the Board and the theoretical basis for the Lincoln School, but also under the leadership of Otis W. Caldwell, Lincoln had become a model convert to life-adjustment goals (the NEA Committee on the Reorganization of Secondary School Education's famous seven cardinal principles, for example) that directly contradicted Eliot's own strictures in the older, college-dominated Committee of Ten. What kind of a school was it, historians still want to know, that could combine cultural epoch theory, the doctrine of interest, and parvenu notions of social efficiency with the relatively remote, patrician sensibilities of founders and supporters like Eliot? What kind of a school was it that would teach vocational math and science to its upper and upper-middle class students, but not Latin and Greek, the traditional foundations of elite school culture?

Judging from the sheer number of its publications (118 between 1917 and 1927 alone), the large number of annual visitors to the school, and the school's generally positive reception, including an endorsement from the New England Association of Colleges and Secondary Schools, the Lincoln School was, despite its many internal contradictions, a professional and popular success throughout much of the 1920s and 1930s. It made solid contributions in those functional areas commonly associated today with the work of university laboratory schools. It provided a limited number of Teachers College students with clinical teaching experience; it engaged in curriculum design and development; it provided an observation and demonstration site for teachers from around the nation and from abroad; it ran its own experimental research institute, promoted staff development and student teaching; and it distributed its printed materials in national journals and in mass mailings to schools throughout the United States. It led the field in curriculum research and development for over twenty years until May, 1940, when a Special Committee of the Board of Trustees of Teachers College issued a report recommending the amalgamation of the Lincoln School with the Horace Mann School, a decision that would rock the school to its foundations. The trustees based their recommendations on the conclusions of an earlier faculty report, the so-called Gulick Report. Although hastily organized and poorly researched (no classes were ever visited and no attempt was made to interview staff members or to assess and compare school outcomes), the Gulick Committee nevertheless concluded that the purposes, philosophies, and methods of the two schools were essentially the same. The Horace Mann School, once a demonstration school for Teachers College, had for some time also engaged in experimentation. For reasons of both intellectual and practical economy, the time had come to merge the two schools, declared the Report. The Committee also expressed its concern that what had been intended as a laboratory school for working out broad, public problems had become "a special service for the socially and economically elite," serving the upper 25 percent of American society and ignoring "the less forward groups that make up the great bulk of the school population."[8]

The tendency of laboratory schools to become exclusive, expensive schools for the benefit of faculty children and the socially and economically advantaged, the Report concluded in ringing tones, is "to be deplored because it gets in the way of carrying out experiments and demonstrations which are of value to education as a whole." The origins of the school as a project of the General Education Board; its awkward administrative relationship with Teachers College (until 1924 four trustees from the Board—Abraham Flexner, George Vincent, Wickliffe Rose, and Charles Howland—sat on the Lincoln School governing board); and its narrowly selective admissions policies, high tuition costs, and the demographic profile of its average student (white Protestant middle-class) all raised serious doubts about the school's mission as an experiment, with large public purposes, in modern education.[9]

The Gulick and Trustees' Reports stung the large family of Lincoln School supporters, including not only the school's staff and Parent Teacher Association but also its retired director, Otis W. Caldwell, and its most famous theoretician and camp follower, Abraham Flexner, into a spirited defense of the school and its historic prerogatives. To the charge that Lincoln was a preserve for the children of New York's cultural, political, and business elite, the Parent Teacher Association acknowledged that the great majority of American agricultural and industrial workers went unrepresented in the school, and to the extent that school authorities attempted to obtain a racially and economically balanced student population, it was a "highly selected" balance. Nevertheless, the Association maintained that these conditions inhered in the experimental nature of the operation. Tuition costs had to be necessarily high to subsidize small classrooms, a large and expensive physical plant, a small teacher-student ratio (ranging from 1:6 to 1:10), and faculty salaries commensurate with the professional expertise and experience of the staff, most of whom held advanced degrees in their respective specialties. It took a peculiar kind of parent, wealthy but also progressive in sympathies, to support such a school. "True experimentation in the educational field," argued the Association, "requires a parent body of fairly high intellectual level, willing to cooperate and capable of carrying out and furthering in the home the processes undertaken and developed in the schools."

Seventeen years earlier in an address to the Parent Teacher Association, Flexner identified three interrelated factors of school success which would have reinforced this belief: (1) the child's native intelligence; (2) the attitude of the parents, which will determine "whether he tries or not"; and (3) the general social environment, including the social standing and influence of the parents and of the child's own peers. Social class—what Flexner called "the tone of the society" to which Lincoln School parents and their children belonged—did matter, if only to supply "expert intellectual leadership" and the exemplary character traits necessary in "this vast, crude, rapidly growing democracy."[10]

If Lincoln was less selective than the average private preparatory school, it would have been stretching the truth to argue, as a reporter for *The New York Times* suggested in 1921, that "a number of multimillionaire households are balanced by the children of coachmen and butlers, and of mechanics or small shopkeepers." As Jesse H. Newlon reported for the Eight Year Study (1933–1941) of the Progressive Education Association, an examination into the scholastic competence of the graduates of thirty progressive schools throughout the United States, the clientele of the Lincoln School was predominantly upper-middle class with most of its students drawn from the business and professional class. The original location of the school at 646 Park Avenue between 66th and 67th Streets, one of the most expensive pieces of real estate in the city, guaranteed this distribution. In 1923, the school moved to the Upper West Side into one of the newest and best equipped facilities in New York. The six-story building sat on an entire city block and included an indoor swimming pool, two gymnasiums, two rooftop playgrounds, shop and studio equipment, a pottery room and kiln, and by one account, the most pedagogically advanced science laboratories in the country. John D. Rockefeller, Jr. sent his sons, John, Laurance, and Nelson, to the Lincoln School and kept a close correspondence with the school's director, Otis Caldwell, who in turn kept the school's benefactor and most famous parent informed not only of his children's progress but of Lincoln's growing stature as a center of progressive school reform as well. Rockefeller, in turn, lauded the school's efforts to teach the more abstruse subjects like mathematics "in a way to give them life and to relate them to the practical affairs of life." He was "deeply interested" in these and other contributions the school was "making to the solution of the problems of education" and thanked Caldwell on a number of occasions for keeping him informed about them. Before Lincoln opened its doors at 425 West 123rd Street, Rockefeller and his wife and children took a Sunday afternoon in April of 1922 to "go all over" the new school building. "We were perfectly delighted with it," he wrote Caldwell. "It is a real achievement."[11]

The planned amalgamation of Lincoln and Horace Mann in 1940 threatened that achievement. Flexner gave the school's commencement address in 1939, using the occasion to criticize the Gulick Report and set the historical record straight and to scandalize the Trustees of Teachers College, whom he accused of plundering Lincoln's large endowment, approximately three million dollars by that time, so as to reduce the financial losses at the Horace Mann Schools. The Lincoln School, Flexner told the audience of students, parents and staff members, had been conceived and developed from the beginning as an experimental school, with the full understanding and agreement of then Dean James E. Russell. What Flexner did not tell the gathering was that, in the eyes of the General Education Board, the agreement with Teachers College was and always had been a marriage of convenience, Flexner and Eliot pushing all along for the establishment of an independent research institute with an independent board of trustees and independent funds.[12] The minutes, memoranda, and correspondence of the Board dating from as early as 1910 to the main period between 1914 and 1917 confirm this view.

The creation of the Lincoln School represented a considerable departure from the General Education Board's earlier policy of general philanthropy, carving out for it new ground in educational policy-making and administration. But it was also a kind of goal line for the Board, the end of a long drive toward educational reform that began in the post-Reconstruction South and moved irresistibly northward over the decade and a half between 1902 and 1917. That drive ended at the Lincoln School, a finished facility, fully staffed and operational, embodying the cumulative ideas, experiences, and lessons of half a generation in educational philanthropy and survey writing. In statements to the press and in discussion with other educators, principals at both the Board and Teachers College were careful, however, to describe the Lincoln School as a joint venture of the two institutions, the former providing immediate and long-term financial support, the latter the intellectual direction and day-to-day administration. Caldwell's dual appointment as the school's new director, hand-picked by the General Education Board, and as an education professor in the College's Division of Natural Science, served as much to preserve the College's preeminence in the partnership as to maintain the illusion of that partnership in the first place. Before accepting the directorship of the new school, Caldwell made it clear that he was "not interested in becoming a school principal to conduct just another school for Teachers College." The school must be distinctive," he wrote Flexner, "and must furnish large opportunity for experimentation to those who are to be engaged in it."[13] Caldwell had proven his value to the Board as the author of the science section of its recent survey of the progressive Gary, Indiana Schools. With his dual appointment, the General Education Board gained a seat of considerable influence both within the Lincoln School and within Teachers College itself, one of the nation's oldest and most distinguished teacher training institutes.

The suggestion that Teachers College or that Columbia University itself may have influenced the original decision to build the Lincoln School runs completely counter to actual discussions at both the Board and Teachers College ranging over the seven years leading up to the school's official opening in September, 1917. These records reveal that the Lincoln School was conceived in opposition to the ideas and inroads of the pedagogues, not in deference to them. Representing the Board's interests, Flexner was hardly a bystander in that contest, registering his opposition time and again to professors at the College like Edward L. Thorndike, who thought the school should incorporate "highly technical experiments and investigations." What the Board envisioned (and had pledged to support) was a school whose chief purpose would be the development of modern subject materials, not a school that simply ran psychological-pedagogical studies of "minute process problems." "Efforts to deal effectively with such subject matter," Flexner wrote Dean Russell, "cannot wait upon experimental investigation of that kind."[14] Nevertheless, until the full story emerged in 1939, the opposite belief—that Teachers College had established the Lincoln School for purely experimental purposes—prevailed in most of the educational literature and in a great deal of the private correspondence between the main actors, including Caldwell, Flexner, Eliot, Russell, Thorndike, and John D. Rockefeller, Jr.

What might have motivated all this obfuscation and by 1940 a sort of cult of dissimulation surrounding the circumstances of the Lincoln School? Was it because the Board, fearing that adverse criticism directed against it might undermine the Lincoln School experiment before it could be proven, wanted to shift the focus of public attention to the more legitimate Teachers College? Or did the nature of the Board's involvement in school reform and in the Lincoln School in particular lead to conflicts with Teachers College, which it too considered best to keep out of the public eye? Finally, how do such questions bear, if at all, on the more prosaic concerns of course content, curriculum development, and teaching methods that challenged the school's staff and director on a daily basis? Is there any relationship between the *real politick* of educational reform and experimentation and the school's actual curriculum, one based on an appreciation of the role of science and scientific method both in education and in every round of life and work? We may never fully answer these questions but, using them as a guide, we can come to a better understanding of the inclusive history and background of the Lincoln School and the General Education Board.

The Influence of the General Education Board

In 1910, when the Board's activities in the South were at their height, Charles W. Eliot suggested to his friend and fellow Board member, Walter H. Page, that it was precisely the Board's work in the South which had made the agency so exciting and visionary. That work, he said, raised a standard for the future: "The best work the Board has done seems to me to be the agricultural instruction and the promotion of the establishment of High Schools in the South. I cannot help thinking that such a Board ought to be chiefly interested in promoting pioneering and experimental work." A few months earlier he wrote the president of the Board, Wallace Buttrick: "I am hoping that you are going to propose . . . some big, new independent and constructive project, not in aid of other people's undertakings, however good, but a demonstration of the feasibility and efficacy of the new sort of education, an education intimately connected with the working lives of the people. This is the thing that most needs to be done in all parts of our country. . . ." In 1914, Frederick T. Gates approached Flexner about the possibility of establishing "some model trade school." Looking back to the groundwork laid in the South and forward to the Board's next project, a survey of the progressive school system in Gary, Indiana, the senior Rockefeller aide drew for Flexner the picture of a non-traditional, liberal arts education, one with "at least enough political economy to rub in the truth that at bottom nothing but increased skill and efficiency will increase the wage."[15]

But Flexner had his own ideas. Fresh from a study of medical education for the Carnegie Foundation for the Advancement of Teaching, the former Kentucky schoolmaster envisioned a privately endowed research institution doing for education what the Rockefeller Institute for Medical Research and Johns Hopkins University Medical School (the beneficiary in 1915 of a gift by the Rockefellers to support full time clinical teaching) were doing in the field of medicine. Like medicine, education had become "a technical affair in respect to which laymen can make very slight specific contributions." Traditional schooling had become a form of "educational blood-letting" and "molasses and sulfur." The schools of tomorrow, on the other hand, were "clinics where children are observed." The success or failure of the Lincoln School—presumably the first of such educational "clinics"—would determine, Flexner argued, the nature and extent of similar efforts in the future.[16]

Before the Lincoln School, the prospects for a radical transformation of education had been gloomy. The Gary schools were too large and diffuse, their educational program too incoherent and tied too closely to public purse strings to achieve the necessary results. Educational reform, the Board asserted in 1918, was "an experimental task, needing special facilities and conditions." In a letter to Gates in 1915 pleading the cause of the modern school, Flexner suggested that by hiring a select body of teachers to teach a select body of students the Board could break the "vicious circle" of overcrowding and bureaucracy. Buoyed by the financial and moral support of the GEB, the Harvard Law School and Johns Hopkins Medical School were showing the way. Unlike the current system of public schools, they "made a break in ineffective methods and started new processes which have reacted powerfully upon institutions that could not, of themselves, have started any innovation."[17]

The aims of the proposed Lincoln School were experimental from the start. On May 25, 1916, the Board met at its New York offices to conclude the basis for an agreement with Teachers College. "The school is not to be a model for universal imitation," stated the agreement, "so much as a productive institution for the experimental study of problems and methods and for the preparation of tested school materials," adapted, it added, to "the needs of modern living." Notice that the proposed merger of Horace Mann, a demonstration school from the beginning, and Lincoln, an avowedly experimental school, flew directly in the face of this original policy. If the experimental work of the school was to remain "adventuring," insisted the staff at the height of the controversy in 1940, it would have to be kept clearly separate from the demonstration function, which was best handled by a special school for that purpose or by "affiliated schools." Combining the two functions in one school was "untenable"; "unsound"; "doomed to failure." Lincoln's relatively small, selective population and its higher per pupil costs were justified by the results it was getting, which according to the elder Russell, had made the Lincoln School the most closely watched experiment station in the educational world. Moreover, as the school's Parent Teacher Association argued, without the support of a parent body "of a fairly high intellectual level, willing to cooperate and capable of carrying out and furthering in the home the processes undertaken and developed in the schools," true experimentation would be impossible. These and other protests proved futile, however, and what the father started the son ended. "If experiments are to be started," wrote Dean William F. Russell in his Annual Report of 1939, "experiments are to be stopped. If anything new is to be done, in the long run something old must be abandoned."[18]

The classical defenders of liberal culture, the school's most vocal critics in the beginning stages of its development, could finally breathe a sigh of relief. Yet their own objections to Flexner and Eliot's modern school bore little resemblance to the legal, bureaucratic or economic concerns raised by Teachers College. Rather, at stake was the survival of culture itself, in a battle of all against all for "the supremacy of noble ideas," in the words of the Secretary of the American Academy of Arts and Letters in 1917. To the school's "frankly utilitarian" purposes, including, most damning of all, the elimination of Greek and Latin from its "all-science" curriculum, the Secretary contrasted "the undiscovered country of the spirit," wherein lay the sympathetic, the altruistic, the noble side of human achievement.[19]

These liberal critics had found much to hate in the program of the Lincoln School, which they had already concluded was devoid of emotion, imagination, poetry, beauty, and art. For their own part, Flexner and Eliot rejoiced at every new victory over "the scholastic vested interests." Informed that Princeton had eliminated the Latin requirement for admission, Flexner wrote Eliot in 1918, "The outer defenses have fallen at Princeton!" He added cheerfully, "Once you make a loophole, all the sheep will soon go through it." Eliot had to remind his youthful friend that "a loophole is not well adapted for the passage of sheep. They need a wider opening than that. I believe that the opening you and I have made in a rather solid wall of tradition is wide enough, not only for sheep, but for some larger animals." In a letter to Flexner two years earlier, Eliot ventured the hope that "a few specimens out of the rising generation can through organized effort be trained in your way."[20]

The Shape of the Lincoln Curriculum: Art Imitates Life

For Flexner, the question was whether, as he put it to the Dean of Teachers College, "industrial and domestic processes [can] be culturally interpreted to growing boys and girls."[21] If the Lincoln School was to fulfill its role as a cultural interpreter of the new industrial state, it would have to train people where it found them and not for some ideal life in the future. "Instead of studying in order that we may later become citizens of the world," Caldwell told Lincoln's first graduating class in 1921, "we now become citizens of the world by directly engaging in activities in which true citizens should engage."[22] Caldwell and his staff constructed an interactive or "experience" curriculum to accomplish what the school's reigning authority, Teachers College professor L. Thomas Hopkins, called "the reconstruction of the present life and living of the individual." Curriculum materials revolved around the life of the school and the local community rather than around *a priori* ideas of what constituted a "proper" education.[23] Thus a study of the boats that ply and plied the nearby Hudson River became a third graders introduction to history, geography, reading, writing, arithmetic, science, art, and literature; a classroom topic like "living in a power age," became an eighth grader's introduction to farm and factory life. Following Flexner's dictum that "The Modern School" [curriculum] "includes nothing for which an affirmative case cannot now be made out," the junior high school mathematics course at Lincoln concentrated on "rigorous discipline in things worthwhile." It avoided drills that, in the words of Raleigh Schorling, a math research-practitioner at Lincoln, became "uninteresting ends in themselves." Courses were to be arranged "from the point of view of the children and from the consideration of social needs," not for the sake of some preconceived notion of mental discipline or college-entrance requirements.[24]

The staff of the elementary division of the Lincoln School prepared a list of eight criteria for selecting large units of work that would become the core of the elementary school curriculum. These units would have to approximate "real life situations" in which students took a natural interest.[25] A first grade unit on Farm Life, for example, would make use of the child's love of animals and inborn affinity for nature. Introduced to the proper names and functional relations of farm life, the pupils then acted them out in dramatic play:

[T]ake the cows to pasture, get the corn from the crib, take the milk to the city, go to church, plow in the field, stack the hay, and converse with each other about farm affairs. All that and much more must be done before the true values in meanings come out of any center of work.[26]

Work and play went hand in hand in a reading lesson designed to sentimentalize the joys and struggles of farm life:

> Work!
> My work begins.
> I sing, I sing.
> My work is hard.
> I sing, I sing.
> My work is done.
> I sing, I sing.
> I sing at work.
> I sing at play.
> So I go singing
> All the day.[27]

How close this bland, undifferentiated version of the contentments of farm life came to "real life situations" or to the "real purposing and real projects" of the ideal elementary school curriculum is hard to say, but it did appear to meet the last and perhaps most important curriculum-making criterion, the development of "desirable habits." An early introduction to the laws of plant and animal husbandry taught "personal and group responsibility, initiative, cooperation, good judgment in proportion to experience, economical methods of study and work, [and] power to plan ahead." The study and recreation of actual farm conditions (or what students were persuaded to believe were actual farm conditions) taught lessons in selection, cultivation, and conservation apparently as important for the city-dweller as for the farmer.[28]

While the junior high school industrial arts curriculum called for the same broad appreciation of the values of work and efficient production, intelligent judgment and planning, shop teachers were so naive as to think they could duplicate actual industrial conditions in the school shop. Frequent excursions to local industries where working conditions were often exploitive, physically degrading, and, unlike the image of farm work, completely joyless taught these teachers (and their students) differently. The field trips were an important revelation for students who having labored under one illusion, agricultural peace and harmony, were now kept from laboring under another, the glories of mechanized industry. What they found instead on these excursions, according to a 1925 report on the industrial arts curriculum at Lincoln, was that real factories and shops lacked adequate lighting and ventilation, divided and farmed out their work to jobbing shops, enforced stupefying, almost inhumane rates of production, discouraged advancement, and rewarded specialization.[29]

Although undoubtedly troubled by these experiences, junior high school students at Lincoln nevertheless came away with a generally positive view of the Industrial Revolution and its consequences. From the rest of their course work, especially in the social studies, they received a different impression than their field experiences and their senses had taught them. Thus sometime around 1925, three eighth grade students depicted the Industrial Revolution as, respectively, a rising sun, dispelling the darkness of an earlier age when all goods were manufactured in the home by hand and when transportation and communications systems were universally "bad"; a cyclone born of the French Revolution and the "discovery of America" that destroyed "the old home" of sticks and stones and ushered in "the new home" of steam, power looms, bridges and better transportation; and an egg hatching three chicks representing factories, transportation, and steam. Seventh and eighth grade history lessons—whether focused on the Industrial Revolution, the French Revolution, the War of 1812, or the unification of Germany—were presented as "an orderly relation of events which show the processes whereby man has gradually made a wonderful progress." This grand narrative provided a soothing palliative for the social and industrial injustices that seethed just outside the school's windows and pricked but otherwise left unaffected the social conscience of the school's young elites. The daily course work would, in any case, serve the important purpose of understanding, ordering, and domesticating these evils.[30]

In attacking these and other social problems (and the long list Lincoln's researcher-practitioners compiled, included race, immigration, health and eugenics, crime and delinquency, "women's position and divorce," and many more) the goal was always to secure "application of the spirit and methods of the natural sciences to the social sciences" and thereby to substitute "positive modes of action for negative restrictions and purgings." Science teaching was valuable because it taught good citizenship defined as "the increased respect which the citizen should have for the expert" in an age which had become "amazingly complicated [and] incalculably difficult to understand," and in which the salient feature was "the political and economic ignorance and indifference of the common man."[31]

Mathematics and biology received special consideration at the Lincoln School, both in its integrated classroom work and in the ensuing research studies, for didactic purposes far exceeding their value as introductions to quantitative reasoning and the origins and functioning of life. As the study of dynamic life systems, biology provided persuasive physical evidence for the heuristic assumption of heterogeneous or correlative experience; it reinforced the modern, empirical description of experience set out by Dewey[32] and other educational pragmatists; and it added a patina of scientific respectability to the extreme hereditarian doctrines of the New Education, the widely held hope that, in Caldwell's words, "the next generation of men and women shall be physically, intellectually, and morally as effective as the laws of heredity will enable us to make them."[33]

If biology served to unify high school science instruction around the life activities of the individual, mathematics demonstrated the social and interactive base of those activities. Following a period of reform between 1916 and 1923, secondary school mathematics teachers began to emphasize the "non-informational outcomes"[34] of classroom teaching and education. A National Committee on Mathematical Requirements (NCMR), formed in 1916 by the Mathematical Association of America and supported by a grant from the General Education Board, announced in its final report that the days of abstract division, factoring, fractions, simultaneous equations, and radicals were over. Raleigh Schorling, a math teacher at the Lincoln School, and David Eugene Smith, chairman of the NCMR and a regular correspondent of Wallace Buttrick, represented the Board's interests on the Committee. They lobbied to make mathematics simpler, more interesting and accessible, and above all, useful. Complex computational exercises led, in their view, to "nothing important in the science" and added "little to the facility in the manipulation of algebraic forms." Raleigh, Smith, and the rest of the NCMR, backed by the General Education Board, pushed for mathematics work of "a more profitable nature," work in the "real use" of algebra, geometry, and computation that emphasized their applicability in the occupational world.[35] At the Lincoln School and at cooperating schools in one hundred other cities, the new biology and practical mathematics formed the conceptual basis for teaching in all the sciences and spread to the study of English, history, civics, and vocational subjects.[36]

When Caldwell spoke, as he often did, of "the biological foundation of education," he was thinking of the students, teachers, administrators, textbooks, classwork, homework, laboratory, school plant, and playground facilities that together in any school formed a single, interdependent whole.[37] This interlocking system of parts possessed, like the human body itself, a kind of homeostatic norm any deviation from which might plunge the entire enterprise into chaos and confusion. The functionalist theory of society attracted educators like Caldwell precisely because it appealed to such putative biological truths, enabling them to understand and control complex social systems and their constituents. It appealed to powerful foundations like the GEB for similar reasons.

Events after 1920 show that by the end of the decade the General Education Board and its parent organization, the Rockefeller Foundation, were channeling millions of dollars of aid to general education and basic research in the biomedical and behavioral sciences. At a meeting in May of 1922, the Trustees decided that "the fostering of general science education was a logical, fundamentally important, and fruitful enterprise for the Foundation." Pursuant to this, a Division of Studies was formed in December of 1923, and in 1925, it was authorized "to make surveys of the sciences involved in the field of human biology and to mature and bring to the Rockefeller Foundation from time to time specific projects to be considered on their own merits." Between 1923 and 1929, the Foundation contributed over four million dollars to biological projects in American secondary schools and universities. Over the same period, the International Education Board, organized in 1923, contributed another four million in aid to institutions and for the support of fellowships, traveling professorships, and publications in the field. Although the GEB contributed only 5.3 percent to biology from a total budget of 12.1 million, 56.1 percent of that amount still remained unassigned by 1929 when its natural science activities were transferred to a special division of the Rockefeller Foundation. Designated the Natural Sciences Division, the new group spent in the first three years of its operation over half of a 7.6 million-dollar-budget on biological research.[38]

In 1933, in its most magnanimous gesture to date, the GEB allocated ten million dollars to underwrite a program of general education along biomedical, biophysical lines. The theoretical rationale for such a program had existed for over a decade. In the famous Report of the NEA Committee on the Reorganization of Secondary Education (1918) and in numerous general science textbooks, science education followed a biomedical model, combining heredity, natural science, and socialization theory. It was neither new nor surprising that six of the seven aims of general education specified by the Rockefeller Commission were all variants of man's "understanding of himself as a biological organism" or that, in the preliminary report of the Commission's Science Committee, the subject of eugenics should appear under the heading "Immediate Personal and Social Life." The future of man would depend on the reproductive patterns of his children. The science courses the Rockefeller Commission envisioned would, as part of a general program of life adjustment, teach that "superior parents breed superior children."[39]

"Science cannot continue to remake affairs," Caldwell wrote, "unless it proceeds promptly to a new kind of study of man himself." Ruling out psychology and psychiatry, it is biology which, quoting Julian Huxley, "must be his chief servant." In *Biology in the Public Press* (1923) and *Biological Foundations of Education* (1931), Caldwell presented the generalizations of science in terms of the equilibrium of man and his physical, social, and psychological environment. Only with biological knowledge of the human organism and its environment could educators bring about the hoped-for reconstruction from which, Caldwell believed, everything else—social peace, industrial harmony, economic prosperity, individual health and happiness—would automatically follow.[40]

Biology seemed especially appropriate because it promised to teach the sense and observational values that were likely to guide intelligent social reconstruction. While rural life was naturally conducive to these values, they had to be artificially re-created in urban schools, where "large machines" turned out, in Charles W. Eliot's view, uniformly unhealthy, unintelligent, and unskilled young adults.[41] The daily exposure farm children enjoyed to the sights and sounds of the country—where survival depended upon sharp senses and quick reflexes, a close observation of nature, and an understanding of the laws of plant and animal husbandry—taught invaluable moral, practical, and civic responsibilities. Urban progressives sought to replicate those virtues in city schools through elementary nature study, school gardens and zoos, agricultural courses, and the general science course, which drew on materials from all three. Skill of eye, ear, and hand became the *sine qua non* of a modern science education. An early advocate of such training, Eliot lumped together observational training, science instruction, and another pressing need, national preparedness in a 1918 speech defending the new Lincoln School:

> The sciences, including chemistry, physics, and biology, are given ample time on the programme of the Lincoln School, and are taught exclusively by a sound laboratory method. The effort of the teachers is not only to teach their pupils to see, hear, smell, and touch accurately, but [also] to learn the scientific method of recording accurately and of reasoning justly from the record. . . . Outside of the medical and engineering professions, very few educated Americans today can practice either scientific observation or reasoning. To correct this condition of things is a matter of extreme urgency; for without this correction the Republic will not be safe in war or prosperous in peace.[42]

Caldwell thought these goals could be best achieved by transposing biology, practically synonymous in his mind with general science, to the first year of high school, thus inverting the usual order of chemistry, physics, biology, and geography.

John Woodhull, head of the Natural Sciences Division of Teachers College, questioned Caldwell's plan to teach biology in the first year. He doubted whether students were more interested in "green things and living things" than they were in chemical and industrial processes. In any case, "interest" was not always the best determinant of educational value. "If pupils are more interested in one subject than another, that ought not to be the only argument, nor the principal argument, for putting that subject in a certain place in the curriculum." Clearly the child needed some way of ordering and making sense of the constant barrage of external stimuli and information characteristic of modern industrial life no less than traditional farm life. But to teach observation mechanically, to approach the observational senses as though they were an essential muscle group requiring routine exercise, seemed to Woodhull to defeat the purpose of scientific observation. Observational skills, in Woodhull's view, emerged more readily in a "logical" sequence of subjects—chemistry, physics, biology, geography—than in a "psychological" sequence. In the physical laboratory, wrote Woodhull, one could "represent the large phenomenon piecemeal, and thus build up the conception of the whole, and at the same time develop the constructive imagination which is needed to grasp the processes of nature." Thus physics, preceded by chemistry, would "prepare the way" for later important work in biology and geography.[43]

Woodhull's arguments fell on deaf ears. The clique forming in his department around Caldwell and the Lincoln School effectively blocked his efforts to retain the old sequence of science courses. In a letter to Woodhull in 1920, the Dean of the College made his own feelings clear: "The outstanding superiority of the Lincoln School in its science work suggests that we should make use of it in the science teaching in the College." Not only would the new sequence go forward at the Lincoln School, as proposed, but the science education program at Teachers College itself, Russell said, should also reflect the change. Some evidence suggests that Woodhull, who resisted such reorganization, felt pressure from the Dean and members of his department, including Caldwell, to take a sabbatical in 1920-21 and after that, early retirement. Woodhull's subsequent retirement removed the last obstacle to the administration's plan for a new science sequence and opened the door to closer programmatic relations generally between the science departments at Lincoln School and Teachers College.[44]

The Social Relations of Mathematics

Like biology, mathematics had been gaining new interest and prestige in the high school curriculum. Between 1900 and 1920, it grew from one of several isolated requirements to become, with biology, the ideological center and driving force of general education. The older, more mechanical approach to mathematics education emphasized the manipulation of numeric symbols in complex factoring problems. A new generation of mathematics teachers—using simple graphs, tables, equations, and formulas—sought to illustrate the underlying principles of order and design, function and relationship. Less concerned with logical axioms and postulates than their predecessors, they sought to expose students to spatial relations and patterns in their immediate environment. For William Betz, whose course in intuitive geometry at the Lincoln School drew national attention in the 1930s, the training his students received in "space intuition" and "plastic thinking," the ability to approach any problem from a variety of directions and with a variety of tools, was "a basic feature of all mental work."[45]

The National Committee on Mathematical Requirements concluded in 1923 that inculcating functional "habits of thinking" was the single most important objective of the junior and senior high school mathematics course. Functional thinking—the ability to predict how changes in one quantity in an algebraic expression affected all the others—led to "maximum efficiency" both in solving mathematical problems and in the day-to-day operation of the farm, the factory, the counting-house, and the home. Functional thinking was "vital" to the establishment of "good citizenship," "maximum efficiency," and the maintenance of social order.[46] In life, as in "all machinery, the geometric figures formed are in continual motion," according to one Committee member, "and the shapes of the figures formed by the moving parts change." The "functional idea" prevented the study of objective space relations from becoming static, a study of fixed forms and their demonstrations. It breathed movement and proportionality into the vast array of geometric forms, whether they were found in the machine process, the operation of the stock market, or the radiating lines of the starfish. In an essay on "Geometry and Nature," twelve-year-old Beatrice Wadhams showed how well she had absorbed the lessons of the new mathematics when she referred to those ubiquitous relations of "equality, congruence, similarity and symmetry."[47]

Following the recommendations of the Committee on Mathematical Requirements, Schorling and Caldwell brought the Lincoln School to the forefront of the new mathematics, with its rejection of formalism, its departure from pure number work and rote memorization, and its emphasis on such normative values as "appreciation," "correlation," and "function." The junior high school mathematics course—the first and for the majority of students probably the only mathematics course they would ever take—included such units as "Practical measurements," "The use of geometry in architecture," "Interest," "The secret of thrift," "Making money earn money," and "Household measurements." By emphasizing their applied aspects, the materials of mathematics would be both "vitalized" and "socialized" to meet the needs of modern industrial society.[48]

Lincoln schooler, twelve-year-old Breading Furst, learned that he and his friends needed mathematics "constantly" in their daily lives.

> In everyday life [he wrote] you constantly need mathematics. When you get up, you figure briefly how long it will take you to go to school, or how long it takes you to get dressed. When you get to school, you have to buy something and you have to know how much it costs. You have to pay for it and watch that you always get the correct change. You are often asked how far you live from school and you can answer that only by measuring the distance, or letting someone else measure it.[49]

For Breading's teacher, William Betz, measurement was the basis of all geometry and an important "weapon" in the battle of life. Without it, "science would be lost, machinery would go out of use, and the civilization of our industrial age would vanish. The mind of man would be weakened through the loss of its keenest weapon. Thought would no longer be precise, or if precision were ever attained, it could not be communicated."[50]

Yet precision had never been a goal of general mathematics, least of all of intuitive geometry. "There should be no struggle for precision in the statement of a principle," wrote Betz's colleague, Raleigh Schorling. The rules and definitions of intuitive geometry were a "summary of experience," a moving average that changed as "the pupil grows in experience." The significance of their study lay less in analytic thinking or precision in measurement than in the broad, normative values of equality, symmetry, congruence, and similarity buried "in the very nature of things." Such values, educators agreed, formed the basis of a rational perception of both the spiritual and the physical worlds. As Betz himself was fond of saying, from Plato, "God always geometrizes."[51]

Mathematics was "a fundamental reality of the domain of thought," in the words of E. H. Moore, former president of the American Mathematical Society and father of the modern mathematics reform movement. Mathematical instruction was the domain of the "trained engineer," an adept in the ways of computation, mechanical and graphic drawing, and experimentation.[52] Accordingly, the mathematics laboratory became a central feature of the new mathematics education. The first such laboratory was developed in that distant cousin of the Lincoln School, John Dewey's University of Chicago High School. There the traditional mathematics classroom, with its rows of anchored desks, underwent a transformation into something more akin to a modern science laboratory, with long flat-top work tables and movable furniture to accommodate class projects and "differentiated tasks." When organizing the mathematics department at Lincoln, Raleigh Schorling adopted this plan, arguing that it maintained the student at an "unbelievable" level of enthusiasm. Less costly than a science laboratory or school shop, it used the tools of the civil engineer: slide rules, inexpensive sextants, surveying equipment, balances and engineer's notebooks. The laboratory gave "concreteness and greater reality" to mathematics and taught pupils "things worth knowing" and "worth doing." Thus "socialized," the laboratory assumed an importance, Schorling hoped, that could "no longer be doubted."[53]

Just how all this emphasis on applied mathematics encouraged such values as "open-mindedness" or fostered a critical attitude toward experimental results often remained vague in the writings of the mathematics reformers.[54] Perhaps this is why they placed so much stress on the observation of student responses to course materials and teaching methods. In the course of every experiment, Schorling explained,

> A record will be kept of pupils' successes, failures, interests, the sufficiency of explanation, the adequacy of the practice material, the clearness of the terminology, the degree to which the subject matter is taken from the experiences of the children, and the suitability of the projects which are included . . . ,[followed by] a systematic use of measurement to test the pupil's mastery of each unit of material and growth in skill, information, and mathematical power.[55]

But even in this appraising, the science educators fared badly. Their psychological studies of student responses and learning curves, their efforts to create an objective measure of appreciational values and to gauge the social effectiveness of science teaching, while bold and original, left them increasingly out on a cognitive limb and with instructional materials that verged dangerously on pseudo-science. Nevertheless, the General Education Board faithfully published the records and data from these tests, delivering them into the hands of teachers and administrators at public, private, and normal schools throughout the country. Textbooks like Schorling's *General Mathematics* (1917), a compilation of his Lincoln School experiments, became a junior high school standard. Experimental courses in science and mathematics as well as in social studies, English, modern language, and industrial arts gave rise to a whole new secondary curriculum designed to develop, according to a report of the staff, "well-knit personalities adjusted to the social order in which they live."[56]

Traditionalists representing both the sciences and the liberal arts put up a bitter, ultimately futile resistance to the primacy of general science and practical mathematics in the curriculum. They resented the hegemonic role of the Lincoln School and indirectly of the General Education Board in setting the direction of course development and experimentation. What they could not prevent and what posed a much greater challenge to traditional thinking was the growing professionalization of teaching and educational administration. Strong ideological ties between the nation's teachers colleges, their laboratory schools, and the philanthropic organizations that funded and encouraged their work guaranteed a broader audience and a wider outlet for the new educational practices, but did not interdict the rise of the expert—a central event not only in the decline of traditional studies but in the consolidation of a reorganized curriculum.

Lincoln's Modern School Philosophy: Innovation and Accommodation

The modern school philosophy Flexner, Caldwell, and Eliot developed and the General Education Board adopted sought to create a consensus on the educational needs of the country at a time of worldwide crisis. After 1914, a cult of preparedness, extending from the government's War Industries Board and the economic demands of total war to high-level discussions at the National Research Council, gradually permeated educational circles. In its postwar configuration, preparedness was more a "temper of mind" (to use John Dewey's description of another, related movement, pragmatism) than a well-defined set of policies.[57] Its enemies included direct democracy, income redistribution, social legislation and idealistic political solutions like Wilson's Fourteen Points and his League of Nations—"will-o-the-wisps" that put the country at a disadvantage in the race between democracy and international communism. In education, preparedness took the form of a new spirit of up-building: a building-up of the body, of the character, and of institutions, "the purpose [of which]," wrote Nicholas Murray Butler, "is not simply to strengthen and perpetuate what others have found to be useful and good, but rather by building upon that, to carry both the individual and the race forward in their progress toward fuller self-expression and more complete self-realization." The progressive idea of human perfection—and preparedness itself—was rooted in the pragmatist's conception of experience. If, as Dewey and other educational progressives argued, experience was the starting point of all inquiry and inquiry in turn the basis of all real knowledge, it was clear that the school, a main center for the production of knowledge, should have as its principal task the rationalization of experience.[58]

What exactly did this rationalization entail? In general terms, it required breaking with the past and beginning a new, more active engagement in the present. Here Dewey contrasted the traditional concept of empiricism in which experience was regarded as discontinuous, inner, and psychical—a "contemplative survey of existence" devoid of living connections, bearings, ties to or truths of the present—with an idea of experience that took into account human "undergoings" and focused not on the past or future but on "things which are coming (are now coming, not just to come)." When it was educative, experience formed a connection not to "what is past and done with" but to a better life in the future—that is, to a reality that, far from being static, is in a constant agitation of change and adjustment. It was the duty of the schools, and of science teachers in particular, to demonstrate this evolutionary law, extrapolating from everyday life a sense of "future possibilities" as well as adjustments. At the practical level, Dewey's world of endless possibilities provided the rationale for a new science of common entities and phenomena, instilled new organizational values and skills, and reinforced the problem-solving approach of the trained engineer, the competent physician, and the laboratory expert.[59]

The Lincoln School set out, in part, to realize these objectives, to take the approved progressive practices of the day—less as ideal types than as raw materials—and, through repeated classroom experiment, to test the strength and efficacy of those materials. It was engaged in free inquiry, but in a centralized way and with as much attention to logic, as the means of systematizing and handling hypotheses and data, as to the psychological methods for which it became justly famous. These investigations, one should understand, the school carried out unapologetically under the watchful eye of the world's largest private educational philanthropy, the General Education Board. Whether the representatives of the Board gave expert service on a "constructive basis," as Dean James Russell believed, or simply meddled in areas where they had no business, the Board itself carried through the majority of its plans with relative impunity. Organized into "cultures of trusteeship," groups like the General Education Board, headed by powerful industrial statesmen, could give voice to and represent public concerns without, it seems, the fear of public accountability. The Lincoln School passed into history in 1940, but its legacy as an private experimental school remains as a testimony to the ambiguous position of the charitable trust in a democratic society.[60]

"Agreement, refutation and sheer incomprehension, all mixed together"—this description of the development of science, an activity at once "progressive" and "degenerate," moving crab-like between new and novel discoveries and the more-or-less fixed structures of the past, fits more closely the large and varied body of Lincoln's experimental work than the idealizing descriptions of either its critics or its defenders. In the management of novelty, "the actual processes of decision and assimilation," observed Jerome Ravitz, "are too complex to be plausibly reduced to simple models; and that while genuine progress does not depend on mere chance, it does depend on judgments . . . for which no simple and certain rules can be laid down." If this is a fair description of the modern research program, then the Lincoln School failed by its own standards to meet the requirements of critical self-study and evaluation, assimilation, and change that are its hallmarks. "The best teachers do not wait for emergent situations which call for inquiry," Caldwell wrote. They lead a search for "the needed problems," make every effort to "add to knowledge," and concern themselves primarily with instrumental ends, with "evidence of effective and purposeful education."[61]

The functional orientation of the course work at the Lincoln School—its slavish adherence to the immediate needs and demands of the present—made the elimination of waste and inefficiency in industry, culture, and one's personal habits the mark of a good science education as well as the animus of good scientific curriculum-making. Harold Rugg—whose social science pamphlet series for the seventh, eighth, and ninth grades led Lincoln School students through "the mushroom growth" during two hundred years in industry, transportation, communication, and credit—may have been right when he complained of the "huge gap between the curriculum and American life."[62] In practice, however, closing the gap may have only solidified the school's role in the social reproduction process, committing it to a philosophy of accommodation and adjustment to "interdependent" social realities. Each individual had his or her appointed role in a complex, differentiated society in which each part, it could be shown, depended in one way or another on every other part. Thus eighth graders at Lincoln learned about labor unions and industrial strikes but learned about them as aberrations of a earlier form of industrial organization—individualistic, speculative, competitive—that left workers with few practical alternatives. On the other hand, the students learned that because modern life had become "so interdependent, . . . some means of avoiding strikes in settling labor disputes"—collective bargaining, arbitration, or the ballot box, for example—was "very essential."[63] Made to see every side of a complex issue, whether it was a lesson in social studies or a problem in geometry, Lincoln students learned the value of balanced and discriminating judgment but knew few passions that might have moved them to sacrifice these qualities or to submerge them in some large cause.

Conclusion

The Lincolnian "Class Poem 1921" conveys something of the spiritual desolation of a fair and impartial education:

There stands a man who watches those who start out.
He sees them drop unnoticed things of value
For which he stoops and searches in the dust.
He is one who went out and has returned
With nothing.

I leave the window and look about the empty room.
They have all gone. I cannot warn them. . . .

'Tis just as well.
Youth's saving gift, I think, is that it will not look,
And cannot see.

I take a last glance back and gently close the door behind me;
I catch a friendly hand that's half-outstretched;
And I am part of the crowd.[64]

Students and teachers at the Lincoln School were caught between two worlds. One resembled a pre-industrial world of apprenticeship in which children and adults, living together in close proximity, were trained for productive employment and citizenship; the other resembled a new world of educational professionalism in which domestic and household responsibilities were removed from the home to the school and in which experiments in educational effectiveness too often became "treatments" for a growing list of modern ailments. The school could never quite decide what it was: an experiment in progressive practices? a hedge against those practices when they shifted dangerously over toward bureaucratic centralism? or the harbinger of something entirely new and novel and distinctly modern? This last possibility was allowed to die early, a sacrifice to child-centeredness, to subject-matter fetishism, and to an experimental tradition that controlled for these factors but otherwise ignored them for larger, correlative and integrative purposes.

Abraham Flexner seemed to betray a sense of this desolation, and perhaps of the dangers lurking in the modern school concept he helped so much to develop, on a visit to two of the school's classrooms during its first semester of operation in 1917. In Mr. Buckner's ninth grade civics class, the students appeared ill-prepared, their opinions, which Mr. Buckner spent "the major part of one hour" trying to elicit, "crude" and untutored; and the assignments too lengthy. In Mr. Glenn's eighth grade science class several students engaged in "idle and disturbing chatter" and "the posture was careless." In both cases Flexner worried that while everyone's opinions seemed in full circulation, very little "real knowledge [or] hard work and definite learning" was taking place. "Fun and interest must be the outcome of the work," Flexner reported in a memorandum to the General Education Board, "though not at the expense of the work."[65]

Having vanquished in his own writing the shibboleths of formal discipline and mental training, the specter of Flexner, one of the leading fathers of the modern school movement, recoiling at his own creation is almost as strange as the specter of Eliot, Flexner's patron, adopting it in the first place. Was fate playing a cruel trick on these two men, or had the ideas they came to embody already passed out of existence, to be replaced by shadow plays and forms that lacked their original substance and meaning? In the actual development of the Lincoln School, the research function—with which Flexner and Eliot, generalists of an earlier age of scientific pedagogy, had had an ambivalent relationship from the beginning—came to overshadow and dominate the teaching function. Teaching came to serve research, when the original intent of the school had been quite the opposite. Yet, looking back, it is hard to imagine how a school at such cross-purposes with itself could have achieved anything else. The genie—of scientific expertise and professionalism, of positivistic problem-solving, and of childless child-centeredness—had escaped the bottle.

THE DALTON SCHOOL: THE TRANSFORMATION OF A PROGRESSIVE SCHOOL

Susan F. Semel

A coeducational, independent day school located on the fashionable Upper East Side of Manhattan founded in 1919 by Helen Parkhurst on West 72nd Street, the Dalton School moved to its East 89th Street location in 1929.[1] At present, the Middle School and High School, grades 4 through 12, are housed in a ten-story brick building at 108 East 89th Street. The Lower School, grades K through 3, occupies a series of cleverly connected townhouses at 53, 61, and 63 East 91st Street. A new physical education facility, opened in 1992, is housed in a luxury apartment building at 200 East 87th Street.

Although Helen Parkhurst founded Dalton as a progressive school, with the financial backing of Mrs. W. Murray Crane, the wife of the owner of Crane Paper Company, the school has strayed far from the original intentions of its founder. Today, Dalton is a competitive, elite, college preparatory school with tuition costs above $17,000 per year.[2] Few parents who apply know or care about Dalton's progressive roots. This chapter examines the gradual transformation of the Dalton School's progressive pedagogic practices from its beginnings to the present.[3]

The Parkhurst Years (1919–1942): Curriculum and Pedagogy at Dalton

It was probably around 1915–1916 that her fortuitous relationship with Mrs. W. Murray Crane began, the woman who was to provide Helen Parkhurst with the financial support she needed to found her school. A mid-Westerner by birth, transplanted by marriage to a pastoral factory town in

Dalton, Massachusetts, Mrs. W. Murray Crane was the second wife of one of the wealthiest men in America. The Crane family business, founded in 1801, is printing paper: paper for stationery and paper for the United States Mint. The Cranes had three children: two boys and one girl, Louise, the youngest, born in 1913. It was the education of Louise Crane that Helen Parkhurst was invited to Dalton to supervise. There is little documentation regarding just how and precisely when Helen Parkhurst began her school for Louise Crane and three or four of her friends in the Crane family house in Dalton. What is of particular significance is the relationship begun by the two women: one rich, powerful, and an important patron of the arts; the other, a practitioner of modest means, and a messiah of progressive education.

Parkhurst's school in Mrs. W. Murray Crane's house lasted, according to Winthrop Crane, for one year;[4] she then went on to implement the Dalton Plan in the public high school in Dalton. This too, lasted for one year. Although difficult to document, it has been suggested that the relative brevity of the experiment was due to parental resistance, perhaps portending the fate of similar experiments in public high schools in New York City. It was after this abortive experiment in the public sector that with the encouragement and financial support from Mrs. W. Murray Crane, Helen Parkhurst opened the Dalton School in New York City in 1919. Her school, originally called The Children's University School, was renamed the Dalton School in 1920; a compromise perhaps, since Helen Parkhurst, according to informants, wanted to name the school after her benefactress who declined the honor (and perhaps the publicity) in favor of the name of the town from which the Crane family originated. Her particular progressive pedagogical plan, originally called the Laboratory Plan, was also renamed the Dalton Plan in keeping with the new name of the school.

Helen Parkhurst founded the Dalton School at a time when "progressive private day schools began to emerge in growing numbers."[5] Often the creations of talented practitioners aided by wealthy women who shared their progressive visions, these schools were for the most part child-centered, reflecting the idea that, "each individual has uniquely creative potentialities and that a school in which children are encouraged freely to develop their potential is the best guarantee of a larger society truly devoted to human worth and excellence."[6]

The Dalton School followed Helen Parkhurst's particular philosophy, which she referred to as "education on the Dalton Plan," an innovative synthesis of the ideas of John Dewey and Carleton W. Washburne. The latter, architect of education on the individual system, which allowed students to proceed through their studies at their own pace, introduced his method in the public schools of Winnetka, Illinois.[7] Parkhurst's book, *Education on the Dalton Plan*, was translated into many languages, including Spanish, Italian, Japanese, Russian and Dutch and Dalton Schools were established in the United Kingdom, Japan, The Netherlands, Russia, and Chile.[8]

Although the connection is difficult to document, Parkhurst almost certainly knew of Carleton Washburne, in view of the striking similarities of their work.[9] Parkhurst, however, called her approach the Dalton Laboratory Plan, and emphasized the laboratory, or "lab," as students and her faculty members came to call it, as her own unique creation and one of the principal concepts of her plan.

Helen Parkhurst formulated The Dalton Plan during a time when many educators were concerned with attending to the needs of the child, rather than fitting the child into an existing structure. She was, above all, concerned with providing students with a better way to learn, a way that would permit them "to pursue and organize their studies their own way."[10] She desired to create

> a community environment to supply experiences to free the native impulses and interests of each individual of the group. Any impediments in the way of native impulses prevent the release of pupil energy. It is not the creation of pupil energy, but its release and use that is the problem of education.[11]

The guiding principles of her plan were freedom and cooperation. By freedom, Parkhurst intended the student to work free from

> interruption . . . upon any subject in which he is absorbed, because when interested he is mentally keener, more alert, and more capable of mastering any difficulty that may arise in the course of his study.[12]

To this end she abolished bells, for she believed that children acquire knowledge at their own rate and that they must have time to learn thoroughly. As Parkhurst saw it, "Freedom is taking one's own time. To take someone else's time is slavery."[13]

By cooperation, Parkhurst meant "the interaction of group life."[14] Concerned with preparing students to live in a democracy, she attempted to create an environment that maximized cooperation and interaction between student and student and students and teachers. Believing that "education is a co-operative task," she set out to implement her principle through the work problem:

> Under the Dalton Laboratory Plan we place the work problem squarely before him (the student), indicating the standard which has to be attained. After that he is allowed to tackle it as he thinks fit in his own way and at his own speed. Responsibility for the result will develop not only his latent intellectual powers, but also his judgment and character.[15]

In September, Dalton students would confront the year's work in each subject all at once. They would be required to discuss their plans of action with their teachers, for Parkhurst considered it essential that both students and teachers understand their tasks. Later, students might discuss their plans with their fellow students; they might modify their plans in accordance with peer recommendations; they might even abandon their plans and start over. Students would have participated, nonetheless, in planning their studies with both faculty members and peers, interacting with the community in a spirit of cooperation.

In addition to planning, cooperation could occur in such student activities as clubs and committees and the "House system," the latter a signature Dalton innovation. Helen Parkhurst conceived of the House, particularly her high school, as the arrangement of the student population into advisory groups representing all four grades and meeting with a teacher-advisor four times a week for a total period of ninety minutes.

House meetings might consist of students planning their work with their advisors, discussing problems of scheduling appointments with teachers, or perhaps assembling in groups to discharge their various responsibilities to the rest of the community. House discussions might approach the more personal level, too. The group might consider student attitudes, habits and experiences, anything with a definite bearing on community life within the school. Thus while House fostered the spirit of cooperation among students, it also developed the qualities of independence and social awareness.[16]

Other important components of The Dalton Plan were the contract system and the assignment. In the Children's University School and then in the early stages of the Dalton School, the curriculum was divided into "jobs" encompassing twenty day-time periods. Students "contracted" for their tasks and signed a contract agreeing to complete them.[17] The students' tasks appeared as the assignment—"an outline of the contract job with all its parts."[18]

To "free" the children and to encourage growth in independence and responsibility, the Dalton School set large blocks of time each morning from nine to noon called "lab time." Each teacher had his or her own "lab," and students would be expected to utilize the resources of their teachers in order to fulfill their contracts. Lab could be either a group or an individual experience and the lab rooms contained both textbooks and "adult books" to facilitate learning.

Graphs recorded student progress. At the beginning the school used four graphs: an instructor's laboratory graph, a pupil's contract graph, a House graph, and an attendance graph. An instructor's graph posted in each lab would show how many units of work the students had accomplished, twenty units being equal to one assignment. Subject teachers and students alike could use these graphs to measure progress; for the teacher it served as a means of determining when to call a "conference" during which a group of students at the same level might discuss certain problems they shared. These graphs also allowed the students to measure their achievement in relation to the group as a whole.

The pupils' contract graph permitted them to record their progress in all subjects. It became known, later on, as the "unit card" because, like the instructor's graph, it contained space for twenty units divided into four sections for each week of the twenty-day period. The House graph emphasized the entire number of units of work completed and contained a space for individual House members to record their progress. It served mainly as a tool for the House Advisor. The attendance graph, posted on a bulletin board, was accessible to students and they took responsibility for recording the time they arrived each morning.

Flexibility, then, remained the keystone of the plan. Teachers called conferences as needed. Classes met, too, as needed, and consisted of grade meetings to discuss problems common to that age group. During Helen Parkhurst's regime, the school exuded informality, spur-of-the-moment decision-making, abundant energy, eager engagement of both faculty and students, and always the element of surprise. Harold Thorne, a former teacher now deceased, was fond of recalling, "You could come back to your classroom on Monday and someone else would be teaching there."[19]

Students were recruited from the immediate neighborhood and from the artistic and academic communities of the city, a mix of families consisting of affluent Anglo-Saxon Protestants and German Jews, artists, writers, and academics (the latter groups often awarded scholarships). A diversity in social class and occupation thus characterized the school.

But even as she conceived it, Helen Parkhurst's Dalton Laboratory Plan was far from perfect. Former students complained of a lack of structure, of conferences called without warning, and of disruptions at those times when projects needed to be completed. Teachers had to be reeducated in Dalton ways. With the emphasis on process, they were often insecure with curriculum. Measuring whether a student had realized his or her potential and had become a contributing member of a community remained a largely unsettled problem.

The Dalton Plan flourished in the lower grades, particularly from four through eight. The need to meet college entrance requirements, kept it out of the High School until 1933, when Dalton became part of a group of independent schools participating in the Eight Year Experiment.

Helen Parkhurst had founded a school with a particular philosophy and a special environment where teachers had lab rooms and classrooms and educational vocabulary indigenous to the institution. But perhaps her greatest contribution to education may have been her emphasis on process rather than product. She saw the Dalton Plan as "a vehicle for the curriculum, that is, a new way of school living, permitting children to acquire flexible habits to put behind ideas."[20] She sought to instill in her students "good habits" because she appreciated the need to adjust to new situations with facility as the primary principle of living. She believed she was creating an environment that would allow her students to make "adjustments and do things in terms of principle . . . to get the right mental habits for life." As she stated in her Caxton Hall Lecture, the trouble with the education given to us in the past is that it really was not a preparation for the particular kind of living that we are enjoying today. Statesmen, teachers, all professions are baffled by problems that we face but do not solve. We must have flexible individuals in the future, who can do their tasks which we, in our ignorance, are unable even to discern today.[21]

To recapitulate, Parkhurst's Dalton Laboratory Plan was original in its language only; it actually was a synthesis of the ideas of leading progressive educators of her day—especially as previously mentioned, Carleton Washburne.[22] Washburne's "individual system" and Parkhurst's Dalton Laboratory Plan had much in common. Both embraced the idea that children should progress at their own pace, and both used the method of individualized instruction to this end. Both emphasized the idea of group life through projects, student government, clubs, and committees. The two offered similar content in their projects; for example, Greek Olympic, Games which became institutionalized at Dalton, were part of the fifth grade curriculum in Winnetka. Both used some standardized form of measurement for student progress: Parkhurst used unit cards or progress charts; Washburne used goal cards. Both adopted systematic approaches to individualized work: Parkhurst used assignments that followed a particular set structure, while Washburne used "specially prepared individual progress materials."

The Influence of the Eight Year Study (1933–1940)

After the school had existed for little over a decade, an assessment of the Dalton Plan became possible when Parkhurst agreed to participate in the Eight Year Study, generated by the Progressive Education Association. A Commission on the Relation of School and College, formed under the leadership of Wilford M. Aikin, consisted of 26 members "concerned with the revision of the work of the secondary school and eager to find some way to remove the obstacle of rigid prescription."[23] By 1932, an experimental solution had emerged in a plan that invited cooperation among a select group of 28 schools[24] and most of the nation's colleges and universities permitting the schools to be released from the usual subjects and unit requirements for college admission for a period of five years, beginning with the class entering college in 1936. Practically all accredited colleges and universities agreed to this plan. Relatively few colleges require[d] candidates to take College Entrance Board Examinations.[25]

Dalton School psychologist Dr. Genevieve L. Coy, served on three subcommittees of Records and Reports established by the Commission; Dr. Hilda Taba, the school's curriculum coordinator, served as an associate on the Evaluation Staff of the Commission, headed by Dr. Ralph W. Tyler.

The Eight Year Study proved to be an exciting event and period for the Dalton School community and former staff members have been eloquent about this period in the school's history. Former students, too, recalled the excitement of participating in an educational experiment that invited staff members, students, and parents to discuss frequently the purposes of education and to speculate on what should be taught. Educational researchers have since characterized this feeling as "the adventure of living."[26] The Dalton community certainly appears to have shared in this feeling of adventure.

When placed in another perspective, however, one might view the Eight Year Experiment as an extension of Parkhurst's Dalton Plan into its High School. The curriculum had to be reorganized so as to reflect a particular four-part philosophy of education already present in the Primary and Middle Schools:

(1)   the development of many sides of the child's na-
      ture—intellectual, emotional, esthetic, spiritual;
(2)   provision for individual differences;
(3)   the development of that self-discipline in the pupil which
      makes it possible for him to use freedom;
(4)   the growth of an active appreciation of, and concern for,
      the needs and achievements of other individuals and
      peoples.[27]

The philosophy of the High School incorporated these precepts, placing a strong emphasis on "appreciation of individual differences" and "social awareness" so that the clear overall purpose of a Dalton education was to prepare the student to live in a democratic society. Curriculum, Parkhurst stated, should not be presented as subjects in "water-tight compartments" but should rather be integrated, cutting across subject lines . . . which might help the student orient herself towards large problems of the present world." Thus, she defined the school's objectives as:

(1)   the development on the part of the student of a personally formulated and cherished outlook on life. This is the overarching objective of the program, and it is, finally, the *integrating force for the individual*.

(2)   the development of intellectual powers: generalization, consistency and persistency in thinking, planning and through an attack upon problems; transfer of ideas from one field of action to another, etc.

(3)   the development of intellectual tools; basic concepts and information in significant areas of knowledge, ability to read with purpose, ability to discriminate in reading and in observation, facility in oral and written expression, etc.

(4)   the development of a self-awareness that leads to satisfying and joyful living. This is the over-arching objective *for the student*, though perhaps never formulated. It will be realized through location of interests, pursuit of interests, understanding of self—through social relationships, plan of imagination in all areas of school activity, etc.[28]

The curriculum was organized so that students would "form a unified point of view on some of the problems of modern life" and the technique of selecting large problems for students to work on was adopted in order for them to comprehend their environment better. The course of study in the Dalton High School for four years follows:

Grade 9: Life in New York City, considered as a metropolitan community.
Grade 10: The Political, Economic, and Cultural Trends which have given character and differentiation to Life in the United States today.
Grade 11: The Impact of European Culture on Our Life Today.

Grade 12: Outstanding, International Problems and America's Relation to them.[29]

Dr. Ralph W. Tyler candidly assessed the impact of the Eight Year Study on the Dalton School in a letter to Professor Bode, a member of the Directing Committee. Tyler stated that the data on Dalton were far more complete than for any other school in the Eight Year Study, and that "achievement of the girls in the new high school program is outstanding." On reading tests, Dalton high school seniors proved superior to the average college sophomore; on writing samples, seniors exceeded the average college juniors. After having attended a government assembly, Tyler concluded that the students exhibited an impressive verbal ability, that the "girls speak as effectively as the ordinary college graduate." He also found evidence of growth of critical thinking and the easy transfer of ideas into new areas. The outstanding features of Dalton's program, for Tyler, were that teachers worked together cooperatively taking advantage of the city to augment the curriculum, that high school girls learned about human behavior and family problems through working in the nursery school division, and that he found, in general, greater coordination of educational efforts between family and home. Tyler concluded that "such a significant contribution to American education ought to be continued."[30]

Although Tyler enthusiastically supported what he saw happening at Dalton, what might be unique and exciting to the Dalton community had already become familiar among the other study participants. Core or integrated curriculum designs existed as learning strategies in the majority of the participating schools. The evaluators cited Dalton, however, as particularly outstanding in its community studies that relied heavily on field trips and in its articulation among all fields and grade levels.[31]

But what did students themselves think? In a document Helen Parkhurst entitled "Working Together," which grew out of a three-day conference at the school, the students agreed that the school made them aware of themselves and that they were cognizant of the need "to collect their own evidence [and] not accept knowledge passively." In particular, freedom, responsibility, and comprehension of the process whereby knowledge is obtained were frequently mentioned both in this document and by former students, too. They also cited personal growth, social consciousness, and the spirit of cooperation as qualities gleaned from the Dalton learning experience.

The Eight Year Experiment, begun in 1933, lasted until 1940, and it made a significant impact on the Dalton community and influenced the course of studies in the High School for many years thereafter. In addition, a policy toward college admissions had been established. As Charlotte Keefe Durham, then director of the High School, noted in a letter, "I never sent a mark to colleges and, as you know, many of you were welcomed into excellent colleges."[32] For many years after the Eight Year Experiment ended, grading continued to be minimized. Not until the 1960s would it again become an issue with faculty members, students, and parents.

Helen Parkhurst and her staff worked tirelessly during this experimental period to perfect their notion of Dalton's philosophy of education and to implement it in the curriculum. She delegated the running of the High School to Charlotte Keefe Durham; however, Mrs. Durham notes that when Parkhurst was Headmistress "she was central and final in its management—very few ideas came from the faculty."[33] She characterizes Parkhurst as "a benevolent, creative, autocrat,"[34] who "cared passionately about freedom for children and went to great lengths to originate plans for that and student responsibility, e.g., the nursery, Dalton Plan."[35]

That Helen Parkhurst was enmeshed in every aspect of school life was an understatement. She would visit the homes of their students, befriend parents, and open previously untapped channels of communication between school and home. A believer in conferences as an effective vehicle of communication, she held many during her administration in which students, parents and faculty participated. A three-day Parents Education Conference held in May, 1938, dealt with studying the needs of the children and their education "to acquaint parents with the kind of work and activities the students are engaged in throughout the school."[36] During one meeting, students presented their views of what sort of teacher they preferred; parents expressed their views of what sort of teacher they would like to have as their child's instructor. Teachers reported on what kind of parents they would "appreciate."

Helen Parkhurst also was fond of appearing at student assemblies to discuss the Dalton Plan. She would also call students at random to her office as individuals or in groups to discuss personal or communal concerns. In addition, she instituted a reporting system, not just for parents of Dalton students, but for nurses and governesses who were concerned with the welfare of their charges. Parkhurst's commitment to the school community was contagious. Parents, too, became so involved with the education of their children that one was moved to write a letter to the student newspaper testifying to that effect:

> Being a parent of a daughter who has been practically brought up in Miss Parkhurst's school, I feel it almost a sacred duty to follow the activities of the school and the principles it teaches. I have watched with pleasure the splendid progress of my child in her studies and in her general development and I often ask myself what are some of the outstanding characteristics that my child has been imbued with through her contact with her teachers and her superiors. One of the most striking of these, I would say, is the clear development of her own logical thinking and her persistent demand for logical reasoning on the part of her parents, also.
>
> A Dalton Admirer[37]

The most telling portrait of Parkhurst, however, can be found through reading the minutes of the board of trustees and by interviewing former board members. What emerges is a picture of an administrator who did as she pleased, regardless of what the board mandated. She was, of course, supported by certain board members who were close personal friends, such as Helen Parkhurst's patroness, Mrs. W. Murray Crane, and Mrs. Evangeline Stokowska. Mrs. Stokowska often accompanied Parkhurst on trips both school-related and personal; she also provided financial support when additional funds were necessary. The antique, renaissance-style cabinets that once graced the second floor corridors were said to have come from Stokowska's apartment; likewise, the elaborate gold threaded drapes that were transformed into angels' costumes for the Christmas Pageant. Helen Parkhurst also received support on the board, first, from Benjamin Buttenwieser, a wealthy and prominent member of the New York German-Jewish community who had an immense respect for education and believed in Parkhurst's ideas; then, when Buttenwieser left to join the Navy, from his wife, Helen, a lawyer. Parkhurst also commanded the loyalty of trustee Lloyd Goodrich, art historian and curator of the Whitney Museum, whose son was the recipient of a scholarship. It is alleged that those members who forcefully opposed her were pressured until they resigned for either "reasons of health" or "business responsibilities." Parkhurst was able to manipulate the board successfully until the advent of Mr. Richardson Wood as president. Then her style of leadership led to her undoing.

As stated in the minutes of the Board for September 26, 1929, the responsibilities of the head of the school were as follows:

> The Head of School shall have full charge of the educational policy of the school and its administration, for both of which she shall be responsible to the Board of Trustees.[38]

The head of the school was also mandated to "regulate the course of study, school sessions and vacations, admission, suspension and expulsion of pupils."[39] Only later, in 1936, did the board act to curb the power of the headmistress by creating a small educational advisory board consisting of three teachers, Miss Keefe, Miss Seeger, and Mrs. Mukerji, to act in concert with Helen Parkhurst on matters concerning educational policy "and to accept responsibility of maintaining budget limits established by the Board."[40] Any payments made by the school had to have the signatures of Parkhurst and two of the three teachers on the advisory board. These three teachers, however, were close to Parkhurst and sources interviewed stated that they were likely "to do her bidding."

There is much evidence that Helen Parkhurst acted with calculated insouciance in regard to money matters. In 1937, she spent $250 on publicity photographs of the school, although unauthorized to do so by the board. She cavalierly stated that the PTA would pay the bill. The board, however, objected, stating that the PTA was not responsible for the debt and that Parkhurst should pay for the photographs herself. Yet, the PTA willingly paid the bill, for Parkhurst was quite successful in her ability to coopt the parents.

While Helen Parkhurst may have carefully thought out her educational philosophy, she certainly did not devote the same amount of meticulous planning to school policy. A particular example of shoddy planning was the infamous merger with the Todhunter School in 1939, "a conservative, fashionable school for girls—totally unrelated to Dalton ideals."[41] According to several sources, the Todhunter School presented a number of desirable elements to Parkhurst. First and foremost, it had $17,000 in its building fund which might be added to Dalton's construction fund. It also had Eleanor Roosevelt on its board, Bernard Baruch's daughter as a student, and a population drawn from wealthy East Side Protestant families. Dalton teachers were not consulted about the merger nor was the board consulted about Parkhurst's plan until she had informally mustered support from some board members.

"The merger," states Charlotte Keefe Durham, "was a disaster. Confusion and questionable financial plans followed from both sides."[42] Few Todhunter students came to Dalton; those who did left the following year. Parkhurst, nevertheless, managed to keep the $17,000 from the Todhunter building fund and applied it the following year to her fund to expand the 89th Street building.

Yet another incident of thoughtlessness and dictatorial management on the part of Helen Parkhurst was her "New Milford Experiment" or "City and Country," as one trustee referred to this scheme. Apparently no one involved seems to know exactly how it came about, what its purpose was, when it was first implemented and how it was financed—although there is much speculation, especially in regard to the latter. There is, however, much agreement on the fact that the site was chosen because Helen Parkhurst had a country house in New Milford, Connecticut.

The first mention of New Milford is found in an editorial in *The Daltonian* on December 1, 1937, entitled "Integration of Work and Play." It comments favorably on Helen Parkhurst's notion of obtaining a small house in the country where some members of the high school might go for a week and combine academic studies with nature studies and winter sports. Students interviewed who had participated in New Milford were unclear as to why they were there. One viewed it as "a lark"; another stated it to be "the most miserable experience of my life." *The Daltonian* of February 28, 1941, reported that on March 1st, students from the junior and senior classes and the faculty would go to New Milford for one month in which they would devote their weekdays to academic studies and spend their weekends taking field trips. Apparently the students were boarded in dormitories and fed in a communal mess hall. It was thought that these facilities were constructed to house city children who might have to be evacuated because of the war. As to the ownership of the property, one informant speculated that Parkhurst had purchased the site through remortgaging the 89th Street building. There is no evidence to support this latter piece of speculation. It is a fact, however, that Parkhurst could not account for the sum of more than $40,000 over the budget, according to board minutes. According to another informant, the faculty who participated in this experiment were "good sports"; however, it was felt that there was an undercurrent of resentment for the authoritarian, insensitive manner in which it was implemented. Indeed, it must have been quite difficult for faculty members with families to absent themselves from home for a full month.

Parkhurst's building expansion program, which she undertook in 1940, illustrates her lack of concern for board approval and perhaps serves to underscore her feeling that the school was hers to direct as she saw fit. Parkhurst decided to implement a plan to build additions to the east and west wings of the school. Without giving the board notice, she sent letters to parents asking for contributions, the percentage to be determined by the amount of tuition paid to support her program. Ultimately she did obtain board approval but only after she had procured loans from two parents totaling the full amount of the projected expenditure.

Helen Parkhurst's Achilles heel was money. She raised it successfully but spent it imprudently. In 1938, she reported to the board in her annual message that the cash deficit of 1929 had been completely eliminated. Yet, in 1940, because of lack of funds, the faculty had to pitch in and donate a percentage of their salaries to the school to prevent the staff from being cut. Two years later, in 1942, after declaring a financial deficit of $91,764.65, the school went into bankruptcy. Where did the money go? Many informants interviewed stated that Parkhurst used school funds for personal gain and that she whimsically granted scholarships. Whatever the case, the climax leading to the inevitable denouement occurred in 1942, when the board under the presidency of Mr. Richardson Wood, editor of *Fortune Magazine*, investigated the school's finances. Concurrently, the faculty, particularly in the high school, split into two factions. Many of its newer members voiced strong opposition to Parkhurst's dictatorial approach in determining academic policy. The schism unleashed such passion that for years thereafter, one loyal Parkhurst supporter, Dora Downes, refused to speak to members of the opposition.

According to board minutes, during a private meeting on April 30, 1942, in which Helen Parkhurst, Richardson Wood, Charles D. Hilles, and Stanley Isaacs were present, Parkhurst agreed to resign. Subsequently, a formal announcement of her resignation was made in a board meeting on

May 5. A letter written by Helen Parkhurst tendering her resignation was accepted by the board and her contract was to be terminated as of June, 1942.

There is much evidence to support the proposition that Helen Parkhurst did not accept her fate lightly. One faculty member reports that Parkhurst, in an attempt to quell the faculty revolt, called an assembly of high school students, locked the faculty out, told the students not to go to classes, assured them that no one would fail, and promised to sign the diplomas of graduating seniors.[43] She also contacted former board members and powerful parents to muster support. During the board meeting of May 13, thirty-five telegrams and notes from parents were delivered to the chairman, expressing opposition to or disappointment in Parkhurst's resignation. The most pathetic series of events, however, were those that involved students being called into Parkhurst's office to be confronted by the once powerful headmistress, now begging them to go home and tell their parents, "I'm good, really I am."

One former trustee suggested that Parkhurst was guilty of financial "hanky panky." It is more than likely, however, that she viewed the school as her creation, her property, so that by the end of her administration she was incapable of distinguishing between what belonged to her and what belonged to the institution. Benjamin Buttenwieser, a trustee during Parkhurst's administration, said of her, "when she was on the ship she was captain." Her tragedy was that she failed to comprehend that the ship she commanded was only temporarily entrusted to her.

By the time she resigned in 1942, the Dalton Plan was firmly established from the nursery school through the High School. The Dalton School had established itself as a child-centered progressive school that attempted to balance Dewey's concerns for a democratic community and individual development.

The Durham Years (1942–1960): Progressivism with an Aura of Tradition

Charlotte Durham, a teacher and administrator under Parkhurst since 1922, became headmistress in 1942 and she inherited an innovative, experimental, but financially troubled institution.[44] By the time of her retirement in 1960, the Dalton School had achieved a healthy balance between academic excellence and artistic endeavor, and between freedom of the individual and responsibility to the community. She established a sense of tradition while maintaining the spirit of Parkhurst's more chaotic progressivism, and under her guidance Dalton gained acceptance within New York's elite independent school establishment. During this period, moreover, Dalton's transformation from an experimental progressive school to a more traditional elite college preparatory school began.

Charlotte Durham stated that she never repudiated Helen Parkhurst's ideas but saw to it that they functioned in an orderly way. Under Durham, the Dalton Plan began in fifth grade. House, as a system of organizing and communicating with students, continued from the lower Middle School through the High School. It consisted of multi-age groups, meeting for a fixed period five times a week. A teacher designated as a House advisor presided. Student activities revolved around Houses; House advisors administered student progress reports.

In fact, House became such an important social unit that the House reports (really "citizenship reports") written by House advisors went to a college along with the academic reports of an applicant. Much debate raged (and still rages) about the merits of a multi-age House. Many faculty members considered it an excellent way for older and younger children to learn about each other developmentally: It afforded an easy way for the Dalton community to get to know itself both vertically, and horizontally. Other faculty members, however, felt that multi-age Houses led to isolation by grade, since eighth graders would remain alone rather than mix with younger children and freshmen would remain with freshmen rather than assimilate with upper classmen. Furthermore, although Houses were small, numbering usually sixteen members in the High School (four students from each class), the group dynamics must have been difficult to orchestrate.

Lab became a fixed block of time consisting of the first two periods in the daily schedule five days a week. Lab commitments were written into the assignment. They were usually extensions of the assignments or accommodated remediation as in High School English teacher Dora Downes' famous "correct writing labs," in which students would sit on kitchen chairs, often for hours, attempting to fathom precisely what grammatical errors the red marks in the margin indicated. Lab was conducted in the same room where the teacher held conferences and usually involved groups of four or more students. Students would be responsible for organizing their groups and scheduling appointments on the teachers' calendars. Although the organization of lab became flexible in the Middle School, student responsibility in the planning of time prevailed there too. The faculty seems to have been concerned with students using lab effectively; the students seem to have been concerned with the availability of the faculty. These concerns still plague both the faculty and the students.

Conferences called when a group of students reached the same point in the assignment were now scheduled into the student's day three times a week. In essence, the conference became the class. Class, as a grade-level academic meeting, ceased to exist.

Assignments—a way of apportioning work to students in large blocks of time, usually four weeks, continued in many forms. Some were creative, suggesting projects and activities that complemented the curriculum, while others listing required reading and page numbers were more prosaic. Apparently the individual teacher determined the shape of the assignment. Often it failed to sustain the excitement and engagement students felt in a conference or lab.

Unit cards in the Middle School and progress charts in the High School allowed House advisors to check on their advisees' progress. They also served to remind students of work yet to be done.

Student government continued both in the Middle and High Schools and although it possessed little decision-making powers, it served as a learning experience in the democratic process. A government period was fixed on the schedule each week as were student committee meetings, revolving around government. Thus, each student was expected to participate in government, if not in an open assembly, then on a committee.

Community service, a central idea in a school committed to educating students responsive to the needs of society, expanded under the leadership of Nora Hodges, a language and social studies teacher. On the assumption that "effective education for citizenship comes from direct association with the community," the students spent one afternoon each week during their junior and senior years in hospitals, settlement houses, nursery schools, political campaign headquarters, and such social service agencies as the Federation of Jewish Philanthropies and the Lighthouse for the Blind.[45] They were visited on these sites by teacher-coordinator—Nora Hodges—and formally evaluated. Records of their performance went to the colleges along with their academic grades.

A popular concept in progressive circles during the 1920s was that of "city and country." City children for lengthy blocks of time visited the country to learn firsthand how butter was made, where eggs came from, how bake hay, and so forth. They would see produce grown and come to understand how particular staples they took for granted came into being. Helen Parkhurst attempted to introduce the "city and country" idea to Dalton through the New Milford Experiment and the Otis trip, both extended trips Dalton students made to the country.

But the New Milford Experiment floundered because of the cloudy financial arrangements Parkhurst had made concerning the farm property in New Milford, Connecticut. The Otis trip to George Dillman's farm in Otis, Massachusetts, continued however and became an established third-grade event under Durham. Twice a year Dalton third graders visited Dillman's farm and learned not only about plants and domesticated farm animals, but also about living together in groups.

Under Charlotte Durham, Dalton changed from a helter-skelter, crisis-prone school to an organized, established educational institution. Visitors to Dalton during Charlotte Durham's administration would have been hard pressed to label the school "progressive" or "traditional." Helen Parkhurst's vocabulary remained, but the school had settled into a routinized way of life: a pattern, historian David Rothman noted, common to many institutions. Additionally, many formal, even downright genteel characteristics, accreted at Dalton rather like those found in more traditional independent schools, such as Chapin, Spence, and Brearley. High School students would be expected to rise when adults entered the classroom; they wore smocks over their clothes, uniforms—actually—the condition of which was carefully supervised by a tyrannical yet caring lady named Margaret who presided over the coat room. Teachers were addressed by their full names, and students appearing in school wearing too much makeup might be sent home. We sense here hardly the atmosphere of a "radical progressive school," where students wore blue jeans and called teachers by their first names.

But much remained to make Dalton seem "different" if not outwardly "progressive" to visitors: Children appeared to be unsupervised in both the lower grades and the upper grades, traveling up and down the stairwells on their own; many different activities took place within one classroom; conferences in the High School were held in semi-circles on kitchen chairs;

and in most instances the teacher was indistinguishable from the students in the semi-circle.

Charlotte Durham was an articulate, educated, genteel woman. Her presence in the school was ubiquitous. Three days a week she would walk through its corridors, stopping to talk with students, visiting classes. She knew each student's name on sight. Her educational philosophy was based on a genuine concern for the child. She saw the school as providing an environment in which "egocentric individuals can be transformed into socially responsible and socially energized people."[46] Ideally, with a Dalton education students would be able to think clearly and independently, "make judgements and discriminate among values," have acquired "sound work habits, proper skills and tools with which to carry out ideas," be "responsible human beings and citizens."[47] Hardly revolutionary ideas in 1947. Did not educational reformers such as Horace Mann and Henry Barnard a hundred years earlier voice similar sentiments?

Charlotte Durham's unique contribution to Dalton was to legitimize the school in the eyes of other independent guild schools. Under her leadership Dalton became a member of the Guild of Independent Schools; meetings were held at Dalton; eventually Mrs. Durham became the Guild head. She also attended meetings of independent boarding school associations, established contacts with colleges and instituted an experimental student teaching program with Barnard College. Significantly, discussions of Dalton as an "experimental school" had been dropped in board minutes by the late forties.

Her task was a difficult one, indeed, during an era when Dalton had a large Jewish enrollment, and other independent Guild schools had little or none; and when Dalton had in its employ Priscilla Hiss, wife of Alger Hiss, during a time when the mood of the establishment in New York City was decidedly against Hiss so much so that Priscilla Hiss often required a police escort from school.

It was, however, mandatory that Dalton change and adopt the characteristics of its "sister schools" if it were to survive. One important factor was that the clientele demanded it. Parents who sent their children to Dalton consisted of three types: those genuinely interested in progressive education, those whose children could not succeed in traditional schools, and those who lived in the neighborhood and chose Dalton because it was convenient or because they were excluded from other independent schools for religious reasons. In the "neighborhood group" fell many Protestant families who often left Dalton for formal and socially acceptable schools after the primary grades. As for the Jewish population, there were few schools open to them which would provide academic excellence, formal tone, and neighborhood accessibility. Because this "neighborhood group" formed the largest segment of the Dalton population, they became a powerful force in influencing the direction of the school.

Another important factor in Dalton's more "traditional" orientation was concern over college admissions. Because the colleges now required knowledge in specific areas, because graduating students became increasingly college bound until the 1950s, when virtually all members of the senior classes went off to college, the curriculum became academically oriented and followed a sequential, chronological progression in English and social studies, skill building in math, sciences, and languages. In the High School, students were required to take four years of English and social studies, three years of science, three years of math, four years of one language or a combination of three years of one and two of another. There was little choice involved on the part of the student as to what courses to elect.

The mood of the country had changed. The Truman and Eisenhower administrations, and in particular the McCarthy hearings, had encouraged a wave of conservatism in politics and conformity in living styles. At the same time, progressive education found itself under attack. In 1949, Bernard Iddings Bell's book, *Crisis in Education*, appeared.[48] In 1953, Arthur E. Bestor's book, *Educational Wastelands*,[49] voiced even more articulate, logical, persuasive arguments against progressive education. Then Sputnik, in 1957, helped to eclipse further the ideas of the progressives who saw the school as a lever of social reform. The schools, according to the new wave of critics, were to become places in which to mass produce scientists who would make the United States "number one" again. This would be done by going "back to basics," squeezing the water out of the curriculum," as Bestor recommended, attending to and rewarding academic excellence.

Charlotte Durham announced her plans to retire in 1959. A search committee for a new head was established and Elizabeth Evarts, former head of the Lower School, was named acting head for the following school year. Some informants state that Mrs. Evarts was Charlotte Durham's choice for successor but that the board felt her vision too limited to meet the needs of the school in the 1960s. She served as acting headmistress from 1960 to

1961. During her tenure the board selected Jack Kittell to succeed Charlotte Durham.

Charlotte Durham served Dalton as headmistress for eighteen years. She reunited a faculty torn by factionalism, revitalized a financially floundering institution, introduced racial integration, continued the Dalton Plan, and routinized and gave the school an air of respectability. All the while she managed to cater to a diverse clientele and retain the special flavor of the school: a healthy balance between academic excellence and artistic endeavor, between freedom of the individual and responsibility to the community.

The Barr Years (1964–1974): Conservatism Meets Progressivism

Jack Kittell's term as Headmaster lasted only three years—from 1961 through 1964. He resigned for health reasons and his desire to return to California. Under his leadership, Dalton began a blueprint for the future; but most informants indicate that the Kittell interlude provided little significant change.[50]

Donald Barr served as Dalton's headmaster from 1964 to 1974. His educational background included the progressive Lincoln School in New York City. He came to Dalton having been Assistant Dean of the Engineering School at Columbia University. Although a product of progressive education, Barr had developed an educational philosophy closer to that of such conservative critics of progressivism as Arthur Bestor.[51] He thought progressive education anti-intellectual and permissive. Thus, during his tenure he sought to inject a rigorous and traditional curriculum into the Dalton Plan. By the time Barr left in 1974, the school had nearly tripled in size, had become co-educational through high school, and had established itself as a fashionable New York independent college preparatory school. Like Helen Parkhurst's Dalton, it was troubled financially.

Barr understood the educational problems of the day: the "de-intellectualized curriculum, the failure to educate in serious subjects, the neglect of academically gifted children."[52] He supported rigorous courses of study based on a rich and varied curriculum. He permitted high school students the freedom to choose their own courses through introduction of a serious elective program; he accelerated able students; and he provided seminars and tutorials.

Under the Barr administration, students in the primary grades (pre-school through third), now called the First Program, began reading instruction whenever they showed an interest. Students in the Middle School studied literature along with grammar and spelling; students in the High School, choosing their electives as if in college, also had to take a one-semester course in composition, poetry, novel and drama. Languages began in the Middle School; science was introduced in the First Program and taught at all levels by specialist teachers from the department. In addition to biological and physical sciences, such behavioral sciences as psychology and anthropology were offered in both the Middle School and High School. Social studies began in the First Program and continued through the High School, the last two years consisting of elective courses. Two sequences, presented chronologically and introduced in the first and last years of the Middle School, consisted of world history, including American and Asian history. Math began with "simple counting in the earliest years of school" and continued throughout the divisions. Students could elect math courses to suit their achievement level; thus certain students might study calculus in grade nine, others in grade eleven. Additionally, Barr placed a strong emphasis on the arts, a tradition established by Helen Parkhurst and fostered by Charlotte Durham.

High school students and some middle school students with "special interests," could arrange tutorials. With faculty sponsorship, seniors could undertake a Senior Project—for example, the equivalent of a master's essay on the subject of his or her choice, produce and direct a play, compose and perform a work of music. Thus, the curriculum accommodated student interest and it gave high school students and some middle school students a measure of autonomy in choosing their individual courses of study. Additionally, it provided for individual differences, as talented students could move ahead rapidly while others could elect courses to match their achievement level.

Barr's educational philosophy kept objective tests from Dalton High School classrooms. Teachers understood that the only valid form of testing was the essay, which allowed students to share the thought processes that led them to their answers. Donald Barr also criticized the College Examination Board in his book *Who Pushed Humpty Dumpty?*[53]

It is difficult to argue with the logic and eloquence one finds in Barr's book, especially when he stated that if objective tests are to be given, the child should be allowed to review his answer sheet with the examiner, for "It is not in a child's command of facts or skills, but in his wonderful errors, that we often catch the first shocking glimpse of his talent."[54] The problem many Dalton teachers found, however, was that their students lacked adequate preparation for taking objective tests, so that when they faced the CEEB tests—tests which helped determine the colleges they might attend, their performances often fell short of their capabilities because of the lack of test-taking practice.

In accordance with his disdain for standardized tests, Donald Barr reviewed the admissions process in the school with the help of the Educational Policies Committee and asked the school psychologist and appropriate divisional directors to devise special tests for prospective Dalton students. The ERB tests, judged "valid" by New York's other independent schools, no longer served as determinants for future Daltonians. This policy led to speculation among parents of applicants over just what kind of student the school was looking. Barr, however, clarified this confusion somewhat in the *New York Times Magazine* article on Dalton when he observed that Dalton students had "pizazz," and Dalton students, quick to follow through, began sporting "pizazz" buttons.

Having banned as much objective testing as he could, Barr also took a firm stand against the "canned curriculum." Teachers were encouraged to devise their own materials and were discouraged from attending professional workshops and book exhibits promoting educational matter. Again, Barr's thinking in this area receives expression in his book *Who Pushed Humpty Dumpty?*

Donald Barr and his staff made the Dalton School an exciting place in which students could learn. Subjects were departmentalized; departments were vertically organized, often cutting across divisions; instruction was individualized whenever possible. The staff participated in all disciplines in the Middle and High Schools, which gave faculty members the opportunity to work with students at many different developmental levels. It also enriched the students to have exposure to faculty members with particular expertise at earlier levels.

"House" and "Lab" continued as integral parts of the Dalton Plan: House now specifically concerned with "the social life and personal development" of students; Lab concerned with "quasi-tutorial problems and project sessions." Now Lab rooms for the disciplines gave the students and teachers easy access to one another. Once again the students received assignments in large blocks usually four weeks in duration, and the assignments again served as student contracts, which they could modify with their teachers to accommodate "interests, aptitudes or problems." Progress charts and unit cards gradually fell by the wayside as the school grew in size and boys were admitted to the High School.

Partially out of a commitment to academic excellence, Barr introduced final examinations in the upper Middle School and in the High School. He also undertook to open up the curriculum and provide an elective system in the High School. To address the problem of a larger, more varied, somewhat less academically elite population, he introduced preceptors or tutors, who worked with students either individually or in groups. Originally a strong psychological component had attended the Preceptorial Departments in the Middle and High Schools. But, with shifting personnel and educational philosophies among headmasters, this emphasis has all but disappeared. Faculty members referred students to preceptors or the students could "drop in" on their own. This practice continues, and the Preceptorial Room, especially in the High School, is typically full of students, even more so around quiz and examination times.

Thus Dalton, as it is today, took shape during the Barr administration. Success is measurable here by simply looking at the rich curriculum, interesting and talented student body and staff, impressive physical plant, financial stability, and college admissions. Yet Dalton, under Donald Barr, was rife with controversy that erupted in what could be termed the "Great Schism," in 1970. Furthermore, four years later, the Headmaster resigned without warning.

A number of underlying causes provided for the unrest and tension during the Barr years. The first was the decade itself. The second was the rapid increase in school size and the accompanying dislocation. Almost every informant discussed school size as a problem. Additionally, a report prepared by E. Belvin Williams for the Education Policies Committee of the Board of Trustees, on December 2, 1971, focused on this issue. Statements such as "a sense of smallness, camaraderie and intimacy has been lost," "it feels too big," and "it seems crowded," appear. However, Mr. Williams countered these statements with the opposing view that school mirrors the real world—"e.g., reduced space." Whatever the case, people who experienced Dalton before it became a large school or during the process of its expansion had adjustment problems. Old Dalton families, very clannish, complained about being pushed out of the auxiliary services by the new people who brought money or fundraising expertise to the school or both. Students complained that they did not know their classmates' names or that they could not find seats in the lunchroom. Teachers complained that they no longer had classrooms but shared space, and were reduced to the status of traveling salesmen peddling their wares from classroom to classroom. Parents complained about the way high school students in various stages of undress leaned on the parked cars in front of the school building. The size of the High School enrollment alone was the same size as the entire school enrollment during Kittell's administration. Theft and vandalism increased.

A third factor in the general unrest was the style of this particular headmaster. Of all the heads of Dalton, Donald Barr most resembled its founder, Helen Parkhurst. Both had definite educational philosophies; both had a sense of style—or flamboyance; both loved publicity; and both could talk the most impecunious parents into dipping into their bank account to give a few dollars to Dalton. But "Parkie" was ubiquitous; Barr was not.

Helen Parkhurst administered Dalton almost tyrannically, often at random. But she was forgiven her faults because she was the founder of the school. Not until money problems became overwhelming did the trustees take matters into their own hands. Donald Barr, in style, was much like Parkhurst. He administered the school, in his own words, "by ukase"; he had little apparent rational organization; the crisis-solution method was the most popular way of solving problems. For many years, it worked.

Donald Barr assumed the responsibility for decision-making, arguing, "On my head be it."[55] He held his teachers in disdain, frequently criticizing them at public gatherings. He tolerated bizarre behavior in students who normally would have been expelled; he did not uniformly enforce school regulations.

And he loved to talk. At faculty meetings, parent meetings; on radio, television and in newspapers, magazines, from *The New York Times* to *Penthouse*, Donald Barr willingly gave his opinion on any topic that arose. He was urbane, witty, entertaining—"the give 'em Hell Headmaster." One informant present at fundraising cocktail parties stated that listening to Barr was like watching the *Tonight Show*, with Johnny Carson, nightly.

A fourth and very significant factor promoting unrest and perhaps leading directly to the movement to force Donald Barr's resignation in 1970, came about as a result of his stance on the use of drugs by Dalton students: the drug problem, of serious national proportions, was equally severe, though on a lesser scale, at Dalton. "We consider marijuana a dangerous drug. We have found that most narcotic users have a desire to entice others into their situation. Narcotic use is, therefore, a contagious disease, and its control is a responsibility of the community."[56] To this end, Barr would expel high school students who brought drugs into the school or who sold, gave, or offered drugs to other Dalton students on or off of school grounds. Marijuana users might, at the discretion of the Headmaster, undergo therapy as a condition of remaining at Dalton; in any of these cases, the Headmaster would evaluate the evidence as to the student's involvement. Rules in the Middle School were similar, except that expulsion was at the discretion of the Headmaster; and if the child or parents came forth with the evidence first, the child would not be expelled. Furthermore, a child who had been using drugs would not gain automatic admission to the High School.

Few Dalton parents would question Barr's stance regarding drugs in general; however, many parents were distressed over the school's policy for users "after hours." And many parents did not regard marijuana as a dangerous drug.

Two final factors contributing to Barr's stressful years at Dalton were his positions on politics and on dress, both of which mobilized the parents to action and divided the parent body into two camps.

On November 14-15 in 1969, a Vietnam moratorium was planned which would interfere with the school day on Friday. In Barr's words, "political absences would be treated 'non-politically'"; students who absented themselves would be subject to Saturday morning detention or "call-back." Donald Barr was a conservative in politics. He supported the war and had a son in the armed forces. His politics often rattled Dalton parents and students as he would freely share his ideas with them. Additionally, he supported a controversial, highly visible language teacher whose policies were much along the same lines as his own.

For a school which saw itself as valuing creativity and promoting self-expression, Barr's dress codes came as a shock. They affected both Middle and High School students. They came at a time when youngsters had exchanged the "mod" look for the Beatles fashions: "the hairy, mustached, bearded, beaded, fringed and embroidered costumes of the late sixties."[57] Army surplus was soon to follow.

Again, Barr took a firm stance. In a letter to parents dated March 1, 1967, he stated that "Bizarre or eccentric costumes are more suitable to the stage than to the classroom, and faddism in clothing and hair-style is alien to the philosophy of the Dalton School."[58] In reply, some of Barr's constituents objected to dress codes on the basis that the school should concern itself with children's minds rather than with matters of dress and grooming, and that creativity should take precedence over costume. Barr retorted that "the child who thinks that creativity is indicated by oddity of dress is getting a poor start in life."[59]

These conflicts led to open warfare between segments of the Dalton community. Although difficult to document, it is highly likely that the pro-Barr camp was composed mainly of families who were fairly new to the Dalton community, while the anti-Barr camp reflected Dalton's "Old Guard"—German Jews, Anglo-Saxon Protestants, serious artists and writers—more at home in the Dalton of Charlotte Durham than of Donald Barr. Perhaps the anti-Barr faction felt excluded or eclipsed by the pro-Barr faction; perhaps the school was changing too rapidly and not necessarily in the direction the anti-Barr camp might choose. Whatever the case, the pro-Barr faction ultimately prevailed.

At the raucous PTA meeting on the evening of March 15 in the 89th Street building's gymnasium, the anti-Barr faction found itself under a carefully organized attack. At stake this particular evening was the PTA presidency, occupied by anti-Barr supporter Dr. Myron Hofer, who by virtue of his office occupied a board seat. The objective of the pro-Barr supporters was to call for Dr. Hofer's impeachment and to replace him with Morris Levinson, a pro-Barr supporter.

In the unprecedented meeting several hundred Barr supporters angrily stamped their feet in unison on the gym floor, grabbed the microphone cords, hissed and booed anti-Barr speakers, thus rendering Barr's detractors impotent. These strategies proved successful. Dr. Hofer was impeached and replaced by Morris Levinson. Having met their objectives, one informant clearly remembers *Time Magazine* reporting that at the close of the meeting, participants "staggered out to their limousines and went home."

Donald Barr emerged from the fray of battle victorious. Subsequently, the board membership was reconstituted to reflect members favorable to Barr's conservative educational philosophy. Those who were opposed to Barr stepped down. Yet a scant four years after emerging victoriously from a battle which was publicized nationally as well as locally, Donald Barr resigned as headmaster of Dalton without any prior public indication of his intention to do so.

What prompted this action? The official reason given to the *New York Times* reporter, Gene I. Maeroff, was that Barr was in a disagreement with his twenty-member board "on the question of where the board's authority should yield to the headmaster's judgment."[60] Richard Ravitch, the board president at the time, agreed: "the issue is the prerogative of the board and the headmaster."[61]

It is telling that Barr's support came primarily from parents who found his hardline, conservative stance on dress and drugs particularly appealing amid the mayhem of the late 1960s and early 1970s. Perhaps it is safe to suggest that these same parents took comfort in Barr's more traditional rather than progressive approach to education; an approach that favored traditional demarcation of subject matter over integrated curriculum, and examinations and grades over project presentations and prose reports. In sum, an educational approach that would prepare students for life in the real world of cutthroat competition rather than for life on a hippie commune.

Telling too, is the fact that while the parents supported Barr, the majority of the faculty did not. Rather, they were critical of his style of leadership which, in his own words, was "rule by ukase." Perhaps this style might have been tolerated in a more traditional school at a different time in history; however in 1974 at Dalton, a school that had a strong tradition of respect for faculty opinion and for its inclusion in decision-making issues concerning curriculum and pedagogy, Barr's style was felt to be intolerable. Moreover it had not changed even though prior to the "civil war," many faculty members had been critical of his "highhandedness" and "inaccessibility." Rather, Barr's leadership style seemed to grow even more exclusive as if his victory signaled a vote of confidence for the restoration of the status quo ante bellum. Clearly, faculty expectations of change were at odds with the direction that the headmaster chose to pursue. As one faculty member remarked, it seemed to be a classic case in which "the operation was a success but the patient died."

By the 1970s, the school once again experienced financial difficulties due to expansion, unbridled spending, and a lack of careful planning. Barr, who had presided over a school that experienced unprecedented growth and riches, now had to consolidate the gains made and cut costs across the board. This was not Barr's forte. Barr was, above all, an intellectual, more at home in a library than buried in a ledger. What the job now required was as administrator who could cut costs, balance the budget, while still delivering to students a first-class education. Although Barr had presided over a school that had grown tremendously, nevertheless, he did not institute a rational form of governance for it. Rather, to many observers his way of doing business was thought to be that of reacting to situations as they presented themselves, rather than careful planning and rational implementation. In sum, the school in 1974 required a different type of head than Barr, one who possessed administrative skills rather than pizzaz. While Donald Barr had succeeded in making Dalton a "hot" school, nevertheless, his successor would have to assume the twin tasks of fiscal solvency and rational management in order to ensure the school's future. Whether or not this could be done in a manner consistent with Dalton's progressive heritage would be the challenge for the next head of Dalton.

Donald Barr's tenure as headmaster of Dalton ended in June, 1974. By the time Barr resigned in 1974, the student body increased from about 560 to over 1,200 and the school admitted boys into the High School. He had imposed his own style of academic traditionalism upon the progressive foundation of the school. Dalton became more traditional by moving away from interdisciplinary curricula to more traditional academic disciplines and by creating an atmosphere of academic rigor. Barr had altered but hardly eliminated the Dalton Plan. Most notably, he had succeeded in making Dalton a desirable place for newly affluent New Yorkers to send their children.

The Dunnan Years (1975–1997): Elite Education with Vestiges of Progressivism

Gardner Dunnan served as Dalton's headmaster from 1975 to 1997. He came to Dalton in 1975 after a career as a public school administrator in a number of affluent suburban school districts—the first head to come from the public sector, rather than from an independent school world, or in Barr's case, the university. During his years at Dalton, Dunnan placed the school on sound financial footing, instituted a rational bureaucratic organization, expanded and improved the physical plant, and made a serious commitment to technology. All the while, the school's graduates continued to enter prestigious colleges and universities, reflecting the goals of the current parent body. Today, the Dalton School is an achievement-oriented, rigorous, college preparatory school, with only vestiges of its early progressive practices. Although the staff still pay lip service to the Dalton Plan, and the school is more progressive than most public schools, it is a far cry from the school Helen Parkhurst founded.

We have seen that the Dalton Plan underwent a gradual transformation in the 55 years between Parkhurst and Barr and, although the Dunnan administration tried to preserve elements of the Plan, still the size of school, the conservatism of achievement-oriented parents, outside pressures— particularly emphasis on credentials and standards—and the leadership's reluctance to challenge this emphasis militated against preserving the Dalton Plan. Nevertheless, the familiar components of the Dalton Plan—House, Lab and Assignment—were still introduced in the First Program to varying degrees and still "provide a basic structure for the education of the young, but are most clearly visible in the higher grades."[62] Most clearly visible in the First Program is House, which is described as "the classroom setting" and the House Advisor as the teacher. For the First Program students, [the Assignment] a contractual agreement between the student and the teacher—a primary supplement to daily class and homework—is introduced in the second grade, where given at first on a weekly basis, it outlines for the student a problem or area to study, suggests ways to research and solve the problem, while providing options for satisfying its requirements[63] Laboratory time in the First Program is often classroom work time, "during which students·pursue any of the areas of study for which they have contracted with the teacher or work independently on group assignments."[64]

Thus, in the First Program the Dalton Plan operates primarily through the House, which serves the function of allowing children to perform both as individuals and as members of a group, realizing their individual potentials, yet allowing them to experience "group life." Secondarily, the Assignment, which begins in second grade, invites the children to learn how to budget their time and teaches them responsibility.

While the First Program at Dalton may seem progressive to visitors, and may be progressive compared to other independent schools, it is hardly progressive, noted its former director Stanley Seidman, "in terms of Dewey and Parkhurst."[65] For example, far more mixed grading existed under Parkhurst than at Dalton today; then, too, in Parkhurst's school, students could conceivably work on a single project for an entire year. What *is* progressive about the First Program today, continued Seidman, "is the way in which it encourages autonomy. There is a willingness to let kids become independent and grow on their own; there is much more freedom for kids."[66]

Of the three divisions at Dalton, the Middle School appears to be the most successful at preserving and using the Dalton Plan although, according to the NYSAIS (New York State Association of Independent Schools) evaluators who visited the school in 1985, "The committee was both impressed by and disappointed by the three essentials of the Dalton Plan, House, Lab and Assignment. The applications of these essentials varied enormously from teacher to teacher. Some teachers were devoted to all three; others avoided one or more."[67] Although there have been subsequent attempts to address this critique, they have neither been systematic nor sustained. Furthermore, this situation has worsened as more teachers with institutional memories retire.

In grades six through eight, House now consists of a single grade, usually fifteen to sixteen students in size, and meets either in the mornings or afternoons depending upon the grade level, two times a week for fifty minutes. Students check in with House Advisors between 8:10 and 8:20; they check out in the afternoons, "[It's] just like a pit stop," according to one informant. In grades four and five, the House Advisor is also the student's social studies, English, or math teacher, and House meets daily. In the "lower Houses," attention focuses on providing the House Advisor more time to work with his or her own students. The consensus among informants is that House "is a real thing regarding the House Advisor and the student but it is not connected to the community anymore."

House Advisors introduce Middle School students to Laboratory time or "Lab." Lab times are inserted into the child's schedule, usually for two periods a week. This procedure works well if the teachers the students must confer with are free; however, the nature of Lab time has evolved from an extension of the class (that is, enrichment) to remediation, without ensuring that students needing help will find their teachers accessible. But teachers do have the option of turning one of their class periods into Lab since classes meet four times per week, and one of those times is a double period.

Under Dunnan, Dalton set out to reconsider the role of the Assignment. In a document entitled "Assignment on the Assignment," the Associate Headmaster described the Assignment this way:

(1)   requirements which reflect an awareness of different levels of student ability as well as of different learning styles;

(2)   themes and approaches which make possible the interdisciplinary synthesis for which Dr. [sic] Parkhurst called;

(3)   clear but not overbearing directions which stimulate reflection, inquiry and an authentic encounter with human questions and creates occasions for student-faculty (Labs) and student-student discussions.[68]

Discrepancies between the historical intent of the Assignment and its actual use constantly arise. The result, as one informant noted, is that when children are sick, their mothers call up and ask for homework and books. Neither the parents nor the students appear to realize that the *homework* is the Assignment. Thus the question teachers pose, both in the Middle and High Schools (and it goes unanswered) is, How can they internalize the Assignment within the Dalton community?

According to an issue of *The Daltonian* that featured articles on the Assignment, it is just as problematic for the students and teachers in the High School. One article in particular noted how Assignments vary in quality from class to class and that some teachers use them conscientiously while others do not. Another article noted the students' under-utilization of the Assignment. A preceptor in the High School observed that,

When I ask to see an assignment, I generally get an unwrinkled, pristine assignment never before consulted, and from this I conclude that the assignment seems more a peripheral than an integral part of a student's life. I do not remember the assignment evolving from an individualized, often utilized contractual agreement between student-teacher body of material, but for whatever the reason, I currently see the assignment as less of a contract and more of a calendar of events.[69]

While others concur that the Assignment in the High School has become a "calendar of events," one student thought that the Assignment functioned more as a vehicle for measuring the accountability of individual teachers for the curriculum: "Currently, it [the Assignment] is used to outline a student's work for an extended period of time. I feel that it is also used to keep the teacher on the right path in class." Furthermore, the student continued,

> the fact is, that the function of the assignment has decreased severely over the last decade. What once played a major role in the student/teacher relationship of a Dalton education is now only a symbol. It is used as an excuse to assign more homework under the pretense that the students ration their time in advance so that they have ample time for their work.[70]

But more than just the Assignment has become problematic in the High School. The NYSAIS report of the April, 1986, visiting committee to the school suggested that "The Dalton Plan of House Lab and Assignment be vigorously reexamined . . . at the moment, Dalton is not consistently or fully maximizing the use of this creative concept."[71] Furthermore, the visiting committee recommended that the school determine whether or not the schedule in the High School is conducive to the Dalton Plan; that the school "determine which aspects of the progressive legacy of Helen Parkhurst . . . are viable today" and devote school-wide faculty meetings to this discussion; and that new faculty members attend monthly meetings to discuss "what they have learned about The Dalton Plan and how it works."[72]

House in the High School is as problematic as the Assignment. House once functioned as an important student link to the Dalton community, but in the High School House has varied from single-age grading to mixed-age grading and although the number of students has remained constant at about sixteen, its composition, time slots, and even purposes have varied—at least partly because the High School saw five different directors between 1975 and 1991. While younger students retain an allegiance to House, older students, plagued by the nagging reality of college admissions, appear to play it down. Thus, it may now function primarily as a conduit for information from teachers to students concerning their progress; secondarily, it may function as a vehicle for sharing school-wide concerns or policies. At the time of the NYSAIS report, House had indeed strayed from the original intent, to function as "the *primary* social unit of the school." Thus, the evaluators urged that the Dalton High School restore the House Plan to its original function; develop a curriculum that takes advantage of its informal, nonthreatening forum; and support House Advisors with in-service programs.[73]

House is not a course, and students do not receive grades for it per se; rather they receive House reports, and therefore, House attendance in the High School has been problematic. Its time slots have been shifted; sanctions for missing House have been imposed, then dropped; thus ultimately, attendance in House may depend upon which homework assignments are due or whether the House advisor exudes charisma or wields power within the community (that is to say whether the House advisor is also the headmaster or a key administrator in the High School).

Lab, the final component of the Dalton Plan, has also come under attack, first because of the shrinking amount of laboratory time students actually have, and second, because of the way in which it has been reinterpreted. When he became Headmaster, Dunnan abandoned the three-day, sixty-minute class schedule in the High School in favor of a schedule of four days, with forty-five or fifty-minute periods; thus he reduced both the amount of Lab time for students and the availability of teachers. One informant noted that she felt "there was a perception on the part of the Headmaster that Dalton teachers weren't working hard enough and needed to be scheduled into more classes."

Many faculty members refer to the high energy level teaching at Dalton requires, and indeed, one of them concluded that "Dalton is not just a job. It's an encompassing way of life." Nevertheless, a sense of a lack of trust in the faculty often prevails. Thus, a policy that might have once have been implemented so as to share faculty between divisions of the school or in response to particular schedule concerns may now be seen as carrying out a hidden agenda. Whatever the intent, the reduction of laboratory time and the introduction of more classes inexorably altered the concept.

In previous administrations, Lab functioned as an extension of the classroom. It might be individuals meeting with teachers to discuss topics not broached in class; it might be group labs, organized by students who had similar lab times; it was generally a place to explore ideas and a place for clarification as well. Today, however, informants note that "the concept of

Lab has been remedial—it's a stigma to go to Lab." Furthermore, students interviewed in the March 18, 1988, issue of *The Daltonian* pointed to the futility of going to Lab, since the same person explains again, in the same language, what you failed to understand the first time in class. Some students continue to use Lab wisely but again usually for clarification or as one informant noted, "to haggle over a grade on a paper or exam." Clearly, as the NYSAIS group indicated, the components of the Dalton Plan should be reexamined in light of the demands of the schedule, and perhaps within the context of the different educational and societal concerns that originally inspired Helen Parkhurst to create her progressive vision, the Dalton Plan.

An innovation in curriculum and pedagogy at Dalton, one that illustrates the importance the Dunnan administration attached to technology, is the project called "Education for the Twenty-first Century." Based on the premise that multi-media systems will replace traditional modes of instruction in communication and computation, the project would formulate a new system prototypical of education delivery relying on the intensive use of multi-media information technologies as the primary means of conveying cultural content of education.[74] The project led to the creation of the New Laboratory for Teaching and Learning at Dalton, funded in 1991 by a two-million-dollar gift from a former Dalton parent and trustee, Robert Tishman.

Reactions to the Laboratory for Teaching and Learning have been mixed. Enthusiastic users of multi-media technology endorse it as a welcome addition that promises to enhance classroom instruction, particularly since all the students have e-mail accounts and can communicate with each other and their teachers from home. Others, however, meet the claim that multi-media technology will eclipse book learning with skepticism and view the New Laboratory as "glitz" or window-dressing, more to promote image than contribute substance.

Dunnan considered the Dalton Technology Plan, as it is now called, the key connection between past and present. He argued that technology has become the means through which the Dalton Plan now operates, facilitating problem solving, individualized instruction, and group work. But Dunnan's optimism notwithstanding, whether or not the Dalton Technology Plan reflects the more progressive aspects of Parkhurst's vision, remains an open question. Currently, the Technology Plan is undergoing revision and one can speculate on how central technology will affect instruction and what forms it will take.

Evident in this chapter is the fact that Dalton has undergone a further transformation from Barr to Dunnan. Thus it is necessary to pose the question, what is the ethos, "the enduring values or character of the school community"[75] that emerged during the administration of Gardner P. Dunnan? Informants agree that "clearly the school is a reflection of the personality of the principal"; also, that "there is little institutional memory." Rather, the Dalton Plan is often dredged up "to justify our educational priorities." The consensus is, however, that for Dunnan, "the central value is change." One informant offers three words to describe the Dunnan administration: "change, flexibility, movement." Another source urged as I described my project to her, "Quickly write it before it changes." That Dalton has indeed changed since 1975 when Gardner P. Dunnan became the headmaster of a financially troubled, poorly managed, independent school with a progressive tradition is evident. But the school not only reflects the personality of the headmaster; it is influenced by a larger configuration of teachers, parents, neighborhood, community, and societal concerns. And as progressive education has waxed and waned in educational circles, so has the Dalton Plan with its three components: House, Laboratory, Assignment.

What about Gardner Dunnan's personal style and philosophy of education? That he created a rational bureaucratic model comes through loud and clear. That he was first and foremost, the final decision-maker is not always as evident; in part this is masked by his bureaucracy; in part this was due to his low-key affable, personal style.

Board minutes and correspondence reveal that Gardner Dunnan set agendas for committees of both trustees and faculty. Indeed, it was Dunnan who approached the Faculty Salaries, Benefits, and Conditions of Employment each year to tell the committee what it should reasonably expect and therefore, request in the way of a raise. It is Dunnan as well who dismissed editors of the student paper or its faculty advisor at his discretion, or even a divisional director. What comes through is the fact that a mechanism existed for running the school but the head in this case, nevertheless, exercised his authority as he saw fit.

Discerning Dunnan's educational philosophy is a more difficult task due to the ever-changing, somewhat trendy nature of the slogan he adopted for the school each year. Clearly, from the reading he encouraged the faculty to do, when he first came to Dalton, Dunnan was very much influenced by the revival of progressive education, as defined by Diane Ravitch, or of informal education, according to Cuban. Shortly after he arrived, he invited educational historian, trustee and parent, Lawrence A. Cremin, to address the faculty. Predictably, Cremin urged the school to act boldly and return to its progressive roots; that in the end, colleges would continue to accept Dalton students, just as they had in the Eight Year Study agreement. Further, he urged that Dalton join with other schools and refuse to grade students; rather, assess them through prose reports without grades—the standard report format of Parkhurst and Durham's administrations. This did not occur, although there has been serious discussion recently in the High School of eliminating advanced placement classes, which often results in tracking and competition.

What has occurred in the school has been a concern for academic rigor and accountability. To these ends, the High School has been transformed into a serious, demanding environment in which students in required courses follow common assignments and take common exams. It has become a place where on any given day, visitors to the fifth or sixth floors of the school, predominately High School floors, will witness teacher-centered traditional style pedagogy in action. Sadly, one informant who attempted to be faithful to progressive pedagogy reported that she was accused by her former chairman of not teaching her class because when he walked by her door he did not see her in front of her class. Rather, she was sitting among her students in a circle, a practice he was obviously unfamiliar with.

In Spring, 1997, both Gardner Dunnan and Associate Headmaster Frank Moretti resigned. By the end of the Dunnan regime in 1997, both the Dalton students and the administration reflected the conservatism sweeping the country. Even though issues of alcohol and drugs, AIDS, and cheating on exams proliferate, the driving preoccupation of most Dalton High School students is gaining admission to a *very* select college, preferably an Ivy League institution, and succeeding in business. Thus, as early as grade nine students in the High School enroll in the Stanley Kaplan Test Preparation Service to prepare for the SATs and Achievement tests. The new equation, it seems, is excellence plus achievement equals Eastern establishment (preferably Ivy League) college or university. The Admissions catalogue, the *Alumni News*, and *The Daltonian* all display prominently college destinations of Dalton graduates.

The reasons for Dunnan's resignation reflected this conservatism, especially its concern for the school being a place that teaches morals and values. During the "Year of Values and Ethics," Dunnan "resigned under pressure saying his decision was prompted by trustees' concerns about both the leadership of the school and his personal life."[76] As one New York newspaper reported:

> But on March 11, the Year of Values and Ethics took on a dark, ironic note—ethics qua Friedrich Nietzsche, perhaps—as Dr. Gardner Dunnan, the school's headmaster and master fund-raiser since 1975, announced he was resigning. The reason: He was under pressure from the Dalton board of trustees after an extramarital affair he was conducting with a special education teacher, Francee Sugar, who is also married, became public. "My circumstances have divided the Dalton community," he wrote in his resignation letter. Students were not unaware of their headmaster's romantic situation. "I'd say 90 percent of the school knew for the past three months," a sophomore Dalton student told the *Observer*.[77]

In a *New York Magazine* article about the "fast" lives of New York City independent school adolescents, Dunnan's troubles received attention. One parent, herself a Dalton graduate asked, "Don't you think the role of the headmaster in a school is one of moral leadership? You can't fuck your subordinate and break up your happy home and stake a claim to morality." A fellow parent stated, "The guy put a sign on his butt that said FIRE ME. If a student is caught cheating, how does he deal with that? He's *really* a cheater."[78]

The parent outrage about Dunnan's affair seemed a little ironic at a school historically known for tolerance and unconventional behavior. Although it appears to have reflected a new conservative emphasis on family values, some believe there was more to Dunnan's resignation. Although no informant would go on record, and the Dalton Board publicly praised him for his excellent record as a fund-raiser, some informants indicated that Dunnan and Moretti's spending and other financial matters displeased the Board.[79]

During his long tenure, Gardner Dunnan had to cope with running a financially troubled school, bringing to it a rational form of organization, attracting a steady flow of applicants to its doors, placing its graduates in prestigious colleges and universities while also addressing the pressing need for diversity, for permanent funding and for space. The question unanswered here is this: would it have been possible to address the myriad problems of the school and to have maintained its progressive philosophy as well? Clearly, Dunnan created a school whose graduates attend some of the finest colleges and universities in this country. Clearly, his administration represented a success story but at what cost to the school? His embarrassing departure, although tarnishing his reputation, does not erase his successes, nor should it obscure the larger questions about the future of progressive education his years have raised. The lesson Dunnan offers to progressives is a disturbing one, for he has demonstrated through his administration that survival may necessitate some form of compromise with the school's progressive roots. It is possible that progressive education, such as the Dalton Plan, may not be feasible given the current constraints under which the school operates and that it is best to forget the past. Although copies of an article appearing in the *Phi Delta Kappan*, entitled "To Teach Responsibility, Bring Back The Dalton Plan" were circulated by the headmaster's office to the faculty, the homage paid to Dalton's progressive roots seemed more rhetoric than reality.[80] Whether this was due to a reluctance of the headmaster to commit himself to an educational philosophy which may be unpopular and may prove unfeasible is uncertain. However, it may well be the example of Dalton indicates that progressive education in its original philosophy and practice may have to be drastically altered if it is to survive.

Conclusion

The Dalton of Helen Parkhurst reflected the progressive movements of its time: often chaotic and disorganized, but at the same time intimate, caring, nurturing, familial, and child-centered. It concerned itself with child growth and development and community and social service, and it strove to effect a synthesis between the affective and cognitive domains of the child.

Under Charlotte Durham, who inherited a financially troubled school, Dalton was able to retain its child-centered pedagogy and its caring and familial orientation, while placing more emphasis on academic rigor. It also ran in a more orderly and rational fashion and became perhaps less experimental and more a part of the traditional New York City independent school community. In essence, Charlotte Durham's genius was to create a tradition out of a progressive experiment, using the Dalton Plan as its guiding ritual.

Under Donald Barr, the parent constituency began to change, including a greater proportion of the recently affluent. The curriculum and physical plant expanded, enrollment more than doubled, the High School became coeducational, and the emphasis on academic rigor and achievement intensified still more. Reflecting an actual antipathy for progressive education, which he equated with anti-intellectual and permissive miseducation, Barr began to transform Dalton into a large, academically competitive, fashionable and—even trendy—institution. He created a "hot," desirable school.

Gardner Dunnan continued Dalton's transformation into an organized, efficient, selective and academically rigorous institution. He enlarged the physical plant and initiated the Dalton Technology Plan, which he promoted as the link between the progressivism of Helen Parkhurst and the Dalton of modernity. His resignation in the spring of 1997, after 23 years as head of the school, left many wondering what direction Dalton would take.

Currently, the original Dalton Plan is alive but not necessarily well. Although House, Lab, and Assignment still exist, they no longer serve as the linchpin of the school and they are implemented inconsistently, without a clear focus on their exact meanings and functions. The school now focuses on academic rigor and excellence, with technology as the panacea for an eroded progressive philosophy.

This insistent ethos of achievement and competition troubles many at Dalton who remember the past. As one former student stated, "Perhaps I should just accept the fact that Dalton is no longer guided by the words of Helen Parkhurst and that when we now use the term Dalton Plan, we refer to whatever philosophy the administration is presently purveying."[81] Another, commenting on the change in the school's ambiance during his fifteen years at Dalton from pre-school through twelfth grade, observed that

The Dalton Plan is supposed to be student and teacher working together, developing a relationship, and maybe even being friends. What has happened to Dalton in these past fifteen years? When I was in eighth grade, I was friendly with almost all of my teachers. I would go to them with problems, and they would help me. Now that simply isn't true. With the exception of a few and, of course, my friends, I feel alone at Dalton. I feel it is me against them. Maybe this isn't true for everyone, but it is for me and I felt I had to say something.[82]

One parent and alumna, commenting on the changes stated, "The emphasis used to be on a love of learning. Now it's very directed toward getting people into college and raising money instead of being the wonderful place it used to be if you were interested in learning."[83] A former teacher added, "Dalton [of the past] just didn't fit into the mold of other great schools; it had a lot of creative people who each played their own symphony."[84]

Two revealing anecdotes indicate how far the Dalton School has moved from its progressive heritage. First, when asked about the Dalton Plan, a new Dalton teacher thought it was the school's medical insurance plan. Second, commenting on my book on the school, a recent Dalton alumnus remarked that he never knew Dalton had been a progressive school.

That the Dalton School remains a distinctly different school today is indisputable. Whether the changes it underwent guaranteed its survival or were inevitable in any event is a difficult and complex question that would require a careful evaluation of a multitude of historical, organizational, and sociological factors affecting school change, including the history of educational reform in general, changes in the nation's and New York City's culture, and trends in independent school leadership.[85] What is clear is that the Dalton School has been greatly transformed from the school Helen Parkhurst founded. But of course the world has changed too, and far more dramatically.

BUILDING A NEW DEAL COMMUNITY: PROGRESSIVE EDUCATION AT ARTHURDALE

Daniel Perlstein and Sam Stack

The story of progressive education at Arthurdale begins in the Scott's Run coal camps of northern West Virginia, near Morgantown, just south of the Pennsylvania border. The site of some of the most wretched poverty in the United States, Scott's Run became a focal point of New Deal reformers.[1] They established Arthurdale as a resettlement for impoverished families from Scott's Run and placed education at the heart their program. In its time, during the 1930s, the community was home to one of the United States' most famous experiments in progressive education.

Unlike private schools that catered to affluent families, Arthurdale offered progressive education to several hundred of America's most disadvantaged students. Under the leadership of Elsie Ripley Clapp, Arthurdale developed a system of community-centered schooling. Organizing curriculum and activities around the needs and desires of the poor, Arthurdale's schools not only promoted the development of the individual but also played a pivotal role in the revitalization and transformation of community life. John Dewey thought that Arthurdale possessed "extraordinary significance for education,"[2] and his view was so widely shared that as many as 150 visitors a week found their way to Arthurdale.[3]

Despite its vitality and fame, however, Arthurdale's experiment in progressive education was short-lived. Although community-centered progressive education fostered learning and citizen involvement, local democracy could not counteract the political and economic forces devastating Depression-era America. This chapter explores the relationship between the progressive practices developed in Arthurdale's schools and the social divisions that shaped the lives of its inhabitants. It illuminates the complex role of race and class in progressive theory and practice, and thus illustrates tensions between the sometimes complementary, sometimes competing demands of community and democracy as progressive ideals.

Envisioning Education for Community Revitalization

Arthurdale was one of several subsistence homestead communities established as part of the New Deal's effort to ameliorate the lives of people "stranded" in places where declining industrial production precluded self-sufficiency. Homesteaders received enough land to grow food for their families, thus allowing residents to regain their dignity as they escaped want. Reformers envisaged residents supplementing their small-scale farming with part-time employment. After a 1933 visit by Eleanor Roosevelt to Scott's Run, the nearby Arthur farm was developed as the prototype homestead community.[4]

Scott's Run was an area of extraordinary natural wealth and human misery. Even before the advent of the Depression, overproduction had given way to declining output and initiated years of unemployment and hardship.[5] When the mines closed, electricity and the pumps that supplied the camps with clean water were shut off.[6] Amid one of the richest coal veins in the United States, sewage ran raw in fetid creeks. Inhabitants, observed Associated Press reporter and Eleanor Roosevelt-confidante Lorena Hickok, used the creek water

> for drinking, cooking and washing and everything imaginable. On either side of the street were ramshackle houses black with coal dust, which most Americans would not consider fit for pigs. And in those houses every night children went to sleep hungry, on piles of bug-infested rags, spread out on the floors.[7]

Hunger-weakened families succumbed to malnutrition, diphtheria, typhoid, and other diseases. When Elsie Clapp visited the area in order to assess its educational needs, the snow was deep and the temperature bitterly cold. People in the camps, she found, "lived under conditions near my idea of hell."[8] "You ain't never goin' to make nothin' of us," one miner told Clapp. "We're like them old apple trees out there, all gnarled and twisted."[9] Camp dwellers, Eleanor Roosevelt would recollect at a 1939 press conference, "were like people walking around dead. They were alive, but they were dead as far as any real living was concerned."[10]

Arthurdale's planners realized that merely moving miners and their families from one area to another and giving them land would not produce the glue to bond residents into a living community. At the same time, reformers were convinced that life in the mine camps had left the residents unable to develop such bonds on their own. By means of cooperative communities, homestead planners sought to restore the camp dwellers' capacity to direct their own lives.

Because they simultaneously understood the profound scars of privation and held to the democratic belief that the poor could learn to participate fully in American life, reformers placed education at the core of their work.[11] Arthurdale's dispossessed miners, Eleanor Roosevelt told a resettlement conference, "must be taught to live."[12] The commitment to education was shared by the homesteaders themselves. Shortly before Mrs. Roosevelt's visit to Scott's Run, she received a letter from several women living in the area. "We consider it very important," they wrote, "to have a schoolhouse—also a community house which could be used for a kindergarten on weekday mornings, for recreation and for a reading center in the evening, and a place of worship on Sundays."[13]

Even before the federal homestead project, relief workers had initiated programs to counter the physical and psychological effects of life in the idle coal camps. Together with other private and government agencies, the American Friends Service Committee (AFSC) established a broad revitalization effort. Garden clubs helped people to farm and can their own food. The Mountaineer Craftsman's Cooperative Association provided fulfilling employment by teaching woodworking skills and furniture making, and then helping to market the products. Playground construction provided children safe and happy havens.[14]

The AFSC effort dovetailed with ideals that had long captivated the Roosevelts, who believed that resettlements could simultaneously model a new Jeffersonian civilization and relieve the poor, thus wedding back-to-nature yearnings with social engineering.[15] After her 1933 visit to Scott's Run, Eleanor Roosevelt concluded that an Arthurdale homestead could build on AFSC's efforts and serve as a national research and exhibition center, displaying methods of social reconstruction in much the way agricultural extension stations demonstrated efficient farming practices. Arthurdale, Mrs. Roosevelt envisioned, would be "a social experiment in community life which centers around its school."[16]

Eleanor Roosevelt contributed generously to the development of Arthurdale and recruited others, notably financier Bernard Baruch, to join her in underwriting Arthurdale's expansive educational program. In addition, Mrs. Roosevelt secured expert advice for the settlement. Joining her in planning Arthurdale's school were such noted educators as John Dewey, Lucy Sprague Mitchell, Progressive Education Association President Carson Ryan, AFSC executive Clarence Pickett, and various local education officials from West Virginia. The planners tapped Elsie Clapp as Director of Arthurdale School and Community Activities.[17]

Elsie Clapp came to her work in Arthurdale with impressive credentials as a progressive educator. Born in Brooklyn in 1879, Clapp was a sophomore at Vassar College when she read John Dewey's *School and Society*, and was captivated by the vision of education it described.[18] After studying with Dewey at Columbia University, Clapp served as his teaching assistant on and off for fifteen years. At the same time, she worked at such progressive schools as City and Country and Horace Mann. Clapp's 1928 *Progressive Education* article, "Children's Mathematics," was a model articulation of Deweyan notions of active learning.[19] In 1929, Clapp became principal of the Rogers Clark Ballard Memorial School, a rural progressive school near Louisville, Kentucky, where she gained a national reputation as an authority on progressive education in rural communities.

Based on her work at the Ballard School, Clapp was hired to be director of schools for the new Arthurdale project. Arthurdale, according to Clapp, was "a test and proof of the ideal of rehabilitation."[20] "People who have lived for from three to five years in Scott's Run," she noted, "are unlikely to have come off unscathed."[21] Among the effects of life in the idle mining camps was the atrophying of intellectual life. When a mine ceased operation or a miner became too old to work, Clarence Pickett argued in *Progressive Education*, "the occasion for the use of [the miner's] skill is gone [and] he has then ceased to be able to use his one capacity." Community-building, on the other hand, could restore what Pickett called the "opportunity for the intelligent use of ability."[22]

Reformers believed that in order to promote the revitalization of coal camp residents and restore communal bonds, schools had to move beyond their traditional curriculum and pedagogy. Milburn Wilson headed the Department of the Interior's Division of Subsistence Homesteads. "Only by developing a critical sense, a broader point of view and a creative imagination," Wilson argued,

> does education contribute to the difficult task of adjustment. Only this type of education would permit necessary social experimentation to be carried out in a democratic atmosphere. . . . Only this type of education could lead to the consideration and the questioning of fundamental values.[23]

Just as community life was "born of the interaction of thinking and doing," Clapp echoed, schools ought to be a "place used freely . . . for all the needs of living and learning."[24]

Community Schooling in Practice

School began in the Arthurdale community in the fall of 1934, following the completion of the first fifty houses for the homesteaders. Working even before school buildings had been constructed, Clapp and her staff immediately confronted the problem posed by homesteader morale. Seeing that homesteaders were "deeply stirred by new hope [but that] they could not shake off their ingrained feeling of insecurity," Clapp organized schooling around the conviction "that in every case the child's improvement hinged upon his parents' gains in security and contentment."[25] By making the school the center of social, medical and leisure activities, educators were able to simultaneously meet the health needs of homestead families, to build a sense of community, and to gain the trust needed for education to progress.

The very architecture of Arthurdale's schools reflected progressive pedagogy and a desire to meet community needs. Homesteaders helped design the school structures as well as build them. To convey communal unity, school buildings were similar in style to Arthurdale's homes. All the school buildings were detached both to inhibit the spread of disease and to allow the possibility of expansion, and their designs were based on the needs of the children at each grade level. Plans called for playgrounds, gardens, and plenty of land in close proximity to the woods, where children could relate subject matter to the rural environment.[26]

Elsie Clapp and architect Steward Wagner were particularly proud of how the buildings linked education with community life. The high school housed a greenhouse and school-community library. The recreation building, designed for both school and community functions, had a full-size basketball court, showers and dressing rooms, a large stage for plays and concerts with space in the wings for set construction, and room for community meetings. Because it would be the most heavily used school structure, the recreation building was strategically placed near the main road. The school center building housed the community director's office, a savings bank, canning and home economics rooms, a sewing room, food demonstration rooms, and the cafeteria, where mothers could prepare school lunches for the children.[27] As Steward Wagner observed the school buildings

increased the vitality and the individuality of the community. . . . We realized with each group in the school the way a building may shape and expand the character of the life and work that go on in it.[28]

Arthurdale's teachers made effective use of the progressive organization of school spaces. Along with Clapp and Wagner, early childhood educator Jessie Stanton took the lead in designing the nursery school structure and program. The nursery school was constructed to provide bright, airy spaces where children could play freely. Each nursery school classroom had its own exit to the playground and a sheltered area allowed children to play outdoors even in rainy weather. The nursery school's prenatal program and advisory services helped open the door for the school to reach out into the community. Well known for her work at New York's Harriett Johnson Nursery School, Stanton had come to nursery education through settlement work. Under her leadership, the Arthurdale nursery's expansive program included adult night classes and home visits to educate parents about hygiene, nutrition, and child development. The nursery's well-baby clinics practiced preventative medicine, a form of health care rarely available in the coal camps or the rural areas surrounding Arthurdale.[29]

Field trips throughout the community helped the nursery school children gain a better understanding of their environment, and particularly of the ways people work together for the community as a whole. Besides touring the local school complex, the children visited community construction sites, the community center building, the Mountaineer Craftsman's Cooperative, the local gas station, and the cooperative store. They saw their mothers and fathers working with others to build Arthurdale and create a better community. Even the bus many of them rode to school had been rebuilt by their fathers in the community garage. In the spring months, students observed plowing and planting, integral facets of life for children who often worked alongside their parents in the subsistence gardens that provided the families' food.[30]

Clapp's commitment to the social and educational value of field trips reflected her own experience teaching at Caroline Pratt's City and Country School. Like Pratt's students, the Arthurdale children used data from their field trips in their play back at school. They were encouraged to express themselves through art and storytelling in which they interpreted the events and excitement associated with constructing a community. Glenna Williams would recall decades after working as an assistant teacher in the nursery school how the educational activities were related to community life. Play with blocks, which were cut into quads, introduced fractions by allowing students to visualize the parts of a whole. Students reproduced with blocks what they observed on outings or at home: plows, tractors, barns, farms, houses, a blacksmith's shop, a doctor's office. Sometimes, Clapp observed, the blockbuilding led to unexpected projects; "all, however, reflect[ed] homestead life and living."[31] High school boys in the school shops and the local Mountaineer Craftsmen's Cooperative made the blocks to Jessie Stanton's specifications; thus the children's dramatic play with blocks doubly reinforced the role of the community in their lives.[32]

The physical, mental, emotional, and social health of the children improved dramatically at Arthurdale, and the nursery school became a centerpiece and showplace of the homestead community. "In an emphatic and pervasive sense," Clapp argued, the nursery school was "the heart and spring of community education at Arthurdale." Two things, according to Clapp, impressed visitors to the nursery school: first, "how children respond to patience and kindness from teachers, and second, how children's play reflects the life going on around them."[33]

The efforts to restore and enhance community life contributed beyond the nursery school. Under the direction of Ethel Carlisle, first graders undertook a study of farm life, an essential component of the homestead community. On frequent excursions, first graders made observations of their parents and other homesteaders plowing fields, threshing buckwheat, digging potatoes, or husking corn. Parents interrupted their work to share with the children what they knew and were doing, and the children continued their own discussions back at school. When cows were delivered to Arthurdale, the children inspected them, leading to weeks of discussions and to churning and tasting of butter. When a class garden spouted, the children wrote a group story about oats. By Arthurdale's second year, the first graders had embraced the homestead's cooperative spirit. "If one makes a school bus" with blocks, Ethel Carlisle observed, "the others build a school; if one makes a dairy, the others make trucks that deliver milk."[34]

Eunice Jones's second graders built a replica of the Arthurdale village with scrap lumber they collected throughout the project. As they located building materials, the second graders witnessed the actual construction of their community and planned in detail how their own construction was to take place. Children observed the use of various tools; they learned to use a level and a square in carpentry and a guide line in laying out stone masonry. In constructing their village, they learned such mathematical concepts as the relation of a part to a whole, equivalents, measures and measuring, and fractions. They also learned to cooperate and communicate, as they developed a common interest by working toward a shared end, broadening and enriching horizons that had been severely limited by life in the idle coal camps. The second graders, Jones recorded in her diary, "were so delighted" with their construction project that as they wrote a story about their village "they laughed and laughed."[35]

West Virginia teacher Sara Liston initiated a study of Indian life with her third-grade class. While not initially trained in progressive education methods, Liston adopted an activity-oriented format to implement learning-by-doing at Arthurdale. The students used materials from the local woods to build a small village and trading post: bark for a teepee, branches for meat-drying stands and looms, stones for the fireplace, berries for dyes.[36] Hands-on activities taught both the skills needed in Indian families and the ways Indian society relied on the talents of all individuals, working for the benefit of the group as a whole.

Under the direction of Elisabeth Sheffield, fourth graders integrated subject matter gathered from the cultural history of the homesteaders themselves. An old cabin on the Arthurdale property served as the locus of the fourth grade's study of pioneer life. Children cleaned the cabin and, in the school shop, made split-log benches, crude tables, a candle stand, a cradle, and a churn. They learned to knit, dip candles, dye with native pokeberries, goldenrod, and walnuts, and cook in pioneer style.[37]

Arthurdale's teachers did not neglect the teaching of such traditional school skills as spelling, penmanship and arithmetic; whereas in many schools such activities are supplemented or enriched by field trips, at Arthurdale academics grew out of community activities, highlighting the use rather than mere possession of skills. As they practiced the processes by which wool is made into cloth, Elisabeth Sheffield's fourth graders kept Wool Notebooks, which included detailed guidelines for washing, fluffing, carding, and weaving. When they turned to the processing of flax, their Flax Notebooks included information on rippling, braking, scunching, and hackling. Students also read about flax in the diaries of pioneers. Writing stories about early settlers in their History Notebooks imparted additional academic skills, and creating a drama about pioneer life further integrated hands-on learning, interdisciplinary study, and creative play.[38]

Pioneer activity not only taught manual and academic skills, but it also "quickened and satisfied the children's curiosities and interests, gave room for individual development," and encouraged the students to explore their concerns about family life.[39] In many ways, the experience of Arthurdale homesteaders making new lives in a new environment parallelled that of earlier pioneers. "Pioneer study," Clapp argued, "interprets present-day living to these children."[40] At the same time, pioneer study at Arthurdale allowed homesteaders scarred by the alien-ation and hopelessness of the mine camps to recover a sense of identity and belonging. "In gaining a future," Clapp reasoned, "the homesteaders seemed to have recovered their past, for in a way difficult to describe, the cabin Colonel Fairfax built so long ago on his land assured them that the life they had left when they went into the mines was theirs still."[41]

The log cabin offered educators an opportunity to reach out into the community and for the community to participate in the educational process. When the fourth grade began their study of pioneer life, almost half of the students' grandparents were still living in log cabins. Elders joined students in the pioneer study, and the log cabin inspired both adults and children with "an appreciation of that simple home life of which their mothers told them. They themselves are glad to find respect for their forebears."[42] The fourth-grade project thus both embodied and created a democratic sense of shared interests.

Before the rise of the industrial economy, progressives believed, domestic production had allowed pioneers to control and understand the labor though which they meet their needs. By contrast, Arthurdale's children, Clapp wrote,

> are living in a time long after the industrial revolution. They press a button for light, buy shoes or a dress—or, at least, goods—at a store. They take it all for granted. But after they have carded, spun, and woven wool, they start to understand more about materials; after they have tanned a hide, they begin to know more about what goes into making a pair of shoes; after they have cooked over an open fire; a stove has more value for them.[43]

Educators saw pioneer culture as a form of collective self-realization. By representing the necessity and opportunity for thoughtful activity, pioneer study afforded a powerful contrast to the physical and mental lethargy of the coal camps.

Arthurdale teachers experienced more difficulty with the fifth and sixth graders than with the younger students. The older children, according to Clapp, were less able than their younger siblings to shake off the lingering legacy of life in the camps. Although teacher Inez Funk observed all her students at home in order to guide them, the effects of malnutrition and lack of previous school attendance continued to haunt the children. Their need for remediation in math and reading was coupled with indifference to academic work. Shop seemed to be the only area that engaged the majority, and they readily fashioned such hand crafts and wooden models as dug-out canoes, looms, wool cards, flutes, a seed box, and a hornbook.[44]

The teachers of older students attempted to build on the interest in craft work. The study of West Virginia history and culture began with an examination of the practical activities through which groups of people had developed solutions to the "problems of food and shelter" in their environments.[45] Annabelle Mayor attended Arthurdale's high school and years later she would recall that

> I had weaving and home making but also had other classes. And the thing was, we did not worry too much about what was in the book, getting up and reciting what we read or studied in the book, but how it was applied to what was going on. Science class, math class and shop class were all sort of coordinated.[46]

The secondary students were haunted by their future as well as their past. Lacking job prospects, the older boys had difficulty focusing on school work, so the high school attempted to organize a curriculum that explored possible livelihoods by examining local resources and regional markets. A number of glass factories existed in the area, and students studied inorganic chemistry, geology, and history by studying and making glass. Students conducted extensive experiments to discover the proper fuels and temperature for the furnace they had built; they examined different chemical compounds for etching. The study of glass making clarified the techniques of production, illuminated the local environment, and enhanced academic skills. But Arthurdale lacked the capital with which to test glass making as a means of economic development. Similarly, an investigation of the possibility of opening a dairy led to the realization that "the milk business. . . is one of volume." As Clapp recognized, given the day's economic conditions, the school's program was insufficient to solve the boys' problem.[47]

The high school was more effective in fostering a spirit of cooperation and community within Arthurdale. "I think," recalled one student, "AHS can be considered an excellent trainer of citizenship,":

Not only did it give us the experience, but it gave us enough freedom to use our own creative ability and initiative. And our teachers were friendly guides and not absolute rulers. They taught us to be proud of our community, to utilize the resources and strive to make it the best community that we could. Our education was not divorced from life situation, but was an integral part of our lives.[48]

Pedagogy for Solidarity

Arthurdale's pedagogy of cooperative practical activity illuminated the bonds that unite citizens and the common culture that expresses those bonds. "A society," Dewey had argued in *School and Society*, "is a number of people held together because they are working along common lines, in a common spirit, and with reference to common aims. The common needs and aims demand a growing interchange of thought and growing unity of sympathetic feeling."[49] The fourth grade's log cabin embodied those social and cultural bonds, and Arthurdale, according to Dewey, demonstrated that the spirit of society was best seen and studied through an encounter with matters "local, present, and close by, [not the] pale and shadowy" abstractions that often passed for social study.[50]

All Deweyan education acknowledged the centrality of activity. Community schooling, however, involved more than the progressive commitment to activity-based learning. "A socialized school," according to Clapp, "uses all the means of learning which a progressive school anywhere employs. . . . But a community school has social ends of some sort in view, and arranges its plans and activities and gathers data for these."[51] Community needs and activities, according to the Plan for the School at Arthurdale, were "the laboratory through which the children [got] their educative experiences. . . . This means that the real learning experiences of the school [came] chiefly through the vocational life of the community."[52]

In rural areas, Clapp believed, the school "lives and moves in intimate association with its people. . . . It can, because of its position and the value of its work, penetrate and affect [their] lives."[53] By assuming social functions and being attentive to its surroundings, the school could also enrich its pedagogical work. Through such activities as dental and well-baby clinics, "gradually the desire for health was born, and the old fatalistic acceptance of death and illness, born of misery and poverty and ignorance, vanished." Teaching fathers how to farm their new plots and mothers how to prepare nutritious foods not only relieved the malnutrition of children; the possibility of productive work restored dignity, intelligence and hope to the parents.[54]

Community-centered education blurred the lines between school and other aspects of community life. Many teachers lived among the homesteaders, and Clapp discussed school plans with the many clubs and organizations that educators helped the homesteaders form. Parents made toys given as Christmas presents in the school shop. Parents and teachers worked together making shelves, tables, and bookcases for classrooms. Adult education began when women came together to prepare lunches for schoolchildren. Joining an adult cooking class gave nursery school teacher Ethel Wadsworth an opportunity to talk informally with mothers about their children, and canning lessons led to specific improvements in diet.[55] But in Clapp's eyes, community schooling above all unified educational experience with participation in civic and social life: "There is literally no division between learning and living. . . learning and living are one."[56] Schooling was transformed from an agency delivering a service into a "joint effort . . . not only shared but mutual."[57]

Although Clapp acted as an intermediary between the homesteaders and Washington in such varied matters as electricity rates, construction schedules, and clinic operations,[58] she was convinced that community schooling was grounded in "neighborly contacts" as teachers "shared in the common experience of adjusting to new conditions and, like other homesteaders . . . had to cope with problems of food, heat, shelter." Such teachers were "fellow-workers" who possessed an "authority not of position, but usable knowledge confirmed by actions and events."[59]

Teaching in a community school, according to Clapp, could not be reduced to "imposing" ideas or to "putting over . . . a fixed plan, a formula, or a ready-made organization." Rather, it responded to the community's needs and to "people's feelings and opinions, ways of doing and thinking . . . as they are revealed."[60] In training educators for other homesteads, Clapp presented narrowly technical matters of pedagogy, but she stressed as a "primary essential, the ways and means of working as a member of a community."[61]

At the same time as teachers were a part of the community, they were also its guide, integrating activities and supplying the intellectual framework with which the school could build on local interests, talents and resources.[62] "In rural communities," according to Clapp, "it is the school that introduces what is called culture. It brings the child into contact with facts and ideas which he would never know without its aid—literature, history, science, and world events."[63] Such teaching, according to Clapp, would enable students "to gain the knowledge they did not know they lacked."[64]

Clapp's community school ideal had placed her among the moderates in the Depression-era debates of progressive educators. When George Counts electrified the 1932 meeting of the Progressive Education Association with his address, "Dare Progressive Education Be Progressive?," Clapp was one of those asked to respond. She seconded Counts' view that child-centered education had neglected social problems and social life, but she rejected Counts' call for "indoctrination." Rather than pretending they were all-knowing and dictating ideological critiques of the social order, democratic teachers, Clapp believed, should learn with their students. "The process of living and learning and doing," she replied to Counts, was itself "revolutionizing."[65]

The community school, Clapp envisioned, "forgoes its separateness. It is influential because it belongs to its people. They share its ideas and ideals and its work. It takes from them as it gives to them." As if remembering her debate with George Counts, she continued, "There are no bounds, as far as I can see, to what it could accomplish in social reconstruction . . . . Changes in living and learning are not produced by imparting information about different conditions or by gathering statistical data about what exists, but by creating by people, with people, for people."[66]

The Persistence of Social Division

The ideal of the school as a hub, indeed engine, of democratic community life had deep roots in the history of progressive education. Whether in isolated rural communities or heterogeneous industrial cities, social antagonisms, according to this view, reflected the limited consciousness of those involved and therefore might be overcome by education. Clapp believed that by addressing the concrete problems faced by all, the schools could revive the cooperative, democratic spirit she believed to have characterized rural, preindustrial American life.[67]

Even faced with the systemic dislocations of the Depression, Clapp held to the view that education could create community feeling. This effacement of social divisions, so problematic as broad social policy, generated the considerable solidarity and pedagogical strength in Clapp's work. Ultimately though, the divisions of the wider society shaped Arthurdale, and inattention to them limited even the pedagogical and curricular work at the resettlement.[68]

Although homesteaders had been profoundly scarred by the hopelessness of life in the mining camps, mine workers had also engaged in considerable political and social activity.[69] As Arthurdale supporter William Brooks acknowledged, the Monongahela Valley had witnessed "some of the fiercest labor wars this country has known," and in the 1920s, Scott's Run, from which Arthurdale recruited many homesteaders, had earned the name "Bloody Run" for the militancy of its miners' strikes.[70] "If there had been a leader," Eleanor Roosevelt would remember thinking, "a revolution could have easily started."[71] In their hopes of creating a community free of fundamental conflicts, Arthurdale reformers developed selection procedures for prospective homesteaders designed to weed out radicals. Interviewers, for instance, demanded references from former bosses in order to assess financial prudence and reliability at work.[72]

The obscuring of class antagonism shaped the Arthurdale schools' curriculum as well as other aspects of community life. One might expect that a curriculum based on activity, interest, local conditions, and social life would highlight the most obvious questions confronting students: the structure of the coal industry or the impact of the Depression on their recent misery and the continuing misery of their former neighbors. Clapp had a ready model of class-conscious progressive education. In November of 1932, at a time when Clapp served on the journal's advisory board, *Progressive Education* described Pioneer Youth's West Virginia summer play schools, established with the cooperation of the West Virginia Mine Workers Union and the League for Industrial Democracy. By means of child-centered activity and exploration of the built environment, the schools examined such topics as wage cutting, strikes, evictions, unemployment, and social change. The project developers reasoned that the local children would inevitably reflect on hunger, evictions, police power in defense of class privilege, and the need for a new social order.[73]

A few homesteaders continued to work as coal miners, and occasionally, the life of the mines did surface in Arthurdale's schools. In the dramatic play of two five-year-olds, one claimed to be a miner off to work, to which his "wife" answered, "You better not work in those mines, Dad. You died there once. You better not do that no more. Better get out of those mines, Dad." However, despite the students' occasional interest, teachers viewed life in the mine camps as a period of stagnation and alienation.[74]

The teachers showed more interest in their students' knowledge of traditional ballads than in their dramatic play about coal mining, and they made little systematic effort to integrate mining into the curriculum.[75] A discussion of language defects in *Community Schools* includes a list of terms students retained from the coal fields: "grease monkey," "slate loader," "pit boss," "yellow dog," "undercut." A combined class of fifth and sixth graders studied West Virginia's products and industries, but other than a 1790 iron furnace, extractive industries went unnoticed; the word "coal" was not mentioned in Clapp's description of the class.[76]

Although Fletcher Collins' seventh and eighth graders portrayed a mine union leader in a drama they created, the play contrasted the students' "bleak" coal camp past with their "aspiring future" as homesteaders. Eleventh- and twelfth-grade American industrial history included such topics as unions, child labor laws, and workplace safety in coal and other industries. Still, the students focused on "the relation of inventions to the knowledge and materials then available." The cotton gin, for instance, illustrated how "the change from hand-work to machine-work affected people's lives." The study of industrial history, according to Clapp, was

> really an attempt to understand changes in industry wrought by inventions through learning about the needs and conditions that produced them and the effects of these changes upon people's lives.[77]

The short shrift given in Arthurdale to the class antagonisms shaping West Virginian and American life was less an oversight than a reflection of the pedagogical and political vision of Arthurdale's creators. The Ballard School, which Clapp had directed before going to Arthurdale, included both rich and poor students and her work at Ballard convinced her that the needs of rich and poor children were "not dissimilar."[78] Moreover, she viewed all commercial activity with suspicion. Although the Arthurdale store was a common topic of children's dramatic play, teachers contrasted "the things 'cash money' could buy—while it lasted" with the "enduring" value of home production. The school bank was used to teach the kind of thrift that teachers believed essential to the success of the homestead. Teachers saw children's withdrawing money to buy Christmas gifts as "probably inevitable," but they expressed concern when the children made withdrawals merely to buy candy.[79]

Just as Clapp promoted students' understanding of modern industrial life through the exploration of archaic, small-scale production technologies, she sought to promote cultural activity and appreciation by recognizing and legitimizing the continuing presence of Appalachian folk traditions. Still, instead of exploring the full range of working-class creativity, Clapp promoted a sentimental and sanitized version of local culture. According to Clapp,

> the experience in the coal fields, brief though it had been, had obscured to [Arthurdale residents] their common heritage; and being in the shadow of urban Morgantown, they had been disturbed by the radio, the movies, and bourgeois cultural standards. If the homesteaders' sojourn in the mines had been much longer, there might have been at Arthurdale no basis for culture; but since they had grown up on farms, and had in Arthurdale come back to the land, their cultural roots were hardy and were beginning to find again a non-sulfuric and fostering soil.[80]

Mine camp residents, according to Clapp, "were limited in their dramatic horizons to minstrel shows, black-face comedies in the minstrel style, and the cheap uncopyrighted plays that are sent away for and produced at a church social or at Christmas." In response, teachers sought "to liberate the natural dramatic spirit of these people by directing them to . . . the materials of their rural culture." Ignoring the industrial ballads that animated labor organizing, teachers reintroduced homesteaders to ballads like "Barbara Allen" and "Fair Charlotte," while they eliminated such words of regional dialects as "yarn" for "yours" from student speech. At their first Christmas in Arthurdale, homesteaders celebrated with a program in which the clubs and committees prepared their own plays and traditional musical segments. Thus, a cooperative communal effort recovered the bonds formed by shared interests and culture.[81]

As conceptualized by Clapp and John Dewey, community could not exist in a climate of alienation and distrust. Although the population of the mining camps was, to use Elsie Clapp's phrase, "polyglot," planners excluded minorities.[82] According to Eleanor Roosevelt, Arthurdale homesteaders were "very carefully chosen." All family members were evaluated and "their ancestry" considered.[83] Only native-born whites were selected. Almost all were Scotch-Irish or Pennsylvania German in "upbringing and racial background," predisposing them, Clapp assumed, to generosity and good humor.[84]

Although a quarter of the homesteading applicants were African American, no Blacks were admitted. When the National Association for the Advancement of Colored People protested the exclusion of Blacks and the foreign-born from the homestead, Resident Director Bushrod Grimes explained that the Arthurdale climate was too cold for Blacks, that instructions had come from Washington prohibiting them, and that Black homesteaders would require a separate school. Although most Black applicants were native West Virginians and farmers, relief official Alice Davis claimed that Blacks were viewed with hostility by white former miners, who asserted that the Black applicants had been brought from Alabama to West Virginia as strikebreakers.[85]

The NAACP's campaign to integrate Arthurdale, like Clapp's failure to address the impact of class relations on Arthurdale, illuminates the need to situate progressive evocations of community amid the complexities of social, political and economic relations. The relationship of community to racial justice was explored most notably by a prominent opponent of the NAACP effort, W. E. B. Du Bois. In the mid-1930s, Du Bois had grown increasingly pessimistic about the willingness of white America to accept racial equality and about the cost to Blacks of integration. From his position as editor of *The Crisis*, the NAACP's official organ, Du Bois rejected demands for desegregation. Instead, he argued that separate Black consumer cooperatives, schools, and other institutions enhanced African-American political and economic power and fostered a distinctive and vibrant Black culture. Du Bois's conflict with NAACP integrationism came to a head over the association's Arthurdale protest.[86]

Blacks, Du Bois reasoned, should form their own cooperative communities and farms and should "insistently demand" their rightful share of the federal subsistence funds.[87] At the same time, he argued, "most homestead colonies, particularly those in the South, are not going to select any Negro participants, except as servants and casual laborers." In West Virginia, school segregation was legally mandated, so even if Blacks were allowed to live in Arthurdale, they would be excluded from homestead schools, as well as from economic opportunities and political participation. For Blacks to seek to participate in such homesteads, rather than to "ask for subsistence homesteads of their own," was, in Du Bois's view, "idiotic."[88]

At least in the short term, events proved Du Bois right. As one homestead official explained, the federal government, in planning homesteads, adopted

the existing economic and social pattern to be found in the locality in which the project is to be located. It is thought that local sponsors are best suited to determine the type of project with respect to racial make-up which should be established in any community.[89]

This policy led to a few integrated projects, but most homesteads, whether in the South or in such northern cities as Indianapolis, Flint, and Youngstown, were segregated. Despite repeated meetings between NAACP leaders and Eleanor Roosevelt, the prohibition against the admission of Negro homesteaders stood in place,[90] and for the entire time Elsie Clapp worked in Arthurdale, the community remained all-white.[91]

In demanding integration, the NAACP did little to articulate a communitarian vision. Du Bois, on the other hand, was convinced that although Blacks were circumscribed by racial subordination, vibrant communities sustained African Americans' cultural, political, social, and economic life. Like Du Bois, Arthurdale reformers articulated a communitarian politics, and, like Du Bois, their vision was shaped by the reality of racial exclusion. Unlike Du Bois, the white activists and educators demonstrated no awareness of the role of racism in their politics and pedagogy. Paradoxically, the centrality of racial politics at Arthurdale was evident largely in their silence about racial matters. The dispute over segregation goes unmentioned in Clapp's accounts of Arthurdale.

The desire to avoid racial or ethnic hostilities distorted not only Clapp's account of the homestead community, but also the study of local history and culture at Arthurdale, in which Clapp had such a great interest. Colonial history explored the role of taverns and the impact of land and climate but not the slave system. Despite the invocations of pioneer yeomanry, the first white settler in what became Arthurdale was Colonel John Fairfax, a friend of George Washington whom Washington advised to buy the tract. Fairfax surrounded his own cabin with those of his slaves, and one such cabin survived. Still, all we learn of slavery from Clapp is that Old Watt, the slave whose cabin survived, "worked faithfully for the Fairfax family for many years. He is buried up in the old graveyard." Instead of serving as a backdrop for the study of slavery, Old Watt's cabin served as the site of the fourth grade's investigation of pioneer life, thus, in Clapp's eyes, "satisfying a certain craving [the students] had, just coming from the desolate mine camps, for possessing something of their own." Just as the Arthurdale curriculum obscured class hostilities, it effaced racial antagonisms. Students explored their own families' former cabins but ignored the social context of their heritage.[92]

Conclusion

In the end, teachers could not dissociate Arthurdale from the wider political and social concerns, whether they wanted to or not. Eleanor Roosevelt's well-publicized role in the revitalization effort attracted criticism as well as support to the homestead, and from its inception, Arthurdale was a focal point of the New Deal's adversaries.[93] The very mix of public and private administration that fostered educational experimentation made Arthurdale an easy target of charges of disorganization. As its political and financial costs grew, the resettlement lost the support of Franklin Roosevelt and key policymakers.[94]

Although New Deal homestead planners were fond of quoting Jefferson, they often acted in Hamiltonian fashion. Cooperative practices were nurtured in Arthurdale, but amid the urgency of Depression conditions, Washington decision makers inadequately built local understanding and political support. At times, the teachers' guidance of the homesteaders dipped into condescension, and despite their efforts to integrate themselves into the life of the community, they were rightly viewed as outsiders. Finally, West Virginians read a steady stream of reporting hostile to Arthurdale in the conservative *Preston Republican*, and in this climate, some local school authorities, who resented the iconoclastic community school, felt themselves authorized to avoid cooperating with it.[95]

Although Clapp's work did enjoy enthusiastic grass-roots support,[96] educators, as Clarence Pickett explained delicately, "assumed more experimental-mindedness among the homesteaders than had yet developed."[97] Many of the poor viewed progressive hands-on activities, which held no stigma for children of affluence, as limiting their social mobility, and some parents believed their children to be learning more about shop than math or English. Moreover, although subsistence farming, curing one's own meat, and preparing children's lunches at school might be educative, they were far from restful. According to Eleanor Roosevelt, Clapp's schools succeeded in "creating community feeling," but sustaining community-centered schooling required the mobilization of people.[98] As the reformers' utopian visions incompletely addressed homesteaders' prosaic hopes for comfort and social mobility, the initial glow of resettlement wore thin.[99]

Ultimately, however, neither the teachers nor the homesteaders could decide the fate of the Arthurdale experiment. After the Congress, fearful of government competition with private industry, blocked the construction of a factory in Arthurdale to manufacture post office furniture, hopes to make the project economically viable faded.[100] Financier Bernard Baruch, who underwrote much of the cost of Arthurdale's educational program, noted that the homesteaders' self-sufficiency and dignity rested on economic conditions beyond their control. "Let us not put these people on their feet," he lamented, "unless it is humanly possible for them to stand by themselves when the helping hand is removed."[101] It would be unfair to keep Arthurdale afloat, he confided to Eleanor Roosevelt, "unless the people there are assured of a living. So far as I have been able to see . . . that is not in sight. . . . It is a question of getting industries there. It cannot be a success without work."[102]

By the summer of 1936, even the optimistic Elsie Clapp acknowledged that economic conditions precluded educational experimentation. Without an "industrial solution and security," she recognized, "our educational enterprise cannot go on here."[103] As the donations that supplemented county school funding dwindled, Clapp and the other outside teachers left. Soon after Clapp's departure, the Arthurdale schools became to all intents and purposes indistinguishable from other rural schools.[104]

"A community school," according to Clapp, "is made *with* the people whose school it is." But, as much as Clapp sought and claimed to be a member of the Arthurdale community who shared in its trials, community educating required both "working with others [who are facing new problems] *and* guiding them in that work."[105] Teachers were needed precisely because homesteaders lacked the knowledge, habits, and skills to educate themselves.

Clapp, Roosevelt and their allies understood both the centrality of the students' consciousness and activity in learning, and the need for outside leadership if the full human capacity of homesteaders brutalized by destitution was to be restored. In the shifting metaphor with which she described her work to *New York Times* readers, Elsie Clapp captured the ambiguity of her view of students' capacity. "It's much like surgery," she began. "We remove mental and physical impediments and graft on things that help." Then, without interruption, Clapp abandoned the notion of student defects in need of removal. "Negative thoughts and attitudes," she continued, "do not flourish here. This is virgin soil, and tomorrow is another day."[106]

The establishment of the new community at Arthurdale created the need for and the possibility of learning. Community-centered education brought the social nature of activity into the very structure and curriculum of the school. By de-emphasizing both her own authority and the presence of social divisions at Arthurdale, Clapp was able to work and learn with, as well as teach, homesteaders, and the formerly lethargic and apathetic mining families quickly became active learners.

Clapp and her fellow teachers showed that poor children, no less than rich ones, benefit from activity and discovery in education. They fostered the homesteaders' ability to shape their education and lives, and guided them as they forged a sense of shared purpose and community. Their joint efforts gave real substance to invocations of local democracy. In Arthurdale's schools, one observer remarked, "there is not room for one who will not cooperate with others, just as in the work we must do outside of school."[107]

Rarely has progressive schooling been so intimately linked to the project of democratic community revitalization. Still, Arthurdale's schools both failed to acknowledge the complex ways residents had already developed strategies with which to resist dehumanization even in the brutal mining camps, and it exaggerated the ability of community consciousness to reshape the lives of people enmeshed in modern social and economic relations. A sentimental theory of political economy united the notion that subsistence farming could allow miners to refashion their lives with the hope that progressive pedagogy could enable students to transcend the divisions of industrial life. Just as educators envisioned communities constructing the meaning of their shared life, New Deal reformers imagined a world of subsistence, as if the forces propelling economic concentration and specialization in America could somehow be suspended at Arthurdale.

In his 1932 address, George Counts chastised the dominant strain of progressive education, charging that the ideal "of the pioneer or the farmer, produced by free land, great distances, economic independence, and a largely self-sustaining farm economy, is already without solid foundation in either agriculture or industry."[108] In a complex society marked by fundamental racial and class relations of domination and subordination, rather than by superficial sectarian divisions, the community school could only incompletely achieve its pedagogical, social, and democratic work.

The question of how to foster democratic pedagogical activities within a society structured by inequality remains a vexing dilemma for progressive educators. In one of his last published writings, John Dewey evaluated Arthurdale. Dewey acknowledged that amid all the obstacles to democratic life, traditional pedagogy and authoritarian relations still reigned supreme in American schools. "The educational system," Dewey observed,

> is part of the common life and cannot escape suffering the consequences that flow from the conditions prevailing outside the school building. When repressive and reactionary forces are increasing in strength in all our other institutions—economic, social and political—it would be folly to expect the school to get off free.[109]

Still, Dewey believed that Arthurdale possessed what were in many respects the best public schools in the United States.[110] He vigorously challenged a critic who charged that in her attentiveness to local matters, Clapp had neglected "the larger political and economic problems of the country."[111] Instead, Dewey suggested Arthurdale offered proof that schools could be wellsprings of democracy in America, and that despite all the forces circumscribing progressive reform, teachers could still make "the educative process a genuine sharing, a truly cooperative transaction in which both teachers and students engage as equals and learners."[112]

Part II

SCHOOLS OF TODAY

CLOSING THE DOOR ON OPEN EDUCATION: BUTTERFIELD SCHOOL

Arthur Zilversmit

A visitor approaching Butterfield School in the Chicago suburb of Libertyville today sees what looks like a typical suburban school. Set on spacious grounds, the red brick building is attractive, but unremarkable. Closer inspection, however, reveals some anomalies. First of all, the building has an unusually large media center; at several points the walls do not quite reach the ceiling, and several rooms are far too large for ordinary classrooms. Today's Butterfield School, it turns out, was built on the ruins of an older school. The first Butterfield was destroyed not by storm or fire, but by another, different series of natural events. Over a period of only a few years the community and the school administration chose to abandon an experiment in "open education."

The movement for "open" education was the characteristic expression of the new romanticism of the late 1960s in the ideology of American public education. Progressive education was, as Lawrence Cremin has pointed out, the educational wing of a larger progressive movement, so the impetus to open American classrooms represented an aspect of the romantic individualism and profound anti-institutionalism of the late 1960s and early 1970s. The mood of these educational reformers was often radiantly optimistic about what could be achieved by a new generation of liberated individuals.

If there were a single event that could be said to have initiated the movement for open classrooms and schools, it was the publication by Joseph Featherstone in *The New Republic* of a series of articles extolling recent developments in the English "infant schools."[1] Featherstone's message struck a chord. Within a few weeks of their publication, in the late summer of 1967, they became the focus of intense discussions among parents, teachers, and others interested in reforming education.

The centers for radical new thinking about education were widely scattered, although they tended to be found in university towns like Palo Alto, Pittsburgh, and especially Cambridge, Massachusetts. But news of change spread far and wide and influenced even relatively conservative communities, and the village of Libertyville, Illinois, was one. Here an experimental open classroom school opened in the fall of 1971. By 1981, however, the school had become quite traditional. Libertyville's experiment in open education makes for an interesting tale, and it can tell us something about the nature of reform and the obstacles school reformers face.

An Unconventional Idea in a Conventional Town

Libertyville, in 1960, was overwhelmingly white and middle class. Located about thirty-five miles northwest of Chicago on a commuter railroad line, it was rapidly changing from a quiet, independent village into a suburban community. Its median family income was $8,306; but one-third of these families earned over $10,000 per year. Fifty-seven percent of those employed were white-collar workers. Like other suburban communities in the post-war era, Libertyville was experiencing rapid population growth.[2] In the late 1960s, professional planners and local political leaders were convinced that the population was going to continue to increase—probably at an even faster rate—and that Libertyville would have to begin to plan for a major expansion of its schools.[3]

More specifically, the Board of Education and a special Citizens' Advisory Committee anticipated that the school population would double in the next twelve years; by 1980 the district would have to provide for 4,000 children (2,250 were enrolled in 1968). Thus, in March of 1968, they proposed a radical plan. Libertyville should establish an educational center for the upper grades—a cluster of buildings on a single, large site. This centralized plan would be efficient, and as education came to rely more on such technology as teaching machines, it would be more economical to locate this expensive equipment at one site where it could be available to large groups of children.

The new buildings would be radically different from traditional schools and would foster individualized learning in learning centers, which not only housed the traditional school library but also held films, filmstrips and the other nonprint materials that would inevitably supplement books. The new site would have specialized learning centers for math, science and languages.[4]

The Board of Education endorsed the proposal and the local newspaper lent its enthusiastic support. But the plan encountered a major difficulty when it lost its most important backer in May, when the assistant superintendent in charge of curriculum resigned and was replaced by a man with an altogether different philosophy. While Superintendent W. C. Rardin had endorsed the plan and had helped to sell it to the Board, he was not by temperament or inclination someone who would lead the district on bold, new educational ventures. Rardin, who had joined the district as a teacher in 1946, was an astute politician and an effective manager, but he generally left curricular planning to his assistant superintendents. Moreover, in late June the superintendent suffered a "mild" heart attack and spent most of the summer recuperating.[5] Accordingly, when the new assistant superintendent, Robert Procunier, came to Libertyville, he found himself virtually in charge of the district, and Procunier, it turned out, had his own ideas of how the Libertyville schools should be structured.

Procunier had ties to the progressive education movement. His mentor had been Harold Shane, former president of the Progressive Education Association who had served briefly as Carleton Washburne's successor as superintendent of the Winnetka, Illinois public schools. Procunier's philosophy of education was clearly in the child-centered tradition of the progressives.[6]

When he came to Libertyville, Procunier recalled, "If nothing else I was brash." He read the Citizens' Committee report "and I thought this is just awful."[7] Crowding hundreds of students on a single campus would be a disaster. Far from serving the needs of the individual student, too many children would get lost in this setting. He told Rardin that the plan was wrongheaded and persuaded Rardin to tell the Board that he had changed his mind about the plan he had endorsed a few months earlier. Rardin now argued against the size of the educational park: "We believe that when 450 or more youngsters per grade level are housed in the same elementary building, some important educational goals are overlooked. How does a ten-, eleven-, or twelve-year-old find his identity when he is one of a group of 450 or more?" Rardin recommended that the Board authorize the construction of a modern "upper grade center" for grades four through eight, which, like the original proposal, would be built around a library center on a site near the center of town. At the same time, Highland Junior High School would become an upper-grade center for the southern sections of the town.[8]

Despite the radical shift in the committee's proposal, the administration retained the plan's emphasis on flexible school architecture. Working with an experienced school architect, the district chose an "open space" plan for its new upper-grade center. The movement to build "open space" schools (not to be confused with the "open classroom"), an important trend in school architecture in the late 1950s and early 1960s, developed out of a fascination with new technologies rather than a commitment to any particular educational program. With the availability of sophisticated air conditioning and lighting systems, school boards realized that they could now buy more building for their scarce construction dollars if they relinquished the idea that each individual classroom needed its own windows for light and ventilation. In the interest of flexibility, new schools could be constructed with few interior walls so that the space could be used in different ways as different needs arose. A new emphasis on individualizing instruction, as well as the anticipated rapid development of new technologies for teaching, led school planners to emphasize, as did Libertyville's Citizen's Committee, the importance of flexible architecture that could be readily adapted to new needs and new technologies.[9]

Early in 1969, Libertyville voters approved funds to acquire land and to build the new upper-grade center. It would have few interior walls or corridors. Its 24 "classroom areas," would be built around a learning center. It would have special facilities for art, music, shop and home economics. The community was assured that open space school buildings were more efficient than traditional school buildings and that this kind of school architecture mirrored a national trend. The new upper-grade school curriculum would not be "experimental"; it would continue the current offerings while gradually evolving into a more individualized program. Accordingly, when the new "open space" building, named

Butterfield School, opened in September of 1970, the curriculum was the same as that offered in the other upper-grade building.[10] Yet the open space design of the building did lead to some changes. For example, the lack of walls encouraged teachers to begin working and planning together.

A Change in Plans

Within six months, however, everything changed. Superintendent Rardin announced that instead of being one of two upper-grade centers, Butterfield would become an alternative "open school," serving all of the elementary grades. The driving force behind this radical shift was Assistant Superintendent Robert Procunier. Even before Butterfield opened, Procunier had led a staff study of educational trends and concluded that there was to be a radical shift, "a gradual phasing out of the traditional grade level structure of the school, and an increased amount of flexibility. . . ."[11] The crucial spark proved to be the visit of a consultant, Don Glines, in the fall of 1970.[12]

Glines was one of a small group of radical critics of American education, who came to prominence in the late 1960s. According to Glines, "The present schoolhouse in America needs to go the way of the dinosaur. . . ." Conventional schools, he thought, are "among the most inhumane institutions in America. They closely rival prisons. . . ." It was time for a radical shift in schooling to "create humane alternatives. . . ." As the director of the Wilson Laboratory School at Mankato State Teachers College in Minnesota, Glines had changed the school overnight, instituting a completely open educational program. Since 1968, students at Wilson had complete freedom to choose their own courses and teachers—or to stay home.[13] Although Glines did not use the term, the policies he advocated were characteristic of the burgeoning open education movement.[14]

Glines' enthusiastic account of what was happening at Mankato had a profound impact on a number of the Libertyville teachers and administrators. Procunier recalls that "by the time he was finished . . . I had probably fifteen or twenty people who came up to me and said, 'Look we got to do what he's talking about.' They were excited about it." Shortly thereafter, a group of administrators and board members went to look over the program at Mankato. They came back convinced that they had seen the future of American schooling.[15]

According to the new plan that Rardin unveiled early in 1971, in the next school year, Butterfield would house a grades one through eight alternative "open school," which would allow the children and their parents to choose their courses and teachers. The program would be highly flexible, with an emphasis on self-motivation—learning to learn—rather than on memorization and with an emphasis on individualized instruction as well. Operating from a child-centered point of view, the program would "emphasize the importance of success for the child, and make every effort to eliminate failure." Because of the "ungraded environment," children of different ages would be able to work together. All areas of the curriculum would be open to all students. The new Butterfield school, Rardin told the Board, "will have no formal classes as we know them. . . ."[16]

The Community Reacts

The new plan naturally aroused some opposition. The community had been asked to authorize construction of a new upper-grade school, not an experimental alternative school, and Libertyville citizens began to doubt that the Board was keeping them informed of the changes in its thinking. Parents wanted to know why they had not been consulted before this radical new departure was announced and they worried, too, about discipline in the new program and whether children would be adequately prepared for high school. But the administration and the Board set up special meetings to explain the alternative school program and, in general, the community accepted the new direction. The local newspaper endorsed the Board's decision: "The Butterfield Plan could well establish Libertyville Grade School District as one of the forerunners in American Education."[17] A survey showed that 915 parents planned to send their children to the alternative school. Although there would be room for all of the upper grade children whose parents wanted them to participate, admission to the lower grades would be by lottery and there would have to be a waiting list.[18]

By May, prospects for the successful implementation of the new program looked hopeful, yet three problems persisted. First, and most important, although the new program would begin in only a few months, none of the teachers had any special training for teaching in an open classroom. Virtually all experts on open education (except Glines) agreed that open classrooms required highly trained teachers.[19] The Board did arrange for eighteen teachers to visit the Wilson-Mankato program, but would this be enough preparation for a radical new way of teaching? Second, the principal of the new school would continue to be Emery Babcock, who had been principal when Butterfield was a relatively conventional upper-grade school. Would Babcock have the skills to lead his staff into a radical new program? Third, how secure was the political base of the Butterfield Plan? Those members of the community who were put off by the fact that the Board had not consulted them about the new program would regard it with suspicion, ready to pounce on any problems and inadequacies.

To prepare for the new policy, the district sent eighteen Butterfield teachers to visit the Wilson school and offered to reimburse tuition for any Butterfield teachers who took courses at Mankato State during the summer.[20] Eleanor Moss, one of the teachers who visited Wilson, recalls that the trip was not a success. When they left Mankato, Moss recalled, "We had our doubts." [21]

Initial Success and Support

The first year of the alternative open school proved exciting as students, teachers and staff members adjusted to their new freedom. The program's aim, according to its principal, Emery Babcock, was to create a "more exciting and more enjoyable" place to learn. As Superintendent Rardin told a newspaper reporter, "To the kids, it's 'great,' a change in learning atmosphere that allows them to pick their own courses, choose their own teacher, set their own schedule, and learn at their own pace."[22]

The "open space" building was divided into two areas instead of conventional classrooms: an expressions center (shop, art, music, home economics, physical education) and learning centers (science, geology, math, language skills and so forth). The learning centers were "large rooms, which resemble libraries in the center [and] are surrounded by shells with tables and chairs." According to Rardin, these were designed so that the teacher could "pull together a group of children who are having trouble with a unit or work on a one-to-one basis."[23]

Each "advisor" (Butterfield's term for teacher) was responsible for advising about 20 children (of different ages), and every morning each of them submitted a schedule of classes he or she wanted to attend that day. Students could choose from a wide array of "mini-courses, maxi-courses and one-time courses."[24] Many subjects were given special names intended to attract student attention and enrollment; pupils could choose from courses called "Bellbottoms and Braces," "Splatter and Clatter," "Bones and Stones," and "Rock to Bach."[25] All of the facilities, including the shops and science labs, were open to children at all levels, and older students worked with and helped younger ones. In a sympathetic series of articles, the Libertyville newspaper quoted Assistant Principal Polly Andrews: "For bright students, the sky is the limit. For the low-achievers, it is good, too. They can work at their own speed." The article described the Butterfield teachers as highly enthusiastic. The reporter assured readers that children still got "the basics" but, she added, "the difference is that [they] get only enough of it at one time to digest the material. There isn't really such a thing as 'failure' at Butterfield."[26]

Open classroom schools were usually noisy and certainly looked chaotic, and many visitors used to seeing children sitting quietly in neat rows, listening to a teacher or quietly working at an assigned task were shocked by what they saw. Even the otherwise glowing account in the Libertyville newspaper noted that some children were taking advantage of their new freedom to "goof off." A reporter for a newspaper in the nearby town of Waukegan described Butterfield in much more jaundiced terms. He told the story of a school that reversed all the rules. It had gotten rid of desks and chairs, and the teachers and students sat on the floor. The school condoned "spreading graffiti on the walls." When asked about the philosophy behind the school, "the young principal" said simply, "Be yourself, child. . . . Use all your senses. The teacher hasn't all the answers." The article, entitled "'Be Yourself' theme of Libertyville school," was accompanied by pictures that reinforced the message that Butterfield was out of control: one showed a child "adding to the blackboard graffiti" while another showed a pupil conferring with a teacher while sprawled all over her desk.[27]

Early in 1972, Butterfield still entertained a waiting list for admission, and only a few students had transferred out of the alternative program.[28] But some Libertyville citizens were clearly unhappy with the new program. Unexpectedly, a large group of parents critical of the Butterfield program attended the February Board of Education meeting, to complain that the principles of the Butterfield Plan were beginning to infiltrate another school in the district.[29]

Criticism Mounts

Responding to the criticism, Procunier conducted a survey of Butterfield families. The results were devastating. Discipline (or rather the lack of it) was a major concern. "It appeared to many that 'anything goes,' that there are few rules relating to student behavior, and [that] these are apparently not being enforced." Parents also "felt that they were not kept informed of their child's selection of teachers and courses; that they were not well informed about their children's academic progress." They expressed concern, too, about "regular class attendance, wise use of 'free' time, and procedures for working with students who 'goof-off.'" Parents were dismayed by "what appears to be [a] general lack of respect for teachers and other pupils and the lack of care of or respect for property." They felt that the school needed to be cleaner and more orderly. They criticized the staff for its failure to provide children with "adequate guidance in helping to develop self-discipline." Parents "desired more direct guidance for their children, closer supervision of the daily program for students, provision of adequate quiet study areas for those who need them, an attempt to watch carefully for 'shy' students, and more careful record keeping on children." The conclusions were clear: The program had to be "modified or adjusted to avoid the impression of confusion." Methods had to be developed "to assure children's regular attendance in class and [to] reduce the seemingly aimless wandering of groups of children." If students were to continue to choose their own advisors, procedures had to be developed that would allow them to form relationships with other children of their own age. Despite these devastating findings, the report ended on a note of optimism: "Though most parents recognize problems . . . the majority retain their confidence that the theory behind the Butterfield Plan is valid. . . . It appears apparent that, if the problems cited can be corrected, the parents will continue to support the Butterfield Plan."[30]

As part of the evaluation process, the district hired two consultants from nearby Trinity Evangelical Christian College. Their evaluation focused on a random sample of 360 Butterfield students, comparing them to an equal number from other Libertyville schools in two broad areas, intellectual growth and attitudinal change.[31]

By the time the outside evaluation began, the community was sharply divided and the controversy about open education had become political since two of the three candidates for the school board were highly critical of the current school board. At one board meeting, the president was forced to restrain one of the candidates. The evaluator, he pointed out, "is not on trial here."[32]

Throughout the spring of 1972, opposition to the Butterfield program continued to mount. The Board found that even when it had not planned to discuss Butterfield, its opponents forced it onto the agenda. After a telephone campaign, a group of critics attended the April 27 Board meeting. Irate parents claimed that the plan had sacrificed academics. One member of the audience explained that the parents had come to the meeting "because our children have gone down in their test scores. . . ." Her child "had not accomplished anything in the past year."[33]

Other parents defended the plan. In a "Letter to the Editor," one parent pointed out that her child's attitude toward herself and toward school had turned around—"from dreading the school day previously, to looking forward to it this year." Moreover, she was doing well academically. The Butterfield plan is not right for all children, she conceded, but neither is the traditional school.[34]

By now community interest had reached a peak. More than 400 people attended a special meeting to hear a preliminary version of the evaluators' report and by the end of the evening it was clear the plan was in trouble. While the evaluators found that Butterfield students generally had "a higher self-concept as a learner in five grades," the results of standardized testing showed that one-third of the Butterfield students had "significantly lower academic achievement" scores than non-Butterfield students. The evaluators concluded that the test results indicated that "the Butterfield Plan is likely achieving its specified objectives in terms of a greater affective growth of the students but is less likely to be achieving its objectives of cognitive growth as measured by the Stanford Achievement Test. "[35]

But despite the evaluators' report and the opponents' claims that the Butterfield plan was a failure, parents of Butterfield children continued to support the alternative program. As an editorial in the local newspaper pointed out, fewer than twenty parents chose to move their children out of Butterfield. "What this means is that the Butterfield Plan, the innovative effort to develop new ways of educating children, will operate next year with approximately the same number of students. What it also means is the issues raised in the long controversy over the plan were not matters of concern for the large majority of Butterfield parents—and that continuance of the plan was scarcely threatened. "[36]

Adjustment Foretells Failure

Yet, in the end, the report proved decisive. While Superintendent Rardin announced that he and the Board shared "a total commitment. . . to make the program succeed," he quietly began the process of dismantling the "open education" plan.[37] The revised Butterfield program Rardin announced would include a more clearly defined program of basic skills for each age level in reading, language, math and social studies. Students would now have a basic program that they needed to complete each year. Children with "the same educational needs" would be grouped for review work and drill. Also, more group instruction would be used in certain content areas to give children experience in working together. Student choice would be reduced by eliminating the daily variable schedules which would be replaced by weekly schedules. While optional courses would still be offered, short courses were eliminated and the principal's approval would be required for any course shorter than nine weeks. Objectives for each course would have to be clearly defined before it began so both parents and children would know what to expect. Under the revised Butterfield plan, Rardin pointed out, all children would start in "conventional classes." As they proved their basic skills, they could move into "open" classes. Moreover, "arrangements would be made for children to continue in conventional classes if their parents desired. . . ."[38]

Assistant Superintendent Procunier had read the handwriting on the wall. He resigned to accept the Superintendency in another suburban district; no one asked him to reconsider his decision. Emery Babcock, who had been closely identified with the open program, was forced to resign and, over the summer, the Board appointed a new principal from another suburban district, Prudence Powers, to take his place. When Babcock left, the Board accepted his resignation with unconcealed delight.[39]

Powers recognized that public relations would be her most pressing task. Accordingly, she presented the Butterfield program in glowing terms in her reports to the Board of Education and in interviews with newspapers. At the same time she made it clear to the staff that any bad news should be kept within the family. One teacher recalled that

> When Dr. Powers came in her mandate was put a good face on for the public. It was PR, PR, PR. We were not allowed to send any notes home that were not positive. We were joking, "Your kid is *positively* obnoxious". . . Kids were vandalizing our cars in the parking lot [and] we were not allowed to tell the police. It had to all come out it's a wonderful place and everything was fine.[40]

Despite Dr. Powers' efforts, however, the Butterfield Plan continued to be highly controversial. Parents of children in other schools objected to the fact that Butterfield had better facilities and that children enrolled there in the lower grades could participate in shop, home economics and drama, programs that were not offered in the "traditional program" in elementary schools. Many parents (and teachers as well) saw the very existence of an "alternative" program as a challenge. Did it imply that there was something wrong with their schools? Another important issue was that the district's "traditional" upper grade school, Highland, had become crowded to capacity, which meant that some parents who were new to the community would be forced to enroll their children in the alternative program at Butterfield even if they preferred a traditional classroom setting for their children.

At the end of the second year of the alternative program, Rardin replaced Prudence Powers (who was ill) with Paul Doescher, the principal of Highland, the "traditional" upper grade school.[41] Doescher's mandate was to bring Butterfield back to a more traditional school program. While Butterfield remained an open-space, grades one through eight "alternative" school, its program began to resemble what in the other schools in the district offered, especially in the upper grades. By January of 1974, a consultant reported that the traditional and the alternative programs were "more similar now than they were two years ago." According to former assistant principal, Polly Andrews, after Doescher took over, Butterfield became "completely traditional. It had an open building but a more closed philosophy."[42]

Conclusion

What had gone wrong? Why did open education fail in Libertyville? The failure of the Butterfield experiment at Libertyville was, as Freud might have said, "over-determined." But the most immediate and compelling reasons for the failure of open education in Libertyville were poor planning and poor communications. Ironically, an educational program for making schools more democratic had been imposed administratively rather than developed by parents, teachers and the community in concert.

The original decision to build an open-space school building had not seemed particularly controversial at the time. Moreover, it resulted from the product of a great deal of deliberate planning. But the much more controversial decision to convert Butterfield into an alternative program for grades one through eight came with little community and teacher participation. Procunier sold the idea to Rardin and Rardin, in turn, helped sell it to the Board of Education. As a result, many Libertyville citizens felt that the Board had been dishonest when it had asked for funds to build Butterfield as an upper-grade school.

Equally important, the Board and the administration failed to involve teachers in planning for the change and provided only haphazard training for teaching in an open classroom. As the progressives had learned in the 1920s and 1930s, changing from a teacher-centered to a child-centered school requires highly trained and deeply committed teachers. From the beginning, the teachers at Butterfield enjoyed little or no preparation for teaching in an open classroom.[43] Some of them, moreover, had little interest or enthusiasm for participating in a major change in their profession.

The children who attended Butterfield were no more prepared for this radical change than their teachers. Students who had spent five or six years in a well-structured educational program suddenly received a great deal of freedom and responsibility for developing their own educational program; many of them had great difficulty in recognizing the difference between freedom and license.[44]

Neither the teachers nor the community clearly understood the purpose of the alternative program. If its goal was a better educational program, people assumed that standardized test scores would show that. If it had other goals, what were they and how could they be measured? Once the administration agreed to evaluate the new Butterfield program by comparing test scores there with those in other schools, its fate was sealed. No advocate for open education would argue that a six-month exposure to open education would produce higher scores on the Stanford Achievement Tests. The evaluation, therefore, led to a widespread perception that the program was failing.

Butterfield's plans had been drawn at a time of rapidly rising enrollments, but by the mid-1970s enrollments had begun to decline.[45] This decline, in turn, put pressure on the School Board to control spending. The Butterfield program was inherently expensive because virtually all of the pupils had to be bussed to school. In an era of tight budgets, the elimination of an increasingly unpopular alternative program presented an attractive way to save money.[46]

Also important in accounting for the failure of open education in Libertyville was a radical change in the national mood.[47] In January of 1973, President Nixon's second inauguration encouraged the last of the mass anti-war demonstrations in the Capitol—the "anti-inauguration." It also marked the end of a time when idealistic young people thought they could mount demonstrations to influence national policy. A new "silent majority," emboldened by the electoral victory of Nixon and Agnew, resisted social experimentation. The developing Watergate scandal, the OPEC oil embargo, and rapid inflation induced a new mood of social pessimism and suspicion of government, and the success of Proposition 13 in California marked the beginning of a tax revolt.[48]

Open education had been the educational expression of the ideals of the youth movement of the 1960s with its optimism about human nature. Open education, like progressive education, assumed that what children needed was not coercion, but the opportunity to develop their individual, innate talents. By the mid–1970s, a more cautious and cynical nation saw this optimistic belief as misguided, expensive and, above all, naive.

Still, the failure of the open classroom school in Libertyville had been by no means inevitable. The idea behind the movement—that schooling can be based on children's genuine desire for learning instead of coercion and regimentation—was hardly new. The open classroom was a new expression of progressive education, and if the school administrators had paid more attention to the history of progressivism and the reasons for its successes and failures, they might have designed a program with lasting effects. Too often, however, educators fasten upon an idea like the open classroom and treat it as a panacea to be applied immediately and universally. Educational ideas become gimmicks and under these circumstances even good ideas and good programs pass out of favor quickly, only to be reinvented by the next generation of educators.

In 1981 the Libertyville School Board, forced to close several school buildings because of declining enrollments, decided to end its experiment in open education and turn Butterfield into a neighborhood elementary school.[49] Within a few years, walls were erected to produce self-contained classrooms. The rooms set aside for shop, home economics, and a science laboratory were converted into classrooms or storage areas or were left empty. As a result, today's visitor to Butterfield School sees an attractive, but quite conventional school. The open classroom, open-space school, is gone and is, for the most part, unmourned.

A SMALL SCHOOL GROWS UP: THE FREE UNION COUNTRY SCHOOL

Mary Bushnell

Washington, D.C. sprawls outside of its borders into the neighboring states of Maryland and Virginia, and the busy Interstate 66 west corridor through northern Virginia leads west into a dense suburbia of planned neighborhoods, shopping malls, and business parks. Just where the development currently ends, state highway 29 stretches south, and a two-hour drive brings one to Charlottesville, a university city of about 40,000. Home to Thomas Jefferson's Monticello and the university he founded, Charlottesville attracts "immigrants" from around the country and the world. Few of the long-term locals were born here, but many people who move here seem reluctant to leave.

In contrast to the suburban sprawl of northern Virginia, Charlottesville sits amid farms and pastureland. The rolling foothills of the Blue Ridge Mountains provide an idyllic backdrop for yearly garden and film festivals, the colors of the foliage, and winery tours. Winding country roads lead past family farms, single family homes, large working farms, and grand estates behind security fences. Although the university and city pride themselves on the absence of any customary "town-gown rivalry," Charlottesville and its surrounding county, Albemarle, maintain a pleasant distinction. The city population has remained fairly constant in recent years, but the county population has grown steadily. Many newly arrived as well as city families now settle in the county where property taxes are lower and schools enjoy a better reputation. The majority of the region's Black population resides in the city, leaving a largely Caucasian county population.[1]

To the northwest of Charlottesville, ten miles of winding country roads past acres of farms bring one to the crossroads village of Free Union. Locals regard it as one of the more attractive areas of the county with views of the Blue Ridge Mountains and substantial open land, yet still close to town. Free Union boasts a post office, a general store, three churches, a doctor, and a few businesses including a home-builder and an architect. In addition to these conveniences, Free Union is known for its little school, situated on 4.5 acres of pasture abutting a large farm, one homestead, and a post office.

Free Union Country School is an independent school for preschool through fifth grade students.[2] Founded in 1984 by a group of parents who were disappointed in the administration of the public schools, the small school usually enrolls about 15 students in its preschool and 40 students in kindergarten through fifth grade. The school was not modeled on external educational or religious philosophy. Rather its school philosophy grew out of the founders' schooling ideals. The school continues to pride itself on operating independent of such educational traditions, as Waldorf or Montessori. In a proposal for the construction of the school a founding family wrote, "This education will be offered in an academic, warm atmosphere close to home, instilling a love of learning, out of which will grow individual achievement." That founding quality of exploration and discovery continued:

> In summary, course content could be described as including as broad a scope as possible, aimed at producing a sort of Renaissance child. Physical education will not be overlooked. Such discovery subjects as photography can be introduced, along with time spent on learning to do things with one's hands; elementary wood-working, perhaps, or learning how things work. There is a practical side of life conventional schooling does not prepare children for; we would try to do more of this.[3]

Experiential learning continues to represent the foundation of education as students explore their physical and social worlds through a unit-based curriculum. On the first day of the school year, kindergarten through fifth grade students gather outside for one of the few assemblies of the year. They sit by class, but spread out in the grass rather than sitting still in the seated rows of an auditorium. It is a lovely September day, and the purpose of the assembly is to remind all the returning students and to teach the new students about playground safety. Students from the upper grades act out skits with great enthusiasm as they have been sanctioned to demonstrate inappropriate behavior on the play structures, such as walking up a slide or jumping off play structures.

Following these instructional antics, the director calls all of the children together for a story. With clever voices and gestures, she tells how the possum lost his tail. It is a story of pride and kindness, about treating friends thoughtfully and not showing off. They talk about the meaning and moral of the tale; then the director invites everyone, students and teachers, to stand in a circle, holding hands. She gives a short speech: "We are all friends here. We care about each other. We love each other. Tall and short, we all teach one another and learn from each other. We are a community."[4]

Free Union Country School hardly looks like a school at all. It suggests a modest vacation home with its rustic appeal and comfortable presence. The western boundary of the school property looks over the green pastures of the neighboring farm with only a simple fence to keep cattle on their side. To the north lies the post office, to the south a private home, and the county road defines the east boundary. A gravel parking lot accommodates 14 cars, and a circular drive brings families to the school door. No fences enclose the playground between the parking lot and the buildings, although the separate preschool playground lies immediately adjacent to the road so it is enclosed by a wooden picket fence. A small garden lies behind one building, and climbing structures provide additional recreation for the students. A founding family provided their expertise as landscape architects to transform farmland into an open, beautiful setting for the school.

Instead of cinder- block or brick, the original classrooms were built from notched logs. Wide wooden steps lead to the main door. Large porches extend off each classroom space, providing spacious sheltered areas for messy class projects and sand tables. As the school grew, additional classrooms were built both to accommodate the increased number of students, and to provide such special areas as a centrally located library. Today the school houses four separate classrooms, a director's office, a library, a small science and art projects room, a reception area, a kitchen, and five bathrooms. The two original log classrooms provide a rustic, well-used and cozy setting. The newer classrooms and the library enjoy high ceilings and many windows, inviting children's eyes to gather in their rural setting. Although each classroom hosts particular grade levels, students continually bustle from one part of the school to another, filling the rooms, hallways and porches with their activities. In addition, classes often leave the building to use the fields, trees, and the outdoor air either on the school grounds or on field trips.

Inside each classroom, activity centers provide resources for art projects, writing, multimedia studies with computers and audiotapes, and comfortable reading areas with sofas and pillows. All students gather on rugs or around large tables for their class activities; the fourth and fifth graders also have individual desks in their rooms. Activity centers encourage students and teachers to take advantage of a variety of resources. Classrooms instill in students and teachers a sense of identity with their classroom group, in addition to the entire school.

"There's never enough wall space in here!" One can hear this familiar lament as teachers seek additional space to display student artwork and projects. The students' work covers the walls on a rotating basis; every week brings something new to see. Walking down the steps from the upstairs classroom to the downstairs, one finds the wide stairwell graced with enormous paintings of the solar system, a cavalcade of animals, or house designs. The changing exhibits demonstrate constant intellectual and artistic productivity.

Much of Free Union's uniqueness grew out of its beginning as a parent-run school, and while the school has moved away from direct parental management, it retains many of the qualities the founding families envisioned. A small group of artisans, artists, teachers, and care-givers, these parents created a modest, community-based environment in which children might grow and learn. They wanted their children to leave the school with confidence in themselves and in what they could do. To accomplish these goals, the parents and teachers, then and now, set out to sustain a caring community and a strong curriculum.

The Free Union Approach to Philosophy and Learning

While caring and schooling has been well-discussed in terms of teachers and students in educational literature, other relationships remain relevant in a school.[5] One characteristic of a community-based school like Free Union is the responsibility the caring families extend to the school and its staff. The following example illustrates how students and parents care and appreciate the responsibility they accept for teachers. After agreeing to purchase $15 in raffle tickets from one of her students, a teacher told the child she had just given him her fresh-produce money for the week.

"All that week," the teacher recalled, "the student came in every day with a kind word and a compliment for me. On Friday, I went out to my car and there was a great big basket of fresh fruits and vegetables from the grocery. Another day, a father walked into my classroom, handed me the keys to his car, took my keys, and said he would return my car at the end of the day. When he brought the car back, it had been detailed inside and out. He said that my car was filthy and he decided to clean it up."[6]

As a community school, the caring relationships between students, teachers, and parents go beyond one-to-one relations; they are grounded in the structure of the school and supported by the shared values of the school membership. As this chapter demonstrates, the school events and daily activities serve to socialize new families and old into the evolving culture of the school. The school does not seek to be disconnected from the home; in fact, home continually enters the school by way of the active parental involvement.

Parents founded Free Union Country School to construct a place where their children and teachers and parents themselves would be part of a community. The children benefit from the increased attention of a community in which everybody shares similar values and concerns. Supported by parents, the teachers consciously provide an environment in which the students feel safe and cared for, in which they feel "at home." On the first day of the 1995–1996 school year, one new student joined the twelve children of the first and second grade classroom. Most Free Union students begin in kindergarten or preschool, so this student bore the stigma of "new kid on the block." His teacher regarded his newness as a serious matter, making an extra effort to welcome him. She encouraged the other children, who had known each other for years, to welcome him as a friend, not as a stranger. To de-emphasize that he was the only new student to enter this year in grades one through five, the teacher explained to the class that "you are all new in this classroom," as all of these students had been in a different classroom during their earlier years. She took the first week of school to "figure him out." He was somewhat shy, and she wanted to get to know him as soon as possible. Not waiting for a month to go by, she began immediately to show active and caring attention to him as an individual as well as a member of the class community. Every child receives this level of individual attention and concern to a degree that would be impossible in a classroom of 30 new students.

In fact, all of the Free Union teachers demonstrate respect for their students, and expect that respect in return. They issue warnings in advance of the end of an activity, so that everyone can reach a stopping place of their choosing. They continually praise polite speech in addition to gently calling attention to inappropriate or unkind speech. They ask permission before interrupting a student or offering suggestions to a student who is at work. These and similar behaviors promote an atmosphere of caring and concern for one another through respect for the rights and responsibilities of others. Teachers model respectful behavior for students to observe and emulate.

Teachers frequently demonstrate and reinforce caring and concern. During fire drills, the staff's paramount concern is the safety of the children. They practice the ritual of lining up at the nearest door, exiting the building in a quiet and orderly manner, just as it occurs every month in every school. But in addition to practicing the standard safety procedures, the teachers take advantage of a fire drill to live the ethic of caring and to demonstrate concern for others.[7] Before the first fire drill of the year, the director calls together any new and young students and explains the process and purpose of the fire drill. She tests the alarm while they stand next to, but outside of the building, so that they become familiar with the sound of the alarm and will not be frightened when they hear it for the first time. Some of the young students still are nervous at the loud sound, but gain consolation from the proximity and kind words of their teachers. These students experience the caring of their teachers in the close attention they receive, and the concern teachers express in advance of a potentially disturbing event.

As much as they want school to be "like home" in how it cares for children, the school staff members have a responsibility to clarify rules unique to school. A school requires more careful behavior than a home. Students and teachers interact informally in the classroom and on the playground, but fire drills represent one occasion when firm boundaries must be drawn around the limits of appropriate behavior. When the older students misbehave by talking during a drill, they lose their recess, an uncommon display of imposed discipline. Sitting separated from one another throughout the free play period, the ten fourth and fifth grade students experienced the strongest punishment the school imposes: isolation from peers. They had been punished for misbehaving during a serious exercise. However, their potentially greater crime lay in the poor behavior they modeled for the younger students. The teachers expressed their disappointment that older students had set a poor example. Older students continually hear encouragement to set good examples, to be leaders, to demonstrate that they are old enough to know how to behave. Younger students learn school boundaries by observing them participating in these behaviors.

In designing the school curriculum, the Free Union teachers focus both on how children learn and on content areas of knowledge. "How children learn" refers to the activities students engage in throughout the school day and to how teachers help construct those activities, much as Dewey called on teachers to provide the "conditions" for children to learn through their activities.[8] Free Union teachers believe that students who learn how to learn can apply these skills to any discipline. Elementary school becomes a place, therefore, for learning skills and habits, in addition to acquiring specific information.

Part of the Free Union curriculum and a caring community includes conflict resolution. After one teacher received formal training in conflict resolution, she introduced these concepts to the other teachers who have since incorporated them into their classrooms. The positive results are visible. Early in the school year, one first grader asked his teacher during clean-up time if he could speak to the class about something. After another student shared her collection of seashells during the end-of-day class meeting, the teacher told the class that the young boy had something to share. The first grader spoke with remarkable maturity. "I'm quite disappointed in how the class is taking care of the art center," said the young boy. "It's a real mess and those two students each day who have to clean up the art center are left with a lot of work to do. Everybody's neglect shows a lack of respect toward the area and our fellow students."

The teacher praised the boy: "I couldn't have said it better myself." But instead of dictating new rules to deal with the problem, she turned to the class and asked them to suggest solutions. "What can we do so that this doesn't happen again?" The students called out several suggestions, like "trying really hard." She replied that trying and knowing about it did not seem to be enough to prevent it from happening. She encouraged them to explore other ways to ensure the cleanliness of the area. After further class discussion, she encouraged the children to go home and consider other ways they could keep the area cleaner, then share those ideas with the class the next day.

By encouraging students to identify and address perceived problems in their world, Free Union teachers construct an environment for living and learning democracy. To educate for democracy, schools themselves should be places where children experience and learn participatory democracy.[9] At Free Union, educating for democracy takes place as a result of classroom strategies and parental involvement. The participation of children and adults in classroom and school governance represented one of the goals the educators at Central Park East schools tried to achieve, and the activities and interaction at Free Union bear strong resemblance to Meier's portrayal of Central Park East.[10]

Free Union teachers also strive to balance their curriculum with the needs, abilities and interests of the students. While this orientation partly reflects the school's small size, it is also the school's stated philosophy:

> Our philosophy is based on the belief that children have a natural curiosity and an innate need to learn about themselves and their world. Our teachers' task is to foster this desire to learn by creating a variety of learning situations at a variety of levels. Work progresses through a richly textured curriculum with hands-on multi-sensory activities. While textbooks are valued, they are viewed as resources, rather than as the only educational tool available. The primary goal of all academic work is to stimulate the children's thinking processes to higher levels.[11]

While the current and founding members do not directly attribute their school philosophy to John Dewey, it clearly parallels the child- and curriculum-centered education he promoted.[12] To be child-centered, according to Dewey, does not mean to allow students' interests to direct all learning: "Interests in reality are but attitudes toward possible experiences; they are not achievements; their worth is in the leverage they afford, not in the accomplishment they represent."[13] Dewey never advocated child-centered schooling divorced from curriculum-centered education. At Free Union, to be child-centered translates to teachers cultivating an environment in which each student's unique needs and abilities become known, celebrated, and built upon within the context of their curriculum. Teachers achieve the concurrent and mutually supporting goals of child-centered and curriculum-centered education by celebrating the differences among their children. Students are free to learn, for example, without the stigma of reading on a second grade, or third grade level. Grade levels become guides, not criteria governing when a child should attain a certain learning level.

Although the parents and teachers developed and wrote down the Free Union philosophy during the early years of the school, they recorded the curriculum more recently. The teachers spent the greater part of one school year composing the curriculum for all grades. For the school's first decade, the curriculum went undocumented, although it had been shared by word of mouth. While this practice gave each teacher generous flexibility in utilizing planning skills for a new year's students, it presented a challenge to the new teacher who was unfamiliar with what children had learned in their previous years. In committing the curriculum to paper, the director and the teachers were careful not to "write it in stone." "The students change every year, so the curriculum is going to change," the director commented. "The [written] curriculum is especially for new teachers to have a clue about what they might do. It's also for each of you [current teachers] so that you would know what the earlier grades' teachers did during a year."[14]

The teachers agreed that the written curriculum would chronicle each year's activities, rather than become an unchanging guide, year after year. As they wrote, they cautioned each other against writing a curriculum so concrete that they would be tempted to "teach to the test." They recognized, however, that students need to know and learn certain concepts each year, and they wanted to document these concepts. The curriculum could provide some kind of continuity when teachers leave, as well as assist those teachers who remain.

The excitement in writing a descriptive rather than a prescriptive curriculum lies in the freedom each teacher has to design the best education for her students. Working from a shared understanding of what skills and content children need to learn, teachers base a new year's curriculum on the needs, existing skills, and experiences of the students in their classroom. Writing a new curriculum every year presents extra work for the teachers, and it requires parental trust, but this approach celebrates the uniqueness of each student and group of students in that it assumes that students all have different needs.

The Free Union teachers also consult such external curricula as "Math Their Way" and the Comprehensive School Mathematics Program (CSMP) to support the curriculum they design. Although some appeared in the early years of the school, the school currently uses no textbooks or basal readers. Instead, the teachers build their lessons on experiential learning, literature, research projects, and the resources of parents. While they design the curriculum respectful of individual student needs, they keep track of the curriculum county schools use, and they try to keep pace with the content and general educational goals of the local public schools. Students who either leave or enter in the middle of elementary school find themselves "caught up" and able to adjust, and students entering public middle school in sixth grade are as ready as their peers from other schools.

In addition to these external influences on curriculum, unit-based learning became central to the school's educational structure during its early years. Teachers organize the school year around six-week multi-disciplinary units. During a unit, students immerse themselves in such topics as immigration, farms or space. Units become vehicles for integrated learning between language arts, social studies, science, art and music. In this way, the students learn a subject in a variety of ways and display their knowledge with various media. Free Union's unit-based curriculum resembles John Dewey's occupational pedagogy of "active work." In *The School and Society*, Dewey described the occupational pedagogy he envisioned and he and his wife Alice put into practice at the Chicago Lab School. From Dewey's perspective, this pedagogy engenders several advantages—two of them being experiential learning and cooperative learning—and it prepares children for adult lives by directly referring to that life.[15] Free Union units (Dewey's occupations) encourage the students to learn the curriculum actively.

While the entire school rarely comes together for units, teachers occasionally arrange to overlap the content of their students' research. Before winter break one year, all the students from preschool through fifth grade participated in country studies. During that month, preschool "became" Germany, the kindergarten resembled China, the first and second grade class studied Ireland, and the older (grades three, four and five) students studied India. The students completed some of their projects independently; more often they worked cooperatively in their research and presentations. The International Center at the University of Virginia sent students to describe their cultures, delighting the Free Union students with costumes and stories, music and customs. Country studies began to take over the classrooms as student flags, reports, murals, maps and artifacts decorated the walls. Parents visited the school one evening so the students could demonstrate their new understanding of other cultures with presentations and conversations. Kindergartners paraded through the school in a great dragon dance, introducing their parents to a tour of nations.

While many parents appreciate Free Union's sense of community and small size, they would withdraw their children if the academic education were inferior. Teachers and parents point to the academic success their students enjoy when they move on to public and private schools following their fifth grade graduation. Alumni consistently distinguish themselves in middle and high school by asking questions, finding multiple methods for solving problems, and mediating social interactions with their peers. One public middle-school science teacher was so impressed with the Free Union students who entered his classes that he enrolled his daughter.

Founding a New School

Free Union Country School currently maintains a waiting list of families hoping to enroll their children, and the small elementary school enjoys a solid reputation as a caring place where young children develop into thoughtful, sociable, creative students. Financially, the school enjoys some measure of security from its growing endowment and reliable tuition income. A strong institution, Free Union nevertheless continues to examine itself and locate ways to improve its daily and long-term operations, even while adhering to its original goals. Having settled into its second decade, the young school is now growing up. Its first ten years of growth and development were, however, at times painful and difficult, and the early arduousness speaks to the commitment of the school's teachers, parents and administrators who built the school into the community institution it is today. Its successes may be numerous, but they did not come easily. In fact, Free Union embodies the story of the survival of a small school often uncertain how it would continue from one year to the next. The school was sometimes uncertain in August whether September enrollments would justify hiring back a teacher. "We just kept meeting, and talking about it, and agreed that we would keep working on it until it didn't work anymore."[16]

In 1983, the Albemarle County School Board announced it would close a small public elementary school and reopen it as a larger school. Some of the families near the small school were outraged: they did not want their children attending a larger school. In addition, the change would have required their young children, including kindergartners, to ride a bus 90 minutes to and from school. While the families in this rural area were accustomed to driving long distances, they did not want to impose these journeys on their young children. Facing their concerns, some of the families recalled a 58-student school in Free Union, which had closed in 1962 during a state-wide consolidation of small rural schools.[17] A small group began to wonder if they might be able to open a similar school close to their homes.

Many of these parents had themselves attended small schools. They had watched the growing trend toward consolidation and sought to restore a sense of community to their area with a local school. This part of the county had historically featured working farms, but was increasingly influenced by gentrification. In January of 1984, 16 families met in the basement of the Free Union Baptist Church to discuss their ideas for a school, their desire for small classrooms, and their hope for a school that would be part of the community. As one father who attended the meeting recalled, "There was another thing, too. There were a lot of people in that room who, at one time in their lives, dreamed of starting their own school. . . . A lot of us had read *Summerhill*, and that kind of literature. . . . So there was an energy, there was an excitement about it. That, wow, maybe this could really happen."[18] His wife added her memory:

But until even the very [moment] it started, it wasn't definite that the school was going to start. I remember having a conversation with another parent about whether we should enroll our daughter in another preschool, or if we should count on the school opening. She said, "You know, I'm going to count on the school opening, and if it doesn't, then we'll figure out something else. It was pretty down to the wire."[19]

By September, just nine months after the parents first discussed starting their own school, a wealthy farmer had donated two and a half acres in the center of the village, volunteer labor had erected a log building, a well had been dug, a septic tank installed, teachers hired and a curriculum designed. One mother, a former teacher, volunteered to serve as the school's first director and to teach math. Another parent offered his experience as a music director to teach music. Ten students enrolled that first year in grades preschool through fourth grade, housed in one divided room. Parents cleaned the school, with each family assigned one week in rotation. During the following summer, the parents built a second classroom to accommodate more students. Over the next decade, they built a library, two additional classrooms, two more bathrooms, an office for the director, and a science and art room.

The eclectic group of founding parents included teachers, farmers, carpenters, builders, college professors, small businessmen, and artists. Each family contributed its expertise, some by investigating legal requirements, others by designing the curriculum, and one key family by coordinating the construction of the log buildings: "Everybody had something different to share. We all had different skills."[20] Although they came from a variety of backgrounds and socioeconomic levels, every family shared the desire to be closely involved in their children's education. The public schools denied them sufficient involvement, so they invested their considerable energies into a school of their own.

The topic of parental and community involvement in schools dominates current educational reform literature.[21] These studies strongly suggest that students succeed in those schools where their parents or other community members become heavily involved. Partnerships and collaboration emerged in the 1990s as key elements of successful schools, and the parental involvement at Free Union certainly supports these findings—although not without some difficulties and adjustments soon to be discussed.

The New School Develops

Parent involvement constituted the central driving force in the founding of Free Union Country School, and it continues to characterize the small school. Yet designed as a parent-run, though not a cooperative school, Free Union continually raised the issue and tested the assumptions of exactly what qualifies as "involvement." The founding parents agreed to be involved physically, building the first classrooms themselves, cleaning the school every week, assisting teachers in the classrooms, providing administration, and maintaining the grounds. By supplying much of the labor needed to run the school, parents could keep the tuition low. As new families came to the school, however, they often brought less of the pioneer spirit. In addition, the school attracted an increasing number of two-income households with parents who could not afford the time to volunteer several mornings a week. These families tended to support the school with their money, rather than their labor. While in the first years parents cleaned the school and maintained the grounds, today those tasks are contracted out. One parent reflected, "The assumption was, 'everybody in their time.' When you could [volunteer], you could. There were years when I was less involved."[22]

As the families changed, so did the school. But it was more than a matter of a new collection of families introducing new ideas. As the school matured, the families and staff members too recognized new needs and concerns. While the founders emphasized parent involvement, the growing school developed a need for increased professionalism. In the school's third year of operation, the parents hired a full-time director. Despite her meager salary, she remained at the school for eight years and, by all accounts, improved the quality of teaching, increased the school's resources, and sustained its general community feeling. "We used to wonder what we would do when [Sue] was no longer director, because she gave so much time and energy to the place."[23]

In 1993, Free Union Country School applied to the Virginia Association of Independent Schools (VAIS) for accreditation. In its report, VAIS conveyed its strong admiration for the Free Union classroom strategies, but it expressed concern that the governance was too weak to support that education. The accreditation review suggested changes aimed at maintaining the high quality of education and ensuring the school's solvency. Most significant among these changes, Free Union is no longer designated a parent-run school. Previously, parents hired the teachers, evaluated their teaching, and remained intimately involved in all aspects of school governance and operation. While an open process of hiring and evaluation suited the founding families, as the school grew in size and stability this loose structure reduced the school's credibility. One teacher interpreted the issue of accreditation this way:

> The main reason we didn't get accreditation is because of the director's role. There was no office for the director, no place in the school where a confidential conversation could be carried on. No place. There was no security of student records.[24]

The director herself was not at issue. Several years after her departure, teachers and parents continue to praise her contributions. She supervised an exciting, vibrant school that continues to reconstruct and adapt itself to its students. The problem was, to repeat, the school governance structure. While the director was remarkably motivated and capable, she had little influence relative to the Board of Trustees, a group of parents and community members who share legal responsibility for the school. The school operated with only short-term goals as the director had no authority to work for the long-term and the Board had yet to regularly address long-term goals. As a result, only a rudimentary organizational structure carried the school forward.

Moreover, the governance procedures were unclear about the duties and responsibilities of the Board, director, teachers, and parents. For the first few years, these blurred roles presented no significant issue. Parents served as members of the Board, as director, and as much of the part-time teaching staff. But as the school grew, other citizens besides just the

parents began to take on these roles; new forms of administrative procedures and decision making became necessary. In addition, as the school
grew, it acquired the greater financial resources for it to remain in
compliance with state requirements for licensure.[25] The founding parents
concentrated too hard on creating a school from scratch to attend to all of
the record-keeping necessary for an accredited school. They started the
school with a strong philosophy, but were not able to construct strong
organizational systems until its second decade.

Although VAIS did not accredit the school because of problems with
governance procedures and the physical plant, the association expressed
its strong commendation of the education at Free Union. In a letter to the
school director, the chairperson of the accreditation team wrote, "We
recognize and applaud you for the school you are, a school where the
mission of a child-centered approach to education is evident in every
room and in every person."[26]

The observed quality of education was very high, but VAIS recommended that the young school design and implement governance procedures for the future. The school immediately undertook to strengthen its
organization. The Board and director attended a weekend retreat to learn
about their responsibilities and tasks. The school members had been like
family—a close, intimate group of neighbors and friends. Over the years,
that closeness presented an obstacle to their ability to run the school as a
business. When the Board, director, and parents faced disagreements over
issues, they sometimes had difficulty addressing them. According to one
parent, resolving issues resembled resolving feuds in a family: "It was
tough for anyone to play the heavy." But recent procedural and structural
changes to the bylaws have eased some of the issues as the respective
roles and responsibilities become better defined.

The parent-ratified Board of Trustees continues to encourage parent
and community involvement in the governing structure, but it provides a
closer accounting of their actions. The new director, hired after the VAIS
study, gained authority to conduct hiring searches and to hire and fire
teachers; the bylaws now clearly delineate her responsibilities and
authority. The school governance today has attained a level of maturity
commensurate with the strength of the founding philosophy.

Parents continue to remain involved in many of the decision-making
processes, although they no longer have direct responsibility for such

sensitive areas as student and teacher evaluations, and finances. In addition to their participation in various committees, parents ratify the selection of Trustees. Also in January of 1996, the director implemented a Parents' Forum, an occasion when families and staff could share information and discuss current school issues, particularly those of direct interest to parents like tuition, building maintenance, and class groupings. Although the Board remains the primary decision-making body on policy issues, the discussions at Parents' Forums now guide Board decisions as parents express their current sentiments.

The continued parent involvement at Free Union matches the level of parent involvement the current educational reform literature advocates.[27] Free Union demonstrates the success of achieving what Goals 2000 recommends.[28] Meier wrote of constructing a "family-oriented school [which houses] authentic forms of collaboration between the school and the family."[29] Coleman and Hoffer have been widely and approvingly cited for their work on the relationship between a school and its surrounding community.[30] These observers and many others call for increased parental involvement in schools as a means of constructing educational quality. Free Union was founded on this principle, and maintains parental involvement as a distinctive, valued feature of its education.

Although the principle of parental involvement remains fundamental, its manifestations have changed over the years, with that change has occasioned some resistance. Fullan concluded that effective and lasting change cannot be mandated. Rather change is a complex and difficult process that requires the participation and knowledge of all involved parties.[31] Even though change may be desirable, the forms it can take—like discarding old blueprints for parental involvement and taking on new ones—may raise hesitation and angst among even the most dedicated participants.

Hesitation in the change process became evident at Free Union Country School. In addition to the annual meeting, the New Parent Forum, and the possibility of their election to the Board, parents today may participate directly in school administration through the Advisory Committee. Meeting monthly, this group of parents and teachers assists the director in translating long-term Board decisions into daily events. At one Advisory meeting, older expectations of parental involvement struggled against newer conceptions of how parents participate in school governance. As one parent commented, "[The new hiring process] is a problem for many parents as what sets us apart from other schools is that here you can have a voice. We don't want to lose that."[32] At issue was teacher hiring. Since the founding of the school, a team of parents had conducted the searches, observed teaching demonstrations, interviewed prospective teachers by committee, and hired all of the teachers. When a new director arrived in 1984, she found her authority strengthened. The Board and, by vote, the parents agreed that she should have the authority and responsibility to hire and fire teachers. The next spring, the director did just that, hiring a new first and second grade teacher and an art teacher. Although she sought and received advice from the current teachers about their new colleagues, she did not directly involve the parents. Some older families took issue with this procedure, even though they recognized that the school had to change. As one parent observed, "We all agree the old way doesn't work, but we still want to be involved."[33]

Throughout these debates over school governance and parent involvement, a central theme emerged: size. How many students (and parents) could Free Union Country School enroll while remaining true to its mission statement? Additional students brought more tuition money which could be applied to teachers' salaries and school programs. Yet if too many students enrolled, an additional teacher had to be added to the budget in order to maintain a low student-teacher ratio. Moreover, any business, even a non-profit business, expects growth and increased professionalism. In short, enrollment increases have affected the school financially, socially and academically.

In addition, growth has profound impact on families and, most importantly, on students. In a small, intimate, family oriented and caring school like Free Union, everyone knows everybody else. The staff and parents work to provide a warm and stimulating educational environment so that every child discovers the joy of learning being in school. Teachers believe students' attitudes toward school grow out of their positive experiences with caring and enthusiastic teachers. But both teachers and parents recognize that when the students leave Free Union, their social and academic skills must stand up to the scrutiny of somewhat larger, less warm and caring institutions. These concurrent goals—a caring school for children now, yet preparation for a larger world "outside"—seem most realistic with a small enrollment that permits a family-like pedagogical approach.

The issue of school size has, of course, provoked educational debate for years. In 1897, the Committee of Twelve on Rural Schools strongly advocated the consolidation of small schools into large, centralized locations.[34] In 1922, University of North Carolina professor Edgar Knight argued that consolidated schools provided better educational services to their communities than small, one-room, multigrade schools.[35] The consolidated school and the centralized community became a symbol of social progress.[36] Throughout the 1920s, school reformers continued to urge the consolidation of small schools into centrally located, large schools, but the communities affected often resisted their arguments.[37] Nevertheless, during the 1950s and 1960s, "Big schools became the rule, not the exception. In a society where bigger was considered better, small districts and small schools were described as backward and inefficient."[38]

By the 1980s, however, the pendulum of size had swung back to favor small schools. Such problems as impersonality, bureaucracy, and diminished contact had become characteristic of larger institutions. Students disconnected from their school communities caused disciplinary problems.[39] In addition, new studies suggested the extraordinary strength with which communities would fight school closure in an effort to preserve their communal centers.[40] While the reaction these studies described could be attributed to romanticizing the past,[41] current reform literature tends to confirm the educational and social efficacy of small schools.[42]

While small schools can be more family-like and provide close relationships, they cannot take the place of family. Schools require different rules of conduct and expectations than families, and although it strives to be nurturing, Free Union continually works to distinguish between home and school behavior. One of the primary goals of kindergarten, for example, is learning how to get along with fellow students and adults. As one teacher explained, although children learn many social skills in preschool, at that young age they usually listen to and respond immediately to teacher requests. In the later grades, teachers often interact with the children familiarly, the way a parent might. Sometimes this more casual approach confuses children and they respond inappropriately. They step across boundaries that have been left unclear without the typical hierarchical relationship between students and teachers found in other schools. At Free Union, teachers are both authority figures and friends. While this unique relationship opens avenues for growth and exploration, it can also interrupt the learning process. One teacher reflected that it is good to have an open and trusting environment that fosters learning, but it becomes a problem for everyone if children find it difficult when they have to stop playing, follow directions, and do what the teacher asks.

Free Union students are learning how to respect and question authority. When a child respects authority, that child recognizes the formality of the classroom as a place of work. "Work" does not mean stale or boring, but it remains distinct from play. At the same time, teachers encourage their students to question authority when they have good reason to do so. Thus, the teachers continually explain why they expect particular responses and behaviors. They do not simply order the children to study in order to earn a grade. In this non-graded school, teachers feel it is more worthwhile to engage students in their own education so that they apply themselves out of enthusiasm for learning.

The Dual-Grade System and Other Features

Another positive outgrowth of the small sizes is multi-grade classrooms.[43] At least two grades share a classroom and a primary teacher at Free Union. About 8 children in each grade stay with the same teacher for kindergarten and first grade, then move to a new classroom and teacher for second and third grades, and finish their stay in the fourth and fifth grade classroom with the upper elementary teacher. In kindergarten, a student is one of the younger children in the classroom learning from older peers as well as the teacher. The next year that student remains in the same classroom with the same teacher and becomes sufficiently comfortable to take on leadership roles. This dual-grade system allows a child to be a follower, then a leader, on alternate years, and both teachers and parents express satisfaction with the system.

Although the school prefers dual-grade classrooms, it alters the pattern to accommodate unusual enrollment numbers. A small number of upper elementary students may combine into a third-, fourth-, and fifth-grade class. A large number of kindergartners enrolled one year, requiring a kindergarten-only class. As a young group, they did not benefit from the constant presence of the older first grade students who could model appropriate behavior. While discrete classes are the norm in most other schools, Free Union considers modeling appropriate behavior a primary pedagogical tool, so teachers try to maintain dual-grade classrooms whenever possible.

While small class sizes represent one of the primary reasons families choose Free Union, size also becomes an issue over which some parents decide to withdraw their children before the end of fifth grade. With only 40 or 45 students in kindergarten through fifth grade, some students find the opportunities for a variety of peer interactions limited, and a few families have concluded that their children need a wider range of same-age peers. Accordingly, they enroll their children in a public school for the upper elementary grades. Some children seem to need a different social environment than Free Union can provide, and the school does not presume to have the one best school for all children.[44] Among the families who choose to stay, however, a general feeling prevails that the cross-age friendships and interactions so common at Free Union provide better socialization for children than large single-age classes.

Parents and teachers alike obviously take into consideration the effect of a small school on social interaction. When the girls of the upper grades began to form a clique that excluded the first and second grade girls, teachers grew concerned. Meeting under the stairs at recess, the older girls formed a club in which they did not want to play with the younger girls. This incident became notable for its exclusion: one group of students excluding another from their activity. In a school where one hears the statement "We are all friends here" repeated with sincerity, exclusion is a serious matter. The younger girls felt slighted and took their concerns to the teachers who carefully considered their complaint. Several days of discussion ensued between the teachers and the director before the teachers felt ready to advise the students. One teacher argued for the need of ten-year-old girls to have their own sense of group and to experience this sense in a safe environment. Another teacher contended that the school was too small to allow cliques and for students to refuse to play with other children: feelings would get hurt. Children's clubs, she suggested, are fine for after school or on the weekends, but not for school time. At issue was the balance between the needs of a small school community and the needs of girls of a certain age. After careful discussion, the school decided to disallow exclusive clubs.[45] Although maintaining community remains a dominant school goal, it suffers challenges that give the school opportunities to reflect on the value of community.

Small size provokes another issue, that of limited teaching resources. Although every Free Union teacher enjoys elementary education skills, each has her own areas of specialization. But how can the school provide children with a variety of teachers (and therefore expertise), yet keep their costs low? In 1995, the school experimented by shuttling children from one classroom to another throughout the day, so they interacted with different teachers. This shuttling also allowed a variety of age and grade groupings. For example, on Tuesdays, the first and second grade class was scheduled to stay in sync with the two other elementary classes (the kindergarten and the upper grades):

8:30–9:00 a.m. Circle time in the first- and second-grade classroom.

9:00–10:00 Reading and language arts in the first- and second-grade classroom. First graders are joined by the kindergartners; a few of the second graders join the third graders in the third-, fourth-, and fifth-grade classroom.

10:00–10:30 Recess with kindergarten through fifth grade.

10:30–11:00 Math with the kindergartners in the kindergarten classroom.

11:00–12:00 Unit time in the first- and second-grade classroom.

12:00–1:00 Lunch and recess with kindergarten through fifth grade.

1:00–2:00 Art with the art teacher in the library.

2:00–2:30 Story time in the first- and second-grade classroom.

2:30–3:00 Cleaning the classroom, circle time, and dismissal in the first- and second-grade classroom.[46]

Throughout the day, students moved from one classroom to another, sometimes accompanied by their teacher, sometimes working with a different teacher. After several months of trying different variations on this schedule, the teachers concluded that the transitions took too much time out of the school day; however, they still wanted to provide all students with the widest range of instructional expertise possible. In an effort to balance these competing concerns, class schedules changed throughout the year as teachers worked to construct the most advantageous schedule for everyone. They determined that shifting children throughout the school day undermined class solidarity in addition to consuming time and decided to not repeat the schedule a second year. A small school can easily experiment with schedules this way, allowing the teachers and students most intimately involved to alter, adopt or discard them. Meier found similar flexibility and the positive benefits of experimenting at Central Park East Schools.[47]

Meanwhile, Free Union Country School feels the constant pressure to maintain the current size of the student body, which is its primary source of funding. The school remains heavily dependent on tuition money—that is to say, the parents—for its budget. While older schools enjoy substantial endowments to support their endeavors, the Free Union endowment has only just begun to produce appreciable income. Older schools may also depend upon alumni for financial support. But the oldest Free Union Country School alumnus currently attends college, and the school can hardly count on its alumni as a financial resource at this time.

The school periodically considers expanding to increase its income among other reasons, and its families might also benefit from a larger student body if increased size provided more scholarships. If a child leaves the school before the end of fifth grade, it is usually for one of three reasons: relocation, the tuition, or the small same-age peer group. Despite its meager resources to offer scholarships, the school remains sensitive to lower-income families who struggle to pay tuition. The school needs higher tuition rates to underwrite teachers' salaries and school programs, yet if the tuition becomes too high, some families would surely turn away. Attempts to find this balance have caused some tension. One parent who has been involved in the school since its inception reflected on this point:

Every year that was the issue. How do we get full enrollment and what kind of tuition can we have to get enrollment? Every year it was, "Well, if you raise [tuition] that much, you're going to lose some families." And for the whole time [Sue] was director, she was always pushing for increased salaries for teachers, and she was also the voice to keep down tuition at the same time. [The Board would] want to raise it $500, which would still make us the cheapest private school in town. "But if you raise it $500," she'd say, "I know you're going to lose families. Three families right now you're going to lose. . . ." And I remember meeting in August wondering whether we were going to open in September, wondering whether we were going to have to let a teacher go, or cut somebody back. And before the end of August, it came through. We had three new kids enrolled. We were running on a deficit for years, in the red for years, and really struggling.[48]

Several parents continue to struggle to pay the current $4,500 annual tuition. While that figure remains lower than the tuition at all other private schools in the area, it represents a sizable investment for parents who would otherwise send their children to a public school. The school's hope is that as it becomes better established in the region and its reputation strengthens, it may become easier to raise scholarship funds and thereby retain lower-income families.

What started as a group of parents seeking a neighborhood school for their children has evolved into a small business. One former school member likens the school to a small start-up company:

The people who are involved in the school now have a different kind of energy and commitment than the families who started the school. Their dedication to the school is no less, but they bring a different set of concerns and issues to the table.[49]

In earlier years, the majority of the parents attended every advisory and Board meeting and, "There were ten opinions for every five people in the room."[50] Today, there is less direct parent involvement, which in some ways leaves the teachers and Board of Trustees freer to do their jobs. But a core group of parents remain intimately involved as classroom aides, part-time teachers, committee members, and active in a wide variety of volunteer projects. Without their considerable efforts every day, the school would look radically different.

The young "business" now has a strong organization and reliable procedures and some of these procedures appear remarkably democratic. The Board of Trustees makes the minutes of their meetings readily available to the school public. The binder of minutes kept in the school reception area invites parents to keep up with Board activities. In addition, parents ratify trustees by secret ballot at their annual meeting. Every year the families and staff members of the school respond to new concerns and changes in the community around them by developing procedures to address these needs—typically, however, in reaction to issues, rather than proactively. For example, at one teacher's meeting, a staff member asked, "What is this school's pregnancy leave policy?" The director's answer was given in jest within the trusting climate of the teachers' meeting, but reflected the school's reactive policies: "Whichever teacher drops first will create the policy."[51] While some families and staff members occasionally campaign for tighter organization and clearer defined procedures, other constituents seek to maintain the personal interactions that have characterized the school's bureaucracy. As one parent explained, "People who are attracted to this school are not form-oriented people."

In the case of pregnancy leave for teachers, that policy decision was postponed easily in light of more pressing and immediate issues. Sometimes, however, the evolution of policy and practice causes tension. Changes in the leadership over the years have left uncertainty about how parents, teachers, the director, and Board members contribute to operations of the school. Following the application for VAIS accreditation, the Board assigned greater responsibility and authority to the school director. However, many parents wanted to remain just as involved in school decisions as they had previously, and these "older" parents sometimes voice their desire to remain involved in hiring decisions. They invariably cite the school's tradition of parent involvement and their own reluctance to change: "What sets us apart from other schools is that here you [as a parent] can have a voice. We don't want to lose that." Although not strictly a parent-run school according to its new bylaws, Free Union gives parents a voice in policy decisions. In addition, the director shares her responsibilities with the Board, which paradoxically causes uncertainty among some parents about who actually leads the school.

As noted, the parents ratify new members of the Board of Trustees every year at the Annual Meeting. The parents of alumni or current students make up the majority of the nine Board positions. As the Board gradually learned its responsibilities, and it found that the range of skills and knowledge needed did not necessarily exist among the school families, it sought out community members for open board positions.[52] In addition, following VAIS recommendations, the Board pushed for several significant changes in one year to create a structure that would protect its classroom success. The VAIS report was perceived to be a "wake-up call" that the school was a gem that could be lost. Some of these changes included raising tuition, altering the teacher hiring process, and clarifying scholarship procedures. With the strengthened role of the director, some parents and now teachers found their old roles and expectations shifting, a less than comfortable position. On occasion the Board, teachers, and parents found themselves at odds. One such occasion, the question "Who decides where the school goes (in the future)?" elicited the following comments from advisory committee members, a group of parents and teachers:

(1)   I feel like the Board is taking us in a direction and the parents know nothing about it.

(2)   The parents have been shut out. Though not intentionally.

(3)   The Board always invites parents, but they're not there. Is it that the meetings are at night? Where are the minutes, anyway?

(4)   People don't get involved if they think everything is okay. They only get involved if there's a crisis."[53]

Uncertainties like these usually reflect communication problems. Parents can be found throughout the school every day, but not all parents. Those parents who volunteer regularly at the school, who work as teachers' aides or at other jobs, and who participate on committees, spend several hours on site every week. Other parents, however, appear only briefly to pick up their children. Every parent has a mailbox in the front office which is filled every week with newsletters, reminders of upcoming events, and notes from teachers. But some of these notices are not always read closely, so critical information often passes by word of mouth among the most involved families. The Board invites all parents to attend the monthly board meetings, but other than those who serve on the Board few choose to attend. The disconnection between the Board and the parents, and the Board and teachers, causes tensions, which the school members recognize and work to resolve. Nevertheless, the school's larger and more bureaucratic organization requires new patterns of communication to replace those that functioned among the former small group of neighbors and friends.

Working through periods of confusion is hardly new for the young school. When new families began enrolling their children after those of the first, founding families, and the school began to grow in a different direction than the founding families had planned, tensions arose among the parents. These second and third waves of parents brought both new concerns, and new skills and ideas that enabled the school to change and develop. "The school began to take on a life of its own," reflected one early parent, "apart from what the founding families envisioned."[54]

Recently, a new wave of parents and teachers have again brought new concerns, skills and ideas. Again tensions have appeared between "old" and "new" families as the school has changed to meet the needs of the parents and, especially, the children. In fact, continual change has become a hallmark. Many parents and teachers compare the school to a growing child: "You try to provide for it all that you can, but it goes its own way."[55] Reflecting on some parents' resistance to change, the director observed, "If the old parents really understood the roots of the school founding, how it was built on change, they'd understand that we're just continuing the tradition."[56]

With all of the difficulties of Free Union Country School during its first decade, and its continuing struggles as it copes with new demands, it remains remarkable for its child-centered and community-based education. This schooling embraces the child and the family, inviting everyone into the school's confines to join in that most important of endeavors: educating the young.

Current Practices and Rituals at Free Union Country School

Throughout the year, school rituals reinforce and celebrate community by reinforcing the connections between home and school. Every day, several parents assist the teachers, either as classroom aides or simply lending a hand here and there. Coming from a wide variety of backgrounds and professions, these parents add valuable and reliable resources and expertise. One mother shares her expertise as a neurophysiologist during science units. Other parents teach art, reading and math. In fact, on one special day in October, the children learn from their parents with no teachers present. At the end of the first marking period, the teachers stay home to write assessments while parents teach special units. Elementary students choose from a range of classes offered in 20-minute segments and designed to take full advantage of the resources available in the school community.

In advance of Parent Teach Day, students write down their first and second choices for activities, similar to college students signing up for limited-enrollment classes. One parent collates all of these choices and constructs the schedule for the day in which students move from one "class" to another. Although the day invites confusion, the director, her assistant, and the parent volunteers keep the classes running smoothly. The children find it great fun to move from hunting and studying bugs in the neighboring pasture, to beading bags, to a workshop on writing and publishing, to baking banana bread, fishing in a local creek, or sewing vests and skirts. Fifth graders explore animal skulls with second graders; kindergartners paint ceramic tiles with third graders. The school walls vanish as students and parents interact in every room and throughout the grounds in myriad exploratory activities.

Other regular events include an open house and potluck dinner to start the year, Halloween games and costumes, a Thanksgiving dinner feast, a winter holiday program, and a field day of Olympics-inspired games. One year the students dressed up as animals and put on a circus. A graduate reflected on that event: "[The circus] really was an absolutely wonderful thing that [a previous teacher] organized. Everybody would dress up as different things. . . . I was a poodle and I scraped my knee. It was a really fun experience."[57] Fund raisers that draw on parent interests and skills occur throughout the year. These events have included a cross country foot race, a yard and plant sale, a holiday wreath sale, a horse show, and a square dance.

Near the end of the school year, a flurry of activity takes over every classroom as the students prepare for the May First maypole dance. Each class sings songs, learns dances and practices weaving ribbons around the maypole to the accompaniment of two teachers on guitar and recorder. Parents bring fresh flowers from their gardens to decorate the maypole and nearly every school family comes out to watch their children dressed for spring performing on the grass field. The culmination of the day comes with the crowning of the May Queen, often a teacher who is leaving the school at the end of the year. Parents and grandparents linger long after the performance with picnic lunches on blankets, sharing news and enjoying the school community.

Graduation always brings tears as the school community bids farewell to its fifth graders. The ceremony is formal, with a promenade of graduating students, ritualized speeches and songs. The parents of the graduates spend the afternoon at the school preparing floral and ivy garlands and bouquets to decorate the steps where the ceremony takes place. Graduates and former teachers often return to observe the ceremonies, contributing a sense of continuity. All of the families bring covered dishes to provide a feast to honor the students and the graduating students and their families enjoy the honor of eating first.

Graduation does not, however, mark the end of the school year. Two days later, all of the children return for a camp-out at a nearby retreat. They enjoy a day of outdoor games and lessons with their teachers, swimming, creek walking, canoeing, nature hiking and outdoor crafting. Then the older students cook dinner for the younger students. Parents arrive at the camp in time to join in the meal and set up tents for the camp-out. As the evening progresses, the students entertain their parents around the campfire with poems, songs, stories and toasted marshmallows. This last night of the school year marks the culmination of years of building friendships among the students and parents, and it can be an emotional occasion for those families who will not return the following year. During the evening entertainment, those families or teachers who have been particularly instrumental in the school receive hand-made quilts made by the students and parents. The quilts symbolize the many hands that come together every day to make the school a strong, nuturing place where children learn.

These special days punctuate a year filled with the excitement of learning. Every day children engage in art, outdoor education, and research. They devour books, reading every day alone and in groups. Loans from the city library supplement the school's own collection of picture and word books. Free Union Country School has, in short, become a place where children blossom and grow, under the caring guidance of their teachers and parents.

A Profile of the Free Union Teachers

As we have seen, the parents of Free Union Country School comprise the backbone of the school. They founded the school, and their involvement distinguishes this school from others in the area. Parents provide not only the financial support necessary for a private school, they also support the school intellectually and emotionally. But as family personalities and needs change with the appearance of new families, so the school adapts to new ways of carrying out its philosophy.

Meanwhile, despite the crucial role parents play in defining and sustaining the school, its teachers enact the school philosophy and values on a day-to-day basis. Teachers come to Free Union with different training and levels of experience but they are all hired specifically "because of their love of children and especially for their respect for children as human beings."[58] Teachers care about the children first, and always consider their learning and growth as the first priority. Lesson plans and the curriculum emerge out of the particular collection of students in a class. As the teacher gets to know that group of students, she continually revises and rewrites her plans for the year both to accommodate and take advantage of their unique qualities.

Because they know their students well, Free Union teachers can easily discern where a classroom activity may need to be changed to keep everyone engaged and learning. Their thorough knowledge of their students' strengths and weaknesses keeps them suspicious of such external evaluations as the Iowa Test of Basic Skills (ITBS) exams administered in the fourth and fifth grades. Although they find value in the test-taking experience, as this will be a common event in the children's futures, the teachers express strong reservations about using the test results to guide any judgment about a child's ability or achievement. "Why do we use this test?" one teacher asked. "Isn't there another we could use that more closely reflects what we teach and believe in? These test scores say nothing about our kids. Nothing."[59]

Ironically, ITBS scores say quite a bit about the Free Union students. Once they have learned how to take the test (a skill they rarely use in a school that resists testing) the students score in the middle to upper percentiles in all areas and continue to test well in their middle and high schools. The teacher's complaint about the ITBS reflects, rather, everything she knows about her students that the test ignores: their ability to apply themselves to a problem, their social skills, and their creativity and curiosity about learning.

Teachers come to Free Union because they appreciate its approach to education and find it a place where they can teach the way their skills and abilities are strongest. Without an external school board or state board of education defining the curriculum and teaching strategies, Free Union teachers are free to work from their strengths and the particular needs and abilities of their students. Given this freedom and the small class sizes, these teachers have been willing to accept lower salaries than they would earn in the public schools. But despite their love for the job, money remains an issue. Like many public school teachers, they often take on additional part-time jobs to supplement their income. Nevertheless, as one teacher observed,

> I don't teach here for the money and benefits. I've chosen to not have a big house with many belongings. I stay here because I can teach here the way that I want to. Maybe I could do that somewhere else, but I am doing it here. I don't stay here for the money.[60]

Those teachers unable to remain for financial reasons still consider Free Union an excellent place for beginning teachers to develop and excel in their profession. When two teachers left, one parent saw their departure as a positive step since they would be applying their valuable experience in other schools, which would reflect positively on Free Union. Yet the school is more than a way station for beginning teachers.

Because of its unique position, it has attracted experienced master teachers who come for the opportunity and support to teach "the way they've always wanted to teach."

While the teachers learn from their students the best way to teach, they also learn from one another and thereby present the students with common values and concerns. As one teacher explained,

> I guess we all start talking like each other after a while, although we weren't that different to start with. But this is such a small place that you hear the way another teacher talks, and you like that, so you start using the same phrases. Like the way we tell children to not do something. Usually I'll say, "You're not welcome to do that here," which I definitely picked up from [another teacher].[61]

Free Union Country School teachers exhibit strong camaraderie. Like the parents, the teachers become friends with each other. They often enjoy coffee in the city after the end of the school day, and they check with each other, not only about teaching issues but about their families and personal lives. Their conversations reveal mutual regard and caring. Their jobs and lives become intertwined as they recognize that balance in their professional and personal lives improves both. When one teacher feels poorly, the others step in without being asked to assist her and ease her day. They celebrate birthdays and other special occasions with quiet affection for each other and concern for reminding everyone that the celebrant is a unique part of a special school.

Conclusion: The Value of Confidence

One founding Free Union family insists that a child who is taught confidence can go into the world and do almost anything. In *The School-home*, Martin described the reactions of her philosophy of education students to a hypothetical caring and compassionate school that incorporates the values of home: "They nevertheless dismiss the ideas saying they will not prepare children for the real world, which is, by their account, a ruthless place."[62] Reflecting this belief, one Free Union family considered the school "too nice" because the rest of the world is not so "nice." But when their children left Free Union, they were shocked to discover that most other schools fail to foster respect among students and between students and teachers. Throughout her discussion, Martin insists that learning about "home matters" represents precisely these skills and values that all children need to live in the world. They are also the lessons society needs to make the world more livable. These ideas arose within Free Union as well, forming a core value around which the school has grown. One Free Union graduate explained that she learned at her elementary school what respect and caring feel like, and this learning has made it easier to find these ideals later in her life.

The transition from Free Union to larger schools can be difficult. One sixth grader felt overwhelmed by the amount of homework assigned her once she started middle school. The teachers hear these concerns from parents and try to increase the homework they require in the upper grades so their students won't be so surprised by the expectations at a different school. But the efforts come at a price. These teachers construct lesson plans, activities, lessons, and curricula every day, and one week a teacher sent home four different reading homework assignments in a class of thirteen students. Since the Free Union teachers create from scratch what other teachers can find in textbooks, they could hardly find time in the day to write extra homework. The homework issue also raises some concern about which responsibilities belong to the school and which belong to the home.

Other alumni experience temporary problems with mathematics and science. The exploratory approach taught at Free Union sometimes translates poorly in other schools. Where Free Union encourages students to find their own way to solve problems, other schools generally insist upon one particular method. Another school may require students to use specific techniques to solve math problems, so that a student "loses points" if the right answer is not "figured correctly." Free Union considers this sort of narrow procedure inhibiting and potentially detrimental to a child's intellectual development.

The issue underlying these discussions is whether a school should be a sanctuary, or whether a school should consciously prepare children for the hard, cruel world they are soon to enter. Should schools teach children to be competitive and look out for themselves first? Or should schools teach children to work together, and treat their friends with respect? Free Union has decided that providing children with a positive, nurturing climate during their formative elementary years provides them with a strong foundation and the personal confidence they need to face the changing world outside.

In the fourteen years since its founding, Free Union Country School has become a respected, even cherished school among its students, alumni and their families. More than one family has moved to the rural area specifically to be near the school. While it is not, and does not try to be, for all students, those families who remain express resolute praise for the school. Parents, students and teachers enjoy a strong feeling of ownership in a school that is, after all, their own.

11

A SCHOOL THAT REALLY WORKS:
URBAN ACADEMY

Mary Anne Raywid

Trying to make schools work—and work for all—is far too often a daunt-ing task.[1] The stories of failure, of good intentions gone awry, of high hopes dashed are all too frequent. Succeeding pages tell a different story, that of the Urban Academy, a school that has thrived and served New York City youngsters well for over a decade. The Academy has an attrac-tive program, a deeply committed staff, and an ambiance that manages to turn "problem" students into members of an intellectual community largely free of the need for disciplinary measures. The school sees its mission as building intellectual capacity and confidence in its students, enabling them to become thoughtful, informed, open, yet critical-minded young adults. There are many indications that it succeeds.

The attempt in these pages is to provide more than a glowing "show-and-tell" account. It is to describe a limited number of the school's attributes in sufficient detail so that interested readers might be able to build on and adapt Urban Academy practice. Additionally, with the hope of occasioning helpful insights, this chapter attempts to identify the features and qualities that seem to make this school work so well.

Urban Academy is a New York City-style school-within-a-school, or mini-school. It is an independent program housed within a building that also houses another, entirely separate program. The High School for the Humanities (HSH) is a large building located on 18th Street between 8th and 9th avenues.[2] It is a semi-selective high school with 1,500 students. Altogether, nine of HSH's rooms have been given to the Urban Acad-emy, a program enrolling 100 tenth through twelfth graders.

Urban Academy students must visit the school prior to an admissions interview and must fill out an application that requires brief thoughtful essays and solutions to general mathematics problems. It is not, however, a selective school, and admission is not based upon achievement or behavior. Indeed, many students entering from other high schools are quite explicit about seeing the Academy as "Last Chance High." Student abilities, achievement, and performance span a wide range, although most Urban Academy students are minority and few are middle-class. What most share is a past that has included difficulties in accepting and dealing with school authority. When they enter, very few see themselves as college-bound. Yet according to Nadine, the staff member primarily responsible for college advisement, 95 percent of Urban Academy's students enter college after graduation. Essentially the only graduates who do not are those who enter the military.

Because the Academy deliberately seeks students of diverse ability, not all become outstanding scholars. SAT scores range from below 400 to above 1,400. Yet, all Urban students graduate, pass all six of the state's required competency tests, and none drop out. Moreover, when students leave Urban Academy, they do so following an experience that has subjected them to constant channeling, prodding, inspiration, and assistance in the intelligent use of their minds—a multi-year immersion in the exercise of higher intellectual processes.

The Urban Academy grew out of an instructional program, an inquiry learning project developed several years ago by its two directors and operated by them in what eventually grew to be twelve New York City high schools. Begun initially as a staff development project for teachers, the program then evolved into a half-day instructional program for students. Eventually, the directors concluded that both youngsters' needs and staff interests might be better accommodated in a full-time school. Thus, Urban Academy opened in 1985 featuring an inquiry approach to learning.

The school's initial staff consisted of interested people the two directors had met in the course of conducting the staff development project or had known earlier. Although some of these people had met one another at summer workshops associated with the demonstration project, they had never worked together and did not really know each other well at the onset.

Staff construe the Academy as "the working laboratory for the Inquiry Demonstration Project."[3] Partly because of its past, partly due to continuing activities, and partly due to its experimental and nontraditional orientation, the Urban Academy characterizes itself as a laboratory school. A steady stream of visitors come to observe, and several faculty still offer in-service courses on the Academy's approach to teachers in other schools.

The Urban Academy staff roster shows 16 members, but this total is misleading because it includes the two co-directors, full-time teachers, part-time teachers, and interns. There are nine full-timers. By virtually eliminating nonteaching personnel, alternative schools such as Urban are able to reduce class size considerably, without major increases in the student-to-adult ratio.

So far as formal status differentiations are concerned, there are only two: teachers and co-directors. Until 1993 there was also an assistant principal who took care of much of the administrative work, but when he left, staff decided together to assume his duties and use his salary for other purposes. Thus, there is presently considerable differentiation as to function among staff, with teachers in effect dividing among themselves most administrative tasks, including admissions, keeping track of attendance, handling student transportation, and academic recordkeeping. These assignments appear to have been determined by mutual agreement and in consideration of individual teachers' interests and special abilities, and they are viewed as permanent until a reason for changing them surfaces (i.e., a request for re-assignment, or an interest in a function on the part of a newcomer). In addition to the teaching staff, the Academy employs one individual who coordinates its community service program and who has major responsibility for facilitating college applications. One secretary serves the entire faculty.

The co-director arrangement at Urban Academy is a novel one on several counts. One of the two co-directors, Herb Mack, functions in the more familiar role of principal and assumes responsibility for coordinating the school's daily operation. Staff look to him for instructions, help, and advice; and he is perceived by students as a strong, supportive, and benevolent, though firm, "father" figure. The co-director, Ann Cook, functions primarily in the role of ambassador to and liaison with the external educational and political community. She is active in and well known to New York City education circles, and she assumes a major role in bringing news as well as new pedagogical ideas into the school. Although Ann regularly teaches at least one course (as does Herb), and is almost always present for staff meetings, she spends a lot of time out of the building and considerable time on the phone when she is there. The co-directorship arrangement at Urban is also novel in that Ann and Herb are long-time professional collaborators. Together they designed and piloted the inquiry approach that is the theme of the Urban Academy. They are also husband and wife, and the parents of three adolescent daughters.

Modifying Student Experience at Urban Academy

According to Wisconsin's federally sponsored Center for School Organization and Restructuring, one of the hallmarks of a "restructured" school is that the experience of being a student or a teacher in such a school is quite different from what it is to be a student or teacher in an unrestructured school.[4] One's task and responsibilities are different, one's days are spent differently, and the school has a different ambiance, all of which leads both students and teachers to feel differently about their association with and roles within it. The "lived experience" of school is transformed for these students and teachers. This is clearly true of school life at Urban Academy. As students readily report without prompting, it is quite different from what they have previously experienced school to be.

Perhaps the most arresting qualities of restructured student experience at Urban Academy accrue from (1) the literally ceaseless efforts to make school a thought-provoking place; (2) the determined arranging and rearranging of the daily schedule to serve programmatic purposes rather than vice-versa; and (3) the unremitting efforts to provide needed support for students.

Providing a Thought-Provoking Learning Environment

The insistence on provoking thought lies at the heart of the inquiry method that is the school's theme and unifying thread. Indeed, the front cover of the Academy's brochure is dominated by a single word: "Why." The opening sentences of the brochure's text elaborate:

> That's what the students at the Urban Academy ask each day, in every class, at every opportunity. When they enter the Urban Academy they become members of an academic community seeking understanding in the same way as inquiring minds have done over the centuries. They ask questions and examine the variety of ways they can be answered.

One of the most noticeable ways in which the Urban Academy differs from many schools as an institution is that these words are not simply words. Urban Academy means what it says it means, and students get what they have been told they will find. The school mission is not simply a "philosophy" statement prepared by some authority to satisfy some regulation or other; rather, it represents a commitment that suffuses everything the school does.

For instance, the goal of arousing questioning and thoughtfulness is reflected in the curriculum and course offerings. Although the Academy offers some standard, discipline-based classes such as American history, algebra, economics, and chemistry, most classes are topically articulated instead, and by topics of concern to urban students. "Telling Stories," "Popular Culture," "Puzzles," "Evolution," "Religion and Society," "American Autobiography," "Utopia/Dystopia," "Animal Rights," and "Women Across Cultures" are a few of the classes from recent semesters. Moreover, students can expect in virtually every course to encounter at least three types of learning: (1) material they recognize as useable now (e.g., knowledge of the city's subway system, museums, or landmarks); (2) content they can use later, that is, the more typical school fare; and (3) treatments that increase reflectivity and thinking ability as well as enhance work habits.

The thoughtfulness theme pervades virtually every class at Urban Academy. This is not easy to accomplish with a student population that would probably not comply with the reading and other daily assignments associated with traditional secondary education. Getting students to tackle activities that must be sustained over an extended period also presents a considerable challenge. One response on the part of the faculty to address these challenges is to probe different facets of a broad topic on different days, introducing more material and complexity as the discussion proceeds.

Most classes manage to present an issue students find genuinely challenging. It is always one that can be tackled at a more penetrating level than simply "getting the facts" or "mastering the basics." For example, Herb's popular "Issues" course one day tackled the question, "What are the most important values?" and on another, "What rights does a parent have and what rights does a kid have?" Avram's "Pop Culture" course required students to draw inferences about musicians' popularity and power from data detailing cassette and CD sales. Barry's "Seminar on Animal Rights" has explored whether or not zoos are inherently inhumane, while the "Women's Studies" class taught by Ann examined the question, "Which is more dangerous: pornography or censorship?" The Library Research Project required of all Urban Academy students each year illustrates another way in which teachers at this school go about making assignments as provocative as possible for students. The project is a demanding and somewhat dreaded requirement, but staff go to considerable lengths to make it palatable and rewarding. One year's assignment asked students to pursue the subject of one article from the front page of the *New York Times* appearing on the day they were born. They had to use both the *Reader's Guide* and a computerized index to identify magazine articles on the topic, find and comment on books from the best-seller lists of the day, and read a review of a film playing at the time. Part two of the project required visiting a different library, comparing its facilities and services with the first, and pursuing scientific abstracts on a question assigned according to the month of birth. Questions included, "How does cocaine affect newborns?" "Which condom is the most effective?" and "What is the latest research on cockroach behavior?" By the time the project was completed in all its parts, students had amassed considerable information about libraries and on the identification and accessing of sources. They had also been required to display skill in acting upon such knowledge, had acquired information bearing on matters of contemporary concern, and had gained an introduction to the pop culture of 15 to 20 years ago.

As this example suggests, efforts to make students think do not end with the in-class efforts of individual teachers; the entire school is organized to provoke adolescents to think. For instance, in the hall outside the Academy's office, there is always posted a bulletin board question based on a prominent current news issue. Recent boards have asked, "Should football be outlawed?" (following an accident in which a professional player broke his neck) and "Should gays be allowed to serve in the military?" (while the issue was being discussed in the press). The question is mounted on a large sheet of poster paper, on which students anonymously pen their responses to the question and to each other. Another sheet of similar size on a nearby board invites graffiti and serves to keep the question sheet, as well as other Urban Academy areas, largely graffiti-free.

Another means of provoking thought is the three-week project that launches each semester at Urban Academy. This is a carefully orchestrated, cross-disciplinary venture that involves the whole school, working in groups of eight to twelve, to tackle the various dimensions of a broad question. Recent project themes have been: "What makes for a good subway system?" "What is community?" and "How does architecture affect lifestyles?" Each project is planned in detail with intensive, day-long group activities. Some exercises and activities are shared by all students and others are differentiated depending on student interests and the talents and focus of individual teachers. For instance, the subway project began with group scavenger hunts to identify sites such as clothing stores, toy stores, city hall, and the main library, and then to verify the fastest route for getting there. After viewing videos on tunnel digging, hearing a panel discuss whether or not the subway system should be abolished, visiting the Transport Museum, and doing particular readings, groups selected differentiated topics to research and pursue, including one led by the science teacher on subway health issues, and others on subway stories, subway advertising, subway station design, public behavior on the subway, and a very intricate one on re-routing the New York City subway system. Fulfilling project requirements is a demanding and intensive venture occupying the full day of students and teachers working together in school and outside it.

After the three-week project period ends, the semester's regular classes begin, yet this initial project serves as a marvelous way to induct new staff, as well as new students, into the life of the Urban Academy. A similar project period in February serves as a welcome, mid-year change of pace. These projects yield extended opportunity for teachers to work together in planning a set of experiences equally novel to beginners and old-timers. Moreover, they provide opportunity for the staff to pursue and model the same sort of inquiry processes they want students to internalize; and they enable students, teachers, and the two groups together to work less formally and more closely with one another than class work typically entails.

Recently, a new way has been added to stimulate student thinking via special-topic seminars on issues of sure concern to students. These seminars are small classes by design, and they make heavy demands on those enrolled. They involve extensive reading assignments (up to 30 or 40 pages weekly), and a paper is due each week. Since the Urban Academy has no library of its own, making it unlikely that daily reading assignments requiring library access could be completed, readings are typically photocopied for students. Seminar students receive weekly packets of carefully chosen articles which form the bases on which their papers are developed.

Events beginning in a recent Animal Rights Seminar class yield further evidence of staff commitment to generating student thinking. Barry, the teacher, was disappointed by students' apparent inability to fulfill his writing assignment, which called for analysis of the materials in the reading packet. He therefore made multiple copies of one articulate, otherwise well-written paper that erred by summarizing one article after another rather than analyzing them. He brought copies of the paper for all to an afternoon staff meeting and distributed them at the start since Herb had placed him first on the agenda. For 45 minutes, the staff discussed the challenge of how to teach students to undertake genuine analysis and what would constitute an adequate response to the assignment. "Analysis" is a frequently used term at Urban, and teachers were embarrassed as well as chagrined that this concept, and how to operationalize it, appeared so elusive. Two teachers agreed to bring selected packets of student papers to a subsequent meeting so that the staff could together explore which papers provide the best analyses and why. The discussion ended with an agreement to return to the matter for general staff consideration after Barry and another teacher had a chance to consider some additional ideas. As this suggests, one of the ways in which Urban Academy staff encourage thought and reflection on the part of students is that they model it, not only in interactions with students but also in their interactions with one another. Little at this school passes as routine and unquestioned.

At another staff meeting, considerable time was devoted to examining an issue of the school newspaper, *Strange Brew*. Staff had earlier been dissatisfied with the production of the paper, which was managed by a skilled journalist part-timer who taught the class enrolling students who wanted to work on the paper. The problem was not the product but the process: although the final production and its content typically was deemed laudable, the instructor was taking rough manuscripts, editing them himself, getting the student authors' approvals, and then putting the revised manuscripts on his computer. The teaching arrangements for the newspaper were changed. The full-time English and computer teacher is now responsible for coordinating production of the paper. Students edit their own articles, typically preparing six or more drafts, and they computerize the material themselves.

The just-distributed "new" paper was discussed at a later staff meeting. Staff offered a number of compliments, but they engaged in serious and detailed examination of the paper, including logical criticism of one piece. They critiqued the paper with regard to both writing substance and style. The discussion also occasioned the suggestion by one teacher for a new publication, an academic journal assembling outstanding student papers.

A statement that hangs on the wall beside Herb's desk, having struck a responsive chord, seems to project the sort of ambiance Urban Academy students have come to expect:

> I fully realize that I have not succeeded in answering all of your questions. . . . Indeed, I feel I have not answered any of them completely. The answers I have found only serve to raise a whole new set of questions, which only lead to more problems, some of which we weren't even aware were problems. . . . To sum it all up . . . in some ways I feel we are as confused as ever, but I believe we are confused on a higher level, and about more important things.

Instituting Scheduling Flexibility

A second way in which the school lives of Urban Academy students and teachers differ quite extensively from the lives lived in most other schools is associated with the way in which the school schedule is viewed. Instead of functioning to control instruction, the schedule at Urban serves as its tool. It is not the all-powerful structure to which everything must conform. Instead, it is designed, and constantly redesigned, to serve the programmatic purposes selected by the staff. When it fails to do so, it is the schedule and not the instructional program that must give way. Although this is more easily accomplished at the end of a semester, when the schedule is regularly redesigned anyway, adjustments can be made in mid-semester.

The schedule at Urban is simply not construed as unvarying. By design, it contains enough day-to-day variation that all must daily be reminded anyway of its components and sequence. Thus, changes are far more easily introduced than when mind-sets call for invariant time segments and sequences.

The design and use of the school schedule at Urban are sufficiently unusual to appear a major reflection of the restructuring the Academy represents. The schedule is made out each semester by Herb, after meetings at which teachers report their needs. A proposed schedule then goes through multiple versions before it is finalized. In the course of resolving conflicts and accommodating needs, the entire plan is scrapped several times and the task launched again from the beginning. The fall version this year represented the sixth such try.

Unlike schedules at most schools, Urban Academy's does not divide the day into equal segments for classes. The first class in a Friday schedule lasts 55 minutes; the second and third, 50 minutes each. Lunch lasts an hour, and the two afternoon classes each last 75 minutes. (Most classes fall within the 50- to 75-minute time frame. Tuesdays, however, have one 90-minute time block.) There are also two 10-minute breaks, one after the second class and one just before the last class of the day. The times to which classes are assigned differ according to teachers' requests. Some classes are always longer, some are always shorter; some teachers may want one or two 50-minute sessions, plus one 75-minute class. Schedules are also developed to accommodate teacher preferences with regard to morning versus afternoon classes, although the more frequent pattern is to shift class time so that a class which meets at 8:30 on Monday may meet at 10:35 on Wednesday. Consequently, students rarely memorize schedules, and Herb posts the schedule for the day outside each of the Academy's rooms early every morning.

A final illustrative manifestation of the use of the schedule to serve the needs of the program instead of forcing instruction to fit into preset time blocks can be found in the building in of nonclass time. The staff meets regularly on Wednesdays from 12:15 to 3:15, as well as on alternate Tuesdays after school. This collaboration time is made possible by having students perform service activities in the community during this time. (All students are required to provide such service weekly, and on a volunteer, unpaid basis. Assignments include such activities as helping in a legislative office, a school, a teenage treatment center, or an animal rescue group.) The "research days" occurring at the end of semesters also introduce nonclass time into the schedule. Over a several-day period, extensive conferences are held with each student, typically assembling all his or her teachers for the discussion. Since all staff are involved in these sessions, the question arises as to what to do with the rest of the students to permit such labor-intensive teacher activity. The answer is a long list of activities from among which students can select. Last year, this list consisted of 17 such activities, including: reading a supplied packet of materials on UFOs (unidentified flying objects), evaluating the reports and the claims made, and formulating an argument about the UFO phenomenon; reading a packet about "ball" lightning and offering an argument as to whether it is real; reading a controversial children's book and making a case as to whether it is appropriate for children; and preparing a thorough resources guide for an area of individual interest.

Providing Enhanced Student Support

A third characteristic of restructured student experience at Urban accrues from the staff's determination to provide whatever is necessary by way of student support. This determination surfaces in many ways, in the school's culture as well as in its structural features and operation.

For example, Urban offers the increasingly familiar advisory groups in which groups of up to twenty students meet weekly to explore school problems together. (The topic of one session of Becky's advisory last year was "What's screwed up around here?") A new set of groups called "organizational tutorials," which involve all students and meet weekly, have also recently been added. These tutorials were started to preserve the integrity of advisory groups while providing a more explicitly academic advisory setting. Prior to the weekly meeting of the small groups of seven to nine, each organizational tutorial teacher checks with each of his/her group members' teachers to see just how the students are doing in each class. Particular emphasis is placed on whether work is being completed, and whether any other class-specific difficulties are occurring for any student. This arrangement was launched in the interests of proactive troubleshooting and to facilitate the identification of emerging cognitive difficulties. The organizational tutorial is a brief (35--minute), highly task-oriented session. The teacher goes around the circle asking for student response on how their work is going and providing feedback from teachers. There are often suggestions about needed priorities, time management, and work organization.

Three kinds of labs are operated to assure that students get needed support: homework labs, course-connected labs, and college labs. The homework labs function as study halls and are operated for those who want them. Because some Academy students are totally without supportive conditions for doing homework outside of school, this elective serves an important function for them. Students enrolled in homework lab get help as needed and must arrive at each session with an assignment to work on, or one is provided for them. Students who do not elect to enroll in a homework lab take an Independent Study class instead, in which they can pursue individual or group projects. Most select the latter, and at the time this chapter was written, one group was reading Dostoyevsky, another was working on conversational Spanish, and a third was doing a videotape of the school.

Another sort of lab is attached to specific courses that make heavy demands in terms of reading or writing. These labs are scheduled for a course assigning an extensive research paper or one assigning a series of short analytical papers requiring a number of rewrites. Their intent is not remediation but the provision of proactive support to enable students to meet demanding standards. This year, for one semester, classes in American History and Television Analysis had labs attached to them, while they were held for the History and Issues courses during the other. Just one of their unusual features is that the lab segment of each course, which meets for one separate and longer period each week, is, by design, taught by a teacher other than the person who teaches the course. Typically, the lab teacher (or teachers) will sit in on the course's regular classes occasionally, to remain aware of course expectations. This enables them to help in ways usual study hall teachers cannot. There are several reasons for assigning staff this way. It affords students additional help, making two sources and two sets of resources available for them to tap. It also leaves the student in charge of carrying out class assignments and satisfying class requirements because the lab teacher's role is to help the student, not to co-teach the course. Lastly, it places Urban Academy staff in yet another kind of collaborative setting, giving them a view of others' teaching and perhaps posing questions about their own.

A third kind of lab has emerged in connection with Urban students' enrollment in college classes, an option open to them. Based on difficulties some have encountered as well as on students' insecurities and hesitations, a teacher now accompanies students and sometimes sits in on the classes in which they are enrolled. The group goes over together to the campus of a local four-year private college or to a two-year city college. Back at the Academy, in a specially scheduled college lab class, whatever support the students need is provided (e.g., help with understanding the material or the instructor's expectations).

A number of other features have also been built into the structure of the Urban Academy in an effort to respond to whatever support needs appear to be emerging. Recently, a new arrangement was added: an optional class on Thursday morning. Attendance is not required first period on Thursdays (from 8:30 A.M. to 9:45 A.M.), and students come in only if there is something they need or want to do. This is a time when some students make dates to talk about specific questions with teachers, while others meet with classmates to work on specific projects or just to talk. Still others use this time to sit and read the newspaper, chatting with whomever comes into the student study/lounge. Several students have offered classes of their own during this optional period, teaching guitar and dance, for example. For most, however, the Thursday session functions as unscheduled time set aside for whatever individualization needs have arisen during the week.

Many other sorts of support are extended to Urban students, although not all of them in typical ways. There are no counselors at Urban because every teacher is expected to fill the counseling role, in the sense not only of academic advisement but also for standing as an interested and concerned adult to any student seeking help. There is a part-time psychologist who deals with problems requiring more attention. He is supposedly available to Academy students for two half-days each week, though he reportedly often gives many more than the hours that are expected of him. Otherwise, he maintains a private practice.

The Academy population is small enough, and there is sufficient psychic closeness in the school, that when a student is in trouble it becomes evident rather quickly. A teacher who happens to spot difficulty or to wonder about whether some exists might first speak with Herb about it, or go first to the leader of the student's advisory group. Or she or he might simply discuss it with another teacher. Spontaneously or by design, the youngster would be engaged by a staff member attempting to discern the difficulty.

Herb has frequent access to the students, who must pass his desk to go from the office/staff room to the student study/lounge next door. He also stocks two small aspirin bottles on his desk with M&Ms. Students stop by constantly throughout the day and help themselves (requiring him to refill the bottles several times a day and to purchase 15 pounds of candy per week). A student stopping for a handful of candy may well become engaged in an exchange with Herb or with another student who is on the same mission. Herb is a father figure to the entire school, and students feel they can ask him for an unusual range of assistance and advice. The notes mounted on the walls around his desk attest eloquently to this:

Hola, Herb: There's a leaky pipe in the women's bathroom. Check it out TODAY.

I hate you, Herb. Love, Bill

Herb, I feel crabby and/or cranky. I'm sick. Please come and get me in Dance A. S. A. P. Jean

Herb, Nancy is driving me crazy. Please help me, Shanti

Dear Herb, I have been diagnosed with "School Burnout"!!! So I'm going home to sleep it off. P.S.: See you tomorrow. Your hardest working student, lane

Dear Herb: i appreciate the fact that you have saved all the letters that i have given you over the years. But you should take them down soon, because i have grown tremendously and find them quite embarrassing. . . . Very happily, May

Lest these messages suggest a highly indulgent environment in which students do as they please, a further look is needed. An observer who concludes that Urban Academy is a permissive school in which student whim and choice govern misses the essence of the school. An important contrast separates Urban Academy from schools where students decide most matters. Students are constantly consulted at Urban; they are invited to participate in decision-making sessions, asked what courses they want to take and with which teachers, and encouraged to express their reactions to events and conditions. What they have to say is listened to not only courteously but intently. What they like and dislike gets serious consideration, as does what they find meaningful as opposed to what they find obscure or inscrutable. They are obviously taken seriously and influence events, but they are not the decision makers at Urban. The teachers are.

An Urban student's choice of courses may be overridden in the interests of achieving an appropriate balance for the class, devising a schedule that makes more sense for the individual in terms of meeting graduation requirements, or separating students staff feel should not be enrolled in the same class. Similarly, regarding curriculum and content, student interests and preferences are taken very seriously, but it is the staff who make the decisions. Though students are the major determinants of what happens at Urban, their influence is not manifested through their votes or statements of preference. It is mediated by staff decisions on what seems indicated in light of student preferences as well as other considerations.

Another way in which the culture at Urban Academy extends support to its students is through the assumptions or "givens" consistently reflected in the school. At most conventional high schools, it is simply assumed that adults are entitled to courtesies denied students. It is also assumed that communication among adults takes precedence over other exchanges. Thus, it is not unusual in most schools for an administrator or another teacher (directly or over a public address system) to interrupt a class or a student-teacher conversation to deliver a message to the teacher or get an answer to a question. This is clearly not standard operating procedure at Urban. Classes and student-teacher conversations have priority and a kind of sanctity. For example, if a student is speaking with a teacher in the hall or at the teacher's desk in the crowded office/staff room, they are rarely interrupted by another staff member, especially if they are talking quietly. Indeed, the norm is the reverse of what typically occurs in schools: staff and other adult conversations may be interrupted by students or teachers, but not student-staff conversations. Commitment, both to showing respect for students and treasuring the importance of "the teachable moment," runs deep. As one of the teachers put it, if a teacher and a student arrive simultaneously at Herb's desk, it is the student and not the teacher to whom he turns first.

A rather different kind of support also prevalent at Urban Academy accrues from the dogged attempt on the part of staff to figure out exactly why their academic expectations of students are not being met, and then to do something about it. Staff consistently reject answers like "They [students] are just lazy," "They were careless," or "They didn't think," in favor of diagnoses that identify specific process deficiencies. As described earlier, when a full class failed to respond appropriately when asked to analyze, the reasons were pursued sufficiently to ascertain that students simply did not know how. Hence, it was clear that they needed help in performing this process, and staff set to work figuring out how to provide the assistance necessary.

In consequence of such an approach, there is a tendency at Urban to render highly explicit much of what other schools simply take for granted. When Academy students are instructed on how to do research papers, for example, the instructions are not just as to length and what note cards and footnotes should look like; teachers attempt to help students understand the nature of the intellectual steps one must go through in doing research. This marks a considerable contrast with customary educational practice, which typically tells students to "analyze," "discuss," or "appraise," and then tests them on whether or not they can do so. Rarely do teachers offer the in-between, the step-by-step guidance on just how one performs these procedures. By contrast, it is characteristic of Urban Academy staff to try to figure out the process and then instruct youngsters on how to conduct it.

Teacher Experience at Urban Academy

Urban Academy teachers work hard, but in several important respects their work appears different from that of teachers in most schools. First, the array of teachers' duties and expectations at Urban is far broader than the teaching of classes. Some teachers perform regular administrative functions like the handling of admissions or the categorizing and recording of credits on student transcripts. Others may be assigned to accompany students to a college course, while still others may conduct the lab portion of a colleague's course. New teachers are expected to audit one or two classes taught by a senior teacher in a related field. New teachers and interns also meet weekly with Herb in small groups to discuss challenges and difficulties raised by either party. All teachers are expected to be available to cover a colleague's class or to assist with it (e.g., by participating in a demonstration or debate) on absolutely minimal notice (such as three minutes). Asking for and receiving help is common among Urban Academy teaching staff.

Although a look at schedules may show a teacher teaching during only three of a day's scheduled five periods, no teachers appear to have prep periods in the form of assigned time that belongs solely to them. Teachers are expected to be available at any time for whatever appears to be needed. Although some might find this an infringement on individual entitlements, it seems closely tied to the deeply rooted conviction at Urban that all are jointly responsible for making the school work and that, when something is needed and one is the logical member to do it or simply the most available member, one does it. Obviously, such an attitude could not long prevail where individuals believed themselves exploited or victimized. It appears to be a sense of reciprocity—a conviction that one can count on comparable support from others when the need arises—that prevents a sense of being exploited.

Urban Academy's teachers work hard in ways that are intellectually demanding and that place a premium on invention and creativity. Working out the curriculum described in these pages is extremely demanding, particularly because change and novelty are seen as assets to sustaining student engagement. By virtue of the quality of effort required, as well as by virtue of other features previously identified, teachers at Urban experience their work as highly professional in nature. They see themselves as performing an intellectually and emotionally demanding task of the highest order of importance. Although—or perhaps because they find almost constant reason to change and improve their efforts, they are proud of what they do and the success with which they do it. They seem to relish the intellectual challenge that their problems sometimes occasion. In multiple ways, Academy staff project the message that educators generally would gain much by emulating their program and arrangements.

The school projects a strong sense of confidence and efficacy. As its descriptive brochure proclaims, "The Urban Academy is recognized as a rigorous academic school serving a diverse population of students who have often been unchallenged in previous settings." As school staff describe this population less formally, it is a group that has experienced difficulty with authority in other school settings. What Urban does is to construe a population that has elsewhere posed disciplinary problems as one posing a primarily pedagogical challenge instead. It seems to work. Few disciplinary problems arise, and virtually none of a confrontational, showdown nature have occurred. The school's sole absolute rule of "no fighting" has never been violated in its eight years, and on the sole occasion when that record was threatened, it was students who stepped in to uphold it.

However, Urban teachers encounter a normal number of adolescent challenges to adult authority and numerous other infractions which, in more traditional schools, might become confrontational occasions. To cite three sorts: lateness is a chronic problem for some Academy students; locker fronts sometimes exhibit displays of questionable taste; and male students often want to wear hats while walking through the hallways of HSH, where hats are forbidden. Academy teachers handle such challenges with careful inquiry into causes and circumstances, receptivity to discussion and negotiation, and often with considerable humor.

Depending on the circumstances, lateness may be viewed more sympathetically by teachers at Urban than at other schools, and it is handled on an individual basis after an effort to determine its reason. In some cases, the solution has been to give the student an alarm clock or to make morning wake-up calls. Other measures have included careful scheduling to lure youngsters into arriving on time, and a support group for tardy students is currently under consideration.

Students whose locker fronts display sexually explicit photographs or language that would undoubtedly offend some are more likely to generate First Amendment discussions with their teachers than personal confrontations. These discussions often yield defenses that staff are quite willing to applaud, even if they do not concede to them. When students who feel they have been wrongfully censored respond with locker fronts somehow proclaiming that, staff are willing to appreciate the students' stance, even though the taboos remain in force.

One of the most important features of Urban's nonconfrontational stance is an overlay of negotiability with respect to matters that are not elsewhere negotiable. Regarding the hats-in-the-hall issue, Ann and Herb express a willingness to negotiate it with HSH officials if the students assign it a priority. As these negotiations will probably necessitate students giving up as well as getting something in return, the two directors ask students what they are willing to surrender: their right to leave the building at noon (which HSH students cannot), or their right to use portable cassette players in homework labs (which HSH students cannot)? When so approached, the hat issue usually recedes, although some rules have been modified through such negotiation between students and staff.

The general absence of confrontational disciplinary problems doubtless contributes to the staff's sense of efficacy. As a result of their being spared a lot of the struggle and unpleasantness that is hard to avoid in other schools, Urban Academy staff enjoy a strong sense of accomplishment, self-sufficiency, and collective competence to cope successfully with the challenges that arise.

The staff at Urban share an extraordinarily close professional community, even though few personal relationships are pursued outside of school. It is apparent, however, that these are people who like, respect, and admire each other enormously; and it would be hard to find a faculty group with members more respectful of one another's knowledge and skills. There is considerable fundamental agreement among Urban Academy teachers. Although they express such agreement in varying degrees of detail and eloquence, they are jointly engaged in sustaining and inducting young people into an intellectual or academic community. Their intent is to occasion cognitive learning and development in the interests of making their students into independent thinkers who can function as adults both receptive to and equipped for further education. They are quite aware of, and continuously responsive to, these young-sters' emotional needs and problems; but they are clear that their own contribution to students' lives is to create a community in which they can truly become knowledgeable, autonomous adults.

The extent to which staff share a single conception of the school's mission is further evident in their formulations of what they are about. The articulations differ from teacher to teacher. For one, the Urban Academy mission is "to provide an empowering education enabling students to establish their place in the world with self-confidence, open-ness, and critical-mindedness," while another sees it as "getting kids to buy into intellectual rigor and to see themselves as intellectuals." Yet, there is sufficient fundamental agreement that all see themselves to be engaged in the same task, pursuing the same ends through a strategy that is also shared: the inquiry approach.

Although adapted in different ways to accommodate different content and different teacher personalities, the shared inquiry approach reflects these features from classroom to classroom: (1) a commitment to maxi-mal openness and receptivity to student responses, including a willingness to pursue hypotheses even when they seem wrong-headed; (2) a commit-ment to exposing students to a variety of information and opinion on all matters considered, thereby expanding their awareness of existing knowledge and theory; and (3) a commitment to problematizing all con-tent, casting the student in as intellectually active and demanding a role as possible.

So understood, the approach appears strongly embraced and consis-tently reflected in all classes. It is broad enough not to pinch. Academy staff do not experience the inquiry orientation as a constraint on their own practice; rather, they report a degree of autonomy that was new to all of them. The inquiry orientation is also sufficiently specific that it would undoubtedly prove alien and restrictive to some teachers. Thus, it can lend consistency to what students experience throughout the school by enabling Urban to stand for something, as distinct from what faculty may stand for as individuals. In turn, this enables both students and staff to select the Academy for what it represents.

Success Ingredients

Just what is it that makes the Urban Academy successful? A number of factors seem to contribute, including some not described here. For example, the fact that the school is part of New York City's Alternative High Schools and Programs unit, an office known to buffer its schools and programs from the city's notorious school bureaucracy, yields the Academy considerable autonomy. Additionally, the school's ability to draw on a variety of resources yields it various forms of expertise and support. Nevertheless, the features that have been described in this chapter are linked by a number of qualities that appear to contribute substantially to the Urban Academy's success.

First, Urban is small—small enough that all associated with the school can greet one another by name. Smallness does not guarantee school success, but there is extensive current agreement to the effect that it is probably necessary to it.[5] Smallness not only permits an obvious sort of personalizing (e.g., task assignment in accordance with staff members' talents and preferences, penalties for infractions according to circumstances and individual situations), in a school that is small, the social order can rest far more extensively on norms and interactions than on rules and regulations—no minor advantage when dealing with adolescents. Furthermore, the staff is small enough that teachers can sit around a table together to discuss and decide issues. At Urban, teachers' desks are all located within a single office/staff room, and they are close enough that it would be difficult to avoid one's colleagues even for a day. Thus, scale may be one substantial factor in the Urban Academy's success.

Second, Urban has a specific focus instead of reflecting the familiar secondary education model and undertaking to appear a scaled-down version of the comprehensive high school. The particular theme or focus at Urban serves as a selection principle for assembling both faculty and students. Those who place a premium on problematizing all schoolwork and on making all classroom encounters thought-provoking, can choose Urban Academy with full knowledge that this is what they will find and be expected to sustain.

Urban's co-directors are convinced that it is not just having a focus but the particular nature of the focus they have chosen that helps explain the school's success. The fact that Urban's is a pedagogical rather than a curricular theme makes it possible to sustain the school's focus across the entire school program and throughout the school day. Contrast this with the more typical magnet school theme featuring a curricular focus (e.g., science and math, performing arts, or computers). Even in those schools that attempt to use one discipline or topic to articulate an entire curriculum (and it is unclear how many do), this is difficult to accomplish. Thus, most substantively themed magnet schools permit more course work in the focal topic or discipline, but the rest of each student's classes may remain quite similar in nature to those in conventional schools. Perhaps, as this suggests, there is more school "transformation" potential in a pedagogical than in a curricular theme.

This suggests yet a third quality that may help explain Urban Academy's success: the consistent dominance and permeation of its mission. The intent to provoke adolescents to use their minds, and to learn to use them well, suffuses literally all that happens in this school—from classes and scheduling to bulletin boards and activities—everything: The priorities at Urban are clear to all involved, and the mission stands as the consistently operative criterion in reaching decisions about everything.

A fourth quality that accounts for Urban Academy's success lies in the fact that the school's co-directors and staff have not contented themselves with the modification of only one aspect of school experience, that is, its instructional approach. Their efforts to engage students thoughtfully have led to considerable curricular change as well as an innovative organization of content. Additionally, staff roles have been modified, novel structures have been introduced, an innovative evaluation system is in place, and more. The point is that a broad, innovative range has been undertaken—of a scope that seems important both in transforming the experience of students and teachers and, perhaps more modestly, even in permitting any change to work. As a number of reformers have observed, school practice and arrangements are so intertwined and mutually supportive that it is necessary to set out to change a great deal in order to succeed at changing anything at all.[6]

A fifth quality that may also loom large in Urban Academy's success is the constant change and revision under way at the school. Urban is not a school content with resting on its past successes. On the contrary, staff seem to assume that virtually all of the school's arrangements and structures are almost infinitely improvable. Thus, almost anything at the school—other than the commitment to an inquiry approach—can, in the staff's view, be modified or replaced. Such a conviction leads directly to the continuing "self-renewal" that Goodlad (1984) found necessary to any school that would not only become good but remain good.[7] At Urban, instead of functioning as constraints to the instructional program, structures such as schedules, curriculum, the kinds of supports extended to students, staffing patterns, and staff roles are all considered alterable.

A sixth and final pervasive situation that probably has a great deal to do with Urban's success is the collaboration that marks most activities in the school. Staff meetings have already been mentioned, and, unlike the meetings familiar to most school staff, at Urban these gatherings typically function as joint problem-tackling sessions. Teachers co-teach classes, or teach the lab course for a colleague's class, or audit a colleague's course, or represent a needed position in a panel or debate for a colleague's course. According to Urban Academy tradition, it is in collaboration with colleagues that problems are identified, tackled, and resolved and their solutions implemented. Such practice undoubtedly has much to do with sustaining the reflection that keeps improvement constant and teacher satisfaction levels high. For it appears more than mere coincidence that Urban Academy is not only an enviably successful program, but one that staff are pleased and proud to be a part of.

A NEW VISION IN PROGRESSIVE PUBLIC EDUCATION: THE STORY OF THE W. HAYWOOD BURNS SCHOOL

Cynthia McCallister

The W. Haywood Burns School, P.S.-I.S. 176, located in the Inwood section of Manhattan, serves children from the communities of Inwood, Hamilton Heights and Washington Heights. Its newly constructed building stands at 204th Street and Broadway, the main traffic artery connecting lower Manhattan with northern Manhattan and the Bronx. Housed within the building are three small, learner-centered schools: the Muscota New School, serving children from kindergarten through grade five, which began operation in the fall of 1993 and was previously housed in another larger school in the district; the Amistad School, a new dual-language school also serving children from grades kindergarten through four; and the W. Haywood Burns Middle School, a new small school serving children from grades five through seven.

The W. Haywood Burns School is dedicated to the memory of its namesake, W. Haywood Burns, a committed African-American social activist, educator, scholar, poet, lawyer, husband and father. As an attorney, Burns worked for the causes of human and civil rights. He was Assistant Counsel for the NAACP Legal Defense Fund; he served as Chief Council with Martin Luther King on the Poor Peoples' Campaign; and he was founding dean of the City University of New York Law School. His reputation as a constitutional lawyer earned him an invitation from the new South African government to help draft a constitution for a democratic multiracial country. In 1995, Burns died in a car accident in South Africa. The school community chose the name of W. Haywood Burns and presented it to the local school board because they felt he personified many of the values they wished to impart to their children.

Just across the street from the school, north on the next block, the old Dyckman farm house stands on a low hill above Broadway, one of the few remnants of the area's pre-urban existence. Its rugged yet quaint eighteenth century design stands in stark contrast to the surrounding urban neighborhood. In the nineteenth century, other farm houses and lavish mansions occupied this section of Manhattan. Just after the turn of the century, when the new subway line linked Washington Heights and Inwood to lower Manhattan, the area became accessible to working- and professional-class families interested in affordable, genteel living. Soon, tenement and luxury residential buildings crowded into every available space. The community appeals to many because of the availability of housing far more affordable than in downtown Manhattan, more than 300 acres of wooded parks, and convenient transportation to downtown Manhattan. These features draw a range of socio-economic groups to a diverse mix of middle- and working-class neighborhoods.

In the past, the community had been home to immigrants from Eastern Europe, Ireland, Germany and Cuba, who had, by the time they moved to the country or into the community, acquired some degree of economic stability. Catholic and Protestant churches and synagogues, German and Eastern-European bakeries and delicatessens, and a sizable number of Irish pubs and news shops bear witness to the community life of the area's former residents, many of whom have since moved to the New Jersey suburbs, upstate New York, and Long Island. Recently, large numbers of Dominicans and Russian Jews have made their home in this northernmost tip of Manhattan. For these groups, coming to the U.S. from economic privation, this community is their first stop in the United States. For many of this community's newest arrivals, poverty complicates the struggle of immigration. Lacking the economic stability their predecessors enjoyed, they often require the full array of social services. Inwood, Washington Heights and Hamilton Grange have recently confronted an unprecedented social instability reflected in the challenges that face Community School District Six. The founding parents, faculty members and administrators of the W. Haywood Burns School are keenly aware of the challenges of educating students in an urban community:

District Six has the highest rate of poverty in the city—40 percent of its families have incomes under $10,000. The 34th Police Precinct has one of the highest levels of drug activity and other crime, including murder, in New York City. In addition, teenage pregnancy is the norm—two out of every three new babies in the community are born to mothers between fifteen and nineteen years old. The District has by far the highest number of students with limited English proficiency of any in the state.[1]

In 1987, when current District Six Superintendent Anthony Amato assumed his position, the district placed last, out of 32 city school districts in math and reading, as measured by standardized tests of academic achievement. With the highest density of population per square mile, the district continues to be the most overcrowded in the city. As a result, school utilization is at 120 percent of capacity. The district also has the largest bilingual population in the State of New York and the fourth largest in the United States, a large proportion of which are immigrants with pressing needs.[2] Parents, administrators and faculty members confront difficult social problems that inhibit student learning, and they recognize they cannot address educational objectives without considering the larger social realities that situate the school.

For immigrant children and their families, meanwhile, education has often represented the promise of economic and social power in a competitive industrial economy. Thus, the teachers, parents and administrators of the W. Haywood Burns School acknowledge that school is an important link between the needs of the community and social services. Accordingly, parent and community involvement have become integral components of the school's organization, vision and curriculum. This chapter presents an account of the origin and development of the W. Haywood Burns School, describing how the participants are striving to enact a student-centered curriculum that emphasizes academic success, social justice, cultural responsiveness and student engagement. This story begins with the W. Haywood Burns School in the midst of its first year, the faculty wrestling with its own resolutions to these questions. This story cannot offer concrete answers. But an account of the challenges and successes of this first year provides a close look at the process of building a progressive school within a large, diverse urban school district. In many ways the questions the W.

Haywood Burns faculty and parents ask echo larger societal questions: How can a sense of community be fostered in a diverse society? How can diversity be maintained in the face of a monoculture? This is also the story of the challenges and early successes of progressive education in an urban setting. The school census report indicates the student body is 70 percent Latino; 17 percent White; 11 percent African-American; 2 percent Asian-Pacific Islander. The faculty is 57 percent White; 29 percent Latino; 12 percent African-American; and 2 percent Asian-American. Eighty-three percent of the students are eligible for the federal free or reduced lunch program, an indication of their level of poverty. Community School District Six includes neighborhoods that serve as unofficial points of entry for Dominican immigrants. Thirty-nine percent of the school population has limited proficiency in English.

Origins of a Student-Centered School of Choice in Community School District Six

The W. Haywood Burns school originated in the parents' need for a learner-centered school of choice in Community School District Six and the Superintendent's willingness to support them with a large amount of administrative and financial autonomy. Until recent times, parents of Washington Heights–Inwood who sought progressive and alternative philosophies of education sent their children to other districts in the City. In fact, Superintendent Amato estimated that at least 2,000 students, out of 28,000 in the district, were bussed to schools in other districts. In an effort to retain some of those students, most of whom were from white, middle-class backgrounds, he sought to recruit students for the new schools being built in the district. In February of 1992, Amato visited local daycare centers to speak to parents about the options for public, alternative schools in the district. A small group of parents became interested in pursuing those options and, as a result, the Inwood Design for Education Alliance (*IDEA*) formed.

IDEA held meetings over a 15-month period in public places around the district to gain support, deliberate about the kind of school desired, and solve problems about how to make the school a reality. Group members shared the responsibilities of visiting schools, reading educational literature, consulting experts, establishing outreach relationships in the community, and writing the proposal they would eventually present to the school board. The proposal outlined plans for a school designed to be a parent-teacher collaborative, emphasizing parent involvement, theme-based learning and offering a student-centered curriculum. The parents desired a school where their children would "learn by doing" in ethnically diverse classrooms reflecting the diversity of the community.

From the outset, *IDEA* members faced both skepticism and hostility from community members who charged them as being, among other things, racists who wanted to take over one of the new schools for privileged children who would be driven to school in limousines. The message conveyed to parents in other schools was that *IDEA* members were using local politicians to obtain special privileges for middle-class children that were unavailable to other children in the district. *IDEA* members saw that their initiative would be defeated unless they worked to oust school board members opposed to their efforts. To realize their dream for a student-centered school in District Six, they knew they would have to elect a slate of candidates to run for the school board and help get Superintendent Amato re-elected. One of the parents, Priscilla Marco, was elected to the school board on a platform of parental choice and school reform. The political groundwork was then in place to activate plans for opening the school.

Parents negotiated with the Superintendent for classroom space and financial and administrative autonomy. They wanted the freedom to choose their own director and teachers; they wanted a separate budget that would enable them to purchase materials; and they wanted the freedom to design the curriculum. The parents chose Leslie Alexander, formerly Director at River East, one of the Central Park East Schools, for the position of school Director. The school, which Leslie Alexander named The Muscota New School, eventually received its own space in a traditional school in the district, which turned out to be, as one parent put it, "a somewhat hostile environment." In any case, Muscota thrived, beginning as a kindergarten through grade three school and eventually adding grades four and five. The school also grew in numbers, eventually serving 300 primary students. Muscota established many connections in the larger progressive education arena including affiliations with the Center for Collaborative Education (CCE) and the Coalition of Essential Schools. Muscota continues its affiliation with these organizations. A more extensive profile of the Muscota New School appears later in this chapter.

IDEA recognized the need to start with a small school within an existing school, but the parents had a long-term goal of eventually serving students throughout middle school. As Muscota outgrew its space, the parents and faculty agreed that a larger space and a more supportive environment would be necessary if the school were to flourish. But they also realized the value of keeping Muscota small, acknowledging the following six benefits:

(1)   Small schools encourage teachers to innovate and "take ownership" of the curriculum;

(2)   Small school size improves students' grades and test scores;

(3)   Small school size greatly improves attendance rates and lowers drop-out rates;

(4)   Female and nonwhite students, in particular, do better in smaller schools;

(5)   Students with special needs, including so-called "at-risk," "exceptional," "disadvantaged," and "gifted" students, are better served by smaller school units; and

(6)   In the small-school environment, security improves and violence decreases, as do student alcohol and drug abuse.[3]

The challenge of expansion is the principal theme of this chapter. How does a school remain small while expanding to meet the needs of increasing numbers of students? With this challenge in mind, the parents and faculty set out to build a larger school that would house Muscota together with two additional small schools sharing the student-centered philosophy. The W. Haywood Burns School would become the enactment of this goal.

Muscota parents asked Superintendent Amato to appoint Lydia Bassett the Interim Acting Principal and head of the planning committee for what would eventually become the W. Haywood Burns School. At the time, Bassett was Director of the Community Service Academy in Salome Urena Middle Academies (SUMA), Intermediate School #218. The Community Service Academy (another small, progressive, learner-centered school serving the community in Washington Heights–Inwood) is an affiliate of the Coalition of Essential Schools and a member of the Center for Collaborative Education. Muscota parents recruited Bassett because of her reputation as a progressive, student-centered educator, as someone who is strongly collaborative, and as a respected member of School District Six respected by the Superintendent and others in the District Office. Lydia Bassett received the 1995 Ellen Lurie Community Service Award, honoring significant contributions to community service in New York City. This award recognized her work at the Community Service Academy. For example, during the 1992–93 school year, the students there worked on a combined total of 25 projects, among them lobbying to make subway stations in the community safer and cleaner, surveying recent immigrants in the community to assess their health needs, and helping to teach reading and math in neighborhood daycare centers. In addition to her skills as an administrator and leader, Bassett also envisioned a school that would help children learn a commitment to community involvement and social activism, and the middle school teachers she recruited brought with them a strong commitment to social activism.

The planning team and other parents drafted a proposal requesting funding and a designation as a New Visions II School. Supported by the Fund for New York City Public Education, the New Visions Schools initiative supports new schools founded upon the principles of faculty autonomy, unified vision and identity among faculty members, and a commitment to a curriculum that incorporates the voices of its participants. This foundation provides administrative and financial support for those who want to establish public schools that feature autonomy over crucial decisions including hiring, resources, curriculum and pedagogy. The planning team's proposal established educational standards that each of the small schools would embrace. It outlined a model student-centered, academically rigorous curriculum. It articulated the belief that the teacher should be an astute observer able to gauge a child's interests, needs and strengths in order to build a curriculum drawing on all the resources the extended community can offer.

The proposal described an educational and community environment in which each child's sense of identity would be nurtured through service learning projects in which small groups of students would "identify problems that concern them, team up with community organizations to help develop solutions, and go out into the community to make a difference."[4] The school would support the needs of the learner, the family and the community; and based on a reciprocal and mutually supportive relationship, the school would inspire the community, the parents and the students to sustain excellence in education. The pedagogical goals articulated in the proposal reflected principles and practices already in place in the Muscota New School and the Community Service Academy, both of which were affiliated with the Coalition of Essential Schools and the Center for Collaborative Education. The principles expressed in the proposal align with the Coalition of Essential Schools' twelve principles of education:

(1)   Schools that are small and personalized in size.

(2)   A unified course of study for all students.

(3)   A focus on helping young people to use their minds well.

(4)   An in-depth intradisciplinary curriculum respectful of the diverse heritages that encompass our society.

(5)   Active learning with student-as-worker/student-as-citizen and teacher-as-coach.

(6)   Student evaluation by performance-based assessment methods.

(7)   A school tone of unanxious expectation, trust and decency.

(8)   Family involvement, trust and respect.

(9)   Collaborative decision making and governance.

(10)   Choice.

(11)   Racial, ethnic, economic and intellectual diversity.

(12)   Budget allocations targeting time for collective planning.[5]

In November of 1995, the Planning Committee was invited to interview with the Fund for New York City Public Education and in early 1996 it received a New Visions Schools planning grant, one of ten recipients from an applicant pool of 176. This grant provided the planning committee resources to make the school a reality. With approval to open the school in the fall of 1996, Lydia Bassett began the process of hiring Middle School and Lower School faculty members and completing administrative and bureaucratic tasks. (The W. Haywood Burns Middle School and the Amistad School were officially named only after the 1996–97 school year was under way and the Parent Teacher Association formed.)

A View from Inside the School

The newly constructed building that houses the W. Haywood Burns School is built of contrasting light and dark rose-colored bricks set against cream-colored panels and window trim. Large copper medallions of the seal of the State of New York and the seal of the New York City Board of Education decorate the front facade. The decor inside is equally attractive, each wing painted in varying shades of a bright blue, green or yellow. The "dining room," as it is called, is paneled in light-colored oak lined with coat hooks, where the children hang their coats before lunch. The panel rises six feet from the floor at which point the walls are painted a bright lemon yellow, intensified in daylight by a row of skylights. Across from the cafeteria, a bold and bright gymnasium features alternating sections of deep rust, light evergreen and golden yellow tiles.

It is a small building compared to the vast and sprawling public schools built in the early half of the twentieth century that typically occupy a large proportion of a city block The small size of the school allows the faculty to get to know their students intimately, and this strong sense of familiarity encourages a sense of school character to develop. "Island of decency" is a fitting metaphor for the W. Haywood Burns School, one of its distinctive features being the pervading sense of care and respect the faculty has for students.

On January 31, 1997, the students of the W. Haywood Burns School celebrated their first five months as a community by staging their first open-house-assembly entitled, "W. Haywood Burns, the Making of a Legend." The auditorium, filled to capacity with students, parents and teachers, was raucous with the excited laughter and chatter of students anticipating their performances. Middle-school director and teacher Gwen Clinkscales welcomed the audience and explained that the students had been studying the life and accomplishments of the school's namesake, W. Haywood Burns, a defender of civil and human rights who fought against injustice and oppression. "What you'll see, she said, "are plays, songs and stories about Haywood Burns. When the students leave they'll repeat these stories and songs, making Haywood Burns a legend."

The assembly featured performances from the students including poems by Maya Angelou and Langston Hughes, folk songs by Leadbelly and Sweet Honey in the Rock, spirituals and civil rights songs. Some student groups offered dramatic interpretations of important civil rights events including the lunch counter sit-in and Rosa Parks' refusal to give up her seat on a Montgomery bus. Another class presented a time-line of important events in the American Civil Rights Movement. The time line opened with the

Brown v. Board of Education Supreme Court decision that mandated an end to segregation in public schools.

One finds it fitting that a movement which began in part as a reaction to injustice in public education should continue to resonate within a public school, which is the case of the W. Haywood Burns School, a public school dedicated to principles of social justice, democracy and community involvement. As principal Lydia Bassett explained in a letter to parents,

> There are many lessons we can draw from the life of W. Haywood Burns—the value of academic achievement, commitment to family and community, and a lifelong dedication to achieving justice and equality in this world. Underlying all of these values is the courage of W. Haywood Burns. We need to have courage to live our lives well. We need courage to stand up for what we believe in, courage to be different or unpopular, courage to continue to work hard in the face of adversity. The spirit of W. Haywood Burns is very important for children to grasp.[6]

The ideals of courage, commitment, community involvement and academic achievement, as demonstrated in the professional accomplishments of the W. Haywood Burns School, appear as well among the faculty members who view teaching as a political act with a moral imperative for working in the best interests of children. In this sense, the goals of the faculty echo the personal vision of the school's namesake, as well as the educational philosophies of John Dewey and Paulo Freire. The teachers aspire to provide children from diverse cultural and social backgrounds with a curriculum that is engaging, academically challenging and responsive to the particular needs of individual students. The organizers of the school recruited and hired the teachers specifically to implement an innovative curriculum based on progressive, student-centered pedagogy; to involve parents and the community in the life of the school; and to promote social justice for culturally, socially and linguistically diverse students.

The principles of student-centered pedagogy can be seen at work in classrooms at every level. But while the teachers in each of the three schools share a commitment to progressive education, they acknowledge a need for enough autonomy to create curricula, devise compatible assessment programs, conceptualize and implement program changes, and cultivate a distinctive identity. This autonomy explains how the faculty of each of the smaller schools articulates the student-centered philosophy. Every school is a product of its participants who, together, shape its culture and character; and this phenomenon lends each of the small schools its distinctiveness. The faculties all agree that the integrity of progressive education works best when schools are small enough to allow participatory decision making and close relationships between teachers and students, and their beliefs characterize the processes of teaching and learning in each school. The following sections illustrate how the progressive pedagogy becomes manifest in each of the smaller schools of the W. Haywood Burns School.

The W. Haywood Burns Middle School

The W. Haywood Burns Middle School offers a rigorous, interdisciplinary curriculum for all students. The program emphasizes intellectual achievement, personal values, essential skills, experiential learning, and the excitement of ideas. Our learner-centered program for young adolescents reflects a coherent and continuous educational framework. The kindergarten through grade eight organization of the W. Haywood Burns School allows students, faculty and parents to collaborate to graduate students who demonstrate academic competence, community responsibility, and an awareness of their personal goals and interests.

Each student's unique potential is nurtured throughout the Middle School experience, emphasizing the development of the whole child. A thematic curriculum engages students in large-scale projects where they develop and demonstrate academic and higher-order thinking skills. Collaborative teachers develop a curriculum that builds on students' interests and talents, supports skill mastery, and continuously monitors student achievement. A nurturing and intellectually stimulating atmosphere supported by parent and community resources, encourages students to develop healthy interests in and out of the classroom.

Building on the strengths of the W. Haywood Burns Lower Schools—The Amistad School and the Muscota New School—the Middle School recognizes that the early-adolescent years are turning points in the lives of young people. Middle school students need a small community where they can be known, where they can forge close relations with adults and peers, and where they can grow their ideas in a rich interdisciplinary curriculum that nurtures and guides their transition from concrete to abstract thinking. A service learning program unites the humanities, math, science and technology with the Washington Heights and Inwood community. What is community? Who am I? How can I effect change in my community? These essential questions guide our students' development as learners and leaders.

The Middle School is organized by teachers working together in teams to provide positive expressions for adolescent energy, to accept and to engage the seesaw pattern of growth during these important years, and to foster a new relationship with their students' parents. Parents and staff work as partners, collaborating for student achievement. An advisory group, facilitated by a teacher-advisor, provides a support network to each child in the school. An advisor monitors each child's academic progress, meets with parents, and ensures that a child is never "forgotten." The school's small size fosters a cooperative, intimate spirit that will allow every child to be known and to participate actively in school life.

Teachers of the W. Haywood Burns Middle School

In this letter to visitors and prospective parents, the Middle School faculty emphasizes the importance of close observation of students as a means of creating a responsive and rigorous curriculum enacted through engaging and empowering learning experiences for adolescents. Visitors who visit classrooms and talk with teachers invariably notice these principles at work.

Gwen Clinkscales, director of the middle school and its math coordinator, moves from one cluster of desks to another, having conferences with students as they work on their architectural plans. Large windows along the east wall of her classroom look onto the playground—a place that happens to be central to students' learning this year. She explains how, early in the year, a student fell from the playground equipment, breaking her arm in two places. The accident caused concern among students who, after a series of long discussions, concluded that the playground had been built for younger children. Gwen explains how middle school students tend to use the equipment in more challenging ways than intended. "So we asked ourselves, 'What would Haywood Burns do about it?' And we agreed he would change it. So the next question was, 'What do we need to do in order to change the playground to meet our needs?'" The students realized they would need to draw up architectural plans, and for that they recognized they would need math skills. This need led to a math-science project focusing on the playground environment. The students began devising architectural plans for playground renovations that take into account the special needs of growing adolescent students. The Salvadori Educational Center on the Built Environment (SECBE), a non-profit organization based at City College of New York, provided assistance to the students and helps them conceptualize and draw up plans for a playground renovation they plan to present to the Parents' Association at the end of the 1996–97 school year. In the process of planning, the students learned math skills that are part of the math curriculum: metric measures, non-standard units of measurement, units, design concepts, scale and tools.

As Gwen Clinkscales explained, "Middle-school kids, if they're engaged, will do the work. If it's meaningful, they'll succeed." A strong emphasis remains on academics, but the middle school teachers also provide children with experiences that are engaging, personally relevant and intended to teach students how to effect change in the world. The teachers continually try to provide students with new and exciting ways to learn. A curriculum with these goals always changes, never remains static. Ellen Meltzer, who teaches a fifth and sixth-grade combination, explained, "We are cognizant of children as a whole—their physical development, age, where they're changing. They need challenge. We try to incorporate skills into activities that will please, challenge and get them onto another level. We are constantly redoing activities based on what they can handle, and there's a constant shifting of activities and goals—a constantly evolving curriculum."

This shifting occurs in response to the observations teachers make of students. As Clinkscales explained, "Each subject has a scope and sequence that aligns with [the district curriculum]." The curriculum evolves as teachers look at the skills as outlined in the scope and sequence, together with observing children and meeting frequently to discuss student progress. "Input comes from a variety of resources: experience as teachers, materials, what's been successful in the past. We establish the best way of getting kids to develop 'literate' skills. To make them feel competent and independent we acknowledge children's abilities," Ellen Melzer explained.

Middle school children should have teachers who know them well. The move from elementary to middle school presents a dilemma. Suddenly a child must interact with seven or eight different teachers; as a result, teachers and students tend to get to know one another superficially. To address this problem, the middle school teachers have implemented an advisory system whereby each teacher is responsible for 15 students. Every Friday afternoon the advisory meets from 1:00 to 2:40, following a basic structure where the group sits in a circle and discusses the issues students bring with them. The advisor becomes the child's advocate. If a child is having difficulty with or is excelling in a subject, that information is passed on to the advisor. As Clinkscales explained it, the advisory is "a way to empower kids and use democratic principles. They elect a leader and co-leader and use a talking stick. They get to practice what they're learning in humanities." (The talking stick is a Native American practice in which group discussion and decision making are accomplished by sitting in a circle and passing the stick from one speaker to the next until all have said their piece.) As a result of advisory discussions, the students decided to hold town meetings as a way to solve problems and discuss such issues as teasing, hurried lunch periods, and short recess times, among others. The advisory also has an activity component where students work on projects under the supervision of their advisory teacher. For example, one class writes and edits a newsletter. Another group serves as the social committee, responsible for planning a school dance. Activities involve students with engaging projects that are fun and educational.

The emphasis on collaboration and shared decision making entails frequent meetings, a prominent feature of the middle-school program. Teachers meet for two hours each Thursday and another hour on Friday. They also schedule blocks of time students spend with cluster teachers (music, art, physical education, computer) so they can meet as a group. Each Thursday afternoon the teachers meet to discuss "Case Studies." During Case Studies, each teacher profiles two students, "one who is doing really well and we can help support, and another student that is not doing as well as we want, to help them do better," as Clinkscales explained. To help teachers view their students' strengths and needs as a first step toward devising instructional plans, each teacher lists observations on chart paper, and as a group, the teachers discuss each case. The Case Studies format helps all of the teachers get to know their students while providing teachers with suggestions from the rest of the faculty. An example of three case study observations appears below:

Student 1
[name]

Strengths
-Beautiful smile
-Becoming more comfortable
-Writes in journal
-More willing to read and speak out
-Works really hard

Needs
-Pronunciation of English
-Beginning reading

Plan
-Activities
-Visit lower school
-Get activities in Spanish and English

Student 2
[name]

Strengths
-Works cooperatively with peers
-Nice person
-Likes art
-Translates for Mom
-Improvement since September

Needs
-Decrease sadness
-Wear glasses

-Needs someone to work with at home
-Should ask for help
-Depressed
-Disorganized
-Low self esteem
-Lack of connection

Plan
-Refer to guidance counselor
-Latch key
-One-on-one
-Buddy up with another student
-Special written daily agenda
-Pair with student in mini course
-Remind her to wear glasses

Student 3
[name]

Strengths
-A doll
-Strong will
-When you give her something she can be successful, she flourishes
-Doing some risk-taking with language
-Great handwriting and copying skills
-Beginning to produce phrases in English
-Understands classroom directives in mathematics
-Asked question in English, confident answering in Spanish

Needs
-Reduce holding back
-Teacher in humanities not clear how much she understands
-Habit of talking all the time in mini-course
-Make humanities class less threatening

Plan
-Listen first then translate
-Make the problem in humanities an advisory agenda item
-In ESL do a reflection on how she is learning English
-Find out routines in humanities and support her in following the routine

As one hears the Middle School teachers talk about their beliefs and practices, one becomes aware of their perception of teaching as a powerful autobiographical experience.[7] The teachers appreciate the opportunity to teach in a school that acknowledges and values their personal histories and the potential benefits they bring to the children of the school. As Ellen Meltzer, who has been teaching for 21 years, observed "My family was involved in the anti-war and civil rights movements [and I see] teaching as a way of living the social beliefs that I have on a daily basis. I always saw schools as a place for social change to work. If we aren't on top of it and work together in school and teach the kids to work together, then there's not much hope for democracy." Gwen Clinkscales grew up in New York City and from an early age was involved in social activism and community involvement:

I was raised in the Black Baptist Church. My father was very involved in the civil rights movement. I was one of 11 African-American kids that integrated a school in Bayside, Queens. Being part of the protest helped me understand oppressed people. I was trained as a teacher, and hold a degree in public administration. I worked for the Consumer Fraud Administration. I also worked a lot in early childhood. I taught in Friends School in California. The curriculum was Piagetan—they were into activity-based learning there. [With the advent of] school decentralization I said I'd never teach in public school. I knew it was designed for people of color to fail. But I came to the recognition that the masses of those children are in public school and realized that if I wanted to help, I would have to work in public education. Working in a school with an umbrella of social activism is the culmination of my interests and passions.

Kathleen Him, a combination fourth and fifth grade teacher, also articulated an understanding of teaching as a way of practicing social activism:

> We come from backgrounds that are political and social. What's so amazing for many of us is our diverse backgrounds. In my previous life I was a lawyer and knew Haywood Burns. I was familiar with his pro bono work in the field with the Gay Men's Council for people of color with AIDS and for gay and lesbian groups. I appreciate bringing my whole self here and being real in front of the kids—looking at each child as a whole. You'll never see a more compassionate faculty to probe and be able to get through to what is there. We are all aware of the social aspects of teaching. I hear teachers say, "I'm not a social worker." But you have to go the extra mile. Curriculum is designed around all that. For example, in my class we're looking at the theme [of environments] through the experience of immigrants and their struggles when they arrived in this country. What kind of environment were they faced with? What did that mean?

Many children in the school come from recent immigrant families, and for them, the curriculum Him describes becomes autobiographical. She understands that a critical awareness of the immigrant's struggle will help those children survive and prosper in their new culture.

The Middle School offers mini-courses as electives designed around themes students and teachers select. They provide an opportunity for teachers to use their expertise and abilities to expose students to an interdisciplinary curriculum. Mini-courses take place on Tuesday for one period and on Thursday for two periods. Theresa Bell's autobiography appears in how she teaches her mini courses:

> My interests are adult literacy and Spanish. I love theater. I am doing a lot with community building around rent and tenant issues. My mini-course has become a fixed group of students working on puppet shows in Spanish. Together we're building the stage, making puppets, blocking, all in Spanish. For many children, their own language is Spanish. Sometimes it takes them by surprise once they

realize that their language has a history, a heritage. That it can be spoken and written. We'll end this year with a nice production in Spanish.

Linda Suss teaches humanities. A teacher in the New York City School system since 1970, she saw the first grants that started mini-schools. She involves her students in a mini-course where they collaborate with senior citizens in the Isabella Home, a live-in facility in the community. Her students have interviewed the residents to find out what their lives are like, and strong relationships between her students and the residents developed over the year. Students also go to a senior citizens community center. All these experiences help them form impressions of what life is like for older people, and to get advice from them. As Suss explained, "Later in the year the seniors will visit. The goal is to involve students in the community and to learn."

The middle school faculty members use contracts with all students to help them meet academic and personal goals. Together with their teachers, students plan, implement and self-assess personally relevant courses of learning. The faculty uses contracts in a variety of ways. For example, in terms of standardized measures of achievement, the students in the W. Haywood Burns school are intensely diverse, each with a unique and particular set of educational challenges. Those students who hope to attend college find the competition for the few seats in the city's specialized high schools intense, and those who seek these places must complete an intensified preparatory curriculum. For these students, contracts provide a structure to help prepare them. The process of test preparation might seem antithetical to progressive pedagogy, and most of the W. Haywood Burns teachers would probably agree. But they are pragmatists as well as progressives, and they understand the demands on students who are part of what is one of the most competitive educational systems in the country. In New York City, standardized test scores determine school placements from preschool through university.

Elizabeth Vasquez, in her third year of teaching, came to the W. Haywood Burns School from the Community Service Academy where she worked with Lydia Bassett: "It was a nurturing environment with constant teacher training and workshops to go to. [Collaboration] was modeled a lot—team meetings, working together, sharing ideas and information, not isolating. I came to Haywood Burns because Lydia was going to be here. She is supportive, open to ideas. I knew this would be a place where I could grow, try new things and fail. Lydia is approachable, nurturing." Vasquez explained how the philosophy of collaborative, community-based learning works in the W. Haywood Burns School: "For example, upper and lower school collaboration is facilitated through having middle school kids help and teach lower grades in reading. New arrivals who do not read can work with eighth-grade students."

W. Haywood Burns Middle School teachers commit themselves to linking academics to real-world concerns, a process that helps students assume a critical, reflective stance toward their own experience to understand better the social, political and cultural conditions that frame their experiences. The teachers in the W. Haywood Burns Middle School view education as a means to help their students control their destinies and become empowered citizens of the American democracy. The teachers strive to implement a curriculum based on the principles of liberatory praxis, where teachers help equip students with the intellectual and cognitive abilities to initiate change in their world.[8] Just as the windows in Gwen Clinkscales' classroom open to the outside world and the problems there to be solved, so do Elizabeth Vasquez's. Her classroom views Broadway. Across the street is an old, one-story warehouse building with a caved-in roof. "It's a real eyesore," Vasquez explained. "The kids and I have been talking about what to do about it. Maybe we should get someone to tear it down. Maybe we could even have a high school built there."

The Amistad School

It is "work time" in Nancy Encarnacion's K-1 classroom. As one of the children explains, work time is when "we play toys, we write in journals, we write on paper, we paint, we fix." The students are gathered in groups at various work stations around the room. One cluster of children works with the Guinea pigs, moving them from large box to small box. "Why are you moving them?" I ask. "To clean out the caca," the children explain, giggling. At the cooking table two little girls are busy cutting bananas and washing grapes to make fruit salad for a snack. Another group of girls sits at a table pounding playdough they recently made in class. Today the dramatic play area is where I meet Fiona, who is European-American and holds a Black baby, and Natalie, who is African-American and is feeding an Asian baby. "Let's get in our gowns," Natalie suggests. The two dress in polyester night gowns. Swaying the baby from side to side as her gown swishes, Natalie says, "We like playin', we like cookin', we like dressin' our babies!"

Two boys work with Legos, and one tells me, "We're doin' bad stuff with Legos." I ask him, "Bad stuff? What bad could you do with Legos?" "We're makin' monsters!" he replied. In another corner three boys are building a school with blocks. Two speak together in Spanish. The third, irritated at being excluded from the play, interrupts in English, and the three begin a discussion in English about plans for the school. Nancy circulates among the children, explaining to them how to go about their "work," offering instructions and explanations in both Spanish and English. Nancy has worked in District bilingual programs and as a pre-kindergarten and kindergarten teacher for the last 20 years. As she explained,

> Throughout these years I've refined my techniques of working in a learner-centered environment geared toward children who are learning English as a second language. They influence my teaching because I'm keenly aware of the second-language learner's learning and emotional needs. These children need a nurturing, risk-free environment where their successes are celebrated. They need to be encouraged to take chances through the age-appropriate activities in language development, science, art, et cetera, in a natural discovery way.

Next door, in Betty Lopez-Towey's class, it's writing time. Instrumental music plays softly in the background as Betty circulates and reminds her students to write their names on their work. "Hot" topics are dinosaurs, *Star Wars*, animals and friends. Writing time in Lopez-Towey's K-1 classroom is also a time to negotiate social relationships. Students compare writing topics, compliment drawing skill, argue about seating arrangements, and tell jokes. As Lopez-Towey explained,

> I love this time, the connections they make—using the print in the environment is how they get their worlds together. Today I worked with two groups of boys assessing [and collecting] unfinished pieces

around the room. I want to work with them on putting their work together and giving it text to make a story. One group was working on *Star Wars*. The other group was working on superheroes.

The rooms are far from the familiar sprawling classrooms, but are small rooms designed to hold small classes. This morning the room is packed with 29 children and five adults—Betty Lopez-Towey and her assistant teacher, Narcissa, two volunteer parents (both fathers) and a researcher. The children's work is displayed around the room. An easel in the meeting area displays a list of choice-time options: math area, cooking area, Bear house, Playhouse, blocks, playdough, sewing table, puzzles, animal study, construction table, water table, painting, writing table, listening table, sand table and typewriter.

Lopez-Towey began her career in education, when as the parent of a Central Park East student she became involved in her own children's education. Upon the recommendation of Deborah Meier, the Director of Central Park East, she returned to college to earn her teaching certificate, eventually becoming a teacher at Central Park East (CPE). Her skill as a teacher was recognized when she became a recipient of the Bank Street Early Childhood Teacher Award. As she explains,

I came to teaching because of my involvement with my own children's learning at the CPE School where I was an active member of a child-centered learning community. As someone who established some basic principles and working practices in a traditional school, I believe that all children, not just children in choice schools, respond to developmentally appropriate environments. At Amistad we have the rare opportunity to build something meaningful and important for our responsive families and for the District.

Work time in Nancy Encarnacion's classroom and writing time in Betty Lopez-Towey's classroom illustrate the kind of engaging, purposeful experiences that characterize the Amistad curriculum. A tour of the classrooms confirms a unifying philosophy of student-centered pedagogy at work. The words and work of children take up every available space on the walls and in the corridors. Real children's books, known as "trade books," fill shelves and boxes around the rooms, replacing traditional basal textbooks—an indication of the teachers' commitment to literature-based literacy programs. Collaboration, talk and social interaction among students and the teachers occur routinely; and students in all classrooms throughout the day work at tables in pairs and small groups. Teachers circulate among students, conversing with them and assessing their progress. The curriculum in each classroom reflects theme-based units, the teachers and students having negotiated the curriculum in accordance with student interests. The faculty agrees that school should provide students with learning experiences in an engaging curricula that promotes academic achievement. Adhering to the mission of the school, teachers emphasize engagement with an emphasis on academic achievement and parent involvement.

The Amistad faculty members all appear to relish the opportunity to take risks and implement an innovative, student-centered curriculum. As Julie Broderick, a second- and third-grade teacher, commented,

> We have all been given an unique educational opportunity this year because we are starting from the beginning. We have been able to begin shaping this school into our collective vision of what education should be. Most educators never get this opportunity. Our faculty is committed to seeing children succeed. Although we are still working towards coming to more of a consensus about what classroom practices facilitate student success, there is a common commitment to the children.

Cara Chambers, another second- and third-grade teacher, echoed this sentiment: "During my three years at [another school], I became frustrated by the 'skill and drill,' teacher-centered methodology that most teachers used. I also wished to have more autonomy over my curriculum, teaching methods and school policies. This frustration led me to apply to other positions [and] the Amistad School was my number one choice."

Amistad teachers recognize the rare opportunity they have to shape a new school with a student-centered philosophy. Jacqueline Avalos, who teaches bilingual students, has been teaching severely emotionally disturbed (SIE) children and inclusion classes for the last seven years. She understands that not all children learn the same way and, therefore, cannot be taught the same way: "They have to be allowed to explore and find their way." As an

Amistad teacher, she enjoys enough freedom to seek different methods and try new approaches. As Nancy Encarnacion commented, "What is special about the Amistad School is that, above all, it promotes child-centered learning. The staff works closely together to ensure that the programs are designed to provide children with enriching classroom experiences that foster exploration and discovery." The faculty's efforts have been successful according to Bilingual Coordinator, Elia Castro, who recollected a recent visit from auditors who came to the School to assess compliance with state and federal guidelines: "I took them around. I was trying to tell them what was going on and [the auditor] said, 'You don't have to tell me, I can see it!'" But Castro also acknowledges that the pressure to meet the District Administration's standards also preoccupies Amistad teachers: "We want to show the Superintendent that we have a different philosophy but are in compliance with the state and the Goals 2000 [Federal Educational Guidelines]."

In a community as linguistically diverse as the neighborhoods surrounding the W. Haywood Burns School, a commitment to student-centered learning also means a commitment to bilingual education. Spanish is the first language for the majority of students in District Six and many have limited proficiency in English. Most of the immigrants living in the District are from the Dominican Republic, and a primary barrier for these students and their families to adjusting to life in the United States and acquiring economic stability is their limited proficiency in English. Superintendent Amato has expressed his concern for addressing the diverse language needs of students in the district, and following his lead the W. Haywood Burns faculty is committed to making the dual-language program a strong priority.

The teachers embrace the discourse of second language and literacy acquisition[9] and strive to create an educational experience for second-language learners that validates their linguistic competencies while enabling them to gain access to mainstream discourses.[10] They are firmly committed to providing the academic support that helps non-speaking and minimum-competency English speaking students acquire English-language proficiency while simultaneously developing cognitive skills in their native language. They are committed as well to helping mono-lingual, English-speaking students acquire foreign-language proficiency. Their goal is to have all of their students bilingual by eighth grade, a goal that aligns with Goals 2000, which recommends that all students graduate from high school with proficiency in a foreign language.

In order to meet the needs of Spanish-speaking children, the W. Haywood Burns faculty members, most of whom speak Spanish, are committed to implementing a dual-language program in the Amistad School whereby English and Spanish are the languages of teaching and learning in each classroom, and a modified dual-language program in the Middle School.[11] This commitment reflects a corresponding interest in developing a nine-year program, bridging the visions and objectives of each small school within the larger W. Haywood Burns community. Marian Brady, Early Childhood Coordinator, sees the developing dual-language program, where the curriculum respects students' diversity and cultural differences, as one of Amistad's most distinctive and attractive features.

Elia Castro, acting Director of the Amistad School, worked with Julie Broderick, Cara Chambers and Lydia Bassett on a Title VII grant to fund an expanded dual-language program. The grant would provide resources to hire master's-level students from Bank Street College. These certified teachers would work as para-professionals in classrooms with the teachers. As Castro explained, "Since they would have a BA in bilingual education, it would be like another teacher." The grant would fund six Amistad positions and two additional positions for the middle school. Castro is currently working with the Muscota New School to develop a service for limited English proficiency (LEP) students, with the goal of starting a dual-language program there too since Muscota already employs four licensed bilingual teachers. The dual-language program would provide a powerful tool to meet the educational needs of students. In a letter to parents, the Amistad teachers articulated their goal:

In our developing dual language program, we believe children have the ability and should have the opportunity to learn in their native language as well as acquire competency in a second language. When children learn language, they also learn culture. Amistad supports the study of other cultures and traditions, with the respect and interest that creates inquisitive learners in a harmonious community environment.

In their first year of existence, focusing on the vast challenges of opening a new school and implementing the curriculum, the teachers have been so far unable to establish a comprehensive dual-language program; it will be the primary challenge facing them in subsequent school years. If awarded, the Title VII grant will provide the financial resources to allow the school to hire one educational aide to help each teacher implement the dual-language program and provide resources for materials and professional development.

Meanwhile, the parents strongly support the student-centered practices in the Amistad School, on any given day a visitor is likely to see parents in the classrooms working with small groups of students. Each of the small schools in the W. Haywood Burns School enrolls students based solely on applications, and most parents select the school out of their interest in the school's philosophy of student-centered learning. Jose Gutierrez volunteers every week during writing time in Betty Lopez-Towey's class where his son is in first grade. He explained one morning what he sees as the special qualities of the Amistad School:

> My son went to [a Catholic primary school]. My son was shy. I don't want him to be shy. Now here, they're gonna be talking to each other. This is the first year that he's happy. Yesterday he was making a lamp, doing different things, how to build things, how to do things. Last night at 8:30 my son said, "I got a great idea. Why don't you read a book to us every night before we go to sleep?" He likes reading.

Second- and third-grade teacher Julie Broderick reiterated this theme:

> Our parents have been very supportive of us during this growing year. We are doing many things this year which are new and non-traditional and we understand that parents are concerned that their children receive the very best academic preparation available. It has taken a great deal of faith and confidence on the part of parents to allow all of us to try different things this year in our classrooms and throughout the school.

Elia Castro summarized what she sees as the qualities that distinguish Amistad from other schools: "Teachers in Amistad believe in the philosophy of child-centered learning and community involvement. Our emphasis on the child and family allows us to nurture the child as a whole. . . they feel the ways teachers care about emotional and physical needs as well as intellectual development. That's what makes us quite different. The way we work with parents is also an important feature of the school. Amistad parents read with the child, cook with the child . . . When visitors walk through the hallways and go through classes, they see it in the children's work and in classrooms. They see adults—teachers and parents—with children. Visitors think they're teachers. And they are."

Faculty collaboration is also an important aspect of the Amistad teacher's expectations. Because the school is new, the Amistad School faculty agrees that collaboration and communication must be actively developed. Marian Brady has an impressive record of experience as a nursery school teacher for 14 years, a public daycare teacher, a sixth-grade teacher, a reading teacher in grades kindergarten through six and a Head Start teacher. Her role is to help the faculty establish a climate of trust and understanding where opinions or questions are valued and where mistakes are addressed with candor. She realizes the importance of building a collective identity based on a shared philosophy, and she recognizes the need to bring about faculty cohesion and school identity. In the months ahead Brady sees her role as helping the faculty set goals to improve performance and job satisfaction, helping them in develop a plan of action and a timeline that specifies ways of implementing instructional innovations, and revisiting specific goals through ongoing dialogues.

The Muscota New School, the other primary school in the building, began the 1996 school year with its identity firmly in place. It had already established relationships with its families, its progressive curriculum and assessment practices were firmly in place, and it enjoyed a brief history of those traditions and rituals that lend a sense of common identity to participants. This history was also present, although to a much lesser degree, among the faculty members of the middle school, several of whom had previously worked at the Community Service Academy under Lydia Bassett's leadership. This shared experience provided a foundation of history and vision for what the Middle School curriculum might look like. While the beginning of the year brought some friction, the faculty was able to work through it to establish an agreed- upon pedagogy and a common vision. But the faculty members of the Amistad School came to the W. Haywood Burns School without a common history, and they are still working to establish their identity as a school. As second- and third-grade teacher Julie Broderick explained, "A big issue for us is the balancing act: How do we juggle the demands of providing a rigorous academic program for our students and work to shape our bigger vision as a school?"

Melissa Martinez, a fourth-grade teacher, agreed: "As a faculty we need to question the curriculum, our philosophy and the general framework that guides what we do while we learn from each other." This is a huge undertaking in the first years of a new school, and Melissa Martinez explained some of the challenges of establishing a sense of shared purpose in the school's first year of existence:

> The Amistad faculty has been working together to create curricular and classroom structures that will enable students to be independent learners. This year, most things are trial and error. But all of us have the same philosophy, so it makes it easier to work together. We have been working hard to get to know each other and our challenges. We all come from different schools and have different backgrounds. To be able to be one—that's the goal.

The Amistad School and the Muscota New School are two separate small primary schools. But while they are separate entities, teachers from each school work closely in informal ways, and the physical layout of the school encourages this collaboration. Classrooms off the first-floor corridor are occupied by Muscota and Amistad classes of students in kindergarten and first grade. Classrooms on the second floor are occupied by second-third and third-fourth combinations. These corridors provide the contact zones where teachers interact and meet informally to share philosophies and practices. The presence of the Muscota teachers has been a source of support for the Amistad teachers, one of whom commented, "If we have wanted their advice, we've asked and they have been receptive, giving [suggestions] and space." Marian Brady credits Muscota faculty members as having been "supportive mentors." While she acknowledges that Amistad teachers have learned from Muscota's experience, she is also aware of the need for the Amistad School to assume its own identity. She explained that the biggest challenge faced by faculty in the first year has been taking on too much at once.

Several of the Amistad teachers came from traditional schools in the district, and in their first year of striving to enact a student-centered pedagogy, they borrowed many of the practices the Muscota faculty follows. For example, Muscota recently developed a model of peer evaluation that the Amistad teachers use as they lay the foundation for planning and implementing their own program of peer evaluation. Several of the teachers of the two primary schools collaborate on the implementation of the Primary Language Record, an assessment tool that incorporates the perspectives of parents and recognizes the child's strengths as a basis from which the curriculum and instruction develop.[12]

The principle of social action and respect for children evidenced in the middle school curriculum appears in the Amistad classrooms as well. While I visited Betty Lopez-Towey, one of her first-grade students said, "Betty, tell Cynthia about Mr. Holmes."[13] Lopez-Towey then recalled the day she took her class to art where a substitute teacher was filling in for an absent teacher. Lopez-Towey was troubled by how the teacher was talking to the children. She decided to pick them up early, and once back in the classroom, they convened in the meeting area. She began the discussion, "I was a little bit troubled by what I heard in art. I didn't like the way Mr. Holmes was speaking to you." Her comment opened the floodgates. In one anecdote after another, the children described how they had been scolded, yelled at, and frightened by the substitute teacher's behavior. "I thought, Lopez-Towey told me, "this was something Lydia needed to hear about, so I asked [the aide] to pull her in." After listening to their concerns, Lydia promised that the teacher would never be asked back and reaffirmed that school should be a place where all children can feel safe and respected. Respect for students and the high value placed on their opinions and insights permeates the way Amistad teachers approach their work. The students' experiences lie at the heart of the curriculum. Julie Broderick acknowledged the fact that students have traveled with the faculty on the challenging journey of opening a new school:

> The most exceptional part of our new school is our student body. They are remarkably unique individuals who are fascinated by so many different things in the world around them. They, too, have

come to a very different educational environment than any which they have been exposed to in past years. They have made a very smooth transition to a more open, learner-centered classroom.

The Muscota New School

Visitors to Muscota rarely have to ask what curriculum the children are learning. It is always very much in evidence in the form of children's work: paintings, drawings, charts, books, models, murals and maps. The classrooms are a rich and colorful display of the work children are doing. What is less visible, unless you spend time in the classrooms and watch it happen, is the process—the way in which learning occurs. Learning takes time and involves serious thought. Children take many different paths to learning and use many different modes: they raise questions and search for answers, read books, tell stories, and go to museums. Other kinds of knowledge is constructed when children go out to observe things in nature, or to look at buildings, parks and bridges. This process is active learning—serious thought that leads to trying things out, to making and to doing. . . .

There's no single source for curriculum. Sometimes a teacher chooses a topic because she or he knows it reflects the common interests of many children. Last year, Vanessa and Rita's class jumped into a study of space which generated from the wide interests of the children after listening to stories of space shuttles and solar eclipses. It was chosen because she knew its potential for providing many different, rich kinds of learning. "Space" was explored in a variety of ways; children made observations and collected information from a variety of sources. They constructed planets and designed murals as evidence of their thoughts.

We are very fortunate at Muscota because each teacher can choose a curriculum that she or he thinks is right for a particular group of children. Planning and preparation take time and thought—they involve finding good books for children to read and use as references, arranging visits to special places, inviting guest speakers, seeking out community resources, and ordering special materials. The interesting thing is that the study can move in many directions once it begins to "take off." When the children bring their individual interests and energies they stretch the curriculum far beyond what the teacher ever imagined. The teacher is ready to support and extend them, as well.

The curriculum is interdisciplinary, linking language, math, science, music, geography and the arts in rich, meaningful ways. Of course, not every child will engage in each activity, but multiple possibilities allow for everyone to find something that is stimulating and satisfying to do and to learn.

The Teachers of the Muscota New School

It is Tuesday morning and the Muscota students and faculty are joining in the school dining room for their Town Meeting, a community ritual for the Muscota New School. It provides an opportunity for the faculty and students to share accomplishments, stories, news of upcoming events, and plans. It is also a means for the faculty and students to cultivate relationships. The teachers of the Muscota New School understand that a sense of familiarity among teachers and students is one of the benefits of working together and learning in a small school. The Town Meetings help secure this benefit. Other rituals become regular features of the school year. Prior to the winter break, the school celebrates "Candlelight Night," when parents, students and faculty members come together to celebrate the holiday season. The school also holds a Madhatter's Ball during the Halloween season.

The principles of faculty autonomy and shared decision making virtually mandate how the Muscota faculty works together. The faculty holds weekly staff meetings it calls "collectives," where teachers share their successes, challenges and plans for the future. The Muscota New School experienced tremendous growth throughout its first four years. It began with a staff of four teachers and now employs twelve fulltime faculty members, all of whom are encouraged to follow their own interests in shaping curriculum. Each of the teachers pursues the ideal of an emergent curriculum whereby the students and teachers together continually shape and develop instructional emphases.

Throughout its four years, the faculty worked hard to establish norms for learner-centered education in its learning community. It developed a system of assessment and evaluation that replaces the traditional report card. Twice a year the teachers write descriptive narrative case reports on each student. Its other innovative practices include a system of peer review. Together the Muscota faculty developed evaluation criteria, and colleagues now conduct the teaching evaluations. This on-going assessment actually gives teachers more autonomy in developing and maintaining professional standards and helps them to grow professionally by observing one another. The faculty appears to have improved as a result of developing and implementing instructional and assessment innovations.

The Muscota New School has always been characterized by a history of a strong parental desire to ensure the school's viability. While wanting to maintain the school's autonomy, the parents recognized the importance of participating in the school operations and decision making. Therefore, they decided that once Muscota moved to the new building they would form a parents' association for the whole school. Accordingly, the Muscota parents and teachers formed a steering committee composed of four parents, three teachers and the director.

The Muscota teachers have developed a strong sense of unity as a result of working closely together since the school opened in the fall of 1993. As mentioned previously, Muscota had been allocated space in a new, but traditional school operated on an educational philosophy antithetical to its own. While the relationship between Muscota and the host school might have been acrimonious, Muscota's existence as a separate entity from the host school probably promoted a sense of "separateness" and "psychic distance" instilling a strong sense of shared identity and autonomy among Muscota faculty members.[14] At present, Muscota faculty members appear to be positioning themselves emphatically in favor of subunit identification (Muscota) and just as resolutely in opposition to school identification (W. Haywood Burns).

At first, Muscota enjoyed complete autonomy from the host school, and its Teacher Director reported directly to Superintendent Amato. But, as Lydia Bassett explained, existing as an autonomous school without the supervision of a principal was never an option for the Muscota New School. Bassett was recruited because of her empathy with the vision of Muscota New School as well as her ability to work in accordance with the overall district mission. With its move to the W. Haywood Burns School, Muscota has assumed a different identity, and now is one of three small schools under the leadership of Lydia Bassett, the building principal.

In spite of the fact that the W. Haywood Burns School follows the principles of student-centered education and set out to become an environment that would support the continued growth of the Muscota New School, some Muscota teachers continue to express concern that being a part of a larger school threatens their autonomy and sense of identity. The literature on small schools emphasizes the importance of the perception of distinctiveness and separateness on the part of faculty and students as strong agents in helping win student and teacher commitment.[15] Meanwhile, a common observation among the Amistad and Middle School faculty is that the Muscota faculty has been reluctant to make connections. "They won't talk" to other faculty members is a comment often heard. This tendency, moreover, limited my ability to represent their perspectives.

Lydia Bassett agreed that issues and concerns need to be publicly voiced to begin the process of addressing them. The institutional governance structures eventually established will determine how the tension over accountability versus autonomy is resolved, and how future issues are addressed. At present the tensions within the W. Haywood Burns School suggest that while groups of parents, teachers and administrators there all have a common purpose—to provide the diverse student population with a meaningful and powerful educational experience—different perspectives exist on how to achieve this goal. Some advocate a large cohesive unit (the school as a whole) standing on a common purpose and vision. Others advocate more autonomy for the small units (the Middle School, Amistad and Muscota). Faculty members of each of the three small schools agree that the challenge facing each of them is how to retain and foster distinctiveness while at the same time contributing to the welfare of the comprehensive nine-year program the larger community of the W. Haywood Burns School promises parents.

While the story of the W. Haywood Burns School currently features some tension, the teachers all share the same objective: to create an educational environment that respects students. One faculty member emphasized the immediacy and importance of the task when she likened the school to that "island of decency" within an often inequitable system, pointing out the importance of preserving the vision of student-centered education in District Six.

Democracy, Autonomy and Community

The W. Haywood Burns School is a microcosm of the larger reality of present-day American urban education where parents, educators, administrators, researchers and policy makers struggle to cope with the complex challenges of meeting the educational needs of students who increasingly represent backgrounds of cultural diversity and poverty. The story of the W. Haywood Burns School serves as a lens through which to view and interpret the larger social, political and cultural issues that influence progressive, student-centered education in urban settings. Through this lens, three important themes come into focus: the possibility of democracy, the importance of autonomy and the need for community.

Democracy. In this era of cultural diversity and economic disparity, urban communities have diverse and pressing needs. Progressive public education offers a possible means to address these needs. Situated within the traditions of postmodern thought, progressive, student-centered education challenges the traditionalist practices that have marginalized the perspectives of women and minorities by acquiescing in centralized authority dominated by the majority, mainstream traditionally white-male viewpoint. By definition, progressive practices respond more directly to the diverse voices of teachers and students than traditionalist approaches because their curricula reflects the needs and interests of students, and the authority to interpret curricula and assess students rests in the hands of the teachers themselves. In many ways, the same criticism has been leveled against the parents who led the struggle to establish a learner-centered school in the predominately Latino and African-American community of Inwood and Washington Heights. But one parent pointed out that with mechanisms in place for parents to become involved with school operations in legitimate ways, all parents in the community have the opportunity to become involved and to learn to use the power structures available.

Progressive education is based on an ethic of action, and action is guided by the lived experience of participants from diverse socio-economic and cultural backgrounds. Progressive urban public schools are thus positioned to serve as tools for a democracy, helping community members acquire the power and voice to play a role in a changing society. The collective experiences of a school's participants shape its agenda. In elite private and suburban schools, where children come mostly from middle class and affluent families, the agenda mirrors the interests of the communities they serve, including the acquisition and concentration of cultural, social and economic capital. In the more inclusive progressive urban schools, the agenda includes social action.

In the case of the W. Haywood Burns School, where the collective experience of students informs the curriculum, issues of economic disparity, poverty, racism, homelessness, immigration, social welfare and health education, among others, provide curricular frameworks. Because the curriculum stems from the lived experiences of economically, racially and culturally diverse students—and their struggles, challenges and successes—it holds a great potential for educating students for participation in a pluralistic, multiracial society. Education is an existential project: experience becomes curriculum becomes experience. By virtue of its mission and the constituency it serves, the W. Haywood Burns School and other progressive urban public schools now find themselves in a powerful position to serve the causes of democracy and social justice by virtue of their missions and constituencies. Lydia Bassett recalled the words of John Dewey as she underscored the importance for all the W. Haywood Burns faculty to remember their common cause: " 'The best school offers what the wisest parent wants for his child.' At W. Haywood Burns we pedagogues must look for a collective wisdom."

Autonomy. Administrative constraints often deny public schools the flexibility needed to implement progressive initiatives. Whereas independent schools enjoy freedom from district- and state-level mandates, as a result of fiscal and administrative guidelines most public schools must adhere to skills-based, traditionalist practices that bear a direct influence on the curriculum. Progressive, student-centered approaches, based on existentialist and phenomenological philosophical traditions, are often at odds with the goals of traditionalist educational approaches founded upon the principles of Aristotelian potentiality. In the face of this conflict, we need to reconceptualize the idea of accountability to effect a change in the way we evaluate students and school systems. The W. Haywood Burns School rests upon the ability of its faculty to work productively for reform within the system rather than fighting it.

The dilemma of accountability is hardly a problem unique to the W. Haywood Burns School. Pressure to teach to standardized tests is an educational reality destined to persist. If lasting, wide-scale systemic reform is to occur, progressive schools must acquire officially sanctioned space and autonomy so that they might create more philosophically compatible measures of accountability. Voices of criticism within the field of educational evaluation now call for a dramatic revision in our evaluation and testing practices. Sternberg addressed this issue when he pointed out that traditional measures of academic achievement tend to measure achievement and ability narrowly according to the ability to memorize and analyze information.[16] In reference to achievement tests, Sternberg observed, "These tests predict school performance reasonably well. They do so because they emphasize the same abilities that are emphasized in the classroom."[17] But Sternberg pointed out that measuring other abilities, those in practical and creative domains are neglected in traditional standardized tests:

> [T]he importance of [memory and analytical] abilities should not be allowed to obfuscate what else is important. . . . In a pluralistic society, we cannot afford to have a monolithic conception of intelligence and schooling; it's simply a waste of talent. . . . The more we teach and assess students based on a broader set of abilities, the more racially, ethnically, and socioeconomically diverse our achievers will be. We can easily change our closed system—and we should. We must take a more balanced approach to education to reach all of our students.[18]

The dilemma of biased evaluation introduces another tension in the W. Haywood Burns School story. Student-centered approaches emphasize practical and creative learning. If progressive, student-centered schools must evaluate themselves and their students according to invalid measures, they will appear to be failing to meet the educational needs of their students. If traditional measurements of accountability continue to be the sole benchmark of educational success, and if the faculties of progressive schools bound to larger traditional school systems lack sufficient autonomy over curricular issues, progressive urban public education has a dim future at best.

The W. Haywood Burns School is indebted to private funding structures that fostered its establishment and growth, and it owes its legacy to a variety of private institutions. The New Visions Schools initiative, the Center for Collaborative Education, the Annenberg Institute for School Renewal and the Coalition of Essential Schools all provide the kind of support needed to achieve systemic public school reform. They offer communities of teachers and parents the financial means to enjoy the autonomy they need to enact progressive educational initiatives. These funding sources exist to seed educational reform. The reform itself can work only when public school districts acknowledge the valuable lessons school-based progressive educational initiatives teach.

Community. The importance of parent involvement is a dominant theme in the W. Haywood Burns story. The school was developed as a result of parents' struggle for alternative education in the district, and those parents invested long, exhaustive hours making their hopes become reality. Their efforts currently focus on the immediate future of the school, but their hard-won successes will continue only to the degree that the faculty encourages their continuing involvement. Within political spheres in the community, the parents' voices protect and maintain the viability of the school, and at the W. Haywood Burns School, one must acknowledge the importance of structures that support authentic parent involvement. Parents hold the key to the future because in community-based education across the country, their opinions carry political clout. If progressive education is to navigate successfully against the mainstream of traditional education, parents will fuel the forward momentum. The W. Haywood Burns School is indebted to a well-informed, committed parent body, together with faculty members who possess the humility and willingness to invest energy in involving parents in the educational experiences of their children. The ultimate success of the W. Haywood Burns School, and the degree to which it will have the freedom to continue, depends on the collaborative efforts of teachers and parents.

Conclusion

Many of the progressive educational reform efforts in both the public and private sectors have their roots in the early twentieth century progressive movement that set out to operationalize the principles of democracy. This movement took place primarily in independent schools with school populations most often composed of children from the affluent upper-middle classes.[19] The stories of independent, progressive schools, successful or not, affluent or not, teach us a great deal. But as Semel and Sadovnik have pointed out, any attempt to impose progressive practices of independent schools onto public urban schools is problematic since independent schools "too closely [mirror] the affluent community in which [they] are located, rather than successfully challenging the values of materialism and affluence."[20] Independent schools, therefore, cannot be held as a "model of democracy in action,"[21] and while their heritage has much to offer progressive public urban education initiatives, "the question for contemporary educational policy is how to translate these lessons into more democratic and inclusive settings."[22] The story of the W. Haywood Burns School illustrates one attempt to make that translation.

Political maneuvering, hard work, time and effort on the part of parents and faculty members—all of it went into the establishment of the W. Haywood Burns School. It continues to be a place where promise and possibility exist in the hearts and minds of its participants; but success will occur for only as long as its participants have the will and the freedom to work toward their vision. Linda Suss made an important point that is relevant to the story of the W. Haywood Burns School: "The New York City school system gets a lot of bad press, but there's a lot to be proud of. There are pockets in the city that are progressive. It starts with leadership and vision."

Parents and the faculty of the W. Haywood Burns School continue to grapple with vision and leadership issues. Through dialogue and discord, consensus and conflict, the collective vision and mission of the school continues to evolve. But underlying this effort is a collective commitment to progressive education, a fierce devotion to the children and a strong sense of both enchantment and dedication. Lydia Bassett expressed the optimism and hope that all of the school's participants felt from the start, the hope and optimism that can sustain this vision of progressive education in the public arena:

> Our school opened only a month ago, but it feels as though we have all been together for much longer than that. The classrooms are filled with students' work and that work is beginning to spill over into the corridors. Children are getting to know each other and they come to school each day to explore new ideas and new friendships. Teachers are working together into the night to enrich the learning experiences of their students. Parents are a presence throughout the day and in the evenings as the Bylaws Committee works to create

the model which will best support parent partnership with the W. Haywood Burns School. In some ways we do not seem like a new school. Perhaps the school is new, but the idea of it has lived in the hearts and minds of all of us for a long time.[23]

13

PROGRESSIVE EDUCATION: LESSONS FROM THE PAST AND PRESENT

Susan F. Semel
Alan R. Sadovnik

Progressive education may be the most enduring educational reform movement in this country, with a life span of about one hundred years. Although as noted earlier, it waxes and wanes in popularity, many of its practices now appear so regularly in both private and public schools as to have become almost mainstream. But from the schools that were the pioneers, what useful lessons can we learn? The histories of the early progressive schools profiled in Part I illustrate what happened to some of the pioneering progressive schools founded in the first part of the twentieth century. But even now, they serve as important reminders for educators concerned with the competing issues of stability and change in schools with particular progressive philosophies—reminders, specifically, of the complex nature of school reform.

As we have seen in these histories, balancing the original intentions of progressive founders with the known demands upon us has been the challenge some of the schools have met successfully and others have not. As contemporary American educators consider the school choice movement and the emergent interest in charter schools they would do well to look back for guidance at some of the original schools representative of the "new education." Particularly instructive, the Dalton School and the City and Country School, are both urban independent schools that have enjoyed strong and enduring leaders, well-articulated philosophies and accompanying pedagogic practice, and a neighborhood to supply its clientele. Moreover, both have weathered the vicissitudes of educational reform movements hostile to progressive education.

In City and Country, we find a school that has managed to keep basically intact (some argue this point) Caroline Pratt's child-centered practices. It does so, in part, because of its small size and because it is a K-8 school, so that parents who are feeling the pressures of college admissions have four more years following City and Country to equip their children with Ivy League credentials. It also attracts parents who consciously favor a progressive school and who are often alumni. It also selects faculty members interested in or graduates of progressive institutions. Significantly, a highly respected core of dedicated long-time faculty members serve to initiate new colleagues into the ways of the school. When progressive education fell into disfavor, the school faced dwindling enrollments; however, neighborhood and "New Age" parents may have been as influential in preserving the school as stable leadership, retrenchment, loyal alumni and the choice real estate that helped to provide financial solvency. Finally, City and Country is proud of its heritage and its leadership is respectful of and continues both to articulate and implement the philosophy of Caroline Pratt.

The Dalton School, by contrast, is a large and very successful K-12 school that has de-emphasized its progressive roots since the 1960s. It continues to voice the rhetoric of Helen Parkhurst but not her practices. Its leadership, beginning with Donald Barr, has been hostile to progressive education and its parent body has increasingly included fewer alumni and more people new to the school. It draws its students from affluent neighbor-hoods, and particularly from its surroundings, and it is mindful of the link between college admissions and a large student body as well as the importance of parents and alumni, who generously support fund drives. Few faculty members now remember the school as progressive; most have retired. In essence, Dalton has survived as a market-sensitive institution that delivers—in its case, college admissions and a first-rate education that would pass muster with E.D. Hirsch's Core Movement.

The Francis W. Parker School appears to walk a fine line between City and Country and Dalton. It continues to thrive in Chicago as a highly successful college preparatory school as well as a progressive school still following some of its original philosophy and practices. It, too, illustrates the importance of leadership as a primary factor in determining the direction of a school, a dedicated faculty with institutional memory and success delivering college admissions. It is, to repeat, highly sensitive to the demands of the marketplace. Moreover, as Stone suggests, the Francis W. Parker School provides us with an important model for teacher education and reminds us, too, that the notion of teachers as curriculum makers has had a long history. Sadly, both Parker and Dalton and to a degree, City and Country—all located in urban areas—unintentionally benefited from school desegregation and the resulting "white flight" of middle and upper middle class students to independent schools.

Competition for admission to selective colleges has had a profound effect on progressive schools such as Dalton, Parker and the Park School. All three schools, especially Dalton and Park, have become elite college preparatory schools, with vestiges of their progressive traditions. Since the 1960s, as college admissions democratized, affluent families have demanded their schools provide advantages in the admissions competition. Thus, independent day schools, and many public schools in affluent suburbs, have attempted to use the methods of elite boarding schools to ensure their students gain admission to selective colleges.[1] While schools like Dalton and Park have lost touch with much of their progressive heritages, they have managed to survive and prosper by adapting to the educational market.

Regrettably, other progressive schools have fared less well. As Newman points out, the Organic School in Fairhope, Alabama has struggled to survive in a changing political climate. Proud of its progressive heritage, its leadership has begun to see its value as the school defines its mission and stabilizes its enrollment. The Organic School also illustrates the importance of location and leadership and the politics of race. The Lincoln School and Arthurdale, two very different schools, ceased to exist: the former, a victim of institutional politics; the latter, a victim of both local and national politics and economic realities.

An examination of the schools described in Part II make it apparent that they resemble many of the pioneering progressive schools. Characteristics like small size, parental involvement, child-centered pedagogy, multi-disciplinary curricula, and teachers as curriculum makers existed in all of the schools profiled in Part I and continue today. Each subscribes to a child-centered philosophy and each practices some form of integrated curriculum, although one rarely finds them referring to earlier progressive models or even using the term "progressive education." Although their methodologies harken back to Deweyan practices, schools like Butterfield come out of the alternative school movement of the 1960s, a blatantly ahistorical period. For some of the newer urban public schools, like Urban Academy and the W. Haywood Burns School, issues of funding may dictate rhetoric since both public and private funding sources tend to suspect the word "progressive." Thus, articulated references to historical antecedents can easily become liabilities. Nevertheless, it is a depressing fact of life, particularly to historians of education, that most American school reformers suffer from historical amnesia and tend to be future oriented. Thus they spend an inordinate amount of time reinventing the wheel, albeit with occasional great success. Contemporary progressive schools have advisory systems and student contracts and often see these as new educational reforms. However, Parkhurst's Dalton Plan included House, an advisory system, and Assignment, a contract between students and their teachers. Bushnell nicely adduces the parents and teachers in the Free Union Country School, who have developed child-centered practices on their own. Dedicated professionals and visionary leaders sensitive to the needs of the children they educate and to the communities they come from help to provide thriving environments at Urban Academy and the W. Haywood Burns School. A less successful effort in innovative, progressive schooling, the Butterfield School presents an instance of well-intentioned efforts to provide children with an alternative to the traditional school. But its creators failed to examine past models, to plan carefully, and to learn from the mistakes and triumphs of former progressive educators.

Still, we can learn much from both the past and present models as we contemplate school reform. Each of the schools profiled here has or had a particular educational philosophy and a pedagogy that followed from it. Teachers, students, parents, administrators were (or are) aware of it and for the most part, subscribed or subscribe to it. That some progressive schools survived and continue to implement progressive practices while others have succumbed to the demands of the marketplace clearly reflects such variables as location, leadership and the temper of the times.

Contemporary reformers often preach the lessons found in the early progressive schools. For example, Henry Levin's "Accelerated Schools" model is based on three principles: (1) unity of purpose; (2) empowerment and responsibility, and (3) building on strengths, all three of which existed in some form in the schools profiled in Part I.[2] Further, Levin stresses the importance of socializing teachers from year to year to ensure continuity. As Provenzo notes, in the past many of the Park School teachers attended the school and returned as teachers. Many stayed for their entire careers and ensured that each generation of new teachers learned the school's philosophy and practices. This had been true at Dalton, Parker and City and Country. Unfortunately, this has become less true in the 1980s and 1990s.

Continuity and preserving tradition also depend on school leadership. The history of the historically progressive schools demonstrates the importance of school leadership, both positively and negatively. Many of the schools had heads who remained for many years and often their replacements taught at the school under their direction. Parkhurst and Durham at Dalton, Pratt and Murray at City and Country, and Cooke and Osborne at Parker are examples of this continuity. Further, as the histories of Dalton, City and Country, Parker, Park and Organic demonstrate, leadership is crucial in determining a school's direction. For example, Barr began the transformation of the Dalton School through the sheer dominance of his personality. After Murray's retirement from City and Country, the school struggled to survive after 63 years of strong leadership by two different women. Parker went through considerable administrative turnover after Cooke, as did Organic after Johnson.

As many of the schools were founded by charismatic leaders, the problem of following in their footsteps remained a problem.[3] In some cases, like Durham at Dalton and Murray at City and Country, charismatic leadership was followed by more traditional leadership, with the founders' progressive vision systematically transformed into ritual. At Park, Organic and Parker continuity of leadership occurred less easily.

The fact that many of the schools profiled in Part I were founded by women provides the opportunity for further research concerning women and leadership. The lives of Marietta Johnson, Mary Hammett Lewis, Caroline Pratt, Helen Parkhurst and Elsie Clapp, and the schools they founded, raise important questions about contemporary feminist theories of school leadership that suggest that women administrators are more caring and connected to their students and faculty.[4] Semel suggested elsewhere that the histories of some of the early progressive schools do not support this contention.[5]

Critics like E.D. Hirsch have accused progressive education of sacrificing academic rigor in the name of affective principles like self-esteem, social justice and equity. Although none of the schools profiled here adopted a core or essentialist curriculum, they all emphasized academic rigor and excellence. These schools indicate that progressivism need not be the enemy of academic standards and that equity and excellence are not mutually exclusive. As the Eight Year study demonstrated, students in progressive schools, including Parker and Dalton, did exceptionally well in college.[6]

Finally, these schools, both old and new, reflect a dearth of knowledge about progressive practices, especially regarding their origins and implementations, about what worked, and about what failed and why? In part, one can attribute this dearth to the failure of specific schools to educate their teachers and parents; at Dalton, for example, one new teacher thought The Dalton Plan was an insurance plan. The problem does not, however, solely reside in progressive schools that have lost their progressive visions. It also resides in schools of education and accrediting agencies throughout this country—institutions that, in general, encourage the teaching of methods and the process of modeling devoid of any historical context or a philosophical base that would encourage critical reflection and that would lead students to ponder what worked, what did not, and why? Few prospective teachers now read Dewey; even fewer know of the work of Colonel Francis W. Parker, Marietta Johnson, Caroline Pratt, Helen Parkhurst or Abraham Flexner. Yet they will graduate from various teacher education programs, subscribing to hands-on learning and use of manipulatives for mathematics. They will introduce integrated units of study, practice cooperative learning and engage students in project work, often through differentiated instruction. They will teach reading through Whole Language, thinking that they are practicing "modern education." Ironically, Dewey would insist that they are.

Progressive Education: Democratic Education for All?

Progressive education has increasingly come under attack as an elite form of education. The paradox of progressive education has been described as democratic education for the elite, often delivered autocratically as well.[7] British sociologist Basil Bernstein has written extensively on progressive education as the education of "the new middle class" or the new managerial class. He has pointed to such pedagogic practices as weak classification (integrated curriculum), and weak framing (implicit pedagogy, internalized, invisible and often coercive discipline) as evidence of the techniques required of those destined to assume decision-making positions of authority in society.[8]

Clearly, this was not what John Dewey had in mind when he opened the Laboratory School, which he hoped to be a model for democratic education. It is ironic that a century later, Dewey's school and other such progressive schools founded under the aegis of "the new education" have become institutions to educate the elite, all too often in traditional educational settings (although visitors from more traditional educational backgrounds might disagree). As we have seen, progressive education in the small, child-centered, mainly independent schools founded in the early twentieth century overwhelmingly attracted elite, white populations. Today, however, progressive, experimental or alternative education has become accessible to diverse populations, particularly in the public sector, while accessibility to the "historical" progressive schools can still be problematic for minorities.

As Heffron points out, the Lincoln School, was founded in 1917 by the General Education Board, a Rockefeller philanthropy originally established to aid Southern education. It was located at 646 Park Avenue, within walking distance of the Rockefeller mansion. All four of the Rockefeller boys attended the Lincoln School, whose principal architects included the traditional educator Charles W. Eliot, and his more liberal protégé, Abraham Flexner. It served as a laboratory school for Teachers College, providing clinical placements for Columbia students participating in curriculum design and development, and providing as well observation and demonstration sites. Logistically, its Republican "Silk Stocking District" location was inconvenient to Teachers College, so in 1920, the school moved to 123rd Street near Amsterdam Avenue.

The Lincoln School located its curriculum in the world in which its student lived. It emphasized "real life" experiences, meeting the students where they were, developing curricula around the life of the school and the local community. As Heffron observes, the Lincoln School was a school "that combined cultural epoch theory, the doctrine of interest, and parvenu notions of social efficiency with the relatively remote, patrician sensibilities of supporters and founders like Eliot." It was "a school that could get away with teaching vocational math and science to its upper and upper-middle class students, but not Latin or Greek, the traditional foundations of elite culture." Indeed, in the spirit of the new educational reforms, the school offered neither Latin nor Greek. Its integrated curriculum, often rooted in science and technology ("relevant" fields of study) is still viewed as paradigmatic for curriculum design.

Although interested in reproducing "actual life on a democratic basis," the school catered to a clientele composed of the upper echelons of New York society and the Columbia University intelligentsia. It had, in Heffron's words, "a small selective population" and "a parent body of a high intellectual level" often with extremely deep pockets. Interestingly, it produced two virulent critics of progressive education: Arthur Bestor and Donald Barr.

In 1907, under the collective influences of Froebel, Dewey, Oppenheim and Henderson, Marietta Johnson started the Organic School in Fairhope, Alabama. An experimental, child-centered "school of to-morrow," it began as a kindergarten in a small cottage in a town established in 1894 by colonists who subscribed to the economic philosophy of Henry George, advocate of the single tax. Like most of the other colonists, Marietta Johnson came from outside the South (Johnson from Minnesota). But according to historian Joseph Newman, they all "drew inspiration from the utopian idealism of *Progress and Poverty*. Working together in an experimental community gave them a sense of self-importance, an identity they enjoyed projecting to outsiders." Although the colonists became divided politically between the socialists and the single-tax adherents, they sustained a powerful sense of community, galvanized by a skeptical view of capitalism. As Newman points out, the Organic School provided the educational experiment dimension to the community, which was an experiment from its inception.

Initially the colony council provided support for the school so it could run as "a quasi-public institution" free to local children. By 1913, it had enrolled 150 white students tuition free, comprising about two-thirds of Fairhope's elementary-school-age population. According to Newman, Johnson "tried to create an egalitarian climate, providing equal opportunities for male and female students, and accepted students from all socio-economic backgrounds represented in the white population—a fairly narrow range in the early days of the community." Johnson also recruited "backward" (disabled) children "for whom the public schools made no provisions."

Because Fairhope had a mild climate, it tended to attract wealthy northerners and midwesterners, who came to winter in the colony or on the eastern shore of nearby Mobile. Thus, another group of affluent, educated and interesting candidates presented itself to Johnson: the children of wealthy midwestern and northern vacationers enamored of progressive education. Finally, as Fairhope became more and more attractive, resembling a New England village with more than 500 residents, it became especially appealing to artists, writers and intellectuals, most of whom sent their children to the Organic School. Significantly, throughout her career, Johnson recruited and raised funds mostly along the East Coast, particularly in affluent bedroom communities like Greenwich, Connecticut.

Johnson's child-centered school impressed John Dewey, who remarked, "Mrs. Johnson is trying an experiment under conditions which hold in public schools, and she believes her methods are feasible for any public school system. Any child is welcome." (Of course, in that time and place "any child" meant any white child.) Today, according to Newman, the school has 60 students, all but one white, mostly from the upper middle class, and mostly from the immediate area. After a troubled past in which the school became a traditional school for white separatists, it struggles both to survive and to recapture its founder's original vision.

Caroline Pratt began the City and Country School as a play group in a settlement house in New York City in 1914. Under the influence of her radical socialist companion, Helen Marot, she tried to interest working-class parents in a school that would teach children about their world through play, particularly with blocks. As she established her school, her idiosyncratic vision of block play and jobs suitable for building a democratic community took on substance. She established, in Dewey's words, "an embryonic community" in which each group had a job or task essential to the maintenance of the school as a whole. Blocks became the vehicles through which children worked together to make sense of their world, first, their immediate environment, then their neighborhoods, until children in the "Sevens" had built a city complete with running water and electricity. This child-centered school continues to use an integrated curriculum that reflects the needs and interests of the children at different developmental levels.

Though City and Country began as a play school for working-class children in the neighborhood (in her book, *I Learn from Children* described her attempts to recruit the children of working people), they did not remain in her school. Parents expressed concern that their children would not fit into traditional schools later on, and ultimately, they withdrew them from her experimental, progressive school. An influx of affluent neighborhood children from families in Greenwich Village—"the new middle class," or struggling artists and writers interested in progressive education—quickly filled the vacuum.

City and Country School has always maintained its "downtown" ambience and its "downtown clientele," who are attracted to its child-centered focus and its emphasis on the school as community. Although committed to democratic education, the school has, from the 1970s on, struggled to remain open in the wake of dwindling enrollments following the death of its second powerful female head, Jean Wesson Murray. Now it accepts full-tuition-paying students almost exclusively. Thus, as in so many of the independent progressive schools that depend upon tuition for their existence, maintaining diversity continues to be problematic.

The Dalton School is located amid some of the most expensive real estate in the world and from its inception, Dalton's student population reflected its location. Parkhurst actively recruited the rich and the not-so-rich-but-famous for her school, providing scholarships for those artists, writers and intellectuals she thought would provide visibility for her educational experiment. Indeed, classes in the early years were composed of children of upper class white Protestants, affluent German Jews (who, because of their religion, found rejection at traditional elite independent schools), along with people in the arts and letters. Never a social reconstructionist school, Dalton sought to mirror life through its students, whose parents reflected different occupations and different economic levels even though creative types and monied businessmen dominated the parent body. Thus, intellectuals, barely able to feed their families (and during the McCarthy era, often blacklisted, as well) would be offered scholarships for their children, who would find themselves seated in the same classroom with the children of the nouveau riche, the old monied Protestants who were interested in progressive education, and upper class German Jews.

Beginning in the 1960s as Dalton became less progressive and more financially solvent, the population changed radically to include up to twenty percent scholarship students of color along with mostly white, new-monied offspring of Wall Street parentage, and the children of highly visible entertainers.

As Perlstein and Stack note, Arthurdale schools depended upon the composition of the community, which was highly selective. Both the race and politics of the workers determined their eligibility for Arthurdale; thus

Blacks and workers whose politics might be viewed as "radical" were excluded. An example of a white, working-class progressive experiment, its schools heavily influenced by Deweyan ideas, it suffered a brief existence. Thus it is difficult to assess how its school might have fared had the community sustained itself. Nevertheless, its history demonstrates the tensions between the social reconstructionist and child-centered strands of progressive education. The debates between Elsie Clapp and George Counts over indoctrination exemplified a major component of these tensions. Furthermore, Arthurdale's refusal to admit Blacks into a community dedicated to egalitarian principles illustrates the importance of both race and class in examining educational inequalities.

The "schools of to-morrow" Dewey lauded as indicative of the "new education" were innovative in their educational philosophies, curricula and pedagogic practices. They did not, however, mirror society, writ large, in their student bodies. The reasons are complex, but generally it seems clear that experimental, progressive education often appealed to those who did not fit or who were excluded from mainstream, elite education as well as proponents of the "new education." The archives of many of these schools support the thesis that they met the needs of a number of children who today might be labeled "learning disabled," by providing individualized instruction and allowing them to progress at their own rates. At Parker and Dalton, German Jews were significantly represented from their beginnings through the fifties, when they began to be eclipsed by Eastern European Jews. Interestingly, as religious quota systems in higher education came under scrutiny, access to other independent schools (and particularly boarding schools) became easier, which may partially explain why the German Jewish presence declined significantly in progressive day schools. This decline was particularly apparent at The Dalton School. Dewey's own school, the Laboratory School, has become an elite school for affluent, mostly white children. Notice that these are independent schools with smaller endowments than mainstream elite schools, and they depend on tuition for their survival.

Of course, not all progressive schools catered predominantly to affluent populations. The Little Red Schoolhouse–Elizabeth Irwin, founded as a public school in Greenwich Village, not far from the City and Country School, became a private school to save its integrity as a progressive, experimental school in the wake of assaults from the public school bureaucratic hierarchy. It subsequently managed to attract a less affluent, though predominantly intellectual parent body. The Downtown Community School, founded in 1944 on the Lower East Side of New York City, mainly for the children of working class families, managed to survive for almost a quarter of a century until its social reconstructionist stance alienated the child-centered faction, thus causing an unbreachable rift.[9] This schism also occurred at a time when independent schools were profiting from "white flight" to the private schools. Fragile from its very beginning, the Downtown Community School could not withstand assaults from both within and without and so it closed its doors.

In the public sector, one finds more cause for optimism. Progressive education certainly existed in Winnetka, Illinois, under the leadership of Carleton Washburne, and in Gary, Indiana until, according to Heffron, it was derailed by administrative progressive bureaucrats. Nevertheless, in New York City, progressive education is alive and well in the public sector. Raywid's discussion of Urban Academy, a public, alternative secondary school in New York City, with a population of poor, urban, minority students suggests that an innovative school with progressive practices, somewhat like those of Central Park East Secondary School, can succeed.

Another new progressive school that invites close scrutiny, the W. Haywood Burns School, P.S.-I.S. 176, is a product of the New Vision Schools program, a New York City Board of Education initiative that, according to McCallister, "supports new schools founded upon the principles of faculty autonomy, [a] unified vision and identity among faculty members, and [a] commitment to a curriculum that incorporates the voices of its participants." Located in the upper reaches of Manhattan (204th Street and Broadway) in a predominantly poor, immigrant neighborhood, it houses three schools within one school, providing a population of 600 elementary and middle-school age children with learner-centered environments, while remaining respectful of their respective cultures. A number of its faculty members who have helped shape the school came from Central Park East, and it will be important to see how well they educate their new students, given both Basil Bernstein's and Lisa Delpit's critiques of progressive education as education that disadvantages working class children and children of color.[10] We need careful empirical analyses of the educational outcomes in this and similar schools in order to settle this question.

Clearly, when independent, progressive schools fall hostage to market forces, they become democratic education for the elite. But were they ever intended to be truly democratic? And what does "democratic" really mean? In their discussion of the Gary Schools, the Deweys were silent on the issue of race, although the Black children there were on a different vocational track than the white children. In the instance of the Organic School, "democratic" education routinely excluded children of color education in the South being rigorously segregated; in Arthurdale, an "egalitarian" community excluded Blacks and union organizers. Is Bernstein right to ascribe the success of progressive education to the new middle class? For many reasons evident in the histories described in this volume, progressive schools certainly have tended to attract this population. In fact, under the label of "alternative education," progressive education has increasingly become an important educational alternative, if not a panacea, for both advantaged and disadvantaged children. The question remains, however, does progressive education, as Lisa Delpit observes, disadvantage them further? Only empirical evidence can answer this question.

Finally, the issue of public and private schooling needs to be critically addressed. Although there are fundamental differences between public and private schools, too often schools like the independent progressive schools profiled in this volume are dismissed because they are private. Such simplistic dismissals ensures that the lessons to be learned from these schools will be ignored. More important, blind praise of public education overlooks their role in the reproduction of educational inequality. Schools like Central Park East, Urban Academy and W. Haywood Burns originated because of the failures of urban public education in educating children from at-risk situations. Conversely, many suburban public schools in affluent neighborhoods are more racially and socioeconomically segregated than many independent schools. As Jay Mathews indicates in *Class Struggle: What's Wrong (and Right) with America's Best High Schools*, the majority of the "best" public schools are in affluent suburbs and educate mostly white, affluent children.[11] Thus, the racial and social class composition of a school may be as or more important than whether it is public or private to understand the role of schooling in either providing avenues for social mobility or reproducing social inequality. Finally, although there has been significant disagreement over their findings, Bryk, Lee and Holland indicate that many urban Catholic schools succeed with students from lower socio-economic backgrounds because of their unifying philosophy and academic emphasis, qualities that exist (or existed) in all of the progressive schools discussed in this volume.[12]

Individualism and Community in Progressive Education

In the past 15 years, a number of social critics from both sides of the political spectrum dissected what they see as the overly individualistic nature of American society.[13] From Christopher Lasch's scathing indictment of American culture in *The Culture of Narcissism*,[14] to Robert Bellah, Richard Madsen, William Sullivan, Ann Swidler and Steven Tipton's analysis and recommendations in *Habits of the Heart*[15] and *The Good Society*,[16] to Amitai Etzioni's more conservative call for a communitarian society in the *Spirit of Community*,[17] American society has been viewed as a nation in desperate need of closer connections between groups and individuals. These critics all recommend that the tensions between individualism and community, so much a part of the history of the United States, be resolved more in favor of community than the trend has been running since the 1960s.

The sociological analysis of the tensions between individualism and community is hardly new. The classical sociology of Emile Durkheim was, at its center, concerned with the effects of the decline of traditional rituals and community during the transition from traditional to modern societies. Durkheim's analysis of the differences between mechanical and organic solidarity in the *Division of Labor*,[18] and his concept of anomie in *Suicide*,[19] examined the need for societies to create rituals and institutions to provide for social cohesion and meaning. Likewise, Ferdinand Tönnies'[20] analysis of *gemeinschaft* and *gesellschaft* provided a sociological analysis of the effects of modernity on community.

Significant similarities exist between Durkheim's sociology of education and the sociological underpinnings of John Dewey's philosophy of education. Central to Dewey's analysis of American education and his call for progressive education was an analysis of the tensions between individualism and community. As Bowles and Gintis noted, Dewey's work attempted to reconcile the tensions between the integrative (community), developmental (individualism) and egalitarian (community) functions of education.[21] Although Bowles and Gintis argued that these functions are inherently contradictory in capitalist society, Dewey believed that schools could help balance the often competing demands of the community and the individual.

In fact, much of Dewey's early writings on education[22] simultaneously called for the need for schools to contribute to individual development and to the development of an "embryonic democratic community."[23] In fact, this tension was historically played out in the two sometimes distinctive branches of progressive education in the 1920s and 1930s: child-centered progressivism, which often resolved the tension in favor of individualism, and social reconstructionism, which often resolved the tension in favor of community.

Thus, social criticism from the 1950s to the present has focused on the tensions between the individual and community. In the late 1950s, in response to the putative conformity of that decade, a number of social critics argued that American society had become overly organizational, bureaucratic and stifling.[24] As Ehrenreich noted, the challenges to authority that percolated in the 1960s had antecedents in a number of cultural and intellectual movements of the 1950s, including the "Beat Generation."[25]

Following the social upheavals of the 1960s and early 1970s, where the tensions between individualism and community often ended in favor of the individual, social critics like Lasch urged an increased sense of community.[26] Lasch suggested that American culture had become a "culture of narcissism" and that such unbridled individualism threatened the core of our civilization. In the 1980s, Bellah et al. provided a critique of American individualism, but at the same time noticed a foundation of communitarianism in American life.[27] They argued a little later that a "good society" was based on democratic institutions that allowed both for individualism and for the connections between individuals within a cohesive community.[28]

In the 1980s and 1990s, analyses of individualism and community acquired considerable political overtones. But with both the left and the right espousing increased community, the political vantage points differ widely. Whereas conservatives seek a return to a community of traditional values and decry the pernicious effects of individualism on the family and on traditional values, liberals and radicals call for an increased democratic community that balances the tensions between individuals and society.[29] For example, Etzioni's more conservative branch of communitarianism argues for a return to more traditional forms of community and, like Durkheim, almost a century before, expresses the need for schools to be agencies of moral socialization and transmitters of community values.[30]

Like Durkheim, Etzioni overemphasizes the cohesiveness of modern societies and underestimates the conflicts between groups over precisely what constitutes a cohesive community and community values. Drawing heavily on Dewey, Lippmann, and Niebuhr—Bellah et al. suggest that the conflicts between groups over competing definitions of community are precisely what democratic institutions ought to resolve.[31] Although Bellah and his colleagues do not suggest these conflicts are easily resolved, they do believe that democratic institutions can create a society that connects individuals to community meaningfully. Echoing the same liberal optimism about the stabilizing force of schooling that both Durkheim and Dewey expressed almost a century before, Bellah et al. look to schools as central institutions in the democratic, communitarian society. Thus, both Etzioni and Bellah et al. look, from somewhat different political vantage points, to schooling as central to community. These contemporary concerns with the role of schools in solving problems raised by the tensions between individuals and community have, as noted earlier, historical roots in Dewey's early writings in the late nineteenth and early twentieth century.

Chapter 1 described nine principles enunciated by the Network of Progressive Educators in 1990 as an example of the types of reforms recommended for improving public education. Further, these principles attempt to balance individualism and community. Unfortunately, contemporary reformers too infrequently look to the past for guidance. One can learn much from the histories examined in this book. Moreover, independent schools rarely serve as models for public school improvement, even though the schools described in both Part I and Part II practiced or continue to practice at least six of the nine principles:

(1)   Education is best accomplished where relationships are personal and teachers design programs which honor the linguistic and cultural diversity of the local community.

All of the schools in Part I had a history of close personal relationships between students, parents, faculty members and the administration. One can attribute this closeness in part to the fact that the roles often overlapped, as exemplified in the case of Eugene Provenzo at the Park School, whose mother taught in the school he attended. In part, one can attribute this closeness to size, since initially, these schools tended to be small and gave the children easy access to one another. Nevertheless, the creation of community was central to their philosophies and each school consciously attempted to create this community, through such mechanisms as assemblies, common projects or jobs, common experiences, like grade trips, and a common pedagogy. Although in many of the schools, conflicts created political and organizational problems, a closely knit community for students remained a hallmark of these schools.

In Part II, the Free Union Country School exemplifies a particular communitarian model of schooling. Parents meant the school to respond to a mutual set of concerns and a particular philosophy of education. They also intended to help govern it and to volunteer their time to teach in it. Free Union is still an embryonic community of child-centered education, and it will be interesting to see how much of its sense of "family" remains as it grows and adopts a more professional stance.

As for honoring the linguistic and cultural diversity of the local community, this principle has worked in the Dalton School, but not necessarily how the Progressive Network intends. The problem is that Dalton does mirror its local community quite well; however, the community is far from diverse. To be fair, the school has over the years attempted to enroll a more diverse and multicultural population, but it has achieved less success in the lower grades where children must rely on their parents for transportation. As an independent school with a high tuition, the school cannot, even with significant scholarship aid, mirror the diversity of society at large. But as we have seen, if homogeneity disqualifies such a school from consideration as progressive, then most independent progressive schools would be disqualified.

This situation is to a large degree also true of City and Country, which never could attract the diverse student body Pratt initially recruited. It, too, has made significant efforts to attract a more diverse student body, but fiscal constraints as well as skepticism of working class parents about the ability of a progressive school to teach their children basic skills hinders these efforts.

Organic and Arthurdale, both committed to principles of democracy, nevertheless restricted admission to their communities. Despite Johnson's commitment to racial integration, the Organic School did not admit Blacks under her direction. Arthurdale excluded Blacks and union organizers in order to maintain stability and order; diversity became a victim of racial and political conflicts.

Finally, noting a lack of diversity in these schools, one should mention in fairness that these schools have defined diversity differently at different times. As Stone reminds us in her chapter on the Parker School, that school defined diversity in terms of ethnicity and social class, reflecting the immediate location of the school and, initially, the social composition of Chicago. A concern for race arose later. Contemporary schools like Urban Academy and the W. Haywood Burns School reflect their neighborhood's linguistic and cultural diversity, but just as the more affluent independent schools do in their way, they also tend to serve particular populations based on race, ethnicity and social class.

(2)   Curriculum balance is maintained by commitment to childrens' individual interests and developmental needs, as well as a commitment to community within and beyond the school's walls.

Historically, all the schools in Part I embraced an explicit commitment to the needs and interests of its students as well as to the community beyond its walls. Arthurdale, for example, attempted to fuse school and community through a social reconstructionist and child-centered approach. That the community it was designed to serve ultimately failed was more of a function of time and place than the school's vision. As well, the Arthurdale community was a carefully crafted community in which one's race and politics determined eligibility for membership. The Dalton School always followed an explicit commitment to the needs and interests of its students, as well as to the community within and beyond its walls. Founded in the spirit of child-centered pedagogy and Dewey's notion of an embryonic community, Dalton was, and to some extent still is, this kind of school. As for commitment to the community within and outside, Dalton has a rich tradition in both areas, a tradition that has faded, but has not disappeared.

City and Country has always been committed to the needs of its students. Founded as a child-centered school, it has continually stressed the developmental and emotional needs of its students in formulating its curriculum and pedagogy. Parker, another child-centered school, at one time devoted an entire year in grade nine to the study of community problems. In the Parker tradition, Urban Academy uses its curriculum to encourage its students to study community problems, thus helping them connect school and society.

(3)   Schools embrace the home cultures of children and
            their families. Classroom practices reflect these
            values and bring multiple cultural perspectives to
            bear.

Perhaps one of the problems at schools like the Lincoln School or Dalton is that they too closely mirrored the affluent community in which they were located, rather than successfully challenging the values of materialism and affluence. Nevertheless, throughout its history, Dalton has attempted to instill in its students a social conscience. This mission has, however, been difficult. City and Country resembles Dalton in this respect, although it has always tried to offer a multicultural curriculum. Additionally, it continues to award scholarships to minority students who have difficulty functioning in traditional settings. Parker attempted throughout its history to connect the school, the home and the society as part of its dedication to Parker's and Dewey's progressive principles.

Set in the Deep South, the Organic School reflected the values of both a quirky single tax constituency and an affluent group of northerners on extended vacations during the mild winters. Although often politically and socially at odds, neither group cared to change the racial make-up of the student body. Arthurdale sought to connect its schools to the home cultures of its families to help them adjust to the economic changes that devastated their lives. However, its schools did not provide a radical critique of these conditions, as social reconstructionists like Counts would have wanted them to do. Certainly Urban Academy, the W. Haywood Burns School and the Free Union Country School reflect their home cultures in both their curricula and their pedagogic practices; however, it is still difficult to judge just how and to what extent these schools integrate cultures unrepresented in their student bodies.

(4)   Students are active constructors of knowledge and learn through direct experience and primary sources.

Historically, all the schools in Part I followed this principle; it is, in fact, what set them apart from their more traditional counterparts. Students remained actively engaged in their own learning, and such progressive experiments as the Otis Farm trip at Dalton and farming at the Park School in Buffalo exemplified experiential education. One finds fewer examples of the principle today, although students at Dalton are probably more involved in their own learning than students at most traditional schools. Students at Francis Parker School and at City and Country have always used the city as a learning laboratory. At City and Country, ubiquitous blocks still invite students to be active constructors of knowledge. Urban Academy and the W. Haywood Burns School use New York City as a learning laboratory and engage their students in their own learning. Burns in particular emphasizes experiential or hands-on learning, which distinguishes it from its more traditional elementary school counterparts.

(5)   The school is a model of democracy and humane relationships confronting issues of racism, class-ism, and sexism.

Although schools like the Lincoln School, Francis Parker and Dalton confronted issues of racism, classism and sexism philosophically (and continue to do so), it is difficult to argue that schools that serve primarily advantaged white children serve as exemplars for progressive concerns of this type. Again, it may be unfair to judge a school this way given its population. Nonetheless, few of these schools model democracy in action. Ironically, the younger schools profiled in Part II that serve less advantaged populations, Urban Academy and particularly the W. Haywood Burns School, seem to be more egalitarian in how they educate children, more tolerant of difference, and more concerned with confronting issues of racism and classism as part of the curriculum and part of daily living. In fact, both schools appear to have been founded on a philosophy of education that mirrors the principles the Network of Progressive Educators set forth.

(6)   Schools actively support critical inquiry into the complexities of global issues. Children can thus assume the powerful responsibilities of world citizenship. (In Chapter 1, this is the eighth principle.)

This has been a traditional hallmark of child-centered progressive schools, particularly those in urban areas. Stone notes the emphasis on global issues in the Parker curriculum. Dalton has, from its inception, been active in educating for global citizenship. Students actively participate in political, environmental, social, and community activities and the curriculum addresses social problems. In many respects, Dalton educators have always attempted to prepare their students for responsibilities like those Dewey envisioned in his writings on democracy and education.

Although City and Country attempted to address this goal at all levels through the eighth grade, the absence of a high school somewhat limited its efforts to educate for global responsibility. Nonetheless, City and Country attempts to prepare its students for democratic participation. Less clear is how this particular curricular thrust operates in the more recently founded schools described in Part II. Clearly, they broach global issues but the extent to which they emphasize global citizenship and particularly world citizenship remains unclear.

Conclusion

The histories of these schools point to the importance of looking first to the past to formulate educational reforms. Many of the practices currently used at innovative, alternative schools like Central Park East Secondary School (CPESS), Urban Academy and the W. Haywood Burns School originated in these schools. As contemporary educators such as Deborah Meier demonstrate, progressive pedagogic practices may work for all children, not just the children of the affluent.[32] Therefore, educational reformers would do well to study the child-centered progressive schools for models of what worked, what failed, and why. For example, all the schools were small enough to create personal communities; and recent high school reforms in New York City, which have built small, alternative high schools as an antidote to large, bureaucratic comprehensive schools, might have been implemented years ago if reformers had only looked to history. Again, the majority of current curriculum and pedagogic reforms, including whole language, authentic assessment, the integrated curriculum, and multicultural education appear in some form in almost all of these schools early in their histories.

We can also learn from the "success" of Dalton, the struggles of City and Country, and the demise of Arthurdale, the Lincoln School, and Butterfield. Their histories teach us significant lessons about school leadership, shared decision making, a sense of community, and the forces that affect school change. In short, they provide models for use to emulate, modify or avoid.

For example, in informal, familial organizations as these schools once were (and some still are) like Parker, Dalton, City and Country, Park, and Organic leadership was not shared, although faculty opinion received respect and the leaders made systematic and sustained attempts to involve parents in or inform them about school philosophy and practices. In fact, one of the greatest paradoxes one notices in these schools is that they supported a democratic education delivered autocratically. Several had dynamic, female founders, focused, even fixated on particular forms of curricula and pedagogic practices. Revered as visionaries, they attracted loyal followings of teachers and parents who heard them lecture, read their educational tracts and duly enrolled children in their schools. They also had wealthy benefactors and benefactresses to underwrite their visions. In some instances—including Dalton, Organic, City and Country, and Parker—strong leadership made it difficult for less charismatic successors to function effectively.

The lesson here is the importance of strong, dynamic, leadership both in founding and maintaining schools with practices at variance with traditional expectations. Additionally, one notices the importance of providing for smooth transitions for the people destined to follow strong leaders. Moreover, the freedom these founders enjoyed in selecting like-minded faculty members bears attention. A common feature in independent schools, this freedom sometimes appears in alternative public schools or choice schools in some school districts, but it is still a rarity. Nevertheless, a faculty that shares the vision or mission of the school is likelier to see to its success.

All of these progressive schools, as we have seen, created a sense of community. Thus, current reformers interested in building school communities can usefully look to these schools for models. Again, one can hardly overemphasize the model presented here of small school size, and a philosophy and pedagogy that creates common experiences, and common traditions for all in the school community: Arch Day, an end-of-year festival at Dalton, in which each grade walks through a flower covered arch; or the open air schooling at Park.

Moreover, the schools profiled in Part I suggest the complexity of school change, particularly when propelled by forces many of these schools could not control. Neighborhood location, for example, helped shape the destinies of many of these schools, particularly The Organic School, Dalton, City and Country, and Parker. The politics of education writ large is another strong influence upon school change. The history of American education in the twentieth century chronicles both the rise and decline of enthusiasm for progressive education, and this shifting attitude definitely helped shape the destinies of these independent progressive schools. Because most depend on tuition, they have accommodated—some more, some less—the demands of the changing "market" in education in an attempt to maintain a healthy enrollment and to balance the budget. Sadly, the marketplace too often controls the destinies of schools that depend on tuition for their existence, and the majority of schools in Part I have been particularly vulnerable since most of them lack "patrician" donors and endowment funds that often support elite boarding schools.

Finally, with respect to the tensions between individualism and community so central to contemporary political and educational debates, the histories of these schools provide significant evidence of how progressive schools have struggled with these tensions. In particular, the Dalton School has, throughout its history, attempted to balance the needs of individuals with the needs of the community. In fact, the Dalton Plan itself was a pedagogical attempt to do exactly that, with House a mechanism for integrating students into the community; Lab, a place for individuals to receive individualized instruction and guidance; and Assignment, a mechanism for individualizing common assignments and accommodating different learning rates. Likewise, City and Country has always emphasized the idea of democratic community central to Deweyan progressivism. Through its community service and jobs component, students become part of a microcosmic democratic society. At the same time, the instruction has always been child-centered and linked to the individual needs of children. Parker has always struggled with these tensions through its progressive school-home-society model; Arthurdale's version of social reconstructionism attempted to create a cohesive community while at the same time stressing child-centered progressivism. The Clapp-Counts debate about indoctrination reflected the significant tensions between the individual and community.

Ideally, these chapters demonstrate how historically progressive schools attempted to balance individualism and community. It has also suggests that many contemporary progressive educational reforms have their origins in the early child-centered schools and that progressive education is alive and well, particularly in the public sector. It is time that educational reformers and practitioners stop reinventing the wheel. It is also time for historians of education to assume active roles in policy conversations. An examination of schools like Parker, Park, Dalton, Organic, Lincoln, Arthurdale and City and Country helps us see that the past has much to teach us. By studying such schools as Urban Academy, The Free Union Country School, and The W. Haywood Burns School, we see as well that the present may hold the same exciting possibilities for children as the "new education," "progressive education," once held.

NOTES

Chapter 1

1. Sections of this chapter are adapted from Alan R. Sadovnik, Peter W. Cookson, Jr. and Susan F. Semel, *Exploring Education: An Introduction to the Foundations of Education* (Needham Heights, Mass.: Allyn and Bacon, 1994); and Susan F. Semel, *The Dalton School: The Transformation of a Progressive School* (New York: Peter Lang, 1992) with permission.

2. E.D. Hirsch, Jr., *The Schools We Need and Why We Don't Have Them* (New York: Doubleday, 1996); John Holden and E.D. Hirsch, Jr. *Books to Build On: A Grade-by-Grade Resource Guide for Parents and Teachers* (New York: Delta, 1996).

3. Arthur Bestor, *Educational Wastelands* (Urbana: University of Illinois Press, 1953).

4. John and Evelyn Dewey, *Schools of To-Morrow* (New York: E.P. Dutton and Co., 1915).

5. Basil Bernstein, *Class, Codes and Control, vol. 3.* (London: Routledge, 1977); *The Structuring of Pedagogic Discourse, vol. 4 of Class, Codes and Control* (London: Routledge, 1990); Alan R. Sadovnik, "Basil Bernstein's Theory of Pedagogic Practice: A Structuralist Approach. *Sociology of Education*, 48:1, pp. 48-64, 1991; *Knowledge and Pedagogy: The Sociology of Basil Bernstein* (Norwood, N.J.: Ablex Publishing Corporation, 1995).

6. Lisa Delpit, *Other People's Children* (New York: New Press, 1995).

7. Lawrence A. Cremin, *American Education: The Metropolitan Experience* (New York: Harper and Row, 1988), p. 88.

8. Lawrence A. Cremin, *The Transformation of the School* (New York: Knopf and Random House, 1961), p. 72.

9. Robert Westbrook, *John Dewey and American Democracy* (Ithaca, N.Y.: Cornell University Press, 1991).

10. John Dewey, "My Pedagogic Creed," in Martin S. Dworkin, ed. *Dewey on Education* (New York: Teachers College Press, 1959), pp. 19-32 (originally published 1897); "The School and Society," ibid, pp. 33-90

(originally published 1899). "The Child and the Curriculum," ibid, pp. 91-111 (originally published 1902).

11. Martin Dworkin ed. *Dewey on Education* (New York: Teachers College Press, 1959), p. 45.

12. Ibid., p. 22.

13. See Laurel Tanner, *Dewey's Laboratory School: Lessons for Today* (New York: Teachers College Press, 1997).

14. Ibid., p. 93.

15. Ibid., p. 41.

16. Ibid., p. 40.

17. Maxine Greene, *The Dialectic of Freedom* (New York: Teachers College Press, 1988).

18. Diane Ravitch, *The Troubled Crusade* (New York: Basic Books, 1983) pp. 43-80.

19. Kieran Egan. "Review of *The Unschooled Mind: How Children Think and How Schools Should Teach*, by Howard Gardner," *Teachers College Record* 94, no. 2, 1992, pp. 402-404.

20. Howard Gardner, "A Response," *Teachers College Record* 94, no. 2, 1992, pp. 410-411.

21. Cremin, *The Transformation of the School*, p. 101.

22. Ibid, p. 114.

23. George Counts, *Dare the Schools Build a New Social Order?* (New York: John Day, 1932). For a discussion of Benne, Counts, and social reconstruction see Michael James, ed. *Social Reconstruction Through Education: The Philosophy, History, and Curricula of a Radical Ideal* (Norwood, N.J.: Ablex Publishing Corporation, 1995).

24. Susan F. Semel, "Basil Bernstein's Theory of Pedagogic Practice and the History of American Progressive Education: Three Case Studies," In *Knowledge and Pedagogy: The Sociology of Basil Bernstein* A. R. Sadovnik. (Norwood, N.J.: Ablex Publishing Corporation, 1995), pp. 337-358; Susan F. Semel and Alan R. Sadovnik, "Lessons from the Past: Individualism and Community in Three Progressive Schools," *Peabody Journal of Education* (Summer 1995), pp. 56-84.

25. Ravitch, *The Troubled Crusade*, p.83.

26. Cremin, *The Transformation of the School*; Patricia Albjerg Graham, *Progressive Education: From Arcady to Academe* (New York,

Teachers College Press, 1967); Ravitch, 1983; David Tyack, *The One Best System* (Cambridge: Harvard University Press, 1974).

27. Cremin, *The Transformation of the School*, p. X.

28. Carl F. Kaestle, "The Public Schools and the Public Mood," *American Heritage* February 1990, p. 74.

29. Ravitch, *The Troubled Crusade*, p. 44.

30. Cremin, *American Education: The Metropolitan Experience*, p. 229.

31. David Tyack, and Elisabeth Hansot. *Managers of Virtue: Public School Leadership in America, 1920-1980* (New York: Basic Books, 1981).

32. Cremin, *American Education: The Metropolitan Experience*, p. 229.

33. Susan F. Semel, *The Dalton School: The Transformation of a Progressive School* (New York: Peter Lang, 1992).

34. Cremin, *The Transformation of the School*, p. 179.

35. Ibid., p. 181.

36. Otto F. Kraushaar, *American Nonpublic Schools: Patterns of Diversity* (Baltimore and London: Johns Hopkins University Press, 1972) p. 81.

37. Cremin, *The Transformation of the School*, p. 202.

38. Kraushaar, *American Nonpublic Schools*, p. 81.

39. For a full discussion of Caroline Pratt's philosophy see her book *Experimental Practice in the City and Country School* (New York: E.P. Dutton and Co., 1924).

40. Cremin, *The Transformation of the School*, p. 213.

41. Joyce Antler, *Lucy Sprague Mitchell: The Making of a Modern Woman* (New Haven: Yale University Press, 1987).

42. Cremin, *The Transformation of the School*, pp. 280-286.

43. Marie Stone, M., ed. *Between Home and Community: Chronicle of the Francis W. Parker School* (Chicago: Francis W. Parker School, 1976).

44. Susan Lloyd, *The Putney School: A Progressive Experiment* (New Haven: Yale University Press, 1987).

45. Edward Yeomans, *The Shady Hill School: The First Fifty Years* (Cambridge, Mass.: Windflower Press, 1979).

46. For a discussion of the Gary schools see Ronald Cohen, *Children of the Mill: Schooling and Society in Gary, Indiana, 1906-1960* (Bloomington: Indiana University Press, 1990); and Ronald Cohen and Raymond Mohl, *The Paradox of Progressive Education: The Gary Plan and Urban Schooling* (Port Washington, N.Y.: Kennidat Press, 1979); for a discussion

of the Winnetka schools see Carleton W. Washburne and Sidney P. Marland, *Winnetka: The History and Significance of an Educational Experiment* (Englewood Cliffs, N.J.: Prentice Hall,1963).

47. See James, *Social Reconstruction Through Education.*

48. Semel and Sadovnik, "Lessons from the Past."

49. Ravitch, *The Troubled Crusade*, p. 76.

50. Ibid., p. 79.

51. A.S. Neill, *Summerhill* (New York: Holt, 1960).

52. Jonathan Kozol, *Death at an Early Age* (New York: Houghton Mifflin, 1967).

53. Herbert Kohl, *36 Children* (New York: New American Library, 1967).

54. Charles Silberman, *Crisis in the Classroom* (New York: Random House, 1970).

55. Joseph Featherstone's articles in *The New Republic* are in *Schools Where Children Learn* (New York: Liveright, 1971); Beatrice and Ronald Gross, "A Little Bit of Chaos," *Saturday Review*, May 16, 1970.

56. Larry Cuban, *How Teachers Taught: Constancy and Change in American Classrooms, 1890-1980* (New York: Longman, 1984).

57. National Commission on Excellence in Education, *A Nation at Risk* (Washington, D.C.: U.S. Government Printing Office, 1983), p. 5.

58. Katherine Borman, Peter W. Cookson, Jr., Alan R. Sadovnik, and Joan Z. Spade, *Implementing Educational Reform: Sociological Perspectives on Educational Policy* (Norwood, N.J.: Ablex Publishing Corporation).

59. Peter W. Cookson, Jr. *School Choice: The Struggle for the Soul of American Education* (New Haven, Yale University Press, 1995).

60. E.D. Hirsch, 1996; Ravitch, 1983; David Tyack and Larry Cuban, *Tinkering Toward Utopia: A Century of Public School Reform* (Cambridge, Harvard University Press, 1995).

61. Semel and Sadovnik, "Lessons from the Past."

62. Network of Progressive Educators, "Statement of Principles," *Pathways* 7, no. 2, 1991, p. 3.

63. Ibid.

64. For a discussion of Central Park East Secondary School see, Deborah Meier, *The Power of Their Ideas* (Boston: Houghton Mifflin, 1995).

65. For a discussion of the Coalition of Essential Schools, see Theodore Sizer, *Horace's School* (Boston: Houghton Mifflin, 1994).

66. Semel, *The Dalton School: The Transformation of a Progressive School.*

67. Bernstein, *The Structuring of Pedagogic Discourse*; Sadovnik, *Knowledge and Pedagogy.*

68. Delpit, *Other People's Children.*

69. See David Tyack and Larry Cuban, *Tinkering Toward Utopia* for a detailed analysis of the history of twentieth century school reform that provides important examples of these lessons.

Chapter 2

1. Ida Cassa Heffron, *Francis Wayland Parker: An Interpretive Biography* (Los Angeles: Book Division Haynes Corporation, 1934), p. 33.

2. John Dewey, *The School and Society* (Chicago: University of Chicago Press, 1899), p. vi.

3. Edward Dangler, "Francis Wayland Parker's Educational Philosophy: Its Origins, Contents, and Consequences" (Abstract of Thesis, School of Education, New York University, 1939), P. 16. (Chicago: Archives of Chicago Historical Society).

4. Ida B. DePencier, *The History of the Laboratory Schools: the University of Chicago 1896-1965* (Chicago: Quadrangle Books, 1967), p. 13.

5. John Dewey, *The School and Society*, *The Child and the Curriculum* In Martin Dworkin (ed.), *Dewey on Education* (New York: Teachers College Press, 1959; original published in 1902), *Democracy and Education* (New York: Macmillan, 1916), and *Experience and Education* (New York, Macmillan, 1938).

6. Lawrence A.Cremin, *The Transformation of the School: Progressivism in American Education 1876-1957* (New York: Knopf, 1961), p. 136.

7. Francis W. Parker, *Talks on Pedagogics: An Outline of the Theory of Concentration* (New York: A. S. Barnes and Co., 1894), p. 450.

8. David Tyack and Elisabeth Hansot, *Managers of Virtues: Public School Leadership in America 1820-1980* (New York: Basic Books, Inc., 1982), p. 15.

9. Dewey, *The School and Society*, p. 15.

10. Parker, *Talks on Pedagogics*, p. 346.

11. Dewey, *The School and Society*, pp. 6-9.

12. Ibid., pp. 14-15.

13. Parker, *Talks on Pedagogic*, p. 338.

14. John Dewey, *The Child and the Curriculum* (Chicago: University of Chicago Press, 1902), p. 9.

15. Francis W. Parker, *Talks on Teaching* (New York: A.S. Barnes and Co., 1883), p.18.

16. Francis W. Parker, *Talks on Pedagogics*, pp. 23-24.

17. Ibid., p. 337.

18. Ibid.

19. Faculty Francis W. Parker School, *Social Motive on School Work: Studies in Education, vol. I* (Chicago: Archives of Francis W. Parker School and the Chicago Historical Society, 1913).

20. Herbart Smith, *Francis W. Parker School Historical Statement* (Chicago: Archives Francis W. Parker School, 1957), p. 1.

21. Parker, *Talks on Pedagogics*, pp. v, 25, 360.

22. Francis W. Parker, *Talks on Pedagogics*, p. 251.

23. Ibid., p. 5.

24. "Autobiography of Francis Wayland Parker," in William A. Griffin, *School Days in the Fifties* (Chicago: A. Flanagan Co., 1906), p. 114.

25. Ibid., p. 118.

26. Tyack and Hansot, *Managers of Virtues*, p. 16.

27. "Autobiography of Francis Wayland Parker," p. 114.

28. Francis W. Parker, "The Farm as the Center of Interest," *Journal of Proceedings and Addresses*, National Education Association, 1897, pp. 527-536.

29. James Campbell, *The Children's Crusade: Colonel Francis W. Parker* (New York: Teachers College Press, 1967), pp. 18, 186.

30. "Autobiography of Francis Wayland Parker," p. 126.

31. Campbell, *The Children's Crusade*, p. 43.

32. "Autobiography of Francis Wayland Parker," p. 117.

33. See Francis W. Parker, "A Sketch of the Work in Quincy Schools from 1875 to 1880," I, *School Journal* 29, June 6, 1885, p. 357. Lelia E. Partridge, "The Quincy Methods Illustrated (New York: 1889). Campbell, *The Children's Crusade*, pp. 75-97.

34. Parker, *Talks on Pedagogics*, p. 435.

35. Francis W. Parker, "An Account of the Work of Cook County Normal School from 1883–1899, *Elementary School Teacher* vol. II, pp. 9–27.

36. "Colonel Parker's Fad Factory," *Chicago Tribune*, January 30, 1899.

37. Campbell, *The Children's Crusade*, pp. 185–194.

38. Heffron, *Francis Wayland Parker*, p. 110.

39. Ibid, p. 32.

40. Parker, *Talks on Pedagogics*, pp. 426–429.

41. "Resignation of Colonel Parker," *Chicago Times Herald*, June 28, 1899.

42. Heffron, *Francis Wayland Parker*, p. 33.

43. Herbert Smith, *Francis W. Parker School Historical Statement*, 1957, p. 1.

44. John Dewey, *The Sources of a Science of Education* (New York: Liveright Publishing Corp., 1929), p. 9.

45. Map of the City of Chicago in 1890 (Chicago: Archives of Chicago Historical Society).

46. Donald Miller, *City of the Century: the Epic of Chicago and the Making of America* (New York: Simon and Schuster, 1996), pp. 178–179.

47. Charles Dudley Warner, "Studies of the Great War—Chicago," *Harper's New Monthly Magazine* 76, December 1887–May 1888.

48. Marie Kirchner Stone, "The Image Binding Chicago Writers," *Lifetime Newspapers* (Chicago: May, 1991), p. 7.

49. Ray Ginger, *Altgeld's America: The Lincoln Ideals Versus Changing Realities* (New York: Harper and Row Publishers, Inc., 1958), p. 96.

50. Anita McCormick Blaine, "Instrument Creating Trusteeship," April, 1901, in Marie Kirchner Stone, *Between Home and Community: Chronicle of the Francis W. Parker School 1901–1976* (Chicago: Archives Francis W. Parker School), pp. 11–14.

51. Martha Fleming, *Morning Exercise as a Socializing Influence, Studies in Education, vol. II, Francis W. Parker Yearbook* (Chicago: Archives Francis W. Parker School, 1921).

52. Heffron, *Francis Wayland Parker*, pp. 319–321.

53. Ibid., pp. 76–81.

54. Parker, *Talks on Pedagogics*, pp. 15–16, 25–47.

55. Francis W. Parker Faculty, *Course of Studies* (Chicago: Archives Chicago Historical Society, 1901–1930).

56. Faculty of the Francis W. Parker School, *Studies in Education*, Francis W. Parker School Yearbook, vol. I–X (Chicago: Chicago Historical Society, 1912–1934).

57. Harold Rugg and Ann Shumaker, *The Child-Centered School* (New York: Arno Press, 1969), p. 44.

58. Interview with Jack Ellison, teacher and principal of the Francis W. Parker School from 1937–1967, April 1996.

59. Parker, "An Account of the Work of the Cook County Normal School from 1883–1899," p. 7.

60. Parker, *Talks on Pedagogics*, p. 447.

61. Marie Kirchner Stone, *Survey I and Survey II of Twenty-five Current Francis W. Parker Faculty on Teaching at the School for Twenty or More Years*, April 1993, June 1994.

62. Sue Stern Ettelson, "The Parker School Legacy," p. 238; Edward Yeomans, "The Francis W. Parker School Legacy to Shady Hill School," pp. 288–289; Nathaniel French, "Urban to Suburban: the North Shore Country Day School," pp. 290–292; in Stone, *Between Home and Community*. See Edward Yeomans, *Shady Hill School: the First Fifty Years* (Cambridge, Mass.: Windflower Press). Heffron, *Francis Wayland Parker*, pp. 116–124.

63. See Carleton Washburne and Sidney Marland, Jr., *Winnetka: the History and Significance of an Educational Experiment* (Englewood Cliffs, N.J.: Prentice Hall, Inc., 1963), pp. 5–9. Jack Ellison, "A New Approach to Teacher Education," in Stone, *Between Home and Community*, pp. 286–287.

64. Interview Jack Ellison, teacher and principal Francis W. Parker School, 1937–1967, April 1996.

65. See, for example, Flora Cooke, "Colonel Francis W. Parker and His Influences on Education, *Progressive Education*, December, 1937, pp. 583–587.

66. Minutes of Trustees of Francis W. Parker School, 1901–1930, McCormick Family Papers (Madison: Wisconsin Historical Society).

67. Carol Lynn Gilmer, "Flora Cooke: Grand Old Lady in Education," in Stone, *Between Home and Community*, pp. 40–45.

68. Minutes of the Board of Trustees of Francis W. Parker School, 1932–1940 (Chicago: Archives Francis W. Parker School).

69. "Opening Notice, October 4, 1901" (Madison: Reprint from McCormick Family Papers, Archives of Wisconsin Historical Society) in Stone, *Between Home and Community*, p. 18.

70. Minutes of Board of Trustees of Francis W. Parker School, 1932 –1940 (Chicago: Archives Francis W. Parker School).

71. Heffron, *Francis W. Parker*, pp. 41–42.

72. Minutes of Trustees of Francis W. Parker School, 1901–1930 (Madison: Archives Wisconsin Historical Society).

73. Patricia Graham, *Progressive Education From Arcady to Academe: A History of the Progressive Education Association* (New York: Teachers College Press, 1967), p. viii.

74. Diane Ravitch, *The Troubled Crusade*, (New York: Basic Books, Inc., 1983), p. 43.

75. Wilford Aikin, *The Story of the Eight Year Study*, vol. I (New York: Harper and Brothers, 1943), p.1.

76. *Adventures in American Education: Thirty Schools Tell Their Story* (New York: Harper and Row, 1943), p. 1.

77. Ralph W. Tyler, *Basic Principles of Curriculum and Instruction* (Chicago: University of Chicago Press, 1949) pp. v–vi.

78. See *Adventures in American Education*, pp. 296–311, 316, for discussion of these goals and the resultant curriculum.

79. Smith, *The Francis W. Parker School Historical Statement*, pp. 9–10.

80. Marie Kirchner Stone, *Ralph W. Tyler's Principles of Curriculum, Instruction, and Evaluation: Past Influences and Present Effects* (Unpublished Dissertation, Chicago: Archives of Francis W. Parker School, March 1985) pp. 313–317.

81. Smith, *The Francis W. Parker School Historical Statement*, p. 17.

82. *Adventures in American Education*, pp. 313–319.

83. Interviews with Ralph W. Tyler, research director for Eight Year Study, Head of the Division of Social Sciences University of Chicago, and author of *Basic Principles of Curriculum and Instruction (1902–1994)*, February–June, 1994.

84. Mary Jane Grunsfeld and Jack Ellison, "Sarah Greenebaum Distinguished Visitors," in Stone, *Between Home and Community*, pp. 293–295.

85. The preceding two paragraphs are based on interviews with thirteen Francis W. Parker faculty members who had taught at the School for 25 years, Spring, 1995.

86. Smith, *Francis W. Parker School Historical Statement*, p. 31.

87. Stone, *Between Home and Community*, p. 74.

88. Smith, *Francis W. Parker School Historical Statement*, p. 8.

89. Helen LaCroix, "Dr. Cleveland A. Thomas," in Stone, *Between Home and Community*, p. 49.

90. Minutes of Board of Trustees of Francis W. Parker School, 1940–1970 (Chicago: Archives Francis W. Parker School).

91. Smith, *Francis W. Parker School Historical Statement*, pp. 32–35.

92. Cremin, *The Transformation of the School*, p. 353.

93. Marie Kirchner Stone, "Group Reading Project at the Francis W. Parker School" (Chicago: Curriculum Office Francis W. Parker School, 1972).

94. Delafield Griffith, "Mini-Course Experiment in the Middle School" (Chicago: Curriculum Office Francis W. Parker School, 1975).

95. Katherine Haskins Chambers and Marie Kirchner Stone, "Experiential Community Service Project and Evaluation" (Chicago: Curriculum Office Francis W. Parker School, 1980).

96. Lillian Lowry, "Physical Education Electives," (Chicago: Curriculum Office Francis W. Parker School, 1975).

97. Interview with Student Advisees of Marie Kirchner Stone, May, 1976.

98. Survey I and Survey II of Twenty-five Francis W. Parker Faculty at the School for Twenty or More Years.

99. Parker, *Talks on Pedagogics*, pp. 337, 401.

100. Survey I and Survey II of Twenty-five Francis W. Parker Faculty at the School for Twenty or More years.

101. Interview with Jack Ellison.

102. Marie Kirchner Stone, "All-School Approach to Health Education for Grades K-12" (Chicago: Curriculum Office Francis W. Parker School, 1985).

103. Stone, *Between Home and Community*, p. i.

Chapter 3

1. Interview with Mordecai "Mawk" Arnold, director of the Marietta Johnson School of Organic Education, October 31, 1994.

2. Lawrence A. Cremin, *The Transformation of the School: Progressivism in American Education, 1876–1957* (New York: Alfred Knopf, 1961), p. 152.

3. John and Evelyn Dewey, *Schools of To-Morrow* (New York: E. P. Dutton, 1915), pp. 17, 39.

4. Paul M. Gaston, *Women of Fair Hope* (Athens: University of Georgia Press, 1984), pp. 66–68; Robert H. Beck, "Marietta Johnson: Progressive Education and Christian Socialism," *Vitae Scholasticae* 6 Fall 1987, pp. 115–159; Henry George, *Progress and Poverty: An Inquiry into the Cause of Industrial Depressions, and of Increase of Want with Increase of Wealth* (New York: J. W. Lovell, 1879).

5. Paul M. Gaston, *Man and Mission: E. B. Gaston and the Origins of the Fairhope Single-Tax Colony* (Montgomery, Ala: Black Belt Press, 1993).

6. Makato Ogura, "'Organic' Chemistry: The Utopian Visions of Fairhope and the School of Organic Education" (senior essay, Department of History, Yale University, April 1993), p. 6.

7. Ogura, "'Organic' Chemistry," pp. 12–16; Laura Elizabeth Smith, "A Woman and Her Idea: Marietta Johnson and the School of Organic Education" (B.A. honor's thesis, Department of History, Harvard University, March 1991), pp. 5, 36.

8. Smith, "A Woman and Her Idea," p. 5.

9. Upton Sinclair, *Autobiography* (New York: Harcourt, Brace and World, 1962), p. 162.

10. Gaston, *Women of Fair Hope*, pp. 79–80.

11. Ibid., p. 67; Beck, "Marietta Johnson," pp. 116–117.

12. Gaston, *Women of Fair Hope*, p. 67.

13. Marietta Johnson, *Thirty Years with an Idea* (Birmingham: University of Alabama Press, 1974), p. 2.

14. Cremin uses this term in *Transformation of the School*, p. 147, as does Gaston in *Women of Fair Hope*, p. 70. Patricia Albjerg Graham describes her "messianic fervor" in *Progressive Education: From Arcady to Academe* (New York: Teachers College Press, 1967), p. 30. Beck,

"Marietta Johnson," describes the convergence of her educational, political, and religious views.

15. Nathan Oppenheim, *The Development of the Child* (New York: Macmillan, 1898), pp. 8, 11, 7, 9.

16. Johnson, *Thirty Years with an Idea*, p. 8.

17. Ibid., pp. 8, 12-13.

18. Gaston, *Women of Fair Hope*, pp. 71-73.

19. Ibid., p. 73.

20. Ibid., p. 77.

21. Smith, "A Woman and Her Idea," p. 74.

22. Joyce Antler, "Feminism as Life Process: The Life and Career of Lucy Sprague Mitchell," *Feminist Studies* 7 Spring 1981, pp. 134. See also Antler, *Lucy Sprague Mitchell: The Making of a Modern Woman* (New Haven: Yale University Press, 1987).

23. Smith, "A Woman and Her Idea," pp. ii, iv, 8, 78-82.

24. Johnson, *Thirty Years with an Idea*, p. 14; interview with Dorothy Cain, graduate of the Organic School and founder of the Marietta Johnson Museum, Fairhope, October 31, 1994; Gaston, *Women of Fair Hope*, pp. 77-78.

25. Marie Howland, quoted in Gaston, *Women of Fair Hope*, p. 75.

26 C. Hanford Henderson, *Education and the Larger Life* (New York: Houghton Mifflin, 1902).

27. Dewey, *Schools of To-Morrow*, p. 23.

28. Johnson, *Thirty Years with an Idea*, p. 44.

29. Rocco Eugene Zappone, "Progressive Education Reconsidered: The Intellectual Milieu of Marietta Johnson" (M.A. thesis, Department of History, University of Virginia, 1982), p. 24.

30. Ibid.

31. Gaston, *Women of Fair Hope*, p. 81.

32. Dewey, *Schools of To-Morrow*, p. 23.

33. Gaston, *Women of Fair Hope*, pp. 7-9.

34. Interview with Dorothy Cain, October 31, 1994; Smith, "A Woman and Her Idea," pp. iv, 4, 40, 84-90; Gaston, *Women of Fair Hope*, pp. 105-106.

35. Gaston, *Women of Fair Hope*, pp. 78, 81, 100-101; Margaret Mead, *Blackberry Winter: My Earlier Years* (New York: Washington Square Press, 1972), pp. 68-69.

36. Johnson, *Thirty Years with an Idea*, ch. 3; Gaston, *Women of Fair Hope*, p. 82.

37. Johnson, *Thirty Years with an Idea*, ch. 3; Gaston, *Women of Fair Hope*, pp. 83-85.

38. Johnson, *Thirty Years with an Idea*, pp. 40-41.

39. Gaston, *Women of Fair Hope*, p. 85; Dewey, *Schools of To-Morrow*, Preface.

40. Johnson, *Thirty Years with an Idea*, ch. 3.

41. "Welcome to the Marietta Johnson Museum," undated information sheet, Marietta Johnson Museum, Fairhope, Alabama; L. J. Newcomb Comings, "An Intimate History of the Early Days of the School of Organic Education," pp. 3-4, undated typescript, Marietta Johnson Museum. The museum is located in the restored Bell Building on the school's old campus.

42. Dewey, *Schools of To-Morrow*, pp. 30-33.

43. Johnson, *Thirty Years with an Idea*, p. 19.

44. Ibid., pp. 61-62, 65.

45. Dewey, *Schools of To-Morrow*, p. 22.

46. Johnson, *Thirty Years with an Idea*, pp. 64-65, 84-87.

47. Gaston, *Women of Fair Hope*, p. 94.

48. Johnson's correspondence, quoted in Gaston, *Women of Fair Hope*, p. 95.

49. Ibid., pp. 95-96.

50. Johnson, *Thirty Years with an Idea*, pp. 95-96.

51. Ibid., p. 105.

52. Ibid., ch. 6; Gaston, *Women of Fair Hope*, pp. 96-97.

53. *Cinagro* (1931), p. 13, Marietta Johnson Museum. The museum has a collection of yearbooks from the 1920s through the 1980s. All *Cinagros* cited hereafter are in the museum.

54. Gaston, *Women of Fair Hope*, pp. 96-97.

55. Ibid.; Johnson, *Thirty Years with an Idea*, ch. 6.

56. Gaston, *Women of Fair Hope*, pp. 88-91, 100-101.

57. Ibid., pp. 101-103.

58. Ibid., pp. 99, 103.

59. Johnson, *Thirty Years with an Idea*, p. 46.

60. Gaston, *Women of Fair Hope*, pp. 104-106.

61. Marietta Johnson, *Youth in a World of Men* (New York: John Day, 1929); interview with Dorothy Cain, October 31, 1994; Gaston, *Women of*

Fair Hope, pp. 108–109. *Youth in a World of Men* and *Thirty Years with an Idea* have been reissued in a combined edition titled *Organic Education: Teaching without Failure*, available from the Marietta Johnson Museum, 440 Fairhope Avenue, Fairhope, AL 36532. (334) 990–8601.

62. "Organic School Building History," undated typescript in folder "Historical Documents of Organic School Campus," Marietta Johnson Museum.

63. "Then and Now," *Cinagro* (1947), pp. 7–8.

64. Gaston, *Women of Fair Hope*, pp. 109–117. *Thirty Years with an Idea*, which is much more specific than *Youth in a World of Men* about Johnson's work at the Organic School, was finally published by the University of Alabama Press in 1974.

65. Interview with Dorothy Cain, October 31, 1994; videotaped interview with former students Claire Totten Gray, Joyce Totten Bishop, and Madeline Gibbs Scott, December 30, 1991, Marietta Johnson Museum. The museum has a large collection of videotaped interviews with students, parents, teachers, and others involved with the Organic School from its founding to the present. All videotaped interviews cited hereafter are in the museum.

66. "Then and Now," *Cinagro* (1947), p. 8.

67. "History and Progress of School of Organic Education," special edition of *Fairhope Courier* (December 12, 1957).

68. Sam Dyson, *Fairhope: A Universal Community* (n.p.: 1990), pp. 29–35.

69. Ibid.

70. *School of Organic Education News Letter* (December 1940) in box "Miscellaneous Historical and Philosophical Gems," Marietta Johnson Museum. See also the editorial in the *Organic Merry Go Round* (September 27, 1940), p. 2, Marietta Johnson Museum. The museum has a collection of issues of this student newspaper. All *Organic Merry Go Round*s cited hereafter are in the museum.

71. *School of Organic Education News Letter* (December 1940); "Then and Now," *Cinagro* (1947), p. 8; interview with Dorothy Cain, March 8, 1995.

72. "Organic School Building History"; "Now It Should Be Told" *Organic Merry Go Round* (October 1, 1943), p. 2; "Editorials," *Organic Merry Go Round* (September 26, 1941), pp. 2, 6; *The School of Organic*

Education (1940), brochure in free literature distribution box, Marietta Johnson Museum.

73. *The Fairhope Organic School* (1924), brochure in box "Miscellaneous Historical and Philosophical Gems," Marietta Johnson Museum.

74. "Now It Should Be Told," p. 2.

75. Ibid.; *Organic Merry Go Round* (December 19, 1941), p. 1.

76. "Sustaining Funds for School," *Organic Merry Go Round* (February 20, 1942), p. 1; "Campaign Speeds Up," *Organic Merry Go Round* (April 3, 1942), p. 1; "School of Organic Education Incorporated," *Organic Merry Go Round* (February 1943), p. 1.

77. "Organic Corporation Reorganized," *Integration* (January 1943), p. 1, Marietta Johnson Museum. The museum has a collection of issues of this school bulletin. All *Integration*s cited hereafter are in the museum.

78. "Thirty-Sixth Year of Operation," *Organic Merry Go Round* (November 1942), p. 2; "Now It Should Be Told," p. 2; "Organic School Building History."

79. "Then and Now," *Cinagro* (1947), p. 8.

80. Ibid.

81. "Reorganized Organic Takes Final Form," *Integration* (June 1943), p. 1; dedication page of *Cinagro* (1977), p. 3; interview with Sam and Helen Dyson, Fairhope, October 13, 1995.

82. Editorial, *Organic Merry Go Round* (October 1, 1946), p. 2.

83. "Then and Now," *Cinagro* (1947), p. 8.

84. Record of "Special Corporation Meeting at C.A. Gaston residence May 19, 1947," in box "Miscellaneous Historical and Organic Philosophy Gems," Marietta Johnson Museum.

85. "History and Progress of School of Organic Education."

86. "Special Corporation Meeting at C.A. Gaston residence."

87. "Historical Documents of Organic School Campus."

88. "Four New Teachers Join Organic Faculty; Sixteen Old Timers Back for New Year," *Organic Merry Go Round* (October 17, 1950), p. 7.

89. Interview with Dorothy Cain, May 23, 1995; faculty information in *Cinagro* (1952), pp. 3, 6.

90. See, for instance, Barry Cornblatt, "Let's Give the Negro a Chance," *Organic Merry Go Round* (April 30, 1948), p. 3; "Your Best Friend May Be a Communist," *Organic Merry Go Round* (September 30,

1949), p. 3; and Frank Laraway, "Fights and Wars—What They Don't Accomplish," *Organic Merry Go Round* (March 30, 1949), pp. 3-5.

91. Danny Rockwell, "Reminiscing with Marietta's Scrapbook," *Organic Merry Go Round* (November 24, 1948), pp. 8-10; "120 Enrolled in Organic School," *Organic Merry Go Round* (October 18, 1948), p. 1.

92. "Activities of '48-49'," *Cinagro* (1949), p. 29.

93. Organizational chart published in *Cinagro* (1952), p. 5.

94. "History and Progress of School of Organic Education."

95. "Board Adds New Members," *Organic Merry Go Round* (May 1952), p.11 ; interview with Dorothy Cain, May 31, 1995.

96. Interview with Dorothy Cain, May 31, 1995; interview with Sam and Helen Dyson, October 13, 1995; Sam and Helen Dyson, *Marietta Johnson School of Organic Education History, 1907-1992* (n.p.: 1992), no numbered pages.

97. Organizational chart in *Cinagro* (1952), p. 5; Dysons, *Marietta Johnson School of Organic Education.*

98. Enrollment computed from student photographs in *Cinagro* (1958). Most issues of the yearbook played up folk dancing, shop activities, and other distinctive features.

99. "Teacher's Handbook for the Year 1960-1961," in folder "Teacher's Instructions, Dr. Goodwin Petersen, Director, 1960-1961," Marietta Johnson Museum; videotaped interview with former student Frank Laraway, May 20, 1991. *Cinagros* from the 1960s reflect the school's indecision on the matter of life classes versus traditional grades.

100. Cremin details the decline of educational progressivism during the 1950s in *The Transformation of the School.*

101. "Annual Report of the Director, the Marietta Johnson School of Organic Education, Fairhope, Alabama, 1961-1962," p. 6, in folder "Goodwin Petersen," Marietta Johnson Museum.

102. Memorandum "Appraising Student Progress in Developing Desirable Personality Traits" and typed draft "School of Organic Education, General Information" in folder "Dr. Goodwin Petersen, 1960-61, Rules and Regulations," Marietta Johnson Museum.

103. "Annual Report of the Director," p. 1.

104. "A Statement Prepared Preliminary to a Fund Drive as to the Aims of the School of Organic Education at the Direction of Goodwin Petersen

and Oliver Rockwell. Sibillyn Hoyle, January 1962," p. 2, in folder "Goodwin Petersen," Marietta Johnson Museum.

105. Notes on faculty meeting of January 12, 1962, in folder "Teachers Management, Goodwin Petersen—1961-62"; "Class Schedule in School of Organic Education, 1960-1961," in folder "Organic Curriculum, Dr. Goodwin Petersen, Director, 1961-1962"; "Disposition of Programmed 'TEMAC' Materials," in folder "Summer School, Dr. Goodwin Petersen, DIR., 1960-1962." All folders are in the Marietta Johnson Museum.

106. "A Statement Prepared Preliminary to a Fund Drive," p. 3; Goodwin Petersen to Oliver [Rockwell], October 7, 1962, in folder "Goodwin Petersen."

107. *Cinagro* (1965), no numbered pages.

108. The continuing emphasis on folk dancing is reflected in the *Cinagro*s from the Hughes years, particularly the 1966 edition.

109. Dysons, *Marietta Johnson School of Organic Education*. *Cinagro*s from the era provide enrollment data.

110. Information on buildings and other physical assets is in Box 1, "School Newsletters, Articles and Letters Concerning Marietta Johnson and the Organic School," Marietta Johnson Museum; "Organic School Building History"; and Dysons, *Marietta Johnson School of Organic Education*.

111. Interview with Dorothy Cain, October 31, 1994.

112. Joseph W. Newman and Betty Brandon, "Integration in the Mobile Public Schools," in *The Future of Public Education in Mobile: South Alabama toward 2000 III*, ed. Howard F. Mahan and Joseph W. Newman (Mobile: South Alabama Review, 1982), pp. 45-54.

113. Don Chapin, "School Allows Development of Child's Thoughts," *Huntsville Times* (clipping dated 1974 in Book 5, "Newspaper Clippings, Photo, 1922-1990," Marietta Johnson Museum), p. 9.

114. *Cinagro* (1974) provides enrollment data. The admissions policy is stated in a newspaper advertisement titled "Marietta Johnson School of Organic Education" from the 1974-75 school year in scrapbook "The Organic School, 1973-1975," Marietta Johnson Museum.

115. Quoted in Pam Middleton, "Organic Education Is Life, Growth!" *Mobile Press-Register* (July 5, 1970), p. 15-D.

116. Chapin, "School Allows Development of Child's Thoughts," p. 9; Debi Breedlove, "School of Organic Education Offers Unique Education for 69 Years," *Eastern Shore Courier* (June 10, 1976), p. 5-B.

117. Dedication page of *Cinagro* (1977), p. 3.

118. Interview with Sam and Helen Dyson, October 13, 1995. Further information on the trust fund is in Book 1, "School Newsletters, Articles and Letters Concerning Marietta Johnson and the Organic School," Marietta Johnson Museum.

119. Interview with Dorothy Cain, December 6, 1994; "Organic School Appoints Zack W. Lee as Principal," undated newspaper clipping in scrapbook "The Organic School, 1973–1975."

120. "Michael L. Kingsmore New Administrator Principal," mimeographed letter in Book 5, "Newspaper Clippings , Photo, 1922–1990," Marietta Johnson Museum.

121. Graham Heath, "Organic School Principal Resignation Reconsidered," *Fairhope Courier*, clipping dated November 1980 in Book 5, "Newspaper Clippings, Photo 1922–1990," Marietta Johnson Museum.

122. Kathy Burke, "Kingsmore Resigns; Board, Faculty at Odds," *Eastern Shore Courier* (November 3, 1980).

123. Kathy Burke, "Faculty, Parents Side with Mike Kingsmore," *Eastern Shore Courier* (November 13, 1980), pp. 1A–2A.

124. Quoted in Burke, "Kingsmore Resigns."

125. Burke, "Kingsmore Resigns."

126. Mike Kingsmore, "Teaching Kids Organically," clipping dated April 1981 in Book 5, "Newspaper Clippings, Photo, 1922–1991"; Graham Heath, "Johnson Exhibit in Fairhope," *Mobile Press-Register* (March 1, 1981).

127. Quoted in Graham Heath, "Organic Slashes Personnel, Maintenance to Curtail Deficits," *Mobile Register* (January 28, 1982), p. 3-F.

128. Heath, "Organic Slashes Personnel," p. 3-F.

129. Interview with Dorothy Cain, December 6, 1994; "Dahlgren's Honored," *Mobile Press-Register* (September 10, 1981), p. 11-G.

130. Harold P. Dahlgren to Claude W. Arnold, January 3, 1982, in Book 4, "Letters," Marietta Johnson Museum; interview with Dorothy Cain, December 6, 1994.

131. Heath, "Organic Slashes Personnel"; David Plunkett, "Faulkner Campus to Open on Organic Site," *Eastern Shore Courier* (August 27, 1986), pp. 1A, 5A.

132. Plunkett, "Faulkner Campus to Open"; Vickie Fildes, "Mayor Sees Bright Future for Downtown," *Eastern Shore Courier* (February 18, 1987), p. 1.

133. Lesley Alderman, "20 Best Places for Retirement," *Money* magazine's *Guide to Retirement* (1994), pp. 62-73.

134. Interview with Mordecai Arnold, October 31, 1994; interview with Dorothy Cain, October 31, 1994.

135. Sinclair, *Autobiography*, p. 162.

136. Videotaped interview with former student Paul M. Gaston, August 28, 1993. As a historian at the University of Virginia, Gaston has written extensively on his hometown of Fairhope.

137. "Professor Dewey's Report on the Fairhope Experiment in Organic Education," in Jo Ann Boydston, ed., *The Middle Works of John Dewey*, vol. 8 (Carbondale: Southern Illinois University Press, 1979), p. 388.

138 Dewey, *Schools of To-Morrow*, p. 39.

Chapter 4

1. Merle Curti, *The Social Ideas of the American Educators* (New York: Charles Scribner and Sons, 1935).

2. Lawrence A. Cremin, *The Transformation of the School: Progressivism in American Education, 1876-1957* (New York: Knopf, 1961).

3. Arthur G. Wirth, *John Dewey as Educator: His Design for Work in Education (1894-1904)* (New York: John Wiley and Sons, 1966).

4. Also see: Patricia Aljberg Graham, *Progressive Education: From Arcady to Acadame* (New York: Teachers College Press, 1967), George Dykhuizen, *The Life and Mind of John Dewey* (Carbondale, Illinois: Southern Illinois University Press, 1973), as well as older studies such as Katherine Camp Mayhew and Anna Camp Edwards, *The Dewey School* (New York: Appleton-Century Co., 1936), Harold Rugg and Ann Shumaker, *The Child Centered School* (New York: Arno Press, 1969) and Ida B. DePencier, *The History of the Laboratory Schools* (Chicago: Quadrangle Books, 1967).

5. Mary Hammett Lewis, *An Adventure with Children* (New York: Macmillan, 1928). A reprint of Hammett's book edited by Eugene F. Provenzo, Jr. and Therese King Provenzo was published in 1985 by University Press of America (Lanham, Md). A new historical introduction

was provided for the work. I draw heavily on this introduction for the background material in this essay.

6. Cremin, *The Transformation of the School*, p. 381.

7. John Dewey, "The University School," *University Record*, vol. 1, November 6, 1896, p. 417.

8. Lewis (1985), p. 2.

9. Ibid., p. 3.

10. Ibid., p. 3.

11. Ibid., p. 4.

12. Ibid., p. 35.

13. Dorothy Canfield Fisher, "A Peep into the Educational Future," *Outlook*, September 1915, p. 215.

14. See for example, Susan F. Semel, *The Dalton School: The Transformation of a Progressive School* (New York: Peter Lang), Chapter 3 for a discussion of Helen Parkhurst's conflicts with the Dalton School's Board of Trustees.

15. Lewis, op. cit., p. 103.

16. Lewis, 1985, p. 99.

17. Ibid., p. 99.

18. Lewis, p. 93.

19. Ibid., p. 39.

20. Ibid., p. 39.

21. Ibid., p. 41.

22. Ibid., p. 48.

23. See Semel, *The Dalton School*, Chapters 7 and 9 for a discussion of the role of college admissions, parental pressure, and conservative politics in the similar transformation of the Dalton School.

Chapter 5

1. The research presented in this chapter was assisted in part by a grant from the Spencer Foundation. The data presented and the views expressed are solely the responsibility of the author. Parts of this chapter have been adapted from Susan F. Semel and Alan R. Sadovnik "Lessons from the Past: Individualism and Community in Three Progressive Schools," *Peabody Journal of Education,* vol. 70, no. 4, Summer 1995, pp. 56–84.

2. City and Country School Brochure, 1994, p. 1.

3. Caroline Pratt, *I Learn from Children: An Adventure in Progressive Education* (New York: Simon and Schuster, 1948), pp. 26-27.

4. Ibid., pp. xi-xii.

5. For a complete discussion of Caroline Pratt's early years see Pat Carlton, *Caroline Pratt: A Biography* (Unpublished dissertation, Teachers College, 1986).

6. See Joyce Antler, *Lucy Sprague Mitchell: The Making of a Modern Woman* (New Haven and London: Yale University Press, 1987), p. 237; Carlton, p. 144 for more detailed descriptions.

7. Ibid.

8. Robert H. Beck, "Progressive Education and American Progressivism," *Teachers College Record* vol. 60, no. 3, December, 1958, p. 134.

9. Antler, p. 237.

10. Pratt discusses the beginning of her lengthy relationship with Mitchell in her book, *I Learn from Children*. The most complete discussion, appears in Antler's biography of Mitchell, which describes two strong willed women educators working together and practically living together. Initially, Pratt was Mitchell's teacher and Mitchell was Pratt's financial backer; however, as Mitchell became a skilled in her work (and, obviously, opinionated) the relationship deteriorated. Mitchell severed her ties with City and Country in 1928.

11. For a complete discussion of the relationship between Lucy Sprague Mitchell and Caroline Pratt, see Joyce Antler's *Lucy Sprague Mitchell: The Making of a Modern Woman*.

12. Pratt, *I Learn from Children*, p. 8.

13. Ibid., p. 9.

14. Jean W. Murray, "Philosophy and Practice at City and Country," City and Country, unpublished materials prepared for student teachers, c. 1950, n.p.

15. Caroline Pratt, "Making Environment Meaningful," *Progressive Education*. (Progressive Education Association, IV:1, April-May-June 1927), p. 105.

16. Pratt, *I Learn From Children*, p. 48-49.

17. Caroline Pratt, "Learning by Experience," *Child Study*, vol. 11, no. 3, 1933, p. 70.

18. Caroline Pratt, *The City and Country School*. Brochure, City and Country School Archives, New York City, n.d., n.p.

19. Ibid.

20. E. J. Greenhall. "From Play School to C&C or Our School in the Twenties." n.d., n.p. in binder entitled, "Articles about City and Country" in City and Country School Archives, New York City.

21. Comments made at City and Country School on Alumni Night, January 22, 1996.

22. See Susan F. Semel, "Female Founders and the Progressive Paradox," in Michael James (ed), *Social Reconstruction Through Education: The Philosophy, History, and Curricula of a Radical Ideal* (Ablex Publishing Corporation, 1995), pp. 89-108.

23. Caroline Pratt, "The City and Country School." Brochure, City and Country School Archives, New York City, n.d., n.p.

24. Ibid.

25. Pratt, *I Learn from Children*, p. 101.

26. While I believe that many of their child-centered schools did create important communities, the historian Lawrence A. Cremin takes a more pessimistic view in *The Transformation of the School* (New York: Knopf and Random House, 1961). Readers interested in both points of view should consult pp. 201-207.

27. Martin S. Dworkin, ed. *Dewey on Education* (New York: Teachers College Press), p. 49.

28. Pratt, *I Learn from Children*, pp. 179-180.

29. Robert Westbrook, "The Dewey School and Workplace Democracy," *Pathways*, vol. 8, no. 3 (May, 1992), p. 7.

30. Pratt, *I Learn from Children*, p. 15.

31. Jean Murray, unpublished paper, "The City and Country School, Inc." (New York: City and Country Archives, n.d.).

32. Jean Wesson Murray, "City and Country Today" (Parents Newspaper, October, 1958, p. 5, in City and Country Archives, City and Country School, New York City).

33. Jean Wesson Murray, "Experiences in a School," 1961, n.p., City and Country Archives, New York City.

34. Cynthia Beer, "Remembrances of Jean Murray," *Newsletter for Alumni, Parents and Friends* (City and Country School, New York City, Fall/Winter 1995).

35. One faculty informant raised the issue of leadership and gender, speculating that it might have been different in a male-dominated group; that leadership tied to managerial skills might have emerged more readily at that time from a male Executive Committee.

36. On the previous Thursday, the Executive Committee had voted to accept the slate of the "outside board" members.

37. Kathleen Holz, "Principal's Report," in *The State of the School*, City and Country School, New York City, September, 1995, n.p.

38. Interview, October 7, 1996.

39. As inconsequential as the addition of basketball might seem, one should note that progressive schools generally resist (although not with great success in recent years) the inclusion of competitive sports as part of their physical education programs. Many, like the Dalton School, also resisted the practice of debating, since it was thought to encourage children to support beliefs they did not truly believe in.

Chapter 6

1. *The Lincolnian* (New York: Jacques and Co., 1921), p. 4.

2. Ibid.

3. *The Lincoln School of Teachers College* (New York: University Printing Office, Columbia University, 1917), p. 7; "The Lincoln School of Teachers College," *Teachers College Record* 17 (January 1917), p. 92; James E. Russell, "To the General Education Board," April 30, 1925, p. 1. James E. Russell Papers. Manuscript Division. Teachers College, Columbia University, New York, New York (hereafter cite as James E. Russell Papers).

4. The Lincoln School of Teachers College, p. 6; Otis W. Caldwell, "To the Members of the General Education Board," May 21, 1919, 1. Records of the General Education Board. Rockefeller Archive Center, Pocantico Hills, New York (hereafter cited as GEB Records. RAC); The Lincoln School of Teachers College, 1918–1919 (New York: Lincoln School of Teachers College, 1918), p. 10.

5. Martin J. Sklar, *The Corporate Reconstruction of American Capitalism* (New York: Cambridge University Press, 1988).

6. M. H. Willing, "The Value of an Experimental School," *School & Society* (May 15, 1926), p. 612.

7. Paul Shorey, "The Modern School," *Education* 38 (May 1918), p. 675, pp. 671–677.

8. See "The Lincoln School - Teachers College Controversy: A Reply to the Report of the Special Committee of the Trustees of Teachers College, issued May 11, 1940" [n.p.] June 5, 1940.

9. Ibid., pp. 62–63.

10. Ibid., pp. 63–66; Abraham Flexner, *The Factors of School Success*, *An address delivered at a meeting of the Parents-Teachers Association of the Lincoln School of Teachers College, New York, January 12, 1923* (New York: Lincoln School of Teachers College, 1923), pp. 10–12, 14.

11. Elmer Davis, "Four-Year-Old Educational Experiment," Reprint from the New York Times Book Review and Magazine of August 28, 1921, *Lincoln School of Teachers College Publications* No 7 (1921), p. 3; The Commission on the Relation of School and College of the Progressive Education Association, *Thirty Schools Tell Their Story*, Adventure in American Education vol. V (New York: Harper and Brothers, 1943), p. 459; John D. Rockefeller, Jr. to Otis W. Caldwell, April 1, 1922; April 7, 1922. OWC Papers. Mrs. George A. Harrop, Princeton, New Jersey (on loan to the author).

12. See Charles W. Eliot's account of the events leading up to the Lincoln School in "The Modern School," *Education* 38 (May 1918), pp. 662–663; Flexner's account may be found in his "Commencement Address," June 2, 1939. William F. Russell Papers, Teachers College, Columbia (hereafter cited as William F. Russell Papers).

13. Otis W. Caldwell to Abraham Flexner, December 19, 1916. GEB Records. RAC.

14. Abraham Flexner to James E. Russell, December 1, 1916. James E. Russell Papers. See Eliot's account of these events in "The Modern School," *Education* 38 (May 1918), pp. 662–663. William Heard Kilpatrick, whose project method became popular at the Lincoln School, took Flexner's side in the dispute with Thorndike arguing in lieu of "the old subject-matter point of view" for an education in "the life [students] ought to live" (Samuel Tenenbaum, *William Heard Kilpatrick: Trail Blazer in Education* [New York: Harper and Brothers, 1951], p. 228).

15. Charles W. Eliot to Walter H. Page, June 27, 1910; Eliot to Wallace Buttrick, December 21, 1909; Eliot to Buttrick, November 23, 1914 and April 6, 1914; Frederick T. Gates to Abraham Flexner, January

1, 1914. Presidents' Papers. Charles W. Eliot. Harvard University (hereafter cited as Eliot Papers).

16. Abraham Flexner, "Parents and Schools," February, 1916, pp. 22–23. GEB Records. RAC.

17. "Report of the General Education Board for the year ending June 30, 1918" in *Annual Reports on Schools* , 4. William F. Russell Papers; Flexner to Gates, August 17, 1915, 2. GEB Records. RAC.

18. "The Lincoln School of Teachers College Controversy," 1940, pp. 6, 87, 91, 89.

19. "Address to American Academy of Arts and Letters," 1917, Lincoln School Files. GEB Records. RAC; Paul Shorey, *The Assault on Humanism* (Boston: Atlantic Monthly, 1917), pp. 78, 52. "The conflict of science and the Classics," wrote Shorey, "is a dead issue. Science has won an overwhelming victory. And its real competitor in education today is, not classical humanism, but pseudo-science" (p. 52).

20. Flexner to Eliot, May 21, 1918; Eliot to Flexner, May 22, 1918; Eliot to Flexner, July 4, 1916. Eliot Papers.

21. Flexner to James E. Russell, December 1, 1916. James Earl Russell Papers.

22. "Your Education, An address made at the graduation of the Twelfth Year Class of the Lincoln School of Teachers College, on June 10, 1921, by Otis W. Caldwell, Director," *Lincoln School of Teachers College Publications*, no. 16 (1921), p. 5.

23. L. Thomas Hopkins, *Integration: Its Meaning and Application* (New York: D. Appleton-Century Company, 1937), p. 200 and ch. 13.

24. Abraham Flexner, "A Modern School," Occasional Paper no. 3 (New York: General Education Board, 1916), 17; Raleigh Schorling, "Experimental Courses in Secondary School Mathematics." Reprinted from the Reorganization of Mathematics in Secondary Education, A Report by the National Committee on Mathematical Requirements, Chapter 12 in *Lincoln School of Teachers College Publications*, no. 1 (1920), pp. 60–63. See also Raleigh Schorling, "Significant Movements in Secondary School Mathematics," *Teachers College Record* 18 (November 1917), pp. 438–457.

25. Staff of the Elementary Division of the Lincoln School of Teachers College, *Curriculum Making in an Elementary School* (New York: Ginn and Company, 1927), p. 29.

26. Ibid., p. 56.

27. James S. Tippett, *The Singing Farmer* (Yonkers-on-Hudson, N.Y.: World Book Company, 1927), p. 72.

28. *Curriculum Making in an Elementary School*, pp. 32, 41.

29. Charles W. Finley and James S. Tippett, *Field Work* (New York: Lincoln School of Teachers College, 1925), pp. 71-72.

30. Daniel C. Knowlton, *Making History Graphic* (New York: Charles Scribner's Sons, 1925), pp. 29-31 and *Building a Course in the Social Studies for the Junior High School*, revised and reprinted from *The Historical Outlook*, November, 1924, vol. XV, pp. 356-360 (Philadelphia: McKinley Publishing, 1924), p. 6.

31. John A. Hockett, "A Determination of the Major Social Problems of America Life," *Social Science Monographs*, no. 2 (New York: Bureau of Publications, Teachers College, 1927), vi, 70; Otis W. Caldwell, "Contribution of Biological Sciences to Universal Secondary Education," *School Science and Mathematics* 21 no. 2 (1921), p. 108; and Harold Rugg, "Curriculum-Making: The Lincoln School Experiment in the Social Sciences," a reprint from December, 1925 *Teachers College Record* in *Lincoln School of Teachers College Publications* 1, no. 5 (1925), p. 5.

32. Dewey's empiricism began with certain broad deductions about the nature of experience, linking biological with general cultural and ethical phenomena. As he wrote in *Experience and Education*, "If biological development be accepted . . . experience is not identical with brain action; it is the entire organism agent-patient in all its interaction with the environment, natural and social (New York: MacMillan, 1938), p. 36. The trouble here is that by further blurring the line between science and non-science, Dewey and his followers succeeded only in carving out new and greater areas of influence for an empirical science of society oblivious of "the entire organism agent-patient."

33. Otis W. Caldwell, *Elements of General Science* (Boston: Ginn and Co., 1914), pp. 301-2.

34. The phrase was made popular by R. J. Havighurst, the General Education Board's specialist in science education in the 1930s. "There are other outcomes of science instruction and of education which are almost intangible," he wrote. "They consist of the development of mental and moral traits such as tolerance, open-mindedness, tendency to explore basic assumptions, active curiosity, cooperativeness, self-dependence, sympathy" ("Tests and Measurements in the Natural Sciences," memo to the GEB,

November 11, 1934, Natural Sciences, 1934-37. GEB Records. RAC. See also Eliot's criticism of science as mere information gathering in Edward A. Krug, *The Shaping of the American High School* (New York: Harper and Row, 1964), pp. 204-205. Training in the ability to "observe accurately, describe correctly, and reason justly," not information, should be the main goal of general science education (p. 205).

35. See National Committee on Mathematical Requirements, *The Reorganization of Mathematics in Secondary Education* (New York: The Mathematical Association of America, 1923); David E. Smith to Wallace Buttrick, April n.d., 1919, in "National Committee of Mathematical Requirements," GEB Records. RAC. About a month after Smith's letter, the Board in May of 1919 contributed $16,000 toward the Committee's expenses and in February of the following year an additional $25,000 to "complete its work" ("Committee on Educational Research, 1916-1921," GEB Records. RAC).

36. After a visit to the school in 1921, Flexner recorded this impression of an English class in the minor Elizabethan poets: "The exercise left no doubt in my mind that literature is just as susceptible of a realistic treatment as are mathematics and science and that, when so presented, children will respond to the literary stimulus precisely as they respond to such stimulus as concrete mathematics and concrete science" (Abraham Flexner to Charles W. Eliot, March 21, 1921, GEB Records. RAC).

37. See Otis W. Caldwell, *Biological Foundation of Education* (New York: Ginn and Company, 1931) for a full description of this term.

38. "History of Policies and Project Policy: Proposed Program, 1933," Rockefeller Foundation. RAC.

39. "Minutes of the General Education Board," April, 1933, GEB Records, RAC; R. J. Havighurst, "The Function and Purposes of Natural Science in Secondary Education," p. 2; "Preliminary Report of the Science Committee on Secondary School Curriculum," December 19, 1935, Rockefeller Foundation. RAC.

40. Otis W. Caldwell, "Science and the People—Draft," n.d., OWC Papers. Otis W. Caldwell and Charles W. Finley, *Biology in the Public Press* (New York: Lincoln School Publications, 1923). To James McKeen Cattell, editor of Popular Science Monthly, Caldwell wrote, "Great innovations, discoveries of new materials and forces, improvement of health, transportation, vision, etc. are all to the good if men may only learn the

types of reorganization and reconstruction of themselves in order that these benefits may find their proper place" (Otis W. Caldwell to James McKeen Cattell, March 24, 1932, box 9, James McKeen Cattell Papers, Manuscripts Division, Library of Congress).

41. Eliot quoted in Edward A. Krug, *Charles W. Eliot and Popular Education* (New York: Teachers College Bureau of Publications, 1961), p. 142, pp. 143-146. See Theodore R. Mitchell's discussion of Eliot's influence in "From Black to White: The Transformation of Educational Reform in the New South, 1890-1910," *Educational Theory* 39 (Fall 1989), pp. 337-350.

42. Eliot, "The Modern School," p. 667.

43. John Woodhull to Dean James E. Russell, "Arguments to sustain my appeal from the division of the Principal of the high school to transfer biology from the first year of the course," circa 1919, pp. 4, 5. William F. Russell Papers.

44. James E. Russell to John F. Woodhull, November 12, 1920. James Earl Russell Papers.

45. Betz quoted in Raleigh Schorling, *The Teaching of Mathematics* (Ann Arbor, MI: Ann Arbor Press, 1936), p. 171. See E. R. Hedrick, "The Function Concept in Secondary School Mathematics," in *Reorganization of Mathematics*, pp. 64-65, 68-70.

46. Ibid., pp. 64-65, 71-73. See also David Eugene Smith, "Mathematics in the Training of Citizenship" in Schorling, *Teaching of Mathematics*. On the issue of efficiency, Schorling wrote in his report to the National Committee on Mathematical Requirements, "We have sufficient evidence to make us sympathetic with the complaints of the industrial and commercial world resulting from its contact with pupils who have achieved only 50% to 80% accuracy" (*Reorganization of Mathematics*, p. 187).

47. Ibid., p. 70; "Illustrated Mathematical Talks by Pupils of the Lincoln School of Teachers College," *Lincoln School of Teachers College Publications*, no. 3, 1918-19.

48. Schorling, *Experimental Courses in Secondary School Mathematics*, pp. 61-67.

49. "Illustrated Mathematical Talks," p. 25.

50. William George Spencer, father of Herbert, quoted by Betz in Schorling, *Teaching of Mathematics*, pp. 171-172.

51. Ibid., p. 177.

52. E. H. Moore, "On the Foundations of Mathematics" in Schorling, *The Teaching of Mathematics*, pp. 40-41, 43.

53. Ibid., pp. 45-49, 85-86, 84, 22, 101-102.

54. Ibid., pp. 106-107.

55. Schorling, *Reorganization of Mathematics*, p. 241.

56. Ibid., pp. 180-181. See "Summary Report - Survey Committee of the Affiliated Schools of Teachers College," June, 1930. William F. Russell Papers.

57. John Dewey, "What Pragmatism Means by Practical," Jo Ann Boydston, ed., *Essays on Pragmatism and Truth, 1907-1909* (Carbondale, IL: Southern Illinois University Press, 1977), p. 98.

58. One of the best expositions of the preparedness movement is Michael Pearlman, *To Make Democracy Safe for America* (Urbana, Il.: University of Illinois Press, 1984). The post-war cult of preparedness found its best contemporary expression in the writings of James M. Beck. See, for example, *The Passing of the New Freedom* (New York: George H. Doran, 1920) and *The Reckoning* (New York: G. P. Putnam's Sons, 1918). Nicholas Murray Butler, *Is America Worth Saving?* (New York: Charles Scribner and Sons, 1920), p. 375.

59. John Dewey et al., *Creative Intelligence: Essays in the Pragmatic Attitude* (New York: Henry Holt, 1917), pp. 6-13, 21, 53, 111-112.

60. Peter Dobkin Hall, *Inventing the Non-Profit Sector* (Baltimore, Md: Johns Hopkins University Press, 1992), ch. 4.

61. James Earl Russell, "Memorandum," November 23, 1916, 2. James Earl Russell Papers; Jerome R. Ravitz, *Scientific Knowledge and Its Social Problems* (Oxford: Clarendon Press, 1971), pp. 264-265; Otis W. Caldwell, *The Work of the Institute of School Experimentation* (New York: Bureau of Publications, Teachers College, Columbia University, 1931), pp. 1-2.

62. Harold Rugg, "The School Curriculum and the Drama of American Life" in Guy Montrose Whipple, ed. *Curriculum-Making: Past and Present*, National Society for the Study of Education, 26th Yearbook, Part 1 (Bloomington, Il: Public School Publishing, 1926), 1; Rugg et al., "Problems of American Industry and Business (Waste and Conservation)," *Social Science Pamphlets* 3 (1926), p. v.

63. Harold Rugg et al., "The Mechanical Conquest of America," *Social Science Pamphlets* 2 (1925), p. 265.

64. *The Lincolnian*, p. 6.

65. Abraham Flexner, "Memorandum: Visit to the Lincoln School, November 9, 1917," GEB Records. RAC.

Chapter 7

1. Sections of this article are adapted from Susan F. Semel, *The Dalton School: The Transformation of a Progressive School* (New York: Peter Lang Publishing, 1992).

2. See Susan F. Semel, *The Dalton School*, Epilogue, for a discussion of the paradox of progressive education at an elite school. The question of whether a school serving a mostly affluent population can be considered progressive in light of the usual progressive principles of democratic education, equality, and diversity is important. For the immediate purposes of this chapter, I examine *"pedagogical progressivism,"* which I mean child-centered practices, individualized curricula, an interdisciplinary curriculum, cooperative learning, experiential education, and the development of the whole child. For a complete discussion of the history of these practices see Lawrence A. Cremin, *The Transformation of the School* (New York: Alfred A. Knopf, 1961).

3. See Semel, *The Dalton School*, for an analysis of the factors that influenced the transformation. My analysis suggests a multidimensional set of factors, including educational and cultural change, geographic and demographic changes, and most important, school leadership.

4. Interview with Mr. Winthrop Crane, August 8, 1991. There is some discrepancy about when Parkhurst's Plan was adopted in the high school in Dalton, Mass. I have chosen Winthrop Crane's account, although Carleton Washburne dates it at 1920.

5. Otto F. Kraushaar, *American Nonpublic Schools: Patterns of Diversity* (Baltimore and London: Johns Hopkins University Press, 1972), p. 81.

6. Cremin, *The Transformation of the School*, p. 202.

7. For a more complete discussion of the work of Carleton W. Washburne, see Cremin, *The Transformation of the School*, pp. 295–299. See also Washburne's own writings, including, Carleton W. Washburne, *Adjusting the School to the Child* (New York: World Book Company, 1932) and Carleton W. Washburne and Sidney P. Marland, Jr. *Winnetka: The*

History and Significance of an Educational Experiment (Engelwood Cliffs, N.J.: Prentice Hall, 1963).

8. In the United Kingdom, a number of books on the Dalton Plan were published, including C.W. Kimmins and Belle Rennie, *The Triumph of the Dalton Plan* (London: Nicholson and Watson, Ltd., 1923), for which Helen Parkhurst wrote a foreword; A. J. Lynch, *Individual Work and the Dalton Plan* (London: George Philip and Son, 1924); and *The Rise and Progress of the Dalton Plan* (London: George Philip and Son, 1926).

9. Cremin, *The Transformation of the School*, pp. 295-296.

10. Helen Parkhurst, *Education on the Dalton Plan* (London: G. Bell and Sons, 1927), p. 15.

11. Helen Parkhurst as quoted in Evelyn Dewey, *The Dalton Laboratory Plan* (New York: E.P. Dutton and Co., 1922), p. 136.

12. Parkhurst, *Education on the Dalton Plan*, p. 16.

13. Ibid., p. 16.

14. Ibid.

15. Ibid., pp. 18-19.

16. Helen Parkhurst, "Report of the Dalton School to the Commission on the Relation of School and College" (New York: Dalton School Archives, 1937), p. 5 (mimeographed).

17. The younger children were expected to sign contracts; this was not so in the High School.

18. Parkhurst, *Education on the Dalton Plan*, p. 47.

19. Interview with Georgia C. Rice, January 26, 1979.

20. Parkhurst, "Lecture at Caxton Hall," p. 5.

21. Ibid., pp. 9, 10.

22. For a complete discussion of Washburne's influence on Parkhurst see Semel, *The Dalton School*, Chapter 2.

23. Ibid., p. 2.

24. Two more schools in California were later added.

25. Aikin, p. 12.

26. H.H. Giles, S.P. McCutchen, and A.N. Zechiel, *Exploring the Curriculum* (New York and London: Harper and Brothers, 1942), p. 289.

27. Helen Parkhurst, "Report of the Dalton School to the Commission on the Relation of School and College" (New York: Dalton School Archives, 1937), p. 1 (mimeographed).

28. Ibid., pp. 1-2.

29. Ibid., p. 5.
30. Board of Trustees, "Minutes (New York: Dalton School, 1937), pp. 360-362.
31. Giles et al., pp. 136, 239.
32. Correspondence of Charlotte Keefe Durham, February 22, 1979.
33. Ibid.
34. Ibid.
35. Ibid.
36. *The Daltonian* (New York: Dalton School Archives, May 20, 1938).
37. *The Daltonian*, October 30, 1930.
38. Board of Trustees, Minutes, September 26, 1929, p. 5.
39. Ibid., p. 7.
40. Ibid., p. 354.
41. Charlotte Keefe Durham correspondence.
42. Ibid.
43. Incident related by Nora Hodges in an interview, January 24, 1979.
44. For a complete discussion of Parkhurst's resignation and the financial troubles see Semel, *The Dalton School*, Chapter 3.
45. Charlotte Durham, Board of Trustees Minutes, May 14, 1947.
46. Board of Trustees Minutes, May 14, 1947.
47. Ibid.
48. Bernard Iddings Bell, *Crisis in Education* (New York: Whittlesey House, 1949).
49. Arthur Bestor, *Educational Wastelands* (Urbana: University of Illinois Press, 1952).
50. For a more detailed account of the Kittell years, see Semel, *The Dalton School*, Chapter 5.
51. Bestor, *Educational Wastelands*.
52. Richard Hofstadter, *Anti-intellectualism in American Life* (New York: Vintage Books, 1962), p. 103.
53. Donald Barr, *Who Pushed Humpty Dumpty?* (New York: Atheneum, 1971).
54. Ibid., p. 160.
55. Ibid., p. 124.
56. *Handbook: Dalton School* (New York: Dalton Archives, n.d.), p. 52.
57. William O'Neill, *Coming Apart* (New York: Harcourt, 1971), p. 238.

58. Donald Barr, "Letter to Parents" (New York: Dalton School Archives, March 1, 1967), n.p.

59. Ibid.

60. *New York Times*, February 7, 1974.

61. Ibid.

62. Report of the NYSAIS Evaluation Visiting Committee, Office of the Headmaster, March 1984, pp. 1-2.

63. Ibid., p. 2.

64. Ibid.

65. Ibid.

66. Ibid.

67. Report of the NYSAIS Evaluation Visiting Committee, Office of the Headmaster, June 1985, n.p.

68. Frank A. Moretti, "Assignment on the Assignment," February, 1987.

69. *The Daltonian*, May 1, 1991.

70. Ibid.

71. NYSAIS, "Report of the Visiting Committee," Office of the Headmaster, April 13-April 16, 1986, pp. 58-59.

72. Ibid., p. 3.

73. Ibid., p. 34.

74. "The Cumulative Curriculum: Multi-media and the Making of a New Educational System" (New York: Institute of Learning Technologies, Teachers College, Columbia University), September 8, 1991, pp. 15, 43.

75. Gerald Grant, *The World We Created at Hamilton High* (Cambridge, Mass.: Harvard University Press, 1988), p. 172.

76. Elisabeth Bumiller, "Headmaster at Dalton Resigns under Pressure," *New York Times*, March 13, 1997, p. B 3.

77. Deidre Dolan, "The Case of the Happy Headmaster: Dalton Says So Long, Dr. Dunnan," *New York Observer*, April 7, 1997, pp. 1, 32.

78. Ralph Gardner, Jr. "Babes in the Woods," *New York Magazine*, April 28, 1997, p. 54.

79. Nancy Neff, "From the Board of Trustees," *Connections: A Publication for the Dalton Community*, Spring 1997, p. 2.

80. June Edwards, "To Teach Responsibility, Bring Back the Dalton Plan," *Phi Delta Kappan* January 1991, pp. 398-401.

81. *The Daltonian*, March 1, 1984.

82. *The Daltonian*, June 8, 1983.

83. *New York Observer*, p. 32.

84. Ibid.

85. For an attempt at this appraisal, see Semel, *The Dalton School*, Chapter 9; Epilogue.

Chapter 8

1. Portions of this chapter first appeared in Daniel Perlstein, "Community and Democracy in American Schools: Arthurdale and the Fate of Progressive Education," *Teachers College Record* 97 (Summer 1996), pp. 625-650.

2. John Dewey, "Foreword," in Elsie Ripley Clapp, *Community Schools in Action* (New York: Viking, 1939), p. vii.

3. Elsie Ripley Clapp, *The Use of Resources in Education* (New York: Harper and Brothers, 1952), p. 138. On the widespread appeal of community-centered schooling among Depression-era progressive educators, see Samuel Everett, *The Community School* (New York: D. Appleton-Century, 1938).

4. Eleanor Roosevelt, *This I Remember* (New York: Harper and Brothers, 1949), pp. 126-27. Most individual homesteads were between four and seven acres. For a national perspective on the homestead program, see Paul K. Conkin, *Tomorrow a World: The New Deal Community Program* (Ithaca, N.Y.: Cornell University Press, 1959).

5. Phil Ross, "The Scotts Run Coalfield From the Great War to the Great Depression: A Study in Overdevelopment," *West Virginia History* 53 (1994), p. 27.

6. Clapp, *Use of Resources*, p. 4.

7. Lorena Hickok, *Eleanor Roosevelt: Reluctant First Lady* (New York: Dodd, Mead and Co., 1962), pp. 136-137. See also Ronald L. Lewis, "Scott's Run: America's Symbol of the Depression in the Coal Fields," in *A New Deal for America*, Bryan Ward, ed. (Arthurdale, W. Va.: Arthurdale Heritage, Inc., 1995).

8. "Mrs. Roosevelt's Home Project Defended Here," undated newspaper article [1933-34], Elsie Ripley Clapp Papers (hereafter ERCP), Special Collections, Morris Library, Southern Illinois University, Carbondale, IL, Series 4. See also Clapp, *Use of Resources*, p. 7.

9. Clapp, *Community Schools*, p. 116. See also E. Roosevelt, *This I Remember*, p. 129; and Hickok, *Reluctant First Lady*, p. 137.

10. Eleanor Roosevelt, Press Conference transcript, 29 May 1939, in *The White House Press Conferences of Eleanor Roosevelt*, ed. Maurine Beasley (New York: Garland, 1983), p. 115. See also Clapp, *Use of Resources*, p. 13.

11. See for instance Harold Rugg, "Social Reconstruction Through Education," *Progressive Education* 10 (Dec. 1932/Jan. 1933), pp. 11–18.

12. E. Roosevelt quoted in Joseph Lash, *Eleanor and Franklin* (New York: New American Library, 1973), p. 541.

13. Homesteaders to Eleanor Roosevelt, 18 Oct. 1933, West Virginia Regional Collection (hereafter WVRC), Archives and Manuscript 2178, Folder 1, West Virginia University, Morgantown, W. Va.

14. Clarence Pickett, *For More Than Bread: An Autobiographical Account of Twenty-Two Years' Work with the American Friends Service Committee* (Boston: Little, Brown and Co., 1953), pp. 32–35; Nat Frame, *West Virginia Agriculture and Rural Life* (Inwood, W. Va.: United States Department of Agriculture, 1948).

15. Franklin Roosevelt, "Actualities of Agricultural Planning," in *America Faces the Future*, ed. Charles Beard (Boston: Houghton Mifflin, 1932), pp. 332, 348; Conkin, *Tomorrow A World*, p. 83; Tamara Hareven, *Eleanor Roosevelt: An American Conscience* (New York: Da Capo Press, 1975), pp. 91–92. Included in the National Industrial Recovery Act was the provision of $25,000,000 to launch subsistence homestead communities. (United States Department of the Interior, Division of Subsistence Homesteads, *General Information Concerning the Purposes and Policies of the Division of Subsistence Homesteads* [Washington, D.C.: Author, 1933], p. 1.)

16. Mrs. Franklin D. Roosevelt, "Homestead—W. Virginia, 1935" (manuscript intended for *Liberty Magazine*), p. 12, Eleanor Roosevelt Papers(hereafter ERP), Franklin Delano Roosevelt Presidential Library, Hyde Park, N.Y., Box 3032. See also Eleanor Roosevelt, "Subsistence Farm Steads-Reedsville Project," speech, [1936?], pp. 1–3, ERP, Box 3033.

17. Eleanor Roosevelt to Bernard Baruch, 26 Sept. 1935, Eleanor Roosevelt Papers, Microfilm edition (hereafter ERM), reel 1: frame 236; Pickett, *For More than Bread*, pp. 57–58.

18. Elsie Ripley Clapp, manuscript fragment, ERCP, Series 2, no. 32.

19. Elsie Ripley Clapp, "Children's Mathematics," *Progressive Education* 5 (1928), pp. 131-135.

20. Elsie Clapp to Eleanor Roosevelt, 24 Apr. 1936, ERM, 4: 398.

21. Elsie Ripley Clapp to G.W. Amner, 13 Sept. 1935, ERM, 4: 270.

22. Clarence Pickett, "The Education of an American Community," *Progressive Education* 11 (1934), p. 236.

23. Milburn L. Wilson, "Beyond Economics," in *Farmers in a Changing World: The Yearbook of Agriculture: 1940* (Washington, D.C.: United States Government Printing Office, 1940), pp. 925-927.

24. Clapp, *Community Schools*, p. 89.

25. Clapp, *Use of Resources*, pp. 22, 90.

26. Steward Wagner, "School Buildings: Arthurdale, West Virginia," *Progressive Education* 15 (Apr. 1938), pp. 304-319.

27. Clapp, *Use of Resources*, p. 8; Wagner, "School Buildings," pp. 304-319; *Dominion News*, 12 Feb. 1934, p. 2.

28. Wagner, "School Buildings," p. 316.

29. Clapp, *Use of Resources*, pp. 14, 127; and biographical information on Jessie Stanton, ERCP, Series 4. Stanton did not live on the project but visited monthly.

30. Clapp, *Community Schools*, pp. 131-134, 203; Sam Stack, Interview with Glenna Williams, June 1995.

31. Clapp, *Use of Resources*, p. 89.

32. Williams Interview; Clapp, *Use of Resources*, pp. 15, 33; and Charles Pynchon, "School as Social Center," *New York Times*, 5 May 1935, Sec. 9, p. 23. The daughter of one of the original homesteaders from Scott's Run, Williams served as student teacher and then as an assistant teacher at the nursery school between September of 1935 and July, 1936. She then studied briefly at Teachers College.

33. Clapp, *Community Schools*, pp. 191, 216.

34. Clapp, *Use of Resources*, pp. 30-33, 86.

35. Clapp, *Use of Resources*, p. 36. See also Clapp, *Community Schools*, p. 136.

36. Clapp, *Community Schools*, p. 153.

37. Clapp, *Use of Resources*, pp. 43-45, 160.

38. Clapp, *Use of Resources*, pp. 42-44, 100-102.

39. Clapp, *Use of Resources*, p. 106.

40. Clapp, *Community Schools*, p. 143.

41. Clapp, *Use of Resources*, p. 41.

42. Clapp, *Community Schools*, pp. 143, 151.

43. Clapp, *Community Schools*, p. 143. Clapp's list of pioneer activities echoes Dewey's similar 1900 formulation in *The School and Society*. (John Dewey, *The School and Society and The Child and the Curriculum* [Chicago: University of Chicago Press, 1990], p. 10.)

44. Clapp, *Community Schools*, p. 156.

45. Clapp, *Community Schools*, p. 325.

46. Sam Stack, Interview with Annabelle Mayor, June 1995.

47. Clapp, *Use of Resources*, p. 162. See also pp. 121–124 and Clapp, *Community Schools*, pp. 346–347.

48. John Martin Taylor, "A Study of the Graduates of Arthurdale High School to Determine the Influence of High School Training on Occupational Adjustment" (M.A. thesis, West Virginia University, 1941), p. 78.

49. Dewey, *School and Society*, p. 14.

50. Dewey, "Foreword," p. viii.

51. Clapp, *Community Schools*, p. 49.

52. Plan for the School at Arthurdale drafted by the West Virginia Advisory School Committee, *Dominion News*, Morgantown, W. Va., 12 Feb. 1934.

53. Elsie Ripley Clapp, "A Rural School in Kentucky," *Progressive Education* 10 (1933), p. 127. See also Elsie Ripley Clapp, "Social Education in a Public Rural School," *Childhood Education* 9 (Oct. 1932), pp. 24–26.

54. Clapp, *Community Schools*, pp. 97, 173.

55. Clapp, *Use of Resources*, pp. 20, 24, 77, 133.

56. Elsie Ripley Clapp, "Arthurdale—A School," c. 4 Jan. 1936, ERM, 4: 310.

57. Clapp, *Community Schools*, pp. 123, 169.

58. Elsie Clapp to Eleanor Roosevelt, 24 Aug. 1935, ERM, 4: 264–265; and Elsie Clapp to Eleanor Roosevelt, 19 May 1936, ERM, 4: 410–411.

59. Clapp, *Community Schools*, pp. 81, 89, 169.

60. Clapp, *Community Schools*, pp. 169, 355.

61. Elsie Clapp to Miss Schauffler, 31 July 1935, 3, ERM, 4: 247.

62. Elsie Ripley Clapp, "Arthurdale—A School," c. 4 Jan. 1936, ERM, 4: 310.

63. Clapp, *Community Schools*, p. 217. For a positive assessment of the teachers, see Bruce G. Beezer, "Arthurdale: An Experiment in Community Education," *West Virginia History* 36 (Oct. 1974), p. 33.

64. Clapp, *Use of Resources*, p. 56.

65. Elsie Ripley Clapp, "Learning and Indoctrination," *Progressive Education* 9 (1932), p. 270. For an account of Counts' speech and its reception, see Patricia Albjerg Graham, *Progressive Education: From Arcady to Academe: A History of the Progressive Education Association, 1919-1955* (New York: Teachers College Press, 1967), pp. 63-67.

66. Clapp, *Community Schools*, p. 67.

67. See Evelyn Dewey, *New Schools for Old: The Regeneration of the Porter School* (New York: E.P. Dutton and Co., 1919); and Graham, *Progressive Education*, p. 62.

68. Its focus on education for social melioration placed Arthurdale at the margins of the New Deal. For a discussion of why educational policy was not a major element of the New Deal see Harvey Kantor and Robert Lowe, "Class, Race, and the Emergence of Federal Education Policy: From the New Deal to the Great Society," *Educational Researcher* 24 (April, 1995), pp. 6-7.

69. See Glenn Lawmaker, Interview with Charles and Hilda Hendershot, Sept. 1987, Audio tape, WVRC.

70. William E. Brooks, "Arthurdale—A New Chance," *Atlantic Monthly*, Feb. 1935, p. 199. The United Mine Workers had in fact expressed concern that the construction of Arthurdale and other homesteads would disperse workers and weaken organized labor. (Pickett, *For More than Bread*, p. 47).

71. E. Roosevelt, *If You Ask Me*, p. 27. See also see Alice Davis to Eleanor Roosevelt, Aug, 1933, in Lash, *Eleanor and Franklin*, p. 521; and Stephen Edward Haid, "Arthurdale: An Experiment in Community Planning, 1933-1947" (Ph.D. dissertation, West Virginia University, 1975), p. 63.

72. Dallas Earl Riley Case History, 1935, ERM, 4: 350; Wendell Lund to G.M. Flynn, ERM, 4: 269; Hareven, *Eleanor Roosevelt*, p. 95; and E. Roosevelt, "Homestead—W. Virginia, 1935," p. 3.

73. Agnes Sailer, "Miners' Children at Play," *Progressive Education* 9 (1932), pp. 507-508.

74. Clapp, *Community Schools*, pp. 139, 210.

75. Clapp, *Use of Resources*, pp. 137-138.

76. Clapp, *Community Schools*, pp. 160, 330.

77. Clapp, *Use of Resources*, pp. 53, 118-120.

78. Clapp, *Community Schools*, p. 10.

79. Clapp, *Use of Resources*, pp. 41, 120-121.

80. Clapp, *Community Schools*, p. 219.

81. Clapp, *Community Schools*, pp. 231, 256, 329.

82. Clapp, *Community Schools*, p. 218.

83. E. Roosevelt quoted in James R. Kearney, *Anna Eleanor Roosevelt: The Evolution of a Reformer* (Boston: Houghton Mifflin, 1968), p. 160. Roosevelt seems to have opposed the background check, but she was unable to enact a non-discrimination policy at Arthurdale.

84. Clapp, *Community Schools*, pp. 116-7.

85. John P. Davis, memo to Walter White, 25 Jan. 1934, Correspondence, Walter White, National Association for the Advancement of Colored People Papers, Part I, Microfilm edition (hereafter NAACP Papers), 26: 0076-77.

86. Report of the Secretary to Annual Business Meeting, 8 Jan. 1934; NAACP Papers, 14: 265; W. E. B. Du Bois, "The Board of Directors on Segregation," *Crisis*, May 1934, p. 149; and W. E. B. Du Bois, "Does the Negro Need Separate Schools?" *Journal of Negro Education* 4 (1935), pp. 328-335. On Du Bois' effort to articulate a vision of community that embraced social justice, see Thomas C. Holt, "The Political Uses of Alienation: W. E. B. Du Bois on Politics, Race, and Culture, 1903-1940," *American Quarterly* 42 (1990), pp. 307-314.

87. W. E. B. Du Bois, "Segregation," *Crisis*, Jan. 1934, p. 20. A number of researchers have returned to Du Bois' view of segregated black schools as exemplars of sustained community-centered education. See Vanessa Siddle Walker, *Their Highest Potential: An African American School Community in the Segregated South* (Chapel Hill: University of North Carolina Press, 1996); David Cecelski, *Along Freedom Road: Hyde County, North Carolina and the Fate of Black Schools in the South* (Chapel Hill: University of North Carolina Press, 1994); and Van Dempsey et al., "The Demise of Caring in an African American Community: One Consequence of School Desegregation," *Urban Review* 25 (1993), pp. 47-61.

88. W. E. B. Du Bois, "Subsistence Homestead Colonies," *Crisis*, March 1934, p. 85.

89. John P. Muchison, Memo to Clarence Pickett, 23 Oct. 1934, NAACP Papers, 22: 0614.

90. Secretary's report to the March [1934] Board Meeting, NAACP Papers, 5: 804; and Report of the Secretary to the May [9 1934] Meeting of the Board, NAACP Papers, 5: 828.

91. Fletcher Collins and Elsie Ripley Clapp, "Distribution By Ancestral Nationality," ERM, 4: 374.

92. Clapp, *Community Schools*, pp. 144–145, 252. In Kentucky, Clapp also stressed the yeomanry of residents while neglecting slavery and current race relations (pp. 17–18). Her only discussion of race in *Community Schools* concerned a high school drama group. Students created a play *Spade*, derived from Stephen Vincent Benet's *John Brown's Body*. The play recounted the misfortunes of Spade, who fled slavery only to find "in northern industry much the same slaveries that he had escaped from in the South. The group enjoyed the disillusioning ending," Clapp reported, "for they were in their own lives beginning to see that there were no fancy escapes from the realities of everyday living" (p. 265; Clapp, *Use of Resources*, p. 126). Indians make several appearances in Arthurdale's curriculum. In dramatic play, friendly ones visited pioneer cabins; others kidnap a pioneer boy. Indian pottery demonstrated pre-industrial craft. None of this, however, implicated white homesteaders in issues of power and domination or challenged the image of a monolithic regional culture (Clapp, *Community Schools*, pp. 147–148, 154).

93. Wesley Stout, "The New Homesteaders, *Saturday Evening Post*, 4 Aug. 1934, pp. 6–7; "Wirt Will Give Facts," *Dominion News*, 26 Mar. 1934; "Demand Wirt Reveal Names," *Dominion News*, 6 Apr. 1934; Lash, *Eleanor and Franklin*, p. 528.

94. Bernard Baruch to Eleanor Roosevelt, 27 June 1936, ERM, 1:290; Harold Ickes, *The Secret Diary of Harold Ickes: The First Thousand Days, 1933–1936* (New York: Simon and Schuster, 1953), entry for 10 March 1934, p. 152; and Lash, *Eleanor and Franklin*, p. 531; Haid, "Arthurdale."

95. Elsie Clapp to Eleanor Roosevelt, 10 Jan. 1936, ERM, 4: 330–333; Eleanor Roosevelt to Bernard Baruch, 2 Dec. 1939, ERM, 1: 437; E. Roosevelt, *This I Remember*, p. 130; and Clapp, *Community Schools*, pp. 170, 358–362. Because of its school finance formula, Preston County funded only three Arthurdale teachers in the community's first year. The county, moreover, ceded to Clapp the authority to select these teachers,

based upon their ability to adapt to progressive methods. The bulk of Arthurdale's teachers came with Clapp from the Ballard School in Kentucky and were experienced teachers committed to progressive education.

96. A majority of families petitioned Clapp to stay on in 1936. (Elsie Clapp to Eleanor Roosevelt, 16 Aug. 1936, ERM, 4: 435. See also Bernard Baruch to Eleanor Roosevelt, 27 Jan 1936, ERM, 1: 256–257; Baruch to Eleanor Roosevelt, 11 May 1936, ERM, 1: 285; and Conkin, *Tomorrow*, pp. 244–46.)

97. Pickett, *For More Than Bread*, pp. 58–59.

98. E. Roosevelt, *This I Remember*, p. 130.

99. Williams interview; Thomas Coode and Dennis Fabbri, "The New Deal's Arthurdale Project in West Virginia," *West Virginia History* 38 (1978), pp. 291–308; Clapp, *Use of Resources*, pp. 66, 149.

100. "Vetoing Mrs. Roosevelt's Pet Project," *Christian Century*, 14 Mar. 1934, p. 348; Eleanor Roosevelt, Press Conference transcript, 9 Feb. 1942, in *White House Press Conferences*, p. 265; and Bernard Baruch to Eleanor Roosevelt, 18 Dec. 1934, ERM, 1: 220.

101. B. Baruch to E. Roosevelt, 6 Apr. 1936, ERM, 1: 276.

102. Bernard Baruch to Eleanor Roosevelt, 22 June 1936, ERM, 4: 416.

103. Elsie Clapp to Eleanor Roosevelt, 30 June 1936, ERM, 4: 418.

104. Elsie Clapp to Eleanor Roosevelt, 4 Oct. 1936, ERM, 1:302; Clapp to Clarence [Pickett], c. 10 Apr. 1938, ERM, 1: 368–371; Eleanor Roosevelt, Press Conference transcript, 9 Feb. 1942, p. 265; Pickett, *For More than Bread*, p. 63.

105. Clapp, *Community Schools*, pp. 89, 169. Emphasis added.

106. Clapp quoted in Pynchon, "School As Social Center," p. 23.

107. Taylor, "Study of the Graduates," p. 73.

108. Counts, "Dare Progressive Education Be Progressive?" *Progressive Education* 9 (1932), p. 261.

109. John Dewey, "Introduction," in Clapp, *Use of Resources*, p. ix. See also Lawrence Cremin, *The Transformation of the School: Progressivism in American Education, 1876–1957* (New York: Alfred Knopf, 1961), p. 237, n 8.

110. John Dewey to J.A. Rice, 16 Apr. 1936, General File, Box 7, 1933–1936, Black Mountain College Papers, Special Collections, Morris Library, Southern Illinois University, Carbondale Ill.

111. John Dewey to Samuel Everett, 29 Apr. 1940, ERCP, 21, folder 2, file 28. Everett had written a critical review of *Community Schools in Action* for the March 1940 *Curriculum Journal* (typed copy, ERCP, Box 2, folder 28.)

112. Dewey, "Introduction," p. viii–ix.

Chapter 9

1. Joseph Featherstone, "Schools for Children: What's Happening in British Classrooms," "How Children Learn, " "Teaching Children to Think," *The New Republic* (August 19, 1967), pp. 17–21; (September 2, 1967), pp. 17–21; (September 9, 1967), pp. 15–19.

2. Median family income for Libertyville was slightly higher than the median income for the Chicago suburbs, which was $8,158 in 1959. Northeastern Illinois Metropolitan Area Planning Commission, *Suburban Fact Book. Revised With New Tables and 1960–1961 Data* (Chicago: Northeastern Illinois Metropolitan Area Planning Commission, 1962), Tables 1, 4, 6, 10.

3. In January, 1968 the Director of Lake County Regional Planning Commission told the Citizens' Advisory Committee that he predicted tremendous population growth in the county and in Libertyville, *Independent Register*, Jan. 11, 1968, pp. 1, 2.

4. *Independent-Register*, May 26, 1968, pp. 1, 2.

5. *Independent-Register*, Oct. 11, 1973, p. 1; May 19, 1977, p. 3B.

6. Arthur Zilversmit and Khryss Holland, Interview with Robert Procunier, Tinley Park, Ill., July 7, 1994; *Independent-Register*, July 18, 1968, p. 3.

7. Procunier interview.

8. Thermofaxed memo addressed to the Board of Education from W. C. Rardin and the Administrative Staff, dated Aug. 27, 1968, bound in Libertyville Board of Education, "Minutes" book, after the minutes of Oct. 1, 1968 meeting; *Independent Register*, Jan. 23, 1969.

9. Frank H. Moyer, "A Comprehensive Bibliography of Open Education and Open-Space Schools—A Reader's Guide" (Plainfield, N. J., 1972), pp. 1.27, 1.32, 1.33.

10. *Independent-Register,* Jan. 23, 1969, pp. 1, 6.

11. *Independent-Register,* May 21, 1970, p. 2G.

12. Procunier interview, *Board "Minutes,"* Oct. 27, 1970, p. 8.

13. Don Glines, *Creating Humane Schools.* Supplemental Edition. (Mankato, Minn.: Campus Publishers, 1971), pp. 5, 6, 7, 11-20. See also, Don Glines, "Upsetting the Curriculum," *Phi Delta Kappan*, 51 (March, 1970), p. 399, and Don Glines, "Implementing a Humane School," *Educational Leadership*, 28:2 (Nov. 1970), pp. 185-190.

14. Glines, *Humane Schools* mentions the words "open schools" only in passing, as on p. 10. The bibliography includes John Holt and Jean Piaget but not does not include Roland Barth or Paul Goodman.

15. Procunier interview.

16. *Independent-Register*, Feb. 18, 1971, pp. 1, 5.

17. *Independent-Register*, March 25, 1971, p. 4.

18. *Independent-Register*, April 15, 1971, p.14; March 18, 1971, p. 3.

19. See, for example Jenny Andreae, "Stages in Implementation," in *Open Education Re-examined*, Donald A. Myers and Lilian Myers, eds. (Lexington, Mass.: Lexington Books, D. C. Heath and Company: 1973) pp. 23-31 and Bud Church, "Opening Up and Making It Work: A Case Study," in *Open Education: Critique and Assessment*, Vincent R. Rogers and Bud Church, eds. (Washington, D.C.: Association for Supervision and Curriculum Development, 1975) pp. 29-46.

20. *Independent-Register*, March 11, 1971, p. 1; May 13, 1971, p. 9.

21. Arthur Zilversmit, interview with Eleanor Moss, July 20, 1994, Libertyville, Il. Moss, a science teacher, had taught at Butterfield the first year when it was an upper grade center. Like most of the building's teachers, she chose to remain at Butterfield when it became an open school. On the other hand, Assistant Principal Polly Andrews came back from Mankato with positive feelings: Arthur Zilversmit, interview with Polly Andrews, September 7, 1994, Libertyville, Ill.

22. *Waukegan News-Sun*, Jan. 7, 1972, p. 1C.

23. *Independent-Register*, March 23, 1972, p. 1; March 30, 1972, pp. 1-2.

24. *Independent-Register*, March 23, 1972, p. 1.

25. *Waukegan News-Sun*, Jan. 7, 1972, p. 1C; Eleanor Moss interview.

26. *Independent-Register*, March 23, 1972, p. 1; March 30, 1972, pp. 1, 2.

27. *Waukegan News-Sun*, Jan. 7, 1972, p. 1C.

28. *Independent-Register,* Jan. 20, 1972, p. 7; Feb. 10, 1972, p. 1.

29. *Independent-Register*, Feb. 10, 1972, p. 1.

30. R. W. Procunier, "Survey of Parental Opinions Regarding the Butterfield Program," March 12, 1972. The Report was submitted to the Board at its March 14, 1972 meeting. It can be found, along with a letter from Victor Cottrell and Leroy Weinbrenner, Trinity College, to Robert Procunier, March 8, 1972 in the Board "Minutes" book after the minutes for May 8, 1972. A summary of the report was published in the *Independent-Register,* March 30, 1972, p. 2.

31. *Independent-Register,* March 16, 1972, p. 1.

32. *Independent-Register*, March 30, 1972, pp. 1, 7.

33. *Independent-Register,* April 27, 1972, pp. 1, 6. A "Letter to the Editor" from John Bostater, suggested that a small group of opponents had conducted a telephone campaign to bring opponents to the Board meeting, *Independent-Register,* May 4, 1972, p. 4.

34. *Independent-Register*, May 4, 1972, p. 4.

35. Victor Cottrell and Leroy Weinbrenner, "Evaluation of Student Educational Development: Preliminary Report," bound in Board "Minutes" book, after May 8, 1972, minutes.

36. *Independent-Register*, May 18, 1972 p. 4. The editorial cited Charles Silberman's recent popular account of the open education movement, *Crisis in the Classroom*, and praised the school board for being "aware there may be better, or even just as effective, ways to do things."

37. *Independent-Register*, May 11, 1972, pp. 1, 2.

38. "Planned Changes for Butterfield School 1972–1973: Report by Superintendent to Board of Education," May 8, 1972, bound in Board "Minutes" book, after the minutes of May 8, 1972; *Independent-Register*, Sept. 7, 1972, p. 2.

39. *Independent-Register,* June 8, 1972, p. 1; July 20, 1972, pp. 1, 2.

40. Eleanor Moss interview.

41. *Waukegan News-Sun*, July 25, 1973.

42. *Independent-Register*, Jan. 17, 1974, pp. 1A, 6A.

43. Assistant Principal Polly Andrews had had some experience with open classroom techniques and had implemented some of them at one of the district's primary schools. Andrews interview.

44. Assistant Principal Polly Andrews acknowledged that it was a mistake to plunge junior high school youngsters into an open program. Andrews interview.

45. In the fall of 1975 Rardin issued a long range planning document that discussed the possibility of closing an elementary school because of declining enrollments. Enrollments in grades k-4 had dropped 131 in the last five years. *Independent-Register*, Sept. 11, 1975, p. 7a.

46. Budget problems emerged in the spring of 1974. See *Independent-Register*, May 16, 1974, p. 11A, and June 13, 1974 p. 4A.

47. In the summer of 1976, the Board's Long Range Planning Committee noted that "Since 'open' or unstructured educational programs are now being re-examined by many educators and school districts it would seem an appropriate time for the school board to review this dual system to determine if a uniform system of education combining the best of the open and contemporary programs can't be instituted within District 70." *Independent-Register,* July 22, 1976, p. 2A.

48. Anti-tax sentiment emerged in Libertyville in 1979 with the organization of the Libertyville Informed Taxpayers that lobbied for a reduced school budget and succeeded in putting one of its members on the School Board. *Independent-Register*, Sept. 27, 1979, pp. 1A, 5A; Oct. 25, 1979, p. 1; Nov. 28, 1979 p. 1; Dec. 27, 1979, p. 5A; Jan. 24, 1980, p. 4A.

49 *Independent Register*, Nov. 25, 1980, p. 1; Dec. 4, 1980, p. 7D; Jan. 8, 1981, p. 10A; Jan. 15, 1981, p. 1.

Chapter 10

1. In 1990, the county population was approximately 95 percent white, 4 percent black, and 1 percent other races. U.S. Census, 1990; Population and Housing. Washington, D.C.: Government Printing Office, 1992.

2. Unless otherwise indicated, the information about Free Union Country School presented reflects 1995-96 ethnographic research conducted during the 1995-1996 academic year. The author participated in school activities as a teacher and school aide, a substitute teacher, and a computer resource, in addition to attending school meetings and school and family activities throughout the year. Her participation at the school averaged 15 hours a week. She collected historical data about the school conducting archival research that included meeting minutes, planning reports, school correspondence, newsletters and curriculum. Audio-taped interviews with a

selected group of founding and current families supplemented the data collection.

3. "Outline of Proposed Neighborhood School," Free Union Country School Archives, February 1984.

4. Field notes, during September, 1995.

5. Nel Noddings, *Caring: a Feminine Approach to Ethics and Moral Education* (Berkeley, Calif.: University of California Press 1984); Nel Noddings, *The Challenge to Care in Schools: An Alternative Approach to Education* (New York: Teachers College Press, 1992). Meier argues convincingly that "caring and compassion are not soft, mushy goals. They are part of the hard core of subjects we are responsible for teaching" in Deborah Meier, *The Power of Their Ideas: Lessons for America from a Small School in Harlem* (Boston: Houghton-Mifflin, 1995), p. 63.

6. Field notes, during September, 1995.

7. See Noddings, *Caring*, p. 179, for a critical discussion of the ethic of caring as lived through a teacher-student relationship integral to social experience and learning.

8. John Dewey, *The Child and the Curriculum*, in Martin Dworkin, ed, *Dewey on Education* (New York: Teachers College Press, 1959; originally published 1902), p. 111.

9. John Dewey, *The School and Society*, in Martin Dworkin, ed, *Dewey on Education* (New York, Teachers College Press, 1959 Originally published 1899), pp. 33-90.

10. Meier, *The Power of Their Ideas*, pp. 21-24.

11. "Free Union Country School Philosophy," Free Union Country School archives.

12. Dewey, *The Child and the Curriculum*. See Robert Westbrook, *John Dewey and American Democracy* (Ithaca, N.Y.: Cornell University Press, 1991), pp. 98-100, for a cogent discussion of how common misreadings of Dewey neglect his concern for curriculum.

13. Dewey, *The Child and the Curriculum*, pp. 99-100; quoted in Westbrook, *John Dewey and American Democracy*, p. 100.

14. Field notes, during January, 1996.

15. Dewey, *The School and Society*, pp. 40-41.

16. Interview, Free Union parent, April 18, 1996.

17. Albemarle County School Term Reports, Albemarle County Fiscal Services Archives.

18. Interview with a Free Union parent, April 2, 1996; A.S. Neill, *Summerhill School: A New View of Childhood* Rev. ed. (New York: Hart, 1993, originally published 1960). Contrary to the extreme openness and fluidity of Summerhill, Free Union Country is and has been from its inception a child- and curriculum-focused school.

19. Interview, Free Union parent, April 2, 1996.

20. Interview, Free Union parent, April 18, 1996.

21. See, for example, James G. Cibulka and William J. Kritek, *Coordination Among Schools, Families, and Communities: Prospects for Educational Reform* (Albany, N.Y.: SUNY Press 1996); James Coleman and Thomas Hoffer, *Public and Private High Schools: The Impact of Communities* (New York: Basic Books, 1987); Joyce Epstein, "School Family Community Partnerships: Caring for the Children We Share," *Phi Delta Kappan* 76 (1995), pp. 701–712; Mary E. Henry, *Parent-School Collaboration: Feminist Organizational Structures and School Leadership* (Albany, N.Y.: SUNY Press, 1996); Meier, *Power*; Alan Peshkin, *Growing Up American: Schooling and the Survival of Community* (Chicago: University of Chicago Press, 1978); Maike Philipsen, *Parental Involvement in Schools: Case Studies of Three High Schools in a Southeastern Metropolitan Area* (Richmond: Metropolitan Educational Research Consortium, 1996); Barry Rutherford and Shelley H. Billig, "Eight Lessons of Parent, Family, and Community Involvement in the Middle Grades," *Phi Delta Kappan* 77 (1995), pp. 64–68; Claire Smrekar, *The Impact of School Choice and Community: In the Interest of Families and Schools* (Albany, N.Y.: SUNY Press, 1996).

22. Interview, Free Union parent, April 2, 1996.

23. Interview, Free Union parent, April 2, 1996.

24. Field notes, during February, 1996. Although the school did not follow traditional standards of school records security, the close community of the early years encouraged respect for privacy.

25. Free Union Country School operates a preschool, which is subject to state licensure requirements as a day-care facility.

26. Letter, 16 December 1993, Free Union Country School archives.

27. See, for example, Cibulka and Kritek, *Coordination Among Schools, Families, and Communities*; Epstein, *School/Family/Community Partnerships*; Henry, *Parent-School Collaboration*; Meier, *The Power of Their Ideas*; Philipsen, *Parental Involvement in Schools*; Mary Anne Raywid,

"Community and Schools: A Prolegomenon," *Teachers College Record* 90 (1988), pp. 197-209; Rutherford and Billig, *Eight Lessons*; Smrekar, *The Impact of School Choice and Community*.

28. The eighth goal of Goals 2000 reads, "By the year 2000, every school will promote partnerships that will increase parental involvement and participation in promoting the social, emotional, and academic growth of children." *National Education Goals Report: Building a Nation of Learners* (Washington, D.C.: U.S. Government Printing Office, 1995).

29. Meier, *The Power of Their Ideas*, p. 23.

30. Coleman and Hoffer, *Public and Private High Schools*.

31. Michael Fullan, *Change Forces: Probing the Depths of Educational Reform* (London: Falmer Press, 1993).

32. Field notes, during May, 1996.

33. Field notes, during May, 1996.

34. *1897 Report of the Committee of Twelve on Rural Schools* (Chicago, University of Chicago Press, 1897), pp. 391-392.

35. Edgar W. Knight, *Public Education in the South* (Boston: Ginn and Company, 1922).

36. William A. Link, *A Hard Country and a Lonely Place: Schooling, Society, and Reform in Rural Virginia, 1870-1920* (Chapel Hill: University of North Carolina Press, 1986).

37. David B. Tyack, *The One Best System: A History of American Urban Education* (Cambridge, Mass.: Harvard University Press, 1974), pp. 24-7.

38. Diane Ravitch, *The Troubled Crusade: American Education 1945-1980* (New York: Basic Books, 1983), p. 327.

39. Ibid., pp. 327-328.

40. Adrian Bell and Alan Sigsworth, *The Small Rural Primary School: A Matter of Quality* (London: Falmer Press, 1987); Bruce Miller, "Teaching and Learning in the Multigrade Classroom: Student Performance and Instructional Routines," *ERIC Digest* EDO-RC-91-6 (1991), pp. 1-2; Alan Peshkin, *The Imperfect Union: School Consolidation and Community Conflict* (Chicago: University of Chicago Press, 1982); Sara Snyder Crumpacker, "The Experience of School as Place" (Ed.D., University of Virginia, 1992).

41. Andy Hargreaves, *Changing Teachers, Changing Times: Teachers' Work in the Post-Modern Age* (New York: Teachers College Press, 1994).

42. George E. Conway, "Small Scale and School Culture: The Experience of Private Schools," *ERIC Digest* EDO-RC-94-6 (1994): 1-2; William J. Fowler Jr., "What Do We Know About School Size? What Should We Know?" AERA, 347-675 (1992); Craig Howley, "The Academic Effectiveness of Small-Scale Schooling (An Update)," *ERIC Digest* EDO-RC-94-1 (1994), 1-2; Meier, *The Power of Their Ideas*; Bell and Sigsworth, *The Small Rural Primary School*.

43. Fowler, "What Do We Know;?" Howley, "Academic Effectiveness;" Miller, "Teaching and Learning."

44. In his socio-historical account of American education, Tyack, in *The One Best System*.

45. Field notes, during October, 1995, argued that our educational system is notable for its unsuccessful quest for "one best system" that serves all students.

46. The First- and Second-Grade Class Schedule, Free Union Country School, October, 1995.

47. Meier, *The Power of Their Ideas*.

48. Interview, Free Union parent, April 2, 1996.

49. Interview, Free Union parent, May 6, 1996.

50. Interview, Free Union parent, April 18, 1996.

51. Field notes, during September, 1995.

52. For example, there are no lawyers among the current school parents.

53. Field notes, during February, 1996.

54. Interview, Free Union parent, April 10, 1996.

55. Interview, Free Union parent, April 9, 1996.

56. Field notes, during May, 1996.

57. Interview, Free Union alumnus, April 2, 1996.

58. Interview, Free Union school director, April 10, 1997.

59. Field notes, during January, 1996.

60. Field notes, during January, 1996.

61. Field notes, during October, 1995.

62. Jane Roland Martin, *The Schoolhome: Rethinking Schools for Changing Families* (Cambridge, Mass.: Harvard University Press, 1992), p. 161. Noddings and Meier make similar arguments; see Noddings, *The Challenge to Care in Schools* and Meier, *The Power of Their Ideas*.

Chapter 11

1. This article was drawn from research commissioned by the Center on Organization and Restructuring of Schools, supported by the U.S. Department of Education, Office of Educational Research and Improvement (Grant no. R117Q00005-93) and by the Wisconsin Center for Education Research, School of Education, University of Wisconsin-Madison. The opinions expressed are those of the author and do not necessarily reflect the views of the supporting agencies. This chapter has been reprinted with permission from the *Journal of Negro Education*, vol. 63, no. 1 (1994), Copyright 1994, Howard University.

2. Since the original publication of this chapter, Urban Academy moved in 1996 to the Julia Richmond Education Complex at 317 East 67th Street. It is one of eight separate schools within the complex.

3. A. Cook, "The High School Inquiry Classroom," in K. Jervis and C. Montag (Eds.) *Progressive Education for 1992: Transforming Practice* (New York: Teachers College Press, 1991), pp. 149–151.

4. F. M. Newmann (1991). "What Is a Restructured School? A Framework to Clarify Means and Ends," in F. M. Newmann (ed.), *Issues in Restructuring Schools* (Issues Report no. 1), pp. 3–7. Madison, Wis.: Center on Organization and Restructuring of Schools.

5. A. S. Bryk, V. E. Lee, and J. L. Smith, "High School Organization and its Effects on Teachers and Students: An Interpretive Summary of the Research," In W. H. Clune and J. F. Witte (eds.), *Choice and Control in American Education* Vol. 1 (London: Falmer, 1990), pp. 135–226. See also, R. W. Eberts, E. Kehoe and J. A. Stone, *The Effects of School Size on Student Outcomes* (Eugene, Ore.: Oregon University, ERIC Document Reproduction Service no. ED 245 382, 1984). See also R. B. Pittman and P. Haughwout, "Influence of high school size on dropout rate," *Educational Evaluation and Policy Analysis* 9(4): 1987, pp. 337–343.

6. J. David, "The Puzzle of Structural Change," Paper presented at the symposium entitled "Structural Change in Secondary Education," held at the National Center on Effective Secondary Schools, University of Wisconsin-Madison, July 1987. See also H. D. Evans, "We Must Begin Education Reform 'Every Place at Once.'" *Phi Delta Kappan* 65 (3), 1983, pp. 173-177. See also T.R. Sizer, *Horace's Compromise: The Dilemma of the American High School* (Boston: Houghton Mifflin, 1984).

7. John Goodlad, *A Place Called School: Prospects for the Future* (New York: McGraw Hill, 1984).

Chapter 12

1. Public School–Intermediate School 176 Planning Committee. (1995). Proposal to the Fund for Public Education for a New Vision School in Washington Heights–Inwood (p. 3).

2. Anthony Amato, interview by author, New York, N.Y., February 14, 1997.

3. M. Klonsky, *Small Schools: The Numbers Tell a Story, A Review of the Research and Current Experiences* (Chicago: University of Illinois at Chicago, 1996), p. 2.

4. Public School-Intermediate School 176 Planning Committee (1995). Proposal to the Fund for Public Education for a New Vision School in Washington Heights-Inwood, p.1.

5. S.F. Semel and A.R. Sadovnik, "Lessons from the Past: Individualism and Community in Three Progressive Schools" *Peabody Journal of Education* vol. 70, no. 4, 1995, pp. 56–85.

6. Lydia Bassett to the parents of students of P.S.-I.S. 176, New York, N.Y., September, 1996.

7. W.F. Pinar, *Autobiography, Politics and Sexuality* (New York: Peter Lang, 1994).

8. P. Freire, *Pedagogy of the Oppressed* (New York: Continuum, 1993).

9. See P. Rigg and V. Allen (eds.), *When They Don't All Speak English* (Urbana, IL: National Council of Teachers of English, 1989); R. Scarcella, *Teaching Language Minority Students in the Multicultural Classroom* (Englewood Cliffs, NJ: Prentice-Hall Regents, 1990); C. Wallace, *Learning to Read in a Multicultural Society: The Social Context of Second Language Literacy* (New York: Prentice-Hall, 1988).

10. D. Macedo, *Literacies of Power: What Americans Are Not Allowed to Know* (Boulder, Col.: Westview Press, 1994).

11. J. Lessow-Hurley, *The Foundations of Dual Language Instruction* (New York: Longman, 1990).

12. Centre for Language in Primary Education, *The Primary Language Record* (Portsmouth, N.H.: Heinemann, 1994).

13. A pseudonym.

14. M.A. Raywid, "Taking Stock: The Movement to Create Mini-Schools, Schools-within-Schools, and Separate Small Schools." (Urban Diversity Series no. 108. Urbana, Ill.: ERIC Clearinghouse on Urban Education, 1996).

15. Ibid., p. 43.

16. R. Sternberg, "What Does it Mean to be Smart?" *Educational Leadership* 54, 6, March 1997, pp. 20–24.

17. Ibid., p. 20.

18. Ibid., pp. 24–25.

19. S.F. Semel and A.R. Sadovnik, "Lessons from the Past," p. 80.

20. Ibid.

21. Ibid.

22. Ibid.

23. Lydia Bassett to the parents of students of P.S.-I.S. 176, New York, N.Y., October, 1996.

Chapter 13

1. See Caroline Hodges Persell and Peter W. Cookson, Jr., "Chartering and Bartering: Elite Education and Social Reproduction," *Social Problems* vol. 33, no. 2, December, 1985, pp. 114–129; and Peter W. Cookson, Jr. and Caroline Persell, *Preparing for Power: America's Elite Boarding Schools* (New York: Basic Books, 1985).

2. Henry Levin, "Accelerating the Learning of All Students," Robert and Augusta Finkelstein Lecture, Adelphi University, April 20, 1998, Garden City, New York.

3. For an application of Max Weber's leadership typology to school leadership see Susan F. Semel, *The Dalton School: The Transformation of a Progressive School* (New York: Peter Lang, 1992), pp. 164–169.

4. See, for example, Charol Shakeshaft, *Women in Educational Administration* (Newbury Park, Calif.: Sage, 1987).

5. Susan F. Semel, "Female Founders and the Progressive Paradox," in Michael James (ed.), *Social Reconstruction Through Education: The*

Philosophy, History, and Curricula of a Radical Ideal (Norwood, N.J.: Ablex Publishing Company, 1995), pp. 89-108.

6. To some extent this was due to the high social class backgrounds of Dalton and Parker students independent of school characteristics. However, students at the progressive schools included in the Eight Year Study did as well or better than students from similar social class backgrounds from more traditional schools.

7. Ibid.

8. See Basil Bernstein. *Class, Codes and Control, vol. 3.* (London: Routledge, 1977); *The Structuring of Pedagogic Discourse, vol. 4 of Class, Codes and Control* (London: Routledge, 1990); Alan R. Sadovnik, "Basil Bernstein's Theory of Pedagogic Practice: A Structuralist Approach. *Sociology of Education* 48:1, pp. 48-64, 1991; *Knowledge and Pedagogy: The Sociology of Basil Bernstein* (Norwood, N.J.: Ablex Publishing Corporation, 1995).

9. See Susan F. Semel and Alan R. Sadovnik, "Lessons from the Past: Individualism and Community in Three Progressive Schools." *Peabody Journal of Education* (Summer 1995), pp. 56-84, for a discussion of the Downtown Community School.

10. Lisa Delpit, *Other People's Children* (New York: New Press, 1995).

11. Jay Mathews, *Class Struggle: What's Wrong (and Right) with America's Best High Schools* (New York: Times Books, 1997).

12. Anthony Bryk, Valerie Lee and Peter Holland, *Catholic Schools and the Common Good* (Cambridge, Mass.: Harvard University Press, 1995).

13. This section is adapted from Semel and Sadovnik, "Lessons from the Past: Individualism and Community in Three Progressive Schools."

14. Christopher Lasch, *The Culture of Narcissism* (New York: Norton, 1979).

15. Robert Bellah, Richard Madsen, William Sullivan, Ann Swidler and Steven Tipton, *Habits of the Heart* (Berkeley: University of California Press, 1985).

16. Robert Bellah, Richard Madsen, William Sullivan, Ann Swidler and Steven Tipton, *The Good Society* (New York: Knopf, 1991).

17. Amatai Etzioni, *Spirit of Community* (New York: Crown, 1993).

18. Emile Durkheim, *The Division of Labor in Society* (Glencoe, Ill.: the Free Press, 1947; original 1893); *The Elementary Forms of Religious Life* (Glencoe, Ill.: the Free Press, 1954; original 1915).

19. Emile Durkheim, *Suicide* (Glencoe, Ill.: the Free Press, 1951; original 1897); and *The Division of Labor in Society*, 1893/1947.

20. Ferdinand Tönnies, *Community and Society* (New York: Harper, 1957; original 1887).

21. Samuel Bowles and Herbert Gintis, *Schooling in Capitalist America* (New York: Basic, 1976).

22. John Dewey, "My Pedagogic Creed," in Martin S. Dworkin, ed. *Dewey on Education* (New York: Teachers College Press, 1959), pp. 19–32 (original 1897); "*The School and Society*, ibid., pp. 33–90 (original 1899); "*The Child and the Curriculum,*" ibid., pp. 91–111 (original 1902); *Democracy and Education: An Introduction to the Philosophy of Education* (New York: Macmillan, 1916); *Experience and Education* (New York: Mac-Millan, 1938).

23. Dworkin, ed. *Dewey on Education*, p. 41.

24. See for example, C. Wright Mills, *White Collar* (New York: Oxford, 1959).

25. Barbara Ehrenreich, *The Hearts of Men* (Garden City, N.Y.: Doubleday, 1983).

26. Lasch, *The Culture of Narcissism*, 1979.

27. Bellah et al., *Habits of the Heart*, 1985.

28. Bellah et al., *The Good Society*, 1991.

29. See Alan R. Sadovnik, Peter W. Cookson, and Susan F. Semel *Exploring Education: An Introduction to the Foundations of Education* (Needham Heights, Mass.: Allyn and Bacon). Chapter 2 offers a detailed discussion of conservative, liberal, and radical political perspectives on society and education.

30. Etzioni, *Spirit of Community*, 1993.

31. Bellah et al., *The Good Society*, 1991.

32. Deborah Meier, *The Power of Their Ideas* (Boston: Houghton Mifflin, 1995).

INDEX

History of Schools
and Schooling

THIS SERIES EXPLORES THE HISTORY OF SCHOOLS AND SCHOOLING in the United States and other countries. Books in this series examine the historical development of schools and educational processes, with special emphasis on issues of educational policy, curriculum and pedagogy, as well as issues relating to race, class, gender, and ethnicity. Special emphasis will be placed on the lessons to be learned from the past for contemporary educational reform and policy. Although the series will publish books related to education in the broadest societal and cultural context, it especially seeks books on the history of specific schools and on the lives of educational leaders and school founders.

For additional information about this series or for the submission of manuscripts, please contact the general editors:

Alan R. Sadovnik
118 Harvey Hall
School of Education
Adelphi University
Garden City, NY 11530

Susan F. Semel
Dept. of Curriculum and Teaching
243 Gallon Wing
Hofstra University
Hempstead, NY 11550